A
BIOGRAPHICAL HISTORY
OF
AFRICAN AMERICANS

ALTON HORNSBY, JR.

A
BIOGRAPHICAL HISTORY
OF
AFRICAN AMERICANS

Alton Hornsby, Jr.

E-BookTime, LLC
Montgomery, Alabama

A Biographical History of African Americans

Library of Congress Control Number: 2005934749

ISBN: 1-59824-075-7

First Edition
Published October 2005
E-BookTime, LLC
6598 Pumpkin Road
Montgomery, AL 36108
www.e-booktime.com

Cover photographs, l-r, John Hope, Mary McCleod Bethune, Dorie Miller, Fannie Lou Hamer, A. G. Gaston. Cover design courtesy APEX MUSEUM, Atlanta, GA

To my students—past, present and future

Contents

Preface ix

Introduction xi-lx

I. Out of Africa into the House of Bondage 1-29

II. Post Emancipation to Jim Crow 30-91

III. An Era of Civil Rights 92-220

IV. The Search for a Black Agenda: 221-286
Traditions and New Contours

References 287-289

About the Author 290

Index of Subjects 291-295

PREFACE

In the last two or three decades, there has been a plethora of directories, dictionaries and encyclopedias chronicling the lives of notable African American personalities. Foremost among these have been Darlene Clark Hine's volumes, *Black Women in America* (1993, 2005) and Jesse Carney Smith's, *Epic Lives: One Hundred Black Women Who Made a Difference* (1993) and the recently released *African American Lives* by Louis Gates and Evelyn Brooks Higginbotham. However, such monumental works are usually published as large hardback editions intended for use in library reference sections. Most also include living as well as deceased persons which adds to their bulk.

However, not since Edgar A. Toppin's *Biographical History of Blacks in the United States Since 1528* (1971) have we had a scholarly volume on African American biography that was published in a format and size that could be possessed and used individually, as a text for students and as a handy reference for others. This work aims to fill that void. And, to avoid the problem of bulk as well as currency, we have included here only deceased persons.

The book gives an introductory overview to African American history, followed by a selection of notable African American subjects, arranged in four topical and chronological periods. We have aimed for diversity in vocations, gender, and geography. We have been particularly concerned with profiling notable subjects who have not appeared in other dictionaries, directories or encyclopedias.

A work of this scope, of course, has required the assistance of numerous individuals and institutions and I hereby wish to express my deep appreciation to them. They include student assistants, Courtney Gober, Hassan Al-Hassan and Dedric Bonds and typists Ellen Ponder, Bettye Spicer, and Augustus Wood III; and

Gene Steele and his staff at E-BookTime Publishers. Also librarians at the Robert W. Woodruff Library of the Atlanta University Center, the Auburn Avenue Research Library on African American Culture of the Atlanta-Fulton Public Library System, the Atlanta History Center and Emory University were most helpful. And Dr. Augustine Konneh, chair, and my colleagues in the Department of History at Morehouse never wavered in their encouragement and support. However, these may be only representative and not inclusive. Thus, we do apologize to any who have been inadvertently omitted.

INTRODUCTION

I. OUT OF AFRICA INTO THE HOUSE OF BONDAGE

The ancestors of most black Americans came from the area of the continent of Africa known as the Western Sudan. This area extended from the Atlantic Ocean in the west to Lake Chad in the east, and from the Sahara desert in the north to the Gulf of Guinea in the south.

From about 300 A.D. to the late 1500s, three powerful empires dominated the Western Sudan in succession. The empires were Ghana, Mali and Songhai. Each originated as a small, generally peaceful kingdom but subsequently expanded and gained dominance over the entire region. The economies of the Sudan empires were based on farming and mining gold. Although the topography of the Sahara provided an often frustrating barrier, there was continuous trade between the Western Sudanese and the then-known world through the Muslims of North Africa.

The cultivation of crops was most prominent in the savanna, the rain forests of the Guinea Coast south of the savanna, and in the Sahara north of the savanna. West African agriculture was conducted under a system which combined private enterprise and communitarianism. Farm land was owned collectively by the descendants of the first occupant. Individual descendants of the first occupant. Individual descendants of the elder were given parcels of land to cultivate, but once cultivation ended, the land reverted back to the collective community. The administrator of the land, the Master of the Ground, determined the usages of the soil.

While agriculture and gold mining were the principal occupations of blacks living in the Western Sudan, others supported themselves by undertaking numerous crafts, including basketry, pottery, and woodwork.

The first of the great Sudanic empires to gain control of the Western Sudan was Ghana. The Ghanians were mostly black Soninke people who spoke a language in the Manda branch of the Sudanic language group. While Ghana's economy was centered on agricultural pursuits in the various villages, its people also engaged in a lucrative trade from their principal commercial center at Koumbi (Kumbi). The Ghanaians served as middlemen in the trade between North and West Africa, obtaining gold from the mines in Wangara, a forest region south of Ghana, which they exchanged for salt mined by the Berbers and later the Arabs in the northern Sahara. While gold was plentiful in the Sudan, salt was a scarce commodity. Consequently, salt became extremely valuable and was often bartered for gold. The Ghanaians also traded ivory and slaves for textiles and beads which were bought in from North Africa. The government of Ghana levied taxes on all caravans, merchants, and commercial transactions. Once the kingdom expanded, it increased its wealth further by exacting tribute from other peoples whom it had conquered and brought under its control. Because of its vast wealth, many of the residents of Ghanaian cities constructed homes of wood and stone.

Once the Arabs occupied North Africa in the seventh and eighth centuries, Islamic missionaries moved into the Western Sudan and quickly became an important cultural force in the region. At about the same time, the Ghanaians began to raise large armies to subjugate many of their neighbors. Since they were the first West Africans to learn how to smelt iron ore, the Ghanaians were able to make arrows, swords, and other weapons which they used to easily conquer less technologically advanced peoples. One of the more noted kings of Ghana, Tenkhamenen, reportedly had 200, 000 warriors in his army in 1067.

Following a drought, compounded by religious divisions, the Ghanaian empire began to decline in the twelfth century. The weakening of Ghana opened the way for many of its former subject kingdoms to increase their strength and influence in the area. Two of the principal candidates to replace Ghana as the superior power in West Africa were Koniaga, inhabited by the Soso people, and Mali, occupied by the Malians. Led by Sundiata Keita,

Mali defeated Koniaga in the battle of Karina in 1235 and five years later, subdued the once dominant Ghanaians.

The Malians were also a Sudanic-speaking people who live principally as farmers and traders. They constructed a prosperous capital city at Niani on the Niger River. The chief administrator of the nation was the emperor. He ruled, however, through a de-centralized system of regional and local officials, which included *inferbas*, or governors of provinces, and *mochrifts,*, or mayors of important cities. One of the most fabled Malian emperors was Mansa Musa, who rules the empire from 1309 and 1332.

Much of Musa's notoriety stemmed from descriptions of his famous pilgrimage to Mecca in 1324. A contemporary picture drawn by the Arab traveler, Ibn Batuta, in his *Travels in Asia and Africa, 1325-1354,* depicts the emperor being sent on his journey to the sound of drums, trumpets, and bugles. In addition, John Hope Franklin commented in his *From Slavery to Freedom* that Musa's entourage "was composed of 60,000 persons." Franklin reported: "Books, baggagemen, and royal secretaries there were in abundance. To finance the pilgrimage, the king car-ried eighty camels to bear more than 24,000 pounds of gold." The exact amount of the gold carried on the journey totaled more than $5 million.

Once Mansa Musa arrived in the Middle East, he spent so much money, according to Edgar Allan Toppin in his book *A Biographical History of Blacks in American Since 1528,* that he "depressed the price of gold in the great commercial center of Cairo." After running low on funds, however, Musa had to bor-row money from local gold merchants. Following the grand pil-grimage of 1324, the Malian kingdom and its emperor were placed on many of the maps of the medieval world, and Musa was given the title "Rex Melle (Mali) King of the Gold Mines."

In addition to Mali's great wealth, Ibn Batuta also observed that the kingdom was virtually free of crime an astonishing feat for any nation, then as now. But the Malians were not strangers to violence, for they had achieved their control of the Western Sudan through the subjugation of their neighbors. Eventually, the Malians had to defend their hegemony against the growing power of other rivals.

After 1332, Mali was ruled by an increasingly inept group of monarchs. Spending continued to be lavish, and local officials often threatened secession from the central government. The people of Songhai were more unified and were led by stronger rulers. Songhai, then, emerged as Mali's strongest rival for supremacy in the Western Sudan.

The Sunni dynasty of Songhai, which was established in 1335, contested Mali for control of the Western Sudan for more than a century. The empire emerged victorious during the reign of King Sunni Ali Ber in 1473. The Sunni dynasty remained in power through Ali Ber and his son until it was overthrown by Askia Muhammad Toure, one of Ali Bers generals, in 1492. Askia Muhammad expanded Songhai'sboundaries to the salt mines of the Sahara, the Hansa states of the Lake Chad region, and the Mossi of the Volta region.

Askia Muhammad established a government which included an efficient central administration as well as appointed local officials. He also made a great pilgrimage to Mecca between 1495 and 1497. Unlike Mansa Musa, however, Askia had a much smaller entourage and spent his money more wisely. Instead of depleting his funds on lavish goods, Askia engaged the services of several Arabic scholars and physicians. The scholars were employed to teach in the empire's two major universities at Timbuktu and Jenne. Because of these and other accomplishments, Edgar Allan Toppin called Askia Muhammad "the greatest of the emperors of West Africa."

Even before Christopher Columbus sailed for the New World, Songhai had become the largest and richest country in Africa. Much of its wealth and the products of that affluence could be seen in the city of Timbuktu, which became a principal center of learning and trade in the Muslim world. An Arab traveler, Al-Hasan Ibn Muhammad, observed in 1526 that all of the houses in Timbuktu were built of "chalke, and covered thatch." There was also "a stately temple" and a "princely palace" built "by a most excellent workman of Granada." All of the inhabitants, especially the "strangers" residing there, seemed exceeding(ly) rich."

Timbuktu was best known for its multitude of educational

institutions. Boys and men studied history, medicine, astronomy, mathematics, and literature. The scholars who taught in the schools and universities were well maintained at the king's expense.

While Askia Muhammad ruled Songhai effectively and efficiently for more than forty years, the empire began to weaken after his sons deposed the aging emperor in 1528. As Askia neared death, warfare over his succession disrupted the kingdom. Both Askia Ishak I and Askia Dared made valiant but unsuccessful efforts between 539 and 1582 to restore the efficient, centralized rule which had existed under the great Askia Muhammad. Thus, when a smaller Moroccan army equipped with cannons and gunpowder invaded the empire in 1590, they were able, in the words of Benjamin DaSilva, et al. in their look, *The Afro-American in United States History,* to "cut Songhai to pieces. The days of the great lack kingdoms of West Africa were over."

But these great Western Sudanic kingdoms, which served as an ancestral home for African Americans, had demonstrated sophisticated economic activities, a capacity for government which was highly developed, and a complex social structure.

Political life in these African nations consisted of local rule at the tribal and village level, but also a combination of hereditary monarchy and aspects of representative government, particularly at the national or central levels. In some instances, councilors elected their leaders. More typically, however, three hereditary families governed West African kingdoms: royal, electing, and enthroning. The monarch was generally selected from the hereditary royal family, but the hereditary electing family made the selection from among those considered the quintessential members of the royal family. Hence, it was not always a matter of primogeniture, where the deceased king's eldest son ascended to the throne. In many situations, the hereditary enthroning family exercised the right to confirm the choice in installing the new ruler. The character of the monarchs and their influence on their subjects ranged from tyrannical to benevolent, from great nation builders to inept and corrupt charlatans. A common characteristic was that, particularly after the eighth century, almost all of them were Muslim.

While Islamic influence became pervasive in West African life and directly affected governance, economic, social, and intellectual activities among the Sudanese, animistic worship, which advocated the propitiation of the spirit of the ancestors, also persisted. Animism was often practiced through chants, sacred songs, and ceremonial dancing. The oldest living relative or descendant of a common ancestor served as the local priest for this form of religion.

The priest of the more ancient, indigenous religions was also known as the Master of the Ground in the extended family, the most common form of social organization. The extended family was composed of several generations of people who were descended from a common ancestor. They all lived in a common village or similar residential area. Individuals who were not obviously related to the group could often become a part of the family in return for performing services for the actual members of the family. Because of its size, both the usual as well as any extraordinary needs of any member of the family, either legitimate or adopted, could normally be supported within the extended family itself. Most disputes could be settled by the Master of the Ground.

Aside from family, work, and worship, there were African cultural expressions in song, instrumental music, dance, art, and literature. Singing took the form of chants, festive tunes, and lullabies as well as sacred songs. Traditional musical instruments included the flute, guitar, harp, and violin. Dancing was used for ritualistic and recreational purposes as well as religious ones. Because of the multitude of languages within a single empire, writing was limited; most of the surviving literature is, understandably, written in Arabic. However, a rich oral tradition which included such literary forms as fables, legends, and myths flourished. By the fourteenth century, the Griot, a professional storyteller, appeared. This elder usually collected and recited tales for a living. In art, utilitarian, ceremonial, and religious themes were prevalent. Cookware, eating utensils, latches, and pulleys were often decorated. Carvers produced masks, dolls, and statuettes. Generally, Edgar Allan Toppin contends, African art was "non representational, distorting natural shapes, such as the human figure, with marvelous plasticity to achieve a truer artistic reality."

Yet, despite the existence of complex political and social systems and highly developed intellectual and cultural activities, the West Africans were not above participating in the ancient practice of owning other human beings.

Slavery developed along with civilization in ancient Europe, Asia, and Africa. Normally, an individual became the slave of another through birth (the child of a slave often was consigned to slavery himself), through capture (such as a prisoner of war), through kidnapping (particularly as a result of pirate attacks on ships), through sale by a relative or another person, and as a result of capture and sale by slave traders.

African slaves were generally treated as lesser members of the extended family, but were, for the most part, treated humanely and could share in some of the privileges afforded other members of the family. But they could also be sold as chattel by their owners. The largest category of sales was probably the result of monarchs disposing of surplus prisoners who had become slaves.

In ancient times West Africans sold their slaves to Arab traders from northern Africa. By the early 1500s, however, after they had established colonies in Latin America and in the West Indies, Portugal and Spain became increasingly involved in the African slave trade. Portugal placed African slaves on the sugar plantations which its colonists developed in Brazil. Spain used Africans on its sugar plantations in the West Indies. After 1600, England, France, and the Netherlands also began to import African slaves into their colonies in North America.

Many of the African slaves obtained by Europeans were sold or traded by other Africans for cloth, rum, and other items, especially weapons. Guns were a precious commodity in the interminable warfare between neighboring African peoples. Other black slaves were captured by traders on the continent, pirated from ships, or kidnapped elsewhere, including Europe.

The nefarious European slave trade took several triangular routes. One of the routes guided ships from Europe transporting manufactured products to the west coast of Africa, where traders exchanged the goods for slaves. Then, on the infamous "Middle Passage," the blacks were carried across the Atlantic Ocean to the West Indies and sold for huge profits. The slave traders then purchased coffee, sugar, and tobacco in the West Indies to be sold in Europe. Over another route, ships from New England colonies took rum and other products to Africa, where they were exchanged for slaves. These blacks were also transported to the West Indies to be sold. Some of the profits were used to purchase molasses and sugar, which was returned to New England and sold to rum producers.

Most of the slave voyages across the Atlantic took several months. Since the slave trade was conducted for profit, the captains of slave ships tried to deliver as many blacks as possible. Some captains used a system called "loose packing" to deliver their cargo. This meant that fewer slaves than the ships could carry would be transported in the hope that sickness and death among them could be reduced. Other captains, seeking larger profits and believing that many blacks would die on the voyage nonetheless, carried as many slaves as their ships could hold. The blacks were generally chained together below deck all day and night except for brief periods of exercise. These crowded and filthy conditions resulted in stench, diseases, and death. This system was called "tight packing." Approximately twelve percent of all slaves died during the crossings of the Atlantic. Thus, the story of the "Middle Passage" is a tale of horrors.

The Euro-American slave trade continued from the 1500s to the 1800s. Although the exact number of Africans who were enslaved during these four centuries is unknown, the most reliable estimates range from ten million to twenty million blacks. Between 400,000 and 1,200,000 of this total arrived in North America.

Slavery in the New World began in the Caribbean and on the Latin American mainland. The Spanish, shortly after the establishment of Santo Domingo (the first permanent European settlement in the New World) in 1496 employed slaves on their sugar plantations. The first Africans were seen there as early as 1501. After the Spaniards virtually exterminated the Carib Indians, natives of the Caribbean islands, larger numbers of blacks were imported. Fearing that blacks would eventually outnumber Europeans in the region, Spanish authorities soon placed restrictions on their importation. In 1517, Bishop Bartholomew Las Casas and others persuaded King Charles I of Spain to rescind the restrictions in order for Africans to augment the dwindling supply of Indian labor. Subsequently, in 1518 large numbers of blacks were imported directly from Africa. Those newly-arrived slaves were known as *bozal* Negroes, which distinguished them from the group of Africans who were initially transported to Europe and Christianized before being sent to the Caribbean.

The Spanish, Portuguese, and eventually the English developed great plantations in the West Indies where cocoa, coffee, tobacco, and sugar were produced. Slaves grew and processed all of these crops, but most were employed in the furious labor of producing sugar. The Europeans also maintained several colonies on the South American mainland, in such places as Brazil and the territory that now comprises Columbia. Here, in addition to agricultural labor, the slaves worked in mines.

As the black population increased, there was always fear among the settlers that the Africans would rebel against their captivity. Thus, harsh slave codes which mandated severe punishments for insurgency were enacted. These codes served to deter large scale violence, but did not prevent another common form of rebellion-escape. Large numbers of black runaways, known as Maroons, formed camps called *quilembos* (cabins). One of the largest *quilombos was* at Palmares, in the northeastern section of Brazil. Between 1630 and 1697, the Maroons established a succession of three republics at Palmares, which contained a government, enacted laws, and elected a king. Their economy was based upon agriculture and trade, although much of their food and supplies was attained by raiding nearby plantations. Finally, in 1697, an army of settlers broke through the Maroon fortifications and destroyed the community. Several of the republic's leaders committed suicide rather than be returned to slavery.

The patterns of black enslavement which developed in Latin America, including the Christianization of Africans, provided ready examples and precedents for the establishment of an even

Larger "slavocracy" in the English colonies to the north. There, beginning in the first half of the seventeenth century, millions of Africans would begin the long cultural process of becoming African Americans.

The tradition beginning of the history of African Americans in the United States is that period of involuntary servitude from 1619 to 1860, when the large majority of blacks were chattels. Although blacks are known to have accompanied the early explorers to the New World, the first permanent settlers were the twenty blacks deposited at Jamestown, Virginia in 1619. These blacks, who had been captured in Africa and sold to the highest bidders (as many lower-class whites had been similarly captured or kidnapped and sold in Europe) were not slaves, but indentured servants.

African Americans were probably indentured servants in the American colonies until 1640, and perhaps as late as 1650. After serving their period of indenture, (normally seven years), some of these blacks became property holders and politically active citizens. Throughout the seventeenth century, however, the numbers of black servants, slaves, or free were still relatively small. There were about 300 blacks in the colonies by 1650. The first rapid increase in their number occurred during the close of the seventeenth century. By the time of the American Revolution, almost half of the population in several southern states was black. Virginia and Maryland, for example, had a total population of approximately 480,000 at the time of the Revolutionary War, about 206,000 of these people were black. South Carolina's black population was larger than the white one. However, slavery was not confined to the South. The first black slaves arrived in New England probably in 1638. By 1700, there were about 1,000 blacks out of a population of 90,000 in the New England colonies, and at the time of the American Revolution there were 16,000 slaves in the region. Massachusetts and Rhode Island became great slave trading colonies, while Connecticut was the leading New England slave colony. On the eve of the American Revolution, there were about half a million black slaves in the American Colonies.

In the South, the bondspersons were principally employed

in producing the staple crops that were the basis of the southern economy. By 1700 they had proved to e the most reliable form of cheap labor for the southern planters. The typical slave, however, do not work on a large plantation. He would be found more likely on a small farm, with one or two other blacks, where he or she worked along side the master and his family. The majority of blacks were field slaves who worked under one of two systems. The Gang Plan or the Task System. Under the Gang Plan, large groups of blacks, especially on the larger plantations, worked long hours in the fields. In the Task System, individual blacks were given various specific chores to perform. Most urban bondspersons worked under the Task System in such occupations as messengers, domestic servants, and craftsmen. A smaller group of favored slaves (selected principally because of their light skin color, loyalty, or old age) worked in and around the master's house as domestic servants.

The climate and soil in New England prevented huge profits from agriculture, but skilled and unskilled labor was in much demand on small farms and in homes, ships, factories, and shipyards, as well as on fishing and trading ships. Since Native Americans and indentured servants proved to be insufficient laborers, black bondspersons were a welcome supplement. In the Middle Colonies and later states, black slaves were employed in similar occupations and in larger numbers.

Since English law did not define the status of a slave, the colonies were left to adopt their own regulations. Essentially, all the colonies and states aimed first to protect the property rights of the master, and, secondly, to protect white society from what was considered an alien and savage race. The codes grew out of laws regulating indentured servitude, but the slave had practically no rights, while the servant had many.

The first statutory recognition of slavery came from Massachusetts in 1641. Rhode Island passed a law regulating slavery in 1652. Virginia regulations, which were to set the standards for the South, were passed in 1661. The status of the mother would determine whether a child was slave or free. Children born to slave mothers would become slaves. Most interracial unions and unions of slaves and free persons were of black women and white men, so the products of such unions would be classified as slaves. This practice ran counter to the English tradition which determined the status of a child according to that of his father.

Generally speaking, the slave codes prohibited the assembling or the wandering of blacks without permission from masters. Bondspersons could not, for instance, own weapons, testify against white persons, and received harsher punishment for some crimes, lesser for others. An attack, for example, on a white person usually meant severe punishment, while petty theft often went unpunished. A master or any white man could not kill a slave with impunity, but was likely to receive less punishment than for killing a free man. Cases involving relations between slave and master could be tried in special courts without juries. Justices of the Peace and a selected group of planters heard such cases and passed judgment. The strictness of enforcement of slave codes varied from region to region, from colony to colony, from state to state, and even from one plantation to another. The Massachusetts code was less restrictive than the Mississippi one, for example, where blacks could be emancipated or manumitted only with legal approval. Urban slaves were less restricted than rural ones. Slaves on small farms enjoyed more freedom than those on huge plantations.

Physical cruelties were inflicted upon some slaves, primarily for insubordination, refusal to work, slave plots or revolts, and for running away. The cruelest punishment was *likely* to *be* seen on large plantations a received at the hands of foremen or slave drivers. In the view of many, the slave system almost completely distorted the African American's personality. Modern historians tend to indict American slavery not so much for physical cruelty and the psychological effects of the slave system, but because of the harshness of the slave codes, wherein the blacks had little legal protection.

Early historians disagreed vehemently on the question of the slaves' acceptance or rejection of his status and on many related matters, such as whether or not religion stifled resistance or served as a vehicle for leadership and protest. One school, commonly associated with the southern-born historian Ulrich B. Phillips, portrayed a docile, contented African, naturally pliable, and logically a slave. Another school, taking its name from the New England historian Stanley Elkins, assessed the psychological consequences of slavery and concluded that the blacks' personalities were so distorted by the harshness of the system that they assumed a docile "Sambo," character. Still another school, which includes such liberal historians as Kenneth Stampp and the Marxist scholar Herbert Aptheker, saw the slave as rebellious and trouble some to his master. Contemporary historians widely agree that the slave community was a complex environment. Many, perhaps most slaves accommodated themselves to their immediate surroundings, with the realization that open rebellion was futile and suicidal. Others were openly rebellious. Many others sought any means available, other than violent insurrection, to show their displeasure with their bondage. This "day to day resistance" was carefully documented as early as 1943 by historians Alice and Raymond Bauer.

Slaves did, in fact, protest their enslavement from the very beginning. Aside from daily acts of rebellion, which took such forms as escape, destruction of property, feigned illness, and disloyalty, there were a number of plots and at least one major mutiny and one major revolt. Black slaves joined with white servants in a conspiracy in Gloucester County, Virginia in 1663; fifty-five whites were killed in the slave rebellion led by Nat Turner in Southhampton County, Virginia in 1831; and slaves mutineered on the Amistad off the coast of Long Island in 1839. In the final analysis, African American slave plots, mutinies, and revolts resulted in the freeing of only a few blacks, although vicious reprisals often followed such acts. Many more slaves secured freedom by escape and by manumission or emancipation.

The origins of a large free black population in America came after the Revolutionary War. In appreciation of the service of approximately 5,000 blacks in the War for Independence, and as a result of the libertarian and egalitarian spirit inspired by the Declaration of Independence and the war, many masters, especially northerners, manumitted their slaves. Soon individual states in the North decreed the gradual abolition of the institution, beginning with Vermont's action in 1777. In 1776, the population of the United States was about two and one-half million, with more than 500,000 black slaves and approximately 40,000 free blacks. More than one-half of these free blacks lived in the South. The Revolutionary leaders, including George Washington and Thomas Jefferson, anticipated a continuation of this trend toward manumission and emancipation until eventually slavery would disappear from the land. This expectation was to be drowned, almost literally, by the whirling noise of Eli Whitney's cotton gin. The invention of this native of Massachusetts made cotton production increasingly profitable and caused rapid and substantial increases in the slave population. On the eve of the Civil War, there were four million black slaves in the South.

Free blacks in the rural South worked primarily as farm workers or as independent farmers. In the urban areas, North and South, free blacks were employed in factories, such as tobacco plants and textile mills, and also worked in shipyards and railroad construction. There were some independent merchants and many personal servants and artisans. The principal professional occupation was preaching, hence the first black leader of national stature was Bishop Richard Allen of Philadelphia, one of the founders of the African Methodist Episcopal (A.M.E.) Church.

Prior to the American Revolution, free blacks were so small in number that they did not pose a threat to whites in most of the states. Then, during the Revolutionary era, thousands of slaves were freed from Delaware to the North. This rapid increase in the free black population resulted in more severe restrictions. By 1790, free blacks faced regulations similar to those governing slaves. In the early history of New England, blacks could not serve in the militias as combatants (the black military hero, Peter Salem, had to beg his master's permission to serve during the American Revolution), although they could be called upon to work on the roads and other menial tasks. Free blacks could not walk on the streets at night without a pass or visit a town other than the one in which they lived without passes. They could not entertain black or Indian slaves without permission. In the South, they ran the risk of being enslaved themselves if caught without proof of their status. In early Rhode Island history, free blacks were not allowed to keep horses, sheep, or any other domes tic animals. In Boston, they could not own hogs. The possession of weapons was severely restricted. In one New England state, blacks could not possess walking sticks or canes unless demonstrably required for the actual support of the person. There was constant conflict in places like New York as free blacks and whites competed for jobs.

By 1840, the free black population in the United States was almost completely disfranchised. More than ninety percent of the American free black population lived in states which totally, or in part, restricted their right to vote. On the eve of the Civil War, blacks voted with relative freedom and safety only in Massachusetts, Vermont, New Hampshire, and Maine.

Restrictions on the political and civil rights of free blacks were motivated by racial prejudice and, additionally, in the South by beliefs that the group had a disquieting influence on the institution of slavery. Free blacks were implicated in a number of the slave plots and uprisings and their very existence pointed to a different life, although not a very radical one, for black men in America. In the final analysis, a free black in pre-Civil War America was little better off than a slave. The inferior status of this group has led historians to classify them appropriately as quasi-free African Americans.

Despite the inferior civil, social, and political status of quasi-free blacks, many managed to achieve considerable distinction in American society. Although discriminated against in employment and in other economic endeavors, a number of free blacks acquired substantial wealth. Even in the pre-Civil War era, there were prosperous free black communities in Philadelphia, Baltimore, Charleston, New Orleans, and elsewhere. Such black individuals as John Jones and Paul Cuffe acquired considerable fortunes: In the military, the am and sciences, and in religion there were free blacks who distinguished themselves and won recognition even from White America. The free black communities, especially in the North, were vociferous opponents of slavery and discrimination, and the abolition movement of the 1830s and the convention movement of the 1840s and 1850s were interrelated vehicles used by blacks to protest their status in America, whether slave or quasi- free.

Momentous changes in the African Americans occurred in the years between 1861 and 1876. These were the years of the American Civil War, Emancipation, and Reconstruction. Four million African Americans were freed as a result of a war in which many of them participated. Then, for the first time, large numbers of blacks had an opportunity to direct their own social and economic destinies; and some, during the Reconstruction era, were able to assert political leadership. Despite the war and the resulting freedom, however, these were still very difficult years for the black masses as they struggled to survive in a hostile environment, and even the gains made during Black Reconstruction failed to provide lasting security.

After the Confederate attack on Fort Sumter, South Carolina on April 12, 1861 and President Abraham Lincoln's call for 75,000 volunteers to "defend the Union," many northern blacks rushed to answer the president's appeal. The blacks erroneously interpreted the unfolding conflict as a war against slavery. They soon discovered that Lincoln's war aims did not include interference with slavery where it already existed and that they were not to be permitted combat roles. Abraham Lincoln judged that a war against slavery would drive additional southern and border states into the Confederacy and that such a program, along with the employment of black troops, would anger most northern whites. Blacks and their white abolitionist supporters, in and out of Congress, clearly expressed their opposition to a war whose aims did not include the abolition of slavery, as well as the refusal to employ blacks as troops.

The first year of the Civil War was for the most part a frustrating one for Abraham Lincoln and the Union. In addition to inept military commanders, he had to contend with apathy and even disloyalty in the North; the possibility of an alliance between the Confederacy and cotton seeking European nations; abolitionist and African American agitation; runaway slaves crossing into Union lines; unauthorized slave emancipation by military leaders; and the employment of blacks in fatigue duties by the Confederacy. There was also the continuous matter of preventing the secession of additional slave states. By the summer of 1862, President Lincoln concluded that the emancipation of certain slaves and the eventual employment of black troops had become military necessities. There were risks involved in such an act: the Border states might join the Confederacy; many northern whites might become alienated; and morale in the Union Army might be lowered. On the other hand, England and the rest of Europe would not likely oppose a war against slavery; abolitionist sentiment in the North would enthusiastically support the effort; and thousands of blacks would be lost to the Confederacy while thousands more could be drawn to the Union.

The Emancipation Proclamation specifically excluded all slave states and areas loyal to the Union, hence preserving the Border States for the North and having little immediate effect in most of the South, which the Confederate Army controlled. At the same time, the Proclamation and the employment of African American troops convinced blacks and abolitionists that the "Day of jubilee" was at hand. Bells rang from the spires of northern black churches and blacks rejoiced when the emancipation edict took effect on January 1, 1863.

The moral crusade known as abolitionism had sprung up during the 1830s. This new, militant movement resulted from the efforts of such New England and Midwestern reformers as William Lloyd Garrison, James Finney, Lewis Tappan, and Theodore Dwight Weld. Ile talents of former slaves Eke Frederick Douglass, Henry High land Garnett, and Harriet Tubman, as well as members of the free black communities in the North, were joined by the efforts of white reformers. These people were successors to the Quaker protectors of earlier centuries, the moderate abolitionists of the eighteenth and early nineteenth centuries, and the colonizationists of the early 1800s, who would rid the land of the African American problem by shipping blacks back to Africa or to other foreign lands. In 1863, the abolitionists' long and painful efforts finally received political sanction at the highest level when emancipation became a war objective, even though prompted not by moral suasion or moral right, but by military necessity.

Almost 200,000 blacks fought for the Union during the Civil War. Although they faced discrimination of one type or another throughout the conflict, many rendered distinguished service and won commendations from the Commander-in Chief himself. A few rose to the ranks of officers. About 40,000 blacks died in the fight for freedom most of these deaths were disease-related, reflecting the poor medical attention received by black soldiers as well as the disproportionate number of blacks on the front line and other hazardous duties. The Confederacy debated the use of black troops until 1864, but when the decision to employ them was grudgingly made, the war was nearing its end.

II. FROM EMANCIPATION TO JIM CROW

The generous terms of surrender which General Ulysses S. Grant offered the Confederates on April 9, 1865 were symptomatic of much of northern white opinion at the close of the Civil War. It certainly reflected the attitude of President Lincoln toward the seceded states which should, in his view, be returned to the Union as expeditiously as possible in a spirit of leniency and reconciliation. Lincoln's mild Reconstruction program was aborted by an assassin's bullet on April 14, 1865, but his successor, Andrew Johnson, a southerner, continued the lenient policies toward the white South. Following Lincoln's example Johnson (who did not believe in African American equality) supported ratification of the Thirteenth Amendment abolishing slavery, but did not push African American enfranchisement or the protection of civil rights. He tolerated anti-black violence in Louisiana, Tennessee, and Mississippi, as well as the Black Codes enacted by the southern white or "Johnson" governments in 1865 and 1866. These codes, reminiscent of the ante-bellum slave codes, proscribed the African American to an inferior status once again in southern society.

Republican leaders in Congress correctly viewed the Johnson program as a motivation to restore white Democratic supremacy in the South. Some of these leaders, motivated by a desire to institute Republican Party supremacy in the region, and others motivated by a sincere interest in protecting African American civil rights, combined to form a solid front of opposition to the president's programs. The "Radical Republicans" favored a harsh program of southern Reconstruction, one which would delay the reentrance of the southern states until Republican strength could be garnered; until the blacks could be enfranchised with the premise that they would form a bloc of southern Republican votes; and one which would guarantee civil rights for

African Americans. In addition, the Republicans believed that southern white Democratic agriculturists should not be allowed to regain economic and political ascendancy in the nation.

In 1866 and 1867 the Republican leadership, using the party's majorities in Congress, took the Reconstruction of the South from President John son's control and instituted their own program. Their plans included an extension of the Freed men's Bureau (originally proposed by Lincoln) to help freed blacks and poor whites eat, attain clothing and shelter, secure job protection, receive medical attention and some education. African Americans were to be made citizens of the United States and granted all rights and privileges enjoyed by other American citizens. This was accomplished through the Civil Rights Act of 1866 and the Fourteenth Amendment (ratified in 1968). The blacks' right to vote was to be insured through the Fifteenth Amendment (ratified in 1870).

The Radical Republican Reconstruction program that was guided through the House by the Pennsylvania egalitarian Thaddeus Stevens and through the Senate by Charles Sumner, a Massachusetts humanitarian, paved the way for the first large scale participation by blacks in the state conventions in the South. These conventions were called in 1867 and 1868 to establish new fundamental laws to replace the pro-Democratic, anti-black documents instituted by the Johnson governments. In South Carolina, more blacks than whites attended these conventions, and in Louisiana the races attended in equal numbers. Elsewhere, northern whites ("carpetbaggers"), some of them economic and political opportunists, and southern whites ("scalawags"), political and economic allies of the northern Republicans, dominated the conventions. The latter group had exercised the greatest influence in the new southern governments, except in South Carolina, where blacks had a majority in the Legislature through out the early years of Radical or Black Reconstruction.

Although blacks never really controlled any part of the southern governments (with the exception of South Carolina) during the whole Reconstruction era (1865-1877), they voted in large numbers and elected, members of their own race and sympathetic whites to offices ranging from city councilman to

United States Senator. There were, for example, four black lieutenant governors, twenty U.S. congressmen, two U.S. senators, three secretaries of state, a state supreme court justice, two state treasurers, and numerous other minor black officials. P.B.S. Pinchback served briefly as acting governor of Louisiana.

Black voters and elected officials tended to pursue an attitude of charity and reconciliation toward their former slave masters and their descendants. They refrained from passing or supporting vindictive legislation and insisted that southern whites reap equal benefits from the reformist acts which they passed. The Black Reconstruction governments, despite examples of waste and corruption, made great strides in the physical reconstruction of the South: in providing free public schools; in eliminating anachronistic penal institutions; and in guaranteeing civil rights. In these matters, black and white alike could look for a better life.

The growing Republican strength in the Northwest, economic ties between northern and southern capitalists, anti-African American intimidation and violence by the Ku Klux Klan and other hate groups, and the economic helplessness of black Americans eventually caused the waning of northern Republican enthusiasm for Black Reconstruction. The nadir came with the disputed election of 1876. In return for Republican pledges of federal aid for internal improvements in the South and the withdrawal of the remaining federal troops supporting Radical Reconstruction, southern Democratic leaders allowed Congress to proceed in certifying Rutherford B. Hayes as president of the United States instead of the Democratic contender, Samuel T'ilden. Following his inauguration, Hayes removed the last federal troops from the South, and the remaining Radical or Black Reconstruction governments in Florida, Louisiana, and South Carolina toppled.

Historian Rayford Logan of Howard University and others have called the period between 1877 and 1900 the nadir in African American life and history. Following the disputed election of 1876 and the so-called Compromise of 1877 which settled it, the Republican Party abandoned the Negro and left him in the hands of southern "redeemers," those native whites who reasserted white supremacy. From Hayes through William McKinley, the national government exhibited a "hands off" policy toward the "southern problem." With little or no relief to be expected from state and local authorities, blacks faced an environment reminiscent of slavery. Legalized segregation, discrimination, and political disfranchisement became the order of the day. The United States Supreme Court in 1883 and 1896 conclusively stamped legality on racial separation. In the Civil Rights cases of 1883, the Court struck down the Civil Rights Act of 1875, which, among other things, had guaranteed blacks equal access to public accommodations. In 1896, in the historic *Plessy v. Ferguson* decision, the Court sanctioned the principle of separate-but-equal facilities for blacks and whites. In practice, however, the facilities were separate and unequal. Beginning with a Mississippi law in 1890, one southern state after another adopted ingenious devices for denying the ballot to blacks. These ranged from literacy tests to the infamous white primary, in which blacks were excluded from the most important state and local elections. Ku Klux Klan-type violence, of which the most notorious form was lynching, continued to augment the legal oppression. Out of this nadir, however, were to come two outstanding voices who would leave large imprints upon African American Booker T. Washington and W.E.B. DuBois.

Booker T. Washington was the only black American invited to speak at the 1895 Cotton States International Exposition in Atlanta. Most prominent southern whites were aware of the significant work he was performing at Tuskegee Institute in Alabama, where as principal since 1881, Washington was producing trained black agriculturists, artisans, and teachers. He also encouraged cleanliness, respect for hard labor, and fostered racial harmony. In his address at the Exposition, latter dubbed "the Atlanta Compromise," Washington admonished blacks for agitating for political power and social equality, and called on whites to assist them in education, principally agricultural-industrial training, and economic advancement.

The formula for racial peace and progress which Washington outlined at the Exposition met wide approval from southern and northern whites. The *Atlanta Constitution* called it the greatest speech ever delivered in the South, and President Grover Cleveland sent Washington a congratulatory telegram. While many blacks supported Washington's ideas, others, particularly publisher William Monroe Trotter and scholar W.E.B. DuBois, disagreed with Washington's remarks and launched attacks against him. Although Trotter was his first and most vociferous antagonist, the best known opposition to Washington was W.E.B. DuBois.

The publication of DuBois' *The Souls of Black Folk* in 1903 crystallized the opposition to the "accommodationist" philosophy of Booker T. Washington. A group of black "radicals" led by DuBois and Trotter met at Niagara Falls, Canada, in June of 1905 and adopted resolutions calling for aggressive action to end racial discrimination in the United States. The lynchings, riots, intimidation, and disfranchisement of the previous decade had taught them that temporizing would not guarantee security to black Americans. The Niagara group held other meetings in the United States, recruiting black intellectuals in nearly every major city. The protest group has become known to history as the Niagara Movement.

Following the anti-black riots in Brownsville, Texas, Atlanta, Georgia, and Springfield, Illinois between 1906 and 1908, the Niagara Movement, with the exception of Trotter (who was suspicious of white people), merged in 1909 with a group of white progressives and founded the National Association for the Advancement of Colored People (NAACP). The NAACP became the most militant civil rights organization in the United States, as it sought to obtain racial equality for all Americans.

Despite the activities of the Niagara "radicals" and the NAACP, the policies and practices of Booker T. Washington and his "Tuskegee Machine" remained in vogue, and continued to garner substantial financial subsidies from wealthy white Americans as well as political endorsements from the White House to state and local authorities. The Niagara "radicals" were hard put in their efforts against Washington.

After the death of Booker T. Washington, several members of the NAACP and other individuals gained the ascendancy in

African American leadership, for there could really be no one successor Tuskegee "king pin." White America, however was resistant in accepting these militant demands, and racial oppression continued to be commonplace. Legal and extra-legal discrimination in employment, housing, education, and political disfranchisement were combined with police brutality and atrocious lynchings. Tuskegee Institute kept a running count of lynchings in the United States and published annual reports as many as eighty-three were recorded in one year and it was 1952 before none was recorded. When the United States intervened in World War I, some seemed to believe that the participation of blacks in the conflict would prick the conscience of white Americans and lead to concessions for blacks. Such precedents, in fact, existed in the War for Independence and in the Civil War. The contemporary story, however, turned out to be one of harassment of black soldiers, even while in uniform at home and abroad, and the war itself was followed by one of the worst series of racial clashes in American history. During the summer of 1919, at least twenty-five cities witnessed racial disturbances in what the poet and civil rights reader James Weldon Johnson called "the Red Summer."

The "Red Summer," a product of the post war depression and the growing black migration to large urban areas, produced a wave of disillusionment in Black America. This disenchantment had positive as well as negative effects. In the early 1920s, for example, scores of black intellectuals, centered in Harlem, began producing literary and artistic works depicting Negro life in the ghettoes and often crying for relief from oppression. The Harlem Renaissance, as the new movement was called, came of age in 1922 with the publication of Claude McKays volume of poetry, *Harlem Shadows*. His poem "If We Must Die" was a militant protest against white attacks in the North and lynchers in the South and urged blacks to resist physical assaults against them. Other notable literary works from this period include Jean Toomer's *Canc,* Jessie Fauset's *There Is* Confusion, Countee Cullen's Color, Walter White's Flight, and Langston Hughes' *The Weary Blues.* The era was synthesized in Alain Locke's anthology, *The New Negro.*

In this same period, such singers as Marian Anderson, Roland Hayes, and Paul Robeson carried performances of African American spirituals to new heights while black musicians and composers, including Louis Armstrong, Fletcher Henderson, Duke Ellington, Scott Joplin, King Oliver, and Bessie Smith brought jazz and blues from southern "honky tonks" to the major cities of the North.

Black nationalism was revived in the movement of Marcus Garvey. The West Indian immigrant taught race pride and urged large-scale emigration of blacks to Africa. arvey's would-be African empire collapsed behind the cell doors of the Atlanta Federal Penitentiary, where he was incarcerated after being convicted of mail fraud.

The Great Depression that hit the country in 1929 stung the African American. Most blacks were already on the lowest rung of the economic ladder, now they were in serious danger of touching ground. The Depression, of course, stifled much of the growing militancy among the race while doing little to relieve discontent. Blacks contended that even in the midst of common woes, they were still singled out and made the victims of discrimination. Their plight in the area of employment, for instance, was depicted by the slogan "the last yhired and the first fired." When Franklin D. Roosevelt took office as president in 1933, American blacks were certainly ready for a New Deal.

Such New Deal measures as the Civilian Conservation Corps (CCC), the National Youth Administration (NYA), and the Works Progress Administration (WPA) lifted blacks as well as whites out of the depths of the Depression, but some blacks felt that they did not receive their fair share of the benefits. Since many of the recovery and reform programs were administered by the state and local governments, this meant all-white control, especially in the South. Discriminatory handling of the measures for relief, in many instances, would not be difficult to imagine. In any case, the New Deal Administration was a segregated one. Nonetheless, President Roosevelt established his so-called "Black Cabinet," black advisers on African American affairs. These individuals included Mary McCleod Bethune, an educator, Ralph Bunche, a political scientist, William Hastie, an attorney, and Robert Weaver, an economist. In the end, the New Deal, despite its imperfections, was viewed by blacks as well as whites as an era of progress certainly a marked advance over the Depression years."

The outbreak of the Second World War in Europe, like its predecessor, encouraged a new wave of black emigration to the North. As the nation entered a state of defense-readiness, blacks sought to obtain a share of the increasing number of jobs in defense industries. Again, they met a good deal of frustration resulting from discrimination. Finally, after blacks threatened to stage a massive protest march in Washington, D.C., President Franklin D. Roosevelt issued an executive order forbidding discrimination in defense related industries. Once the United States entered the world dwar, hundreds of thousands of black Americans served with distinction. This service, along with the growing black populations in the urhan centers, a rise in the literacy rate among blacks, and increasing economic opportunities appeared to foster a new determination to end racial discrimination in American life. The NAACP, bolstered by the records of black servicemen, an increased membership, a new corp of brilliant young lawyers, and steady financial support from white philantrhropists, led the way toward freedom.

The existence of segregation and discrimination in the most democratic nation in the world constituted an American dilemma, according to the Swedish social scientist Gunnar Myrdal, who in 1944 had concluded a year-long study of the race problem entitled *An American Dilemma.* The NAACP had long been aware of the dilemma and was determined to resolve it by eliminating segregation and discrimination from American society. The NAACP leaders, like most Americans, revered the constitutional structure of the United States and thus sought to implement its program through legal channels. Prior to World War II, the organization's legal minds were chipping away at the foundations of segregation and discrimination by winning important decisions before the United States Supreme Court. After the war, there was a virtual avalanche. From 1945 to 1954, the NAACP attacked legalized segregation and discrimination in almost every domain and its foundations slowly crumbled. Ingenious devices for denying blacks the right to vote, discrimination in housing, bias in transportation, and segregation in recreation and educational facilities fell victim to NAACP-sponsored law suits, The Supreme Court decisions on school segregation, which are highlighted by the Brown case in 1954, were so far-reaching and portended so much for the future that they inaugurated a whole new era in African American history, the era of civil rights.

III. AN ERA OF CIVIL RIGHTS

The schoolhouse had long been considered an integral part of the democratic process. It was, in fact, a bulwark of American society. Indeed, its ability to socialize individuals made it almost sacred institution. The destruction of segregation and discrimination in the schools could then bring the day closer when America would boast of an integrated society. The school decisions inspired a literal stampede for equality. Court decisions quickly knocked down the remaining vestiges of legalized segregation, Congress, in the face of skillfiil lobbying by black organizations and increasing black voter registrants in the North, began passing laws designed to insure Negro voting rights against extra-legal trickery in the South. President Harry S. Truman issued an executive order banning segregation in the armed forces; several years later, President Dwight Eisenhower signed a bill that prohibited discrimination in housing assistance by the FHA and the Veterans Administration. Civil rights committees were established to investigate and report injustices. Boycotts, such as the famous one in Montgomery, Alabama in 1955-56, broke down Jim Crowism on local buses. With segregation and discrimination by law a dead letter, black groups turned to overt and covert bias in the private sector. Centering their attention on the humiliating separate lunch counters and restaurants, the sit-in technique (aided by the boycott) was revived and used frequently to wipe out discrimination in restaurants and other public accommodations from hotels to cemeteries. The Civil Rights Act of 1964 acknowledged the correctness of sit-ins by, among other things, outlawing discrimination in public accommodations. The American dilemma seemed to be over, all citizens would be free in "the land of the free." The dream which Martin Luther King, Jr. had so eloquently described at the March on Washington in August 1963 seemed near fulfillment.

In assessing the gains in civil rights and human freedoms which blacks had made in a single decade, 1954-1964, it was easy for some to see them as a continuation of the progress aborted by the end of Reconstruction in the 1870s and 1880s. The achievements and the prospects seemed so significant that many felt that the era could properly be called "The Second Reconstruction."

President Lyndon B. Johnson's signature on the Civil Rights Act of 1964 had barely become law when a serious racial disturbance erupted in Harlem. That same summer several other northern cities were the scenes of violence. August, 1965, the County of Watts in Los

Angeles exploded, leaving many dead and injured, and property losses in the millions of dollars. For the next two summers, peaking with the equally destructive Detroit riot of 1967, scores of major racial outbursts, often times sparked by clashes between blacks and white police officers, occurred. The nation sought an answer to these eruptions, particularly at a time when the millennium appeared at hand. The Presidential Commission on Civil Disorders (Kerner Commission) offered its findings in March 1968. In spite of all the court decisions, the sit-ins, marches and boycotts, the average black American was disillusioned with his status in American society, for he still found himself ill-housed, ill-clothed, poorly paid, (if at all), segregated, and discriminated against (through covert and extra-legal means) in all walks of American life. Ingrained white racism, the Commission reasoned) blocked the legitimate aspirations of black people. The slaying of Martin Luther King, Jr., the nation's leading apostle of nonviolent resistance to racism and bias, in April of 1968 increased the disillusionment and, in fact, led to some outright despair. New cries of black nationalism, black separatism, and violent resistance were heard in African-America.

In three and one-half centuries of life in America, the African race has seen momentous changes in the legal and social structures of the country which relate directly to its own status. The legal foundations of segregation and discrimination which kept it in a straitjacket were toppled in the last decade. The attainment of these goals involved a long, painful, often times frustrating and disillusioning struggle. Yet, as the Kerner Commission Report so dramatically depicted, the long fight for dignity and justice was by no means completed, for the real victory would have to involve the repression of white racism. White Americans would have to confront its ingrained and often unconscious bias on the subject of race, and work consciously to erase its effects from the land.

The landslide proportions of Richard Nixon's re-election as president in 1972 case a dark cloud over black America. During his first term, the president had consistently reaffirmed his commitment to racial equality and justice, but at the end of his term many of the most prominent leaders in black America found Nixon's record on civil rights seriously wanting. Some even claimed that there had been an erosion of the gains made under the two previous Democratic administrations. They cited, for example, the presidents failure to appoint blacks to top level positions in the federal government (i.e., under Nixon, the cabinet returned to an all-white status); his nominations of G. Harold Carswell and Clement Haynsworth, both "conservative" southerners, for seats on the United States Supreme Court; his vehement opposition to busing to achieve school desegregation; and his indifference towards desegregated housing and support of black institutions of higher education. The United States Commission on Civil Rights joined its voice with that of the black leaders, charging that the Nixon administration was derelict in its enforcement of existing civil rights laws.

President Nixon used several occasions, including press conferences and meetings with blacks inside and outside of government, to express concern with the disillusionment and disenchantment with his administration within black America. Yet he refused to alter his course. Nixon was prone to cite the phenomenal progress of black Americans in the past decade in the areas of civil rights, economic opportunity, and political development. He seemed to suggest that the remaining problems of blacks were less a matter of race and more of initiative, self-reliance, and economic development, and discussed the need for "black capitalism" and black entrepreneurship. As Nixon approached the election campaign of 1972, he predicted substantial black support for his candidacy and did, in fact, win endorsement from several prominent blacks in his bid for re-election. However, the leaders of most of the major black civil rights orgnizations in the country urged Nixon's defeat, and on election day he amassed only about thirty percent of the total black vote.

The president began his second administration amid the aura of the greatest election victory in American history, while the growing cancer of Watergate still only slowly creeping into his political life. The "Watergate" scandal, whose discovery was attributed to a black security guard, FrankWills, would soon bring down the presidency of Richard Nixon. Meanwhile, the president continued his policies of "benign neglect" toward black America.

The indifference of a national administration toward the peculiar problems of black Americans, combined with a growing economic recession, created a certain amount of confusion among blacks. Ironically, this was also a time of substantial political progress at the local level, particularly in the South. The problem, however, in large measure, was that the local political prowess which blacks were gaining could not be transformed or translated into influence at the national level, and could not halt the growing spiral of black unemployment and underemployment. The indifference manifested by the national administration had its impact in other facets of black American life. The drive for "affirmative action" in recruiting blacks to higher paying jobs seemed to lose some of its furor, as did the preferential recruiting of black students to previously all-white or majority white schools and colleges. The economic decline was a part of the explanation; the cry by some whites of "reverse discrimination" was another, but the complacent tone set in Washington was also of great significance. What should blacks, still the most ill-fed, ill-housed, poorly trained segment of the American population, do now? Would the disillusionment of the past become outright despair? Would there be new Wattses, Detroits, and Atlantas? Would the black masses again take to the streets to vent their frustrations at still not being able to share fully in the American Dream? There were, as always, voices in the black community urging such a course of action, but they were, as in the past, on the fringe of the black mainstream without a substantial following.

During the Nixon nadir, the black mainstream would continue to look to the leadership of the black middle class, as exemplified in the major civil rights organizations the NAACP, the Southern Christian Leadership Council (SCLC), Operation PUSH (People United to Save Humanity), the Urban League for the right path to the Promised Land. That leadership, faced with the political and economic realities of the 1970s and the growing displays of overt racism in the North, could only sprout the old shibboleths of the Civil Rights era and espouse similar strategies. In fact, black American leaders were now faced with problems, policies, and practices that defied simple solutions; such previous tactics as marches, court edicts, or even a brick thrown through a plate glass window seemed to be less than effective. Black America needed influence at the highest levels of political and economic decision-making, and that it did not have.

While the Nixon administration undoubtedly exaggerated the extent of black progress in America in the 1960s, it was nevertheless true that all indexes relating to income, education, housing, and the like revealed numerical and often percentage gains for black Americans during the 1960s. In many respects, Black America was still a colonized nation, but its colonial status was closer to that of America in the 1760s than to Rhodesia in the 1970s. These facts, together with the apparent futility of violent outbursts, seemed to suggest to black America, the masses as well as the elite, that after a decade of disillusionment, a return to the mainstream would best promote physical and psychological well-being. The mood of black America suggested a harvesting of gains to prevent further erosions; to place education above demonstration; to seek whatever securities that were inherent in the middle-class society in America; and to acknowledge the fact that America was still a nation of two societies one black, one white separate and unequal.

The "Watergate" scandal of the early 1970s, in which President Richard Nixon was recorded on tape as allegedly condoning criminal conspiracy, did what black voters had been unable to do in 1972 remove him from office. Nixon's successor, Vice President Gerald R. Ford, a "more moderate" Republican, came into the White House under the major constraint of not having been elected to the Oval Office. The next presidential campaign was less than two years away.

Given the constraints under which he assumed office, Ford, who eventually pardoned former President Nixon, acted in the manner of a caretaker. He continued many of his predecessor's policies while trying "to heal the nation" in the aftermath of Watergate. President Ford made no new major civil rights initiatives and generally opposed "forced busing" to achieve school desegregation. One of his cabinet members, Agriculture Secretary Earl Butz, was forced to resign after uttering a racial slur against blacks.

Ford's propensity for simplicity, particularly in foreign affairs, a continued downturn in the economy, and the "stain" which Watergate left on the Republican Party, particularly its "conservative wing," left the president particularly vulnerable as the 1976 elections approached. Jimmy Carter, a relatively unknown peanut farmer and the former governor of Georgia, emerged from the dose race victorious.

Carter had sprung on the nation during the Democratic primaries as a populist who would strengthen the economy so that both farmers and laborers could reap a better harvest. As a former southern governor, he was a suspect among blacks, particularly in the North. Although the southerner from the small town of Plains had captured the Georgia governor's office as a segregationist, he declared in his inaugural address that the time for racial bigotry in his state was over. Carter won the allegiance of many of Georgia's black leaders, particularly in the capital city of Atlanta. Since Atlanta was the headquarters of the Civil Rights Movement, the Atlanta black leadership cadre, including the father and widow of slain civil rights leader Martin Luther King, Jr. as well as such civil rights veterans as John Lewis and Andrew Young, was highly respected throughout the nation. The Atlanta group was thus able to win over other influential blacks in other parts of the nation to join them in their support of Carters candidacy. Even when Carter stumbled in a speech in Gary, Indiana, in which he discussed "the ethnic purity" of neighborhoods, the Atlanta leadership group stuck with him and helped save him from disaster in Black America. The strong showing which Carter made among blacks in the South, particularly, gave him, according to several journalists and political analysts, his margin of victory over President Ford.

Many blacks apparently believed that they had put Carter in the White House and placed great expectations on him when he took the oath of office in January, 1977. There were predictions of several black Cabinet officers, increased financial support of black institutions, and greater sensitivity toward other special aspirations and needs of Black America. But even after Carter, in an unprecedented and unexpected move, named the black Georgia congressman Andrew Young U. S. Ambassador to the United Nations and appointed Patricia Roberts Harris, a former Howard University law professor, Secretary of Housing and Urban Affairs, some blacks began to grumble that the president had made too few high level black appointments. There were even some complaints that Mrs. Harris, a fair-complexioned, middle class African American, was "not black enough" in her racial consciousness. Harris, a former civil liberties lawyer, bristled at the suggestion.

As President Carter developed his financial policies in the midst of a continuing economic downturn in the nation, Vernon Jordan, the head of the National Urban League, began a chorus of protests that the president was not doing enough to help the most depressed segment of the nation, Black America. In the beginning, Jordan's comments drew few adherents, but shortly thereafter only Carter's staunchest supporters among American's black leadership establishment were withholding criticisms. Carter himself vacillated between bristling and appeasing his black critics. One one occasion, he noted thatg he was under no compilsion to have a "quota" of blacks in his cabinet; on another, he expressed disappointment that he had not been able to recruit more highly qualified, high-level black appointees. On some occasions, Carter extolled the progress that his administration had made in civil rights and in other major issues of concern to blacks; on other occasions, he admitted that much remained to be done.

Yet it was the soaring inflation which brought higher gasoline prices and diminished supplies, and the Iran hostage crisis of 1979 that crippled the Carter presidency. Carter's inability to restore a full, healthy economy and to secure the release of American citizens from Iran brought accusations of a "malaise" at the White House. Finally, when Ronald Reagan, the former Hollywood star and governor of California, who ran an unsuccessful campaign for the Republican presidential nomination in 1976, told voters in the 1980 elections that he would restore the economy and make Americans proud of their nation again, the American electorate turned Jimmy Carter out of the White House. Although black voters still provided Carter with the heaviest support of any segment of the American population, there was less enthusiasm for him in the 1980 election. Many blacks apparently agreed that the president was not forceful enough in solving the problems of the economy or in dealing with terrorists. Others seemed to believe that he had still done too little to advance the major concerns of black America: fuller employment, better education, and enhancement of civil rights.

In the end, Jimmy Carter, by any fair assessment, was the strongest supporter of black America's "Agenda" than any American president since Lyndon Baines Johnson. While only two blacks served in his Cabinet, others were generously sprinkled throughout other high levels of government. They included Clifford Alexander, Secretary of the Army, Mary Frances Berry, Assistant Secretary of Education; and Drew Days, Assistant Attorney General. Carter appointed more black federal judges than all of his predecessors combined. He consulted with such black leaders as Jesse L. Jackson, Martin Luther King, Sr., and Benjamin Mays to a degree much larger than Johnson, and took more initiatives to support black colleges than any of his predecessors. But President Carter's gestures toward black America were not only hampered by a slow economy, but also by a growing white backlash against affirmative action and other preferential and compensatory programs for African Americans as well as continued opposition to school desegregation. In a similar fashion, if not outright overtly, Ronald Reagan had also appealed to such sentiments in his 1980 campaign, wile at the same time declaring himself a proponent of "equal opportunity."

Exponents of one version of a cyclical theory of history relate the nature and character of events of certain periods to the policies and practices of the presidential party or administration in power. Often, such an analysis takes into account the personality of the president himself. For example, both Lyndon Johnson and Jimmy Carter were southerners of somewhat humble origins who later achieved considerable wealth. Even after rising to social and political prominence, however, they tended to eschew lavishness and elitism. Both were raised among substantial black populations in the segregated South. Both overcame their backgrounds to become proponents of racial equality and racial justice. Reagan, on the other hand, emerged from modest means to fame and fortune as a Hollywood star. During his acting career and later as governor of California, Reagan associated primarily with his peers, whose lifestyles reflected glamour and power. Although he later referred to his appointments of blacks to high positions in the California state government, Reagan rarely, if ever, identified with the black masses or their particular circumstances, aspirations, and needs.

While one can make too much of the relationships between the cycles of party and administration policies and practices, and the differing characters of chief executives, it was, nevertheless, true that the "Second Reconstruction" blossomed under Democratic administrations, whose leaders, although men of substantial wealth, exhibited a special sensitivity to all of Black America. The new era of progress and hope first waned under

Republican presidents, one of whom allowed arrogance to place him outside of the law. The "Second Reconstruction gained new life under a southern Democrat who once made a living producing peanuts with poor blacks. This interlude was ended when the Republican governor of California occupied the White House.

IV. THE SEARCH FOR A BLACK AGENDA: TRADITIONS AND NEW CONTOURS

Ronald Reagan appointed only one black person, Samuel R. Pierce, a "conservative" lawyer, to his Cabinet. When Pierce left the White House, he was being investigated by Congress for possible corruption in office. Another Reagan black appointee was William Allen, another "conservative" who left his post as head of the U.S. Civil Rights Commission in disgrace under clouds of mismanagement and buffoonery. President Reagan rarely consulted with members of the black leadership establishment largely because he felt that they were partisan (almost all of them were either Democrats or Independents) and because they continuously complained that he was insensitive to their "Black Agenda." While Reagan did not sway in his opposition to such "Black Agenda" items as affirmative action and mandatory busing to achieve desegregation, he boasted of strengthening the economy and its subsequent benefits to all Americans, including black ones. President Reagan also took offense at any suggestion that he was a racist. However, as he prepared to leave the White House in 1989 after serving two terms, Reagan suggested on network television that some of the black leadership establishment deliberately continued to fan the fires of racism for self-gain, while distorting the declining significance of race in American life as well as his own record in behalf of civil rights and equal opportunity.

While Reagan did sign a bill extending the provisions of the historic Civil Rights Act of 1965 and the legislation creating the Martin Luther King, Jr. federal holiday (both with some initial reluctance), he advocated tax exemptions for segregated private schools and opposed two civil rights bills designed to strengthen the provisions of the Civil Rights Act of 1964. These protections were struck down by a Supreme Court dominated by Reagan appointees. The "Reagan Court" emerged after the president appointed three justices and elevated another to Chief Justice, jurists who were widely suspected of being "conservative ideologues." One of his nominees, Robert Bork, was rejected by the United States Senate. Reagan appointed only two blacks to federal judgeships.

Indeed, it was Reagan's appointments to the judiciary, particularly the United States Supreme Court, which highlighted the "betrayal of the Second Reconstruction." After all, the new era of human and civil rights for blacks, women, other ethnic minorities, and dissidents had begun with the high Court's decision in *Brown v. Board of Education of Topeka, Kansas* in 1954. Then, after blacks took control of their own destinies beginning with the Montgomery Bus Boycott of 1955, the Supreme Court remained steadfast in guarding and protecting their liberties under constitutional guarantees. When Reagan appointees joined the "conservative minority on the high Court, however, affirmative action and other compensatory programs to readdress past discrimination, as well as mandatory busing to achieve school desegregation, were rebuffed time and time again. The concept of "reverse discrimination" gained new prominence as the Court frequently agreed with the complaints of white males, particularly, that they were the victims of bias because of their race or sex.

While the policies of the Reagan administration and the rulings of the Supreme Court may have accurately reflected the current mood of White America, i.e., that the "Second Reconstruction" had achieved its objectives in granting full constitutional rights to African Americans, many blacks continued to blame President Reagan for "rolling back the [civil rights] clock." Some even suggested that despite what opinion polls might say about race conscious policies, the president had a constitutional and moral duty to promote such ideas and programs until the "Second Reconstruction" was, in fact, completed. They often enlisted in their assessments the history of the first Reconstruction which ended when another Republican president, Rutherford B. Hayes, made a "corrupt bargain" with racism in 1876.

During what some black and white leaders, scholars, and

other individuals came to call "the Reagan Nadir," a number of proponents of the "Black Agenda" turned their focus away from traditional politics into independent parties, apolitical postures, or new structures of political activity. Others chose to remain within the traditional structure. Some placed their hopes on the shoulders of the Reverend Jesse Louis Jackson, a veteran African American minister and civil rights leader. The former SCLC leader, through his organizations Operation PUSH and the Rainbow Coalition, emerged in the 1980s as the most popular national black leader since the late Martin Luther King, Jr. In 1984, Jackson sought the Democratic nomination for president and was promptly hailed as the first major black figure to seek that office. But Jackson's candidacy seriously divided the black leadership establishment. Several contended that his candidacy would further polarize the races in the United States, while others believed that it would undermine the solidarity which the Democratic: presidential nominee would need in the general election to defeat Ronald Reagan. Furthermore, the black leadership establishmen insisted that Jackson had absolutely no chance of capturing his party" nomination, let alone the White House.

Jackson persisted, however, insisting that he could win both the nomination and the presidency by galvanizing black Americans, bringing additional minorities (a rainbow coalition) into his ranks, and winning the support of whites "of goodwill." Although his campaign did mispire a significant increase in new blackvoters, particularly in the South, Jackson stumbled with other minorities and whites when he became associated with the Nation of Islam leader Louis Farrakhan, and after making allegedly anti-Semitic remarks himself.

Louis Farrakhan had long been accused of harboring anti-Semitic views. He allegedly called Judaism "a gutter religion" and Adolph Hitter, the Nazi dictator, "wickedly great." At the time these comments were made, Farrakhan was a strong supporter of Jesse Jackson. There were loud out cries from Jews, gentiles, and even some African Americans, particularly when Jackson procrastinated in disassociating himself from Farrakhan. However, Jackson himself created his most crucial political mistake when he was quoted as having privately referred to Jews by the epithet "hymie." After initial denials and vacillations, the presidential candidate apologized, but severe, perhaps irreparable damage had been done to his quest to broaden his Rainbow Coalition beyond black people.

The black opposition to the Jackson candidacy took on more strident tones after the "hymie!' remark. There were more assertions that the Jackson campaign represented divisiveness and futility. At the Democratic National Convention in San Francisco, Andrew Young, the mayor of Atlanta, Georgia, and a colleague of Jackson's in the Civil Fights Movement, publicly severed ties with the African American candidate and seconded the nomination of the leading contender, former Vice President Walter Mondale. Young was roundly jeered by Jackson delegates and supporters and open warfare between pro and anti-Jackson blacks seemed a real possibility in the Golden Gate city. With deep divisions among blacks and barely five percent of support from whites, the Jackson campaign of 1984 was doomed.

No matter what the outcomes were in 1984, the candidacy of Jesse Jackson for the Democratic nomination inspired thousands of blacks to enter or reenter the traditional political process and to pin their hopes on a candidate who espoused, for the most part, a "Black Agenda." Jackson's showing among whites, while not very impressive, was the best ever attained by a black presidential candidate. Furthermore, the barrier against a major African American candidate for a major party's nomination was shattered.

By 1988, even amidst continuing racial divisions, African Americans were mayors in almost all of the nation's larger cities. Other American cities were on the verge of electing blacks to high office and even smaller municipalities, some with minority black populations, had elected black mayors. Black representation in state legislatures, school boards, and state courts were increasing, especially in the South. There was a black lieutenant-governor in Virginia. These trends were encouraging to Jesse Jackson and his hard-core supporters. Despite the results of 1984, they decided that the preacher-politician should make a new effort for the White House in 1988.

The lessons to be learned from the Jackson campaign of 1984 included the imperative to solidify African Americans, particularly the black leadership establishment, to avoid the appearance of being an exclusive "Black Agenda candidate, and to avoid such embarrassing episodes as the Farrakhan affair and the "hymie" remark so as not to alienate white voters. In the 1988 campaign Jackson succeeded remarkably well in unifying blacks; almost all of the nation's prominent black Democrats rallied around his candidacy or remained neutral. He kept arm's length from Farrakhan and made overtures to Jewish leaders (Jackson had begun these gestures during his address at the 1984 Democratic Convention). Jackson carried his populist theme to urban black communities as well as rural hamlets, and carried the white working class laborer as well as the Midwestern and southern farmer. He said he wanted to give hope to the hopeless and make America a better place for all people. Black voters gave him ringing endorsements and Jackson increased his white support at least threefold, but fell short of enough votes to win the Democratic nomination for president of the United States.

Nevertheless, Jackson's primary successes, which resulted in him finishing second with more than 1,200 delegates at the 1988 Democratic Convention, had some immediate and long-range results. It helped to reduce the alienation felt among the black masses and gave many new hope that their agenda could become reality through the traditional political process. Jackson helped to shape his party's platform and secured new high ranking positions for African Americans in the Democratic Party; one of his campaign managers, Ron Brown, was subsequently elected Chairman of the Democratic National Committee. Most importantly, Jackson helped reduce white antipathy to the election of blacks to high offices. Within months of the end of Jackson's campaign, L. Douglas Wilder was elected governor of Virginia and David Dinkins mayor of New York City with substantial white support. However, many believed that Jackson had driven the Democratic Party "too far to the left," which contributed to its defeat in the 1988 presidential election. Also, despite his populist appeals, many still viewed Jackson as the candidate of the "Black Agenda." Indeed, several commentators suggested that while Jackson's efforts may have helped to pave the way for Wilder in Virginia and Dinkins in New York City, these triumphs were only secured by an abandonment of a "Black Agenda" in favor of one which suited "mainstream" White America. Such an agenda deemphasized "race conscious" policies and practices.

To be sure, even in the euphoria among most African Americans over the Jackson candidacies, other, including academicians Thomas Sowell and Robert Woodson, contended that such an adherence to a "Black Agenda" would impair efforts to promote equal opportunity for African Americans. They deplored "race conscious" policies and practices, including affirmative action programs, which they implied lowered black self-esteem and increased racial animosity. Instead, they argued, the African American leadership establishment should encourage initiative and enterprise among blacks and focus their attention on the serious internal problems of African American communities: the disproportionate number of unwed mothers and school drop-outs, drug abuse, crime and violence, poverty, and other social ills. While many in the black leadership establishment had acknowledged such problems, they all too often, the black "conservatives" asserted, placed blame upon white racism and were too dependent on relief from the federal government. The black "conservatives" would have middle income blacks promote their agenda to the black masses which could lead to solutions.

Smaller numbers of blacks during the "betrayal of the Second Reconstruction" shunned the traditional political processes altogether and sought refuge in African national parties, the Nation of Islam and other such groups, or withdrew entirely from structured political involvement. They had apparently abandoned all hope of achieving a "Black Agenda," however defined, in any variation of the American political process. Many of these people were leaders or promoters of a new wave of Afrocentricity, which gained momentum, particularly among intellectuals and students.

The new Afro-centricity or Afri-centricity, which was by no means confined to non-traditional partisans or apolitical blacks, was in reality a continuation of the Black Consciousness Movement of the 1960s and 1970s, whose political anthem was "Black Power" and whose cultural themes were "Black Is Beautiful and I'm Black and I'm Proud." The earlier movement led to many changes in the students, faculties, and curricula of the nation's institutions of higher education. Hand-in-glove with affirmative action programs, the movement changed the physical and intellectual complexion of many educational facilities and even made an impact in libraries, museums, the media, and other institutions. The Black Consciousness Movement was the mother of the Black Studies or Afro American Studies programs, inspired the epic television production "Roots" in 1977, and was instrumental in establishing African and African American history as important areas of scholarly research and study. In literature, its progenitors and leading practitioners included such poets as Gwendolyn Brooks and Dudley Randall; novelists Margaret Walker Alexander, Ernest Gaines, and James Baldwin; dramatists Imanu Amiri Baraka (LeRoi Jones) and Ron Milner, and literary critics Houston Baker, Jerry Ward, and Larry Neal. In art, its promoters included David Driskill, Jacob Lawrence, and Elizabeth Prophet. In music, Bernice Johnson Reagon and Quincy Jones were among the leading exponents of the Movement, while Ossie Davis and Ruby Dee were the leaders on the Broadway stage. Among historians Vincent Harding, Lawrence Reddick, and Lerone Bennett emerged as vocal and prolific adherents. Former SNCC leader Stokely Carmichael and Black Panther founders Huey P. Newton and Bobby Seale were among its political pioneers. Culturally and politically, the older movement was far from monolithic. Although some partisans might argue vigorously for their concept of Afri centricity, the tenets and practices actually ranged from infusion into Euro-centered scholarship and institutions to distinct and separate emphases and institutions.

The earlier Afro-centric or Black Consciousness Movement began to wane during the Nixon presidency. There appeared to be increased apathy, disillusionment, and some return to the mainstream. Enrollment in Black Studies courses decreased as did the demand for them, and new questions were even raised about the academic legitimacy of the discipline. Then, during the "Reagan Nadir," there appeared what some called "a resurgence of racism" in the United States. Black men were assaulted and killed by whites in New York City when they "intruded" into all white neighborhoods. Blacks in Miami, Florida noted at least three times during the 1980s after alleged racially motivated killings of black men by white and Hispanic police officers. Nonviolent demonstrators were assaulted itf Forsyth County, Georgia in 1986 by Ku Klux Klansmen and other white supremacists on the eve of the first Martin Luther King, Jr. national holiday. Black students were subjected to verbal and physical abuse on hundreds of high school and college campuses throughout the nation.

This "resurgence" of racism led to new demands that colleges and universities increase the diversity of their student bodies and faculties and that there be a greater infusion of ethnic studies, particularly African and African American curricula. But some African American youths decided to turn inward, electing instead to attend or to transfer to all-black or majority black colleges in order to "escape the throes of academic racism while immersing themselves in their own culture. Meanwhile'on the nation's black campuses, there were, in addition to demands that such institutions should become "blacker," i.e., a greater infusion of Black Studies and black administrative control, there was a new insistence that these historical institutions be reformed internally, in terms of physical facilities, efficiency, and effectiveness.

As in the Black Consciousness Movement, exponents of the new Afri-centricity espoused a levelling of African American society. They challenged the black social and economic elite to move away from any attempt at assimilating into the white world and to identify with their black "brothers and sisters," regardless of class. Indeed, like the black "conservatives," the Afri-centrists contended that the black elite had an obligation to help pull the black underclass out of its quagmire of poverty, illiteracy, drug abuse, crime, and despair.

The new Afri-centrists tended to be boldly nationalistic in their orientation. They identified closely with the continent of

Africa. Many came to reject the racial designation Negro, as their predecessors had done, and even the term black itself, preferring instead to be known as African American. Some took African names and wore African dress, as in the 1960s movement. New slogans, often proudly worn on tee shirts and other clothing, proclaimed "Black Is Back" and "It's a Black Thing; You Wouldn't Understand" (an apparent taunt to whites). While Martin Luther King, Jr. remained a revered martyr, other civil rights heroes and heroines slipped in esteem among the new Africentrists. The black "radicals" of earlier periods: W E. B. DuBois, Paul Robeson, Angela Davis, and Malcolm *X* were elevated to new heights of respect and admiration. The suggestion was that aggressive, nationalist strategies, not nonviolent assimilationist or integrationist attitudes, were the key to achieving the "Black Agenda."

The intellectual foundation for the new Afri-centricity was laid by black scholars, including Molefi Kete-Asante of Temple University, Maulena Karenga of the University of California, Ronald Bailey of the University of Mississippi and Armstead Robinson of Virginia. These scholars were also leaders in the National Council of Black Studies (NCBS), which had emerged during the earlier movement as a major coordinator, along with the older Association for the Study of Afro American Life and History ASALH) and the Association of Social and Behavioral Scientists (ASBS), of the changing scholarship. Kete-Asante and others wrote that black culture, even human civilization itself (because of its African origins) must be studied and understood with African history, folkways, philosophy, geography, diaspora, etc. at the center.

The Afri-centrist scholars, however, faced strong challenges not only from white intellectuals, but from some black ones as well. Historians, including Nell Painter of Princeton University of Virginia, argued that African American experiences could not be fully understood from a narrow, internally-centered focus. They contended that such matters as class and gender must be strongly considered and, indeed, that these factors may well emerge as more central to the understanding of issues than race. In fact, the research and publication of the peculiar roles of black women in American and African American societies became one of the major fields of scholarship in the 1980s.

Other cultural manifestations in African American life during "the betrayal' included new motion pictures and new musical forms delineating the black experience. A young black filmmaker, Spike Lee, emerged in the 1980s with new media presentations of black people. Lee began his career with a racy comedy, *She's Gotta Have It,* and later established himself in the film industry with *School Daze*, a film about fraternity antics and color consciousness on a black college campus. *Do the Right Thing,* Lee's third film, was probably the best of these productions. With its theme of violent racial confrontation set in the Bedford Stuyvesant section of Brooklyn, New York, it was certainly Lee's most controversial effort to date. Some critics even suggested that the film risked provoking the "race war" that it had so graphically depicted, Nonetheless, Lee's work in *Do the Right Thing* garnered an Academy Award nomination for Best Original Screenplay in 1990.

While gospel, jazz, blues, and soul music remained staples of the African American musical diet in the 1980s, "rap," a new form, appeared. Although rap music could be used for nearly any purpose from comedy to sex to politics was often employed to express a description of, and offer an opinion on, life in the black ghetto. Some of the messages presented as musical essays in verse, addressed such problems as drug abuse, violence against women, inferior education, and gang-related crime. Leading rappers of the period included 2 Live Crew, Run DMC, M.C. Hammer, and Public Enemy.

It should be clear that the new Afri-centrists did not represent a majority view in Black America during "the betrayal". African American aesthetics continued to run the gamut from assimilationist to nationalist. Still there were variations among all people, so that an "assimilationist" and a "nationalist", for example, could both condemn the racist South African system of aprtheid and celebrate the release of African National Congress leader Nelson Mandela from jail in February 1990.

If one holds to the cyclical theory of presidential administrations, then the election of Arkansas Governor Bill Clinton in 1992 raised new hope and optimism in Black America. And Clinton's early pronouncemts and appointments seemed to bear out such confidences. But soon, African American officials in the Clinton administration became the rargets of ethics investigations and were attacked for their policy statements. Commerce Secretary Brown and Agriculture Secretary Espy faced congressional probes; Espy eventually resigned. Surgeon General Joycelyn Elders was forced out of office for her "liberal" views on abortion and sexuality, and Energy Secretary Hazel O'Leary faced constant criticism for alleged excessive spending, particcularly on travel.

Then, as attacks on affirmative action heightenened in the public and private sectors, the president, while staunchly defending the concept, did allow that some programs needed "review." And just before the 1996 presidential election, he signed a welfare reform bill that many black leaders opposed. Nevertheless, black America had little choice but to support Clinton for re-election. Again they voted for him by large majorities and he was returned to the White House for a second term.

As African Americans pondered whether the Clinton administration would move back toward the left or more toward the right in its last term, whether the "Black Agenda" would be promoted, marginalized, or opposed, Black America, itself, continued to be torn politically and culturally, between hip-hoppers and traditionalists. The hip-hop culture, epitomized by rap music, was still attracting and maintaining many adherents, particularly among young blacks. And many of them were still maintaining that revolution, rather than reform, was the answer to black political and social needs. In speeches, writings, and songs, they tended to decry traditional politics, and withdraw from the process. At least, in rhetoric, they still disdained non-violent, direct action as well. Traditionalists, on the other hand, continued to deplore the "pernicious effects" of the increasingly popular "gangsta rap," contending that it glorified violence and drugs and was sexist. It did little to solve the rampant epidemic of crime, violence, illegitimate births, and drug abuse that they believed to be threatening the very existence of African America.

There began to appear, however, a major sign of a possible common ground between the hip-hop and the traditional cultures in Black America. Some rappers emerged as principal proponents of pietist living in such groups as the Five Percent Nation of Islam, an offshoot of Elijah Muhammad's Nation of Islam. Mega-urban black churches sprang up in large cities across the country, and thousands of young blacks particularly supported these churches in which the worship services increasingly included contemporary gospel, jazz, and even rap. Ministries, on black college campuses particularly, drew new adherents, and such ministries, including gospel choirs, even appeared on mostly white campuses.

Still, as the new millennium approached, the state of African America remained much the same as it had been for the past fifty years. It had been a half-century since the Second Reconstruction dismantled "de jure" segregation and struck at legal and extra-legal discrimination. But it had not led to the "promised land" of freedom, equality, and justice. Most troubling were the continuing high rates of semi-literacy and the low rates of higher education; the staggering rates of illegitimate births, drug abuse, domestic and other violence; and the assaults on young black males through injustices in the criminal justice system. These resulted in extraordinarily high rates of incarcerations—much greater than college enrollments among the same people. Many of these ills are the result of stagnant levels of poverty, and many exacerbated the prevalence of poverty. Through it all, no new Black Messiah appeared, and the strategies for solutions remained floating in a sea of division, which often reflected class and gender as well as generational differences. Except during major racial crises such as in urban riot, the beating of Rodney King, or the trial of popular black hero and football star 0. J. Simpson, these differences prevented the unity necessary to achieve impact and influence on policies and actions as was accomplished most effectively during the Second Reconstruction. And so the search continued not only to achieve the "Black Agenda," but indeed to define that agenda.

Amid the continued transculturations of traditional African American culture, by the New Millenium, "cultural warfare" not only existed in White America, but also became increasingly apparent in Black America. The "divide" centered largely around rap music, particularly, gansta rap", and the Hip-Hop Culture that it inspired. Traditionalists decried the gutter language, the sloppy dress and the apparent condoninings of violence, and misognynmy. Hip-hoppers defended their "way of life" as a true reflection of life among the masses of African Americans and hence representative of core black culture.

On the issue of homosexuality, however, many traditionalists and hip-hoppers found common ground—they were both homophobic.

When the Democrats lost the White House in the bitterly contested presidential elections of 2000 and George W. Bush, son of former president George Walker Herbert Bush was inauguarted with pledges to be "a compassionate conservative," many African American traditionalists were skeptical and wary. Bush, the younger, soon proved them correct. For although, he placed African Americans in places where they had never been before—Secretary of State and national Security Advisor—he publicly opposed affirmative action and his economic policies did little to promote new and better jobs for the black disadvantaged.

When terrorists attacked the World Trade Center in New York City and the Pentagon in Washington, DC on September 11, 2001, most Americans, of all races and classes, united behind Bush in a great outpouring of patriotism amid cries for revenge. But when early the next year, Bush led the nation into a war against president Saddam Hussein of Iraq, because the dictator allegedly possessed or was preparing "weapons of mass destruction," support for the administration among African Americans waned, as blacks and other minorities were highly visible in combat in the desert nation and prominent among the casualties.

Meanwhile, after the famed African American comedian Bill Cosby, in 2004 and 2005, began to make critical assessments of the cultural status of Black America; suggesting that some, mostly disadvantaged, African American parents were failing their children in preparing them for, and supporting, their education and that the Hip Hop culture was self destructive, the "cultural divide" among traditionalists and the younger generation as well as between classes was further exposed. While many traditional African American leaders concurred with Cosby's remarks, others, including the theologian and author Michael Dyson dissented, suggesting that Cosby was unfairly making disadvantaged blacks the villain for whatever social pathologies existed in Black America.

I. OUT OF AFRICA INTO THE HOUSE OF BONDAGE

ALDRIDGE, IRA FREDERICK (July 24, 1807-August 7, 1867) Entertainer, was born to free black parents in New York City. He attended the Free African School there, where he developed an interest in the theater. As a teenager, Aldridge debuted as an actor in the city's first African American theater group, called the African Theatre. After the African Theatre closed in 1823, Aldridge emigrated to England where black actors in the 19th century had far greater opportunities. He became an acclaimed Shakespearean actor there, playing such roles as Macbeth, King Lear, and Othello. Although some racist critics demeaned his performances, others proclaimed his the greatest portrayal of Othello ever. He toured extensively in Europe, where he enjoyed an even greater reputation than in England, itself. Aldridge became known as the "African Roscius," after the great ancient Roman actor. In 1863, he became an English citizen, and reportedly never returned to the United States.

ALLEN, RICHARD (1750-1831), Clergy, Abolitionist, Civil/ Human Rights Leader was born in bondage in Philadelphia, Pennsylvania and was sold as a youth to an enslaver in Delaware. He became a preacher shortly thereafter and received permission to hold services in his enslaver's home. Allen preached to both blacks and whites and was allowed, at the same time, to hire himself out. He bought his freedom by hauling salt, wood, and other products, and by laboring in a brickyard. He also became a member of the St. George's Methodist Church in Philadelphia, where African Americans worshipped in the balcony.

While attending services at St. George's one Sunday in 1786, Allen and others black worshippers were pulled from their knees and ordered to move to the reserved worship area for

1

blacks in the church's balcony Out of this incident grew the Free African Society, a quasi-religious organization whose programs included a fund for mutual aid, burial assistance, relief for widows and orphans, strengthening of marriage ties and personal morality, cooperation with abolition societies, and correspondence with free blacks in other area of the country. Its principal organizers were Allen and Absalom Jones, who later became an Episcopalian minister. It was probably the first stable, independent black social organization in the United States. Among the other joint efforts of Allen and Jones were the organization of relief measures for the black population in Philadelphia during the yellow-fever epidemic in 1793 and the raising of a company of black militia during the War of 1812.

In further protest of the discrimination at St. George's, Allen founded the Bethel African Methodist Episcopal Church, the first A.M.E. church in the United States on June 10, 1794. By 1816 the AME Church had been organized nationally—the first all-black religious denomination in the United States. Richard Allen was named the first bishop of the Church. Allen led the AME Church for fifteen years, until his death in 1831. He was succeeded by Morris Brown, an exile from South Carolina who had resided in Philadelphia since 1823.

Meanwhile, Allen, had become the premier national black leader in the United States. He devoted himself tirelessly to the causes of abolition, anti-colonizationism, and civil/human rights. His national stature was most evident in his leadership, although briefly, of the National Negro Conventions. The initial National Negro Convention met at Bethel A.M.E. Church in Philadelphia in 1830. Delegates from Delaware, Maryland, New York, Pennsylvania, and Virginia attended. The convention, under the leadership of Richard Allen (other prominent African American leaders present included abolitionist and shipmaker James Forten and journalist Samuel Cornish), adopted resolutions calling for improvements in the social status of African Americans. The delegates considered projects to establish a black college and to encourage blacks to emigrated to Canada. Neither of these proposals was adopted. Opposition even arose to the mere idea of an African American convention. Yet these ad-hoc conventions continued to convene and occasionally were attended by white abolitionists and reformers. In the ten years before the Civil War, there was a rash of such conventions held in Cleveland, Rochester, and New York City as well as in Philadelphia. One of the most important meetings was in Rochester in 1853, when the National Council of Colored People was formed. This group issued a statement that both denounced racial oppression in America and cited instances of black progress.

ARMISTEAD, JAMES LaFAYETTE (1760-1832) Soldier, was born a bondsman of William Armistead of New Kent County, Virginia. In March 1781 Armistead was granted permission to serve with General LaFayette during the War for Independence and infiltrated the headquarters of British general Charles Cornwallis. Armistead was noted for his written intelligence reports concerning the Yorktown campaign that ended the Revolutionary war.

LaFayette gave Armistead a certificate stating: "This is to certify that the bearer by the name of James had done essential services to me while I had the honor to command in this State. His intelligences from the enemy's camp were industriously collected and more faithfully delivered. He properly acquitted himself with some important communications I gave him and appears to be entitled to every reward his situation... under my hand, Richmond, November 21st, 1784. LaFayette."

As a reward for his services, Armistead was granted his freedom by the Virginia legislature in 1786. Thirty years later, he purchased forty acres of land near New Kent County and raised a family. He was granted an annual pension of $40 in 1819 and in 1824 was personally greeted by General LaFayette upon the general's return too America. Armistead died in 1832.

ATTUCKS, CRISPUS (c. 1723- March 5, 1770) Sailor, of Framingham, Massachusetts, an escaped slave, died with four other Americans in the so-called Boston Massacre on March 5, 1770. Attucks was a bondsman of deacon William Brown of Framingham. In November 1750 he escaped from bondage at the age of twenty-seven. He was in the forefront of the group that taunted British soldiers during the altercation and reportedly was the first to fall from their fire. Massachusetts later honored Attucks with a statue in Boston. In Boston, African Americans held an annual Crispus Attucks Day from 1858 to 1870.

BANNEKER, BENJAMIN (November 9, 1791-October 9, 1806), Scientist, was born in Ellicott, Maryland, the grandson of a white woman. He secured a modest education from a school for free blacks near Joppa, Maryland, but received assistance in his study of science from George Ellicott, a Maryland Quaker, planter, and philanthropist. As a youth, Banneker made a wooden clock which reportedly remained accurate throughout his lifetime. Between 1791 and 1802, Banneker published a yearly almanac, which was widely read, and was also the first black man to publish astronomical materials in the United States. His other publications included a treatise on bees. Banneker is also credited with computing the cycle of the seventeen year locust.

In 1791, Banneker was appointed upon the recommendation of Thomas Jefferson to serve as a member of a commission to survey plans for Washington D.C. That August, he wrote a famous letter to Jefferson appealing for a more liberal attitude toward African Americans, using his own work as evidence of African American intellectual equality. Banneker said in part, "I apprehend you will embrace every opportunity to eradicate that train of absurd and false ideas and opinions which so generally prevail with respect to [blacks]; and that your sentiments are concurrent with mine which are: that our universal Father hath given being to us all; that He had also without partiality afforded us all with these same faculties and that, however diversified in situation or color, we are all the same family and stand in the same relation To Him."

BARBADOES, JAMES (d. June 22, 1841) Abolitionist. Little documentation of James Barbadoes's life remains, despite his activism and leadership among free Negroes in Boston. He was a member of the Massachusetts General Colored Association and a delegate to the Convention of the People of Color in Philadelphia in 1831. Barbadoes was also a founding member of the American Anti-Slavery Society. At a May 1934 meeting of the New England Anti-Slavery Society, Barbadoes urged support for William Lloyd Garrison and his abolitionist newspaper, *The Liberator*. Barbadoes and three others extended an invitation to Garrison to attend a meeting of African American citizens after Garrison returned from England. In the 1830s, Barbadoes ran a barbershop and rented rooms in Boston. He died on June 22, 1841, of "West India Fever" after a doomed mission to settle a group of blacks in Jamaica.

BECKWOURTH, JAMES PIERSON (April 6, 1798-1866), Trader, Explorer was born to a white father and a black slave mother in Fredericksburg, Virginia, the third of thirteen children. Beckwourth signed up as a scout for General William Henry Ashley's Rock's Rocky Mountain Fur Company in 1823 and 1824. He worked as a "mountain man" for the next thirteen years. Beckwourth established his own trading post in St. Fernandez (now Taos, New Mexico) and later in Pueblo de Angles (now Los Angeles, California). In 1846 Beckwourth fought in the California revolution against Mexico and in 1846 in the American war with Mexico. He served as chief scout for General John Charles Fremont on his exploring expedition in 1848. Beckwourth discovered a path in the Sierra Nevada Mountains between the California Feather and Truckee Rivers. This path became a major emigrant route to California. It was later named the Beckwourth Pass.

BETHUNE, THOMAS GREENE (BLIND TOM) (May 25, 1849-June 13, 1908), Musician. By the time Thomas Greene Bethune was four, the blind child, who was born into bondage, was being exhibited as the "musical marvel' of the Bethune plantation in Georgia. The exhibition of Tom, however, soon turned into exploitation as his owners made several fortunes on his talent, including an estimated $100,000 from an 1866 European tour. Colonel James Bethune even used Tom's talent to benefit the Confederacy throughout the Civil War. When Tom was 15, Colonel Bethune gained guardianship of the boy, supposedly with his parents' consent. In 1865, with the end of the war, an attempt was made to liberate Tom from the guardianship that was akin to slavery. That, however, failed and Tom's "guardianship" was eventually passed on to the colonel's son, and later, the son's widow and her second husband who profited off the last fifteen years of Tom's life. Tom reportedly died penniless on June 13, 1908, in Hoboken, New Jersey. His accomplishments included performances before foreign dignitaries and President James Buchanan, the composition of over 100 piano and vocal pieces, and the mastery of over 700 pieces by European greats such as Beethoven and Bach.

BRYAN, ANDREW (1737-1802), **LEILE, GEORGE** (1750-1820), Clergy, In Savannah, Georgia, George Liele and Andrew Bryan organized the American colonies' first black Baptist Church in 1773. Liele and Bryan were both former bondsmen with modest education. When they first began preaching (at very young ages) there were no black denominations. Liele and Bryan preached without compensation. Liele supported himself as a laborer-for-hire after being freed by his previous enslaver. Opposition to black worship eventually forced Liele to flee to Jamaica. Bryan's enslaver defended him against other whites who were alarmed over the growth of the Black Church, and although Bryan bought his wife's freedom, he did not purchase his own until after his enslaver's death, because of a sense of gratitude he had for his enslaver's support of him.

CAESAR, JOHN (d. January 17, 1837) Insurrectionist, led hundreds of slaves in the attack of the St. Johns River plantations on the eve of the second Seminole War. Near the end of the war, he organized a guerilla campaign against plantations in the St. Augustine vicinity, recruiting black and Native American slaves. On the night of January 17, 1837, Caesar was killed in a surprise attack. Nevertheless, his efforts at the beginning and end of the war led to the Treaty of Fort Dade, resulting in freedom for many runaway slaves who might otherwise have been reenslaved.

CINQUE, JOSEPH Mutineer. The most famous slave mutiny in U.S. history took place on the Spanish ship, *Amistad*.in July 1839. A group of Africans, led by Joseph Cinque, brought the captured vessel into Montauk, Long Island, where they were arrested. Former President John Quincy Adams defended the rebels before the U. S. Supreme Court, which granted their freedom.

CROMWELL, OLIVER (1752- January, 1853), Soldier, was reportedly born free in Columbus, Burlington County, New Jersey. He worked as a farmer before joining the 2nd New Jersey Regiment under the command of Colonel Israel Shreve. Cromwell recalled that he accompanied General George Washington when he crossed the Delaware in 1776 and also claimed to have fought in the battles of Princeton, Brandywine, Monomouth, and Yorktown. He received an honorable discharge from the Jersey Battalion-signed by General Washington at his headquarters-on June 5, 1783. Cromwell received a federal pension of ninety-six dollars a year.

CUFFE, PAUL (January 17, 1758-September 9, 1817), Shipbuilder, abolitionist, Pan-Africanist was born in New Bedford, Massachusetts as a free man. His mother was a Native American and his father was African born. As a teenager he became a sailor on cargo and whaling ships. Eventually, he rose to the rank of captain and owned his own fleet.

In 1797, he purchased a farm and built a school for the children in his hometown. An abolitionist and an activist in the cause of civil rights, Cuffe and his brother John unsuccessfully sued the state of Massachusetts for the right to vote.

A devout Quaker, Cuffe became convinced that African Americans should help with the "chistianization and civilization" of Africa. Although opposed by many African American leaders, including Richard Allen, he devised an emigrationist scheme and actually took 38 free blacks, many of them children, to Sierra Leone in 1815. However, Cuffe died before any success could be seen for the venture.

DABNEY, AUSTIN (c. 1760-1834) Soldier, is believed to have been born to a Virginia white woman and a black father in North Carolina. Dabney was enlisted in the Georgia Militia by Richard Aycock. In February 1779, Dabney fought along with white men in the name of colonial independence. He was wounded in battle, ending his military career. Dabney was emancipated in 1786 by the Georgia legislature, and in 1821 he was granted 112 acres of choice farmland in Walton County. His prosperity grew from owning horses during the later years of his life. Dabney was, according to some, Georgia's only genuine black hero of the American Revolutionary War. Dabney died in Zebulon in 1834.

DELANY, MARTIN ROBISON (MARTIN R. DELANY), (May 6,1812-1885) Abolitionist, Pan-Africanist, Physician was born in Charles Town, Virginia (now a part of West Virginia),the son of free African Americans. He was educated in the African Free School of New York City, the Canaan Academy in New Hampshire, the Oneida Institute in upper New York, and the Harvard University Medical School, where he received his medical degree in 1852. Delany attempted to practice medicine in Pittsburgh, but prejudice and poor profits drove him into other areas.

He became a member of the British Association for the Promotion of Social Science and published two books, *The Condition, Elevation, Emigration and Destiny of the Colored People of the United States* (1852) and *Principle of Ethnology* (1879). In 1843, Delany published a newspaper, *Mystery*, and joined Frederick Douglass in the publication of *The North Star* in 1847.

He was also a leader of the national convention movement of African Americans. Following the passage of the Compromise of 1850, with its new Fugitive Slave Act, Delany became convinced that the United States was too inhospitable for people of African descent and turned his attention to colonization. He helped organize an expedition to Nigeria in 1858, negotiated treaties with eight African chiefs who granted lands for prospective African American settlers, and began plans for the expanded production and exportation of cotton in the region. During the Civil War, Delany was a medical officer with the rank of major in the 104th Union Regiment in South Carolina. He settled in Charleston after the war, working with the Freedmen's Bureau, and later served as a justice of the peace there. He was defeated in a bid for lieutenant governor of South Carolina in 1874.

DOUGLASS, FREDERICK (c. 1817-February 20, 1895), Abolitionist, Civil/Human Rights Leader, was born in Tuckahoe, Maryland, in 1817, Douglass was separated in infancy from his mother and had harsh enslavers as a child. While still very young, Douglass became a house servant in Baltimore, where white playmates taught him to read. His first attempt at escape was thwarted, but in 1838, while working as a ship caulker, he managed a successful break from slavery. Further education by anti-slavery groups in the North made Douglass a very lucid speaker and writer.

The publication of the *North Star* in 1847 was one of the factors that led to Douglass's break with William Lloyd Garrison, the noted white abolitionist and publisher of the *Liberator*. Garrison saw no need for two major rival anti-slavery publications, but Douglass and other blacks had become convinced that they must play a more leading role in the abolitionist movement, and that included the printing of a newspaper.

In later years Douglass was appointed to several political and diplomatic posts, including unofficial advisor to presidents Abraham Lincoln and Andrew Johnson, marshal of the District of Columbia, recorder of deeds of the District of Columbia, and minister to Haiti. He also served as president of the Freedmen's Bank in 1874. On March 18, 1877, Douglass was appointed Marshal of D.C. Despite southern opposition and opposition from within his own party, President Rutherford B. Hayes appointed Frederick Douglass marshal for the District of Columbia. On May 17, 1881, President James A. Garfield appointed Frederick Douglass the recorder of deeds for the District of Columbia.

On February 20, 1895, Douglass died in Anacostia Heights, in Washington, D.C. In 1898, a monument was dedicated to him. The tone of the ceremony was set by T. Thomas Fortune, president of the Afro-American League. "The management of the colored race in the South has been a conspicuous failure," he said, "I see other black and yellow peoples about to come under the care of this government. If you rule [them]...as the South has been and is being ruled, you will have revolution upon revolution, and you ought to have it."

DUSABLE, JEAN BAPTISTE POINTE (c.1750-August 28, 1808) Trader, was born in St. Marc, Saint Dominque (now Haiti), the son of a Frenchman who had emigrated to Haiti from Marseilles, France, and an African woman...He was probably educated in France and may have worked as a sailor. He had become a fur and grain trader in the Great Lakes region by the late 1770s, establishing a base at the site of what is now Chicago. Although the British were suspicious of DuSable's relationships with the French in the area, they sent him to represent British trading interests with Native Americans around the St. Clair River, northeast of present-day Detroit. Du Sable returned to his post at present-day Chicago in 1784, where he erected several buildings at what gradually became a major trading center. Du Sable was a "jack-of-all-trades", working as a carpenter, cooper, distiller and miller.

He married a woman from the Potawatomi nation, with whom he had two children, and he became intimately involved in the affairs of his wife's people. But in 1800 he was denied a desire to become a Potawatomi chief. Consequently, he sold his property for what was then the enormous sum of $1,200, and moved to St. Charles, Missouri, where he worked as a farmer and trader. In 1912 the city of Chicago placed a marker in his memory at the corner of Kinzie and Pine streets. In 1987 a commemorative stamp was issued in his honor by the U. S. Postal Service.

ELDRIDGE, ELEANOR (March 27, 1784 or 1785-1865) Businesswoman, was born in Warwick, Rhode Island. She began working for the Baker family at an early age, washing clothes for twenty-five cents a week. During her six years with the family, she became skilled at spinning, weaving, and arithmetic. In 1812 she and her sister began a business of weaving, washing, and soap boiling that enabled Eldridge to buy a lot and build a house, which she would, later rent for $40 a year. By 1822 she had saved enough from her various business ventures to build a large house. Over a period of years she added to the house and began making payments toward a second house. When Eldridge made a trip to visit relatives, it was mistakenly reported that she had died. Upon her return, all her property, valued at $4,000, had been sold. On the advice of friends, she entered a "trespass and ejectment" suit, which she won. However, she could recover her property only after payment of $2,700, which likely went unpaid. In 1838 Eldridge's memoirs were written by Frances Harriet Whipple Greene McDougall.

ESTEVANICO (Esteban) (d. 1539), Explorer, was born in Morrocco, in North Africa. As a bondsman, he became a part of an expedition that left Spain in 1527 to explore the western coast of the Gulf of Mexico. But the explorers' ships were blown off course into what is now Tampa Bay, Florida. Sailing west, the party then became shipwrecked on Galveston Island off the Texas coast. There were only four survivors, including Esteban, who became an especially valuable member of the group because he got along well with the Native Americans who inhabited much of the areas. By 1536, the exploring party had reached Mexico City. Spanish authorities were then made aware that Native Americans had reported that within the area were" the seven Golden Cities of Cibola" that contained many treasures. The party was directed to search for the riches. Esteban was sent out ahead of the others and directed to report back his findings. As he proceeded, in 1539, he became the first non-Native American to enter what is present-day Arizona and New Mexico. However, members of the Zuni nation killed him and the remainder of the party went back to Mexico. When Coronado and other explorers reached the areas at a later time, the "golden cities" appeared to be only the reflections of the sun off of the top of some Native American pueblos.

FORTEN, JAMES (1766- March 4,1842) Shipmaker, Aboltionist, was born of free Afncan American parents in Philadelphia on September 2, 1766. He studied at a Quaker school but at the age of fifteen he quit to serve as a powder boy aboard the privateer Royal *Louis* during the American War for Independence. He was captured by the British and held prisoner for seven months. He eventually spent a year in England where he was introduced to international abolitionism..

Upon returning to America he was apprenticed to a sail-maker, but by 1786 he was a foreman and in 1798 he became owner of the company. The business prospered and in 1832 employed forty Euro-Americans and African American workers.

By the 1830s Forten had become active in the abolitionist movement and was a strong opponent of African colonization. He was one of the most outspoken opponents of the Fugitive Slave Act of 1793. He became a noted pamphleteer (a 19th-century form of social activism) and was an early fund-raiser for William Lloyd Garrison's *The Liberator*. Indeed some scholars credit Forten with convincing Garrison to support African American equality as an essential element of militant abolitionism. Forten was also a founding president of the American Moral Reform Society

GARDNER, NEWPORT (1746-1826), Entertainer, was one of the first black music teachers in America, opened a music store in Newport, Massachusetts. Gardner, born in 1746, was a slave of Caleb Gardner, one of Newport's leading merchants. The bondsman taught himself to read, sing, and write music. One of his compositions, "Crooked Shanks," was included in the collection *A Number of Original Airs, Duettos and Tiros,* published in 1803. He was also active in religious affairs. He was a founder of the Newport Colored Union Church and Society and became a missionary in Africa in 1826, the estimated year of his death.

HALL, PRINCE (1735-December 4, 1807), Soldier, Fraternal Leader, Clergy, a veteran of the War for Independence, received a charter for a Masonic Lodge for blacks on September 12, 1787. This group was chartered in England as African Lodge No. 459. Hall, the first master of the organization, set up additional African lodges in Pennsylvania and Rhode Island during 1797. Hall was born in Barbados, British West Indies, in 1735, the son of an

Englishman and a free black woman. He was apprenticed as a leather worker but abandoned that training to emigrate to Boston. During the Revolutionary War, Hall and twelve other free blacks were inducted into a Masonic Lodge by a group of British soldiers stationed in Boston. When the British evacuated the area, Hall organized a Masonic Lodge for blacks. Hall, a self-educated clergyman, also championed the establishment of schools for black children in Boston, urged Massachusetts to legislatively oppose slavery, and proposed measures to protect free blacks from kidnapping and enslavement. Following his death in Boston on December 4, 1807, the African Grand Lodge became the Prince Hall Grand Lodge, which has become a major social institution in Black America.

HAMMON, JUPITER (October 17-1711?), Poet, born in bondage, published *Salvation by Christ with Penitential Cries on* December 15, 1761, the first known poetical work by an African American. Hammon's enslavers had given him a rudimentary education, including religious instruction, and helped to publish his verse. Scholars do not accord much literary merit to Hammon's work, but he is an important figure because of his place in the chronology of black literature. Hammon is also known for his *Address to the Negroes of the State of New York* (1787), in which he called upon blacks to be faithful and obedient to their masters. Hammon believed that the race should endure its bondage humbly and patiently until it earned its freedom by honest and good conduct.

HEALEY, JAMES AUGUSTINE (April 6, 1830-August 5, 1890) Clergy, **HEALEY, PATRICK FRANCIS** (February 2, 1834-January 10, 1910), Clergy, Educator.
   James Augustine and Patrick Francis Healy were the sons of an Irish immigrant, Michael Healey and a bondswoman, Mary Eliza. Their father sent the brothers to the North for their education, but after being rejected by several academies, the Healys entered a Quaker school on Long Island, New York. Later, they transferred to the College of the Holy Cross in Worchester, Massachusetts, where James was the most outstanding pupil. In

1852, he entered the Sulpician Seminary in Paris, and on June 10, 1854, he was ordained a priest in Notre Dame Cathedral in Paris. Healy's first assignment as a priest was in a white parish in Boston, then he became pastor of the New St. James Church. Healy's stature in the New England Catholic hierarchy continued to rise; in 1874, he was appointed bishop of Maine and was consecrated in the Cathedral at Portland on June 2, 1875. Healy proved to be an energetic and devoted to duty. He ministered to an all-white following, but only occasionally was subjected to racial abuse. Shortly before his death on August 5, 1890, Healy was promoted to the rank of assistant at the Papal Throne.

Patrick Healy, who earned a doctorate in Europe (which some authorities cite as the first PhD ever awarded to an African American), became the 29th president of Georgetown University, the oldest Catholic college in the United States on July 31, 1874. Healy, the first African American to become a Roman Catholic bishop, headed the institution until 1883.

HEMINGS, SALLY (1776-1835) Bondswoman, was believed to have captured the heart of Thomas Jefferson, who at the time was a forty-five-year old widower, shortly after she arrived at Jefferson's Monticello plantation in 1775 as a bondswoman. She accompanied his daughter to join him in France and was apparently educated and financially compensated during the three-year stay. Soon after she returned to Monticello, in 1789, Hemings gave birth to a son. Writings by Jefferson, Hemings children, and Virginia's *Richmond Recorder* evidenced their intimate relationship and Jefferson's paternity to this and probably six other of Heming's children. Hemings was discreetly freed by Jefferson's daughter after his death in 1826.

HILL, PETER (July 19,1767-1820) Clockmaker, was born into bondage in a New Jersey Quaker household, where he learned the craft of clock making from his enslaver. He worked in his enslaver's clock shop until age 27, when he was manumitted. Hill received his manumission document May 1, 1795. On September 9, 1795, Hill married Tina Lewis, a free person of color. Hill went on to open clock shops of his own in Burlington

Township and Mount Holly, New Jersey. Two of Hill's tall case clocks are known to still be in existence: one in Westtown (Pa.) School, the other in the National Museum of History and Technology of the Smithsonian Institution in Washington, D.C.

HORTON, GEORGE MOSES (1797-1883?) Author, was born into bondage on a plantation in Northampton County, North Carolina. He later bargained with his enslavers for the "privilege" of earning money by selling love poems to students at the University of North Carolina. Not able to write himself, Horton dictated his poems to the students. As a result, his earliest works have been forgotten or attributed to others. Horton was taught to write by Carolina Hentz, a writer, abolitionist, and wife of a professor. His first volume of poetry, *The Hope of Liberty* (1829), was not successful enough to pay for Horton's freedom, but it earned him some local fame and later promoted the cause of abolition with two reprintings under the title *Poems of a Slave* (1837, 1838). Horton published two more volumes of poetry in his lifetime: *The Poetical Works of George M Horton, the Colored Bard of North Carolina* (1845) and *Naked Genius* (1865). It is believed Horton died in 1883 in Philadelphia, Pennsylvania.

HULL, AGRIPPA (1759-1848), Soldier, was born free in Northampton, Massachusetts. Hull enlisted as a private in the brigade of the Massachusetts line on May 1, 1777, where he served for the duration of the Revolutionary War. He served his first two years as a private and the next four years as an orderly for General Tadeusz Kosciuszko, the Polish patriot. Hull received his discharge (signed by General George Washington) in July 1783 at West Point. Kosciuszko later met with Hull in New York when the general visited the United States in 1797. Hull married a fugitive slave, adopted another fugitive slave, and farmed a plot of land in Stockbridge, Massachusetts.

JOHNSON, FRANCIS (FRANK) (1792-1844), Musician, one of America's first African American bandleaders, gave a command performance before Queen Victoria at Buckingham Palace in 1838. He was presented with a silver bugle. Johnson was born in 1792 and by 1820 had established himself as a versatile musician, playing with white bands in Philadelphia. When he organized his own band, principally a woodwind ensemble, it won national acclaim for its excellent performances at dances and parades. Frank Johnson's Colored Band, as it was called, even performed on plantations as far south as Virginia. Johnson became noted for his ability to "distort a song into a real, jig, or country dance."

JONES, JOHN (1816-1879), Businessman, civil/human rights leader, was born free in Green City, North Carolina. He was self-educated and became a tailor's apprentice in Memphis, Tennessee, before moving to Chicago in 1845. Jones opened a tailoring business there, from which he amassed a fortune. Using his wealth and influence, Jones led the successful fight against the prohibition of the immigration of free blacks into Illinois in 1853, the "Black Laws "(which confined blacks to "second class citizenship") and school segregation in Chicago. He was elected a Cook County, Illinois, commissioner in 1875 and served for two terms. Jones was also the first African American elected to the Chicago Board of Education. Prior to the Civil War, he was also active in the abolitionist movement, his home being used as a station on the Underground Railroad. Jones died in 1879, leaving an estate valued at more than $100,000.

LANGSTON, JOHN MERCER (December 14, 1829-November 15, 1897) Politician, was born to a Euro-American man and an African American bondswoman on a Virginia plantation in 1829. After his father's death, Langston was sent to Ohio, where he was reared by one of his father's friends. By 1854, Langston was engaged in an active law practice in Chillicothe, Ohio, and in 1855, as the only African American attorney in Brownhelm, he was elected clerk. Langston won a seat on the Brownhelm City Council the following year—making him the first African American to win an elective political office in the United States—a post he held until 1860.

In 1865, he was named president of the National Equal Rights League and in 1867 he became a member of the Board of

Education in Oberlin, Ohio. After his return to the South during Reconstruction, Langston served as inspector general to the Freedman's Bureau Schools (1868-69); teacher, law school dean, and acting vice president of Howard University (1869-76); minister to Haiti (1877-85); president of the Virginia Normal and Collegiate Institute (1885-88); and congressman from Virginia (1889-91). Langston, who died in 1897, was one of the last African Americans elected to the U.S. Congress in the nineteenth century, and was the great-uncle of Harlem Renaissance poet Langston Hughes.

LEIDESDORFF, WILLIAM (1810-1848), Sailor, State Official, was born in Saint Croix, Virgin Islands, to an African mother and a Danish father. Leidesdorff moved to New Orleans, Louisiana, in 1834. After becoming a ship captain he piloted a voyage from New York to California around the southern tip of South America aboard the schooner *Julia Ann* in 1841. Leidesdorff settled in California and built a hotel, school, and steamboat. He served as U.S. vice-counsel for the port of San Francisco from 1845 to 1846.

LOGUEN, JERMAIN WESLEY (1813-1872), Clergy, Abolitionist, was born in Davidson County, Tennessee. His mother, Cherry, was born free in Ohio, kidnapped, and sold to David Loguen, who fathered Jermain. Logue sold Jermain and his mother to a brutal enslaver. After witnessing the constant whipping of his mother, the murder of another bondsperson, and the sale of his sister, Loguen sought his freedom. With the help of Quakers, Loguen escaped on the Underground Railroad to Hamilton, Ontario, where he learned to read and worked as a lumberjack and farmer. He later settled in central New York. After opening a school for black children in Utica, Loguen and his wife moved to Syracuse, where he opened another school and managed the Underground Railroad station there. In 1842 he was ordained a minister of the New York Conference of the African Methodist Episcopal Zion Church and went on to establish several churches between 1840 and 1850. He worked closely with Frederick Douglass on the Underground Railroad, and he wrote for Douglass's *North Star* and *Frederick Douglass' Paper*. The Fugitive Slave Act of 1850 threatened the freedom of Loguen and other runaway slaves, so in 1851 he escaped to Canada. Upon returning to Syracuse, he continued his work with the Underground Railroad, helping some 1,500 slaves escape, including Harriet Tubman, who stayed at his home. He was twice elected bishop of the A.M.E. Zion church and was about to begin mission work on the west coast when he died in 1872.

LOWERY, PETER Minister, became pastor of a black church in Nashville, Tennessee in 1849, making him probably the first African American pastor of a church in the South. Lowery, who was born a slave, had managed to purchase his freedom and that of other members of his family, including his mother, brothers, and sisters, over a period of more than forty years. In his endeavor, he was substantially aided by his wife, Ruth, a free woman of color.

LYONS, JUDSON WHITLOCKE (August 15,1858-June 22, 1824), Politician, was born in Burke County, Georgia. He attended the Augusta Institute (Georgia; now Morehouse College in Atlanta) and received a law degree from Howard University in 1884. Shortly thereafter he was admitted to the bar in Augusta. He began his political career at the age of twenty when he became an elected delegate to a constitutional convention. Two years later he served in Georgia's internal revenue service and was a delegate to the Republican National Convention. He was appointed Register of the Treasury in 1898 and his name was printed on U. S. paper currency—the first African American to be honored in this fashion. In 1904 he was a member of the Republican National Committee. He left his post at the Treasury in 1906.

MALVIN, JOHN (1795-July 30, 1880), Educator, Emigrationist, was born free to a free mother, Dalcus Malvin, and an enslaved father in Dumfries, Prince William County, Virginia. He was taught reading and spelling by an old slave who used the Bible as a teaching guide, and he learned carpentry from his father.

He moved to Cincinnati, Ohio, in 1827 to remain free, and he became a community leader and helped with the Underground Railroad. Malvin married Harriet Dorsey in Cincinnati on March 8, 1829. After his arrests, and brief imprisonment as a "fugitive slave" in 1831, Malvin became interested in emigration and migration. In 1832 he founded the School Education Society in Cleveland to provide a school for black children. Malvin purchased his father-in-law's freedom in 1833. He was a delegate to the National Convention of Colored Freedmen in Cleveland in 1848. During the 1850s Malvin attended meetings of the influential Ohio State Conventions of Colored Citizens and was elected vice-president of the Ohio Anti-Slavery Society in 1858. Malvin worked to end the Black Laws of Ohio, which prohibited blacks from attending schools and imposed a five-hundred-dollar. security bond on blacks entering the state.

At the start of the Civil War, Malvin urged African Americans in Cleveland to organize troops, although it would be several years before blacks would be allowed to serve. One year before his death, Malvin's autobiography was published in the *Cleveland Leader* as a forty-two page booklet entitled *Autobiography*.

MARRANT, JOHN (March 23, 1784-August 14, 1818), Author, was born in New York. He lived in St. Augustine, Florida, for a time before being captured by members of the Cherokee Nation. Marrant was influenced by the Reverend George Whitefield, an English preacher who co-founded, with John Wesley, the Methodist Movement. He served with the British Royal Navy and was a Methodist missionary in Nova Scotia before becoming an author. His writings detailed the events of his own life that led him to his religious convictions. His most popular work, *A Narrative of the Lord's Wonderful Dealings with John Marrant,* describes Marrant's "dealings" with God. Historian Arthur Schomburg reprinted Marrant's Masonic Sermon in 1789 and described him as "undoubtedly one of the first, if not the first, Negro minister of the gospel in North America." Marrant rarely referred to racial matters in his works and thus was never cited in early collected works of African American biographies.

MOLINEAUX, TOM (March 23, 1784-August 14, 1818) Athlete, was born in bondage in Georgetown, District of Columbia. As a boy, Molineaux began to box, following in the footsteps of his late father. His abilities as a boxer won him his freedom and a hundred-dollar prize when Molineaux defeated a slave from a nearby plantation on the bet of their enslavers. He used his prize money to go to London, where boxing was a popular and profitable sport, and he became the first American to fight with distinction abroad. Unfortunately, his success was short-lived; he lost two highly publicized matches with Tom Cribbs, the British champion. Molineaux then entered a downward spiral into poverty and alcoholism. He died penniless in Ireland on August 4, 1818.

NEWBY, DANGERFIELD (1815-October 17, 1859) Insurrectionist, was born in Virginia to a bondswoman and a Scotsman. His father granted all his children freedom upon his death. Newby married and had seven children. Desperate to free his enslaved family, Newby joined John Brown's group. He was killed in the Harpers Ferry raid the night of October 17, 1859; afterwards, his body was beaten and mutilated by the town's citizens. His remains were buried in a shallow grave in Harpers Ferry and later moved to North Elba, New York, where they were laid to rest near the grave of John Brown.

PLEASANT, MARY ALLEN (MAMMY), (c.1800-1904) Businesswoman, Abolitionist, was either born in bondage or as a free woman in Pennsylvania. It is known that she subsequently moved to San Francisco from Boston where she had met William Lloyd Garrison. In California, Pleasant opened a restaurant and boarding house, managed estates, and made loans. She is believed to have rescued slaves who were being held illegally and to have worked to secure blacks' rights to testify in court and ride street cars. Pleasant also reportedly gave money to John Brown to help his attack on Harpers Ferry. But Pleasant, believed to be of African and Native American descent, also holds a prominent name as the planner and operator of the House of Mystery, a brothel. She also admitted to helping one of her women forge a marriage contract in order to gain wealth through divorce.

PLUMMER, HENRY VINTON (1844-February 8, 1905) Clergy, Soldier, Emigrationist, was born in bondage in Prince George's County, Maryland. At eighteen, Plummer escaped from slavery after having been sold at least twice. In 1864 he enlisted in the navy and taught himself to read during his year and a half of service. In 1867, Plummer married Julia Lomax; together they had six sons and two daughters. Plummer began ministering in Maryland congregations while preparing to attend Wayland Seminary in Washington, D.C., from which he graduated in 1879. Upon the recommendation of Frederick Douglass, President Chester A. Arthur appointed Plummer chaplain of the 9th Cavalry in 1884. Championing temperance, Plummer formed the Loyal Temperance Legion for the children of the black troops at Fort Robinson, Nebraska. Although he was popular among the soldiers, his influence may have been viewed as a threat to the white run army. In the months following Plummer's proposed plan for the colonization of central Africa by African American volunteer soldiers, he was accused and convicted of drunkenness. Upon his dismissal, Plummer moved to Kansas where his attempts to return to the service were unsuccessful. He spent the remainder of his life serving his churches.

PRINCE, LUCY TERRY (1750-1821) Author, who in 1749, at age sixteen, wrote "The Bar's Fight," a poem about Native American attack on Deerfield, Massachusetts, where she was a slave. The poem wasn't published until 1855, in Josiah Gilbert Holland's *History of Western Massachusetts*. Prince is considered by some to be the first black American female poet, though Phillis Wheatley published her first work in 1776. Born in Africa, Prince was kidnapped as a child and brought to Deerfield, where she became a slave to Ebenezer Wells. Prince was married in 1756 to Abijah Prince, a free man who bought his wife's freedom. Prince's past probably inspired her civil rights efforts. She succeeded in convincing the governor's council of Guilford, Vermont, where she was living, to order the protection of her family after their fence had been torn down by white neighbors. She also tried, but failed, to get one of her sons enrolled in Williams College. In 1821, Prince died on the family farm in Sunderland, Vermont.

PROSSER, GABRIEL (1776-1800), Insurrectionist, was born in Virginia in 1776. In 1800, the young insurrectionist, along with Jack Bowler, planned to seize an arsenal at Richmond, attack whites in the area, and free the slaves. It was hoped that the revolt would spread throughout the state. Perhaps as many as 1,000 slaves were prepared to participate in what would have been one of the largest slave revolts in U.S. history. Prosser had won such a large following by telling fellow blacks that he was their chosen leader, quoting Scripture to bolster his claim. The rebels had made or obtained swords, bayonets, and bullets in preparation for the uprising when a storm hit the area. Two slaves belonging to Mosby Sheppard betrayed Prosser's plot. Governor James Monroe declared martial law in Richmond and called up 600 members of the state militia. Prosser fled, but was captured in Norfolk on September 25. He was later convicted and, with fifteen others, sentenced to hang on October 7. Another thirty-five blacks were later executed. Although interviewed by Governor Monroe himself, Prosser refused to implicate others. The demeanor of the captured rebels led John Randolph of Virginia to declare that "the accused have exhibited a spirit, which if it becomes general, must deluge the southern country in blood. They manifested a sense of their rights, and a contempt of danger."

RANGER, JOSEPH (c.1760-?) Sailor, was born in Northumberland County, Virginia. Ranger was aboard the *Jefferson* when the British blew it up. He also served on the *Hero*, the *Dragon*, and the *Patriot* during the American Revolution. Ranger was part of the captured *Patriot* crew that was held by the British until the surrender at Yorktown. He served on the *Patriot* and the *Liberator* in the years following the Revolution. He reportedly received the benefits of the Federal Pension Act of 1832, an annual payment of $96 and 100 acres of land.

RUSSWURM, JOHN BROWN (1799-1851), CORNISH, SAMUEL (1795-November 6, 1858), Publishers, Two African Americans, John Russwurm and Samuel Cornish, began publication of *Freedom's Journal*, the nation's pioneer African American newspaper, in New York City in 1827. Russwurm was born to a bondswoman and an American merchant in Jamaica. After studying in Quebec, in 1826, he became one of the first African Americans to graduate from college, when he earned a degree from Bowdoin College. The paper was not very successful, and two years later Russwurm moved to Liberia, claiming that African Americans "had no future in the U.S." in Liberia, he became a superintendent of education and a governor and an editor of the *Liberia Herald* and recruited African Americans to settle in Liberia. Cornish began a second publication, the militant *Rights of All*, which also was short-lived. In 1836, Cornish published *Weekly Advocate* and the following year co-edited the *Colored American*. Most of the African American newspapers founded before the Civil War were principally abolitionist propaganda sheets, with Frederick Douglass's *North Star* being the most successful.

SANDERSON, JERIMIAH BURKE (1821-1875) Abolitionist, gave his first public address at an abolitionist meeting in Nantucket, Massachusetts. (Frederick Douglass also gave his first public speech there.) Throughout the 1840s, the Scottish and African-blooded Sanderson, born and educated in New Bedford, Massachusetts, spoke out against slavery in his state as well as in New York, where, in 1853, he joined the National Council of the National Colored Convention. Although Sanderson did not promote immigration of blacks abroad, he did support the massive migration of blacks to California in 1854 by going there himself. There he helped many black religious, social, political, and educational organizations increase their status in American society.

Sanderson was elected to A.M.E. positions of secretary of the California conference and state delegate to the church's national conference, but died in a train accident on August 19, 1875, before he was able to serve.

SASH, MOSES (1755-?) Insurrectionist, was indicted on January 20, 1787, for taking up arms against the Commonwealth and encouraging others to do the same, according to a Suffolk County, Massachusetts, courthouse document. A second document showed he was indicted for stealing two guns. Reportedly Sash's indictments indicated he played a major role in the rebellion, as the members of Shay's council of war and directors of the rebel strategy were excluded from the indemnity that was granted to less serious offenders. Governor John Hancock later pardoned all participants.

Sash had been born to Sarah Sash and Samson Dunbar in Braintree, Massachusetts, in 1755. During the Revolutionary War, Sash enlisted as a private in Colonel Ruggles Woodbridge's Regiment in August 1777. In May 1781 he reenlisted as a private in the seventh Regiment.

SCOTT, DRED (1846-1857) Bondsman, Plaintiff, filed suit in the St. Louis Circuit Court on June 30, 1847, claiming that his temporary residence in a free territory should have made him a free man. Scott was a semi-literate bondsman whose travels throughout the country-specifically into the free portions of the Louisiana territory, where slavery had been excluded by the Missouri Compromise of 1820, and into free Illinois-formed the basis for the case. The case eventually reached the United States Supreme Court which, ruled on March 6, 1857, that Scott had no standing in the American courts because persons of African descent were not citizens of the United States. Indeed, had "no rights that any white man was bound to respect." Furthermore, the Missouri Compromise was declared unconstitutional, in that Congress had no powers to regulate bondage in the federal territories. The decision was a major blow to the abolitionist cause in the United States.

SMALLS, ROBERT (1839-1915), Sailor, Politician, was born into bondage in Beaufort, South Carolina. He received a rudimentary education through the indulgence of his enslaver. At the beginning of the Civil War, he was employed by the Confederates aboard the steamer *Planter* out of Charleston, South Carolina. In 1862, while the crew of the boat was ashore, Smalls took control of the vessel and turned the ship over to the United States. He also provided Union officers with valuable information about Confederate battle positions. As a result of his heroics, Small became a second lieutenant in the Union's "colored division" and was awarded a bonus of $1500. Smalls' war deeds aided his rise in South Carolina politics and business endeavors during Reconstruction. He later served five terms in the U.S. House of Representatives.

THIERRY, CAMILLE (1814-1875), Author. The 215-page *Les Cenelles* was published as the first anthology of African American verse. Fourteen of the poems were written by Camille Thierry, a New Orleans Creole who lived most of his life in France trying to escape racism. Thierry was asked to contribute to the compilation after he had published his first poem, *Les Idees,* which appeared in *L'Album Litteraire*, a collection of writings intended to promote racial equality.

TUBMAN, HARRIETT (1814-1875) Abolitionist, returned to Maryland and Virginia at least twenty times and is credited with freeing more than three hundred bondspersons. The daring abolitionist was born in Dorchester County, Maryland, in 1823. While working as a field hand as a young girl, she suffered a severe head injury by a weight that an enraged overseer had thrown at another slave. The damage from that blow caused Tubman to suffer from "sleeping seizures" for the rest of her life. In 1844, she married a free black, John Tubman, but remained in bondage. In 1849, her enslaver died and rumors emerged that his bonds persons were to be sold into the Deep South. Tubman, along with two of her brothers, escaped. Fearing capture and punishment or death, the brothers returned to the plantation, but Tubman, using the North Star for directions, marched on until she reached Philadelphia.

In 1850, Tubman returned to Maryland for a sister and a brother, and in the following year she led a party of eleven blacks from the South into Canada, leaving behind her husband, who had married another woman. In 1857, Tubman made one of her last trips into Maryland, rescuing her parents and three additional brothers and sisters. The family then settled in Auburn, New York. The family home, purchased from anti-slavery senator William H. Seward, was later turned into a home for elderly and indigent African Americans. After serving in the Civil War as a nurse and a spy, Tubman devoted all of her energy and earnings to this home during the twilight of her life. Tubman, often called "the Moses of her People," died in Auburn in 1913.

TURNER, NAT (1800-November 11, 1831), Insurrectionist. led the most momentous slave revolt in U.S. history It occurred in Southhampton County, Virginia in 1831. Turner had earlier run away from, then returned to, his enslaver. Approximately sixty whites were slain in the revolt. Turner was captured on October 30 and hanged on November 11. Thirty other blacks were implicated, then executed. The revolt caused near pandemonium in the South. Slave Codes were vigorously enforced, slave patrols were increased, and suspicious blacks were either incarcerated or killed. No other major slave revolt or conspiracy followed the Turner insurrection until John Brown's raid on the U.S. Arsenal at Harpers Ferry, Virginia, in 1859.

VASSA, GUSTAVIUS (OLAUUDAH EQUIANO) (c.1745-1800), Author, abolitionist was born Olaudah Equiano in Nigeria. Vassa enjoyed a childhood filled with tribal unity. At the age of ten, he was kidnapped by nearby tribesmen and sold into slavery. He was brought to Virginia where he was purchased by a British sailor, Michael Pacal, who took him to England. There he began his formal education and was given the name Gustavius Vassa, after the sixteenth-century Swedish king. He traveled with his enslaver across the seas, witnessing fighting between the French and the British in the Napoleonic Wars. He was further educated in London and was baptized in St. Margaret's Church, Westminster, in February 1759. While in Britain, he worked for a while for the government, helping to resettle blacks in Africa. He was, in this capacity, probably the first British civil servant of African descent. In 1789, he published an abolitionist work called *The Interesting Narrative of the Life of Olaudah Equiano, or Gustavus Vassa the African*. The book became a bestseller in Europe.

VENTURE (1729-1805), Author. A compilation of stories called *A Narrative of the Life and Adventures of Venture*, published in 1798, detailed the life of the former Connecticut bondsperson known as Venture A son of the prince of the Dukandarra tribe, Venture was born into bondage in Guinea, West Africa. His birth name, Broteer, was changed to Venture by the slaver who brought him to America. Nicknamed "Black Bunyan," Venture worked to purchase his own freedom at the age of thirty-six, and the freedom of his wife, daughter, two sons, and three other slaves. The *Narrative* described, and possibly exaggerated, the great feats of work that Venture performed, such as carrying a barrel of molasses on his shoulders for two miles. The depiction of the lives of enslaved and free blacks in the eighteenth century Connecticut was a key element in the *Narrative*.

VESEY, DENMARK (1767?-1822) Insurrectionist. After many years as a bondsman he won $1500 in a lottery in 1800 and purchased his freedom. A highly intelligent man, he acquired considerable wealth and influence in South Carolina. Using church meetings as a cover, he plotted a slave insurrection in 1822 aimed at taking over Charleston, South Carolina, killing whites, and, perhaps, fleeing to Haiti if the plot failed. However, he was betrayed by informers, captured and hanged along with 34 bondspersons.

WALKER, DAVID (1796-1830), Author, abolitionist, was born in Wilmington, North, Carolina to an enslaved father and a free mother. His militant anti-slavery pamphlet calling on blacks to revolt was discovered in several areas of the country in 1829. Walker's *Appeal*, published in Boston, stirred slaveholders in several southern states. Walker was a free black who had wandered across the South before settling in Boston as the proprietor of a secondhand clothing store. He had become widely acquainted with anti-slavery and revolutionary literature. The *Ap-*

peal, which was probably smuggled into the South by black sailors, called for mass slave uprisings, with violent reprisals against slaveowners. Although perhaps only a few literate blacks could read it, southern states took extreme precautions. The mails were scrutinized, ships arriving in southern ports were searched, and black seamen were restricted. The circulation of the work became a crime and a bounty was placed on Walker's head. Walker died under mysterious circumstances in 1830.

WHEATLEY, PHILLIS (1753?-1784), Poet, was of Sengalese origins. At an early age, she was brought to North America and purchased by the Wheatley family in Boston. Frail, but precocious, the family gave her only light duties in the home and permitted her to obtain an education. She showed a propensity to study the Bible and to use its passages as a basis for poetry. Later she read the English neo-classicists and emulated them as well. In 1773, she published *Poems on Various Subjects, Religious and Moral*, becoming the second American woman and the first African American to publish a book. Manumitted in 1773, she traveled to London and was received by the Lord Mayor and other influential Londoners. On February 28, 1776, Wheatley had an audience with General George Washington at his Cambridge, Massachusetts, headquarters, so that he might express his appreciation for her poem in his honor. After the death of her benefactors in the early 1780s, Wheatley, herself, fell into destitution and poverty. While modern scholars acknowledge her role in the hierarchy of African American literature, most do not think highly of her writings.

WRIGHT, THEODORE SEDWICK (1794-1847), Minister, Civil/Human Rights Activist, graduated from the Princeton Theological Seminary in 1828, making him the first black to graduate from an American theological seminary. He then took his lifelong post as pastor of the First Colored Presbyterian Church, also called the Shiloh Presbyterian Church. Wright constantly organized and promoted civil rights efforts. Throughout the 1830s, he lectured for active abolitionist movements and, in 1833, helped found the American Anti-Slavery Society. After withdrawing from the organization in 1840 over the growing trend toward Garrisonian radicalism, he helped form the American and Foreign Anti-Slavery Society. In addition to fighting for freedom, Wright pushed for jury trials in fugitive slave cases and black enfranchisement, including an 1840 push for suspension of the property requirement for black voters. Wright was also active in the temperance movement and missions to evangelize African peoples.

YORK (b. 1770- d. 1822 or 1832?) Explorer, was born in Virginia. He set out as part of the Lewis and Clark expedition in 1803, officially as Clark's valet. York was the son of the Old York and his wife, Rose, who were house slaves of the Clark family. During the two-year journey, however, York also served as a diplomat of sorts: he apparently acted as a French-Canadian interpreter for Clark and built friendships with Native Americans by dancing for them. According to some accounts, York returned to Kentucky with Clark and, although reportedly freed in 1825, served as his valet until his death.

II. POST EMANCIPATION TO JIM CROW

ABBOTT, ROBERT S. (1870-1940) Publisher, was the son of an enslaved butler and a field woman who purchased their son's freedom. After her husband died, Mrs. Abbott married John Sengstacke, an editor, political educator, and clergyman. Young Abbott worked on his stepfather's news sheet and received his education at the Hampton Institute.

In 1948, Abbott established the *Defender* in Chicago, Illinois with a staff of former barbers and servants as well as a few recently educated blacks. He attracted good journalists like Willard Motley and also published the early poems of Gwendolyn Brooks. Abbott's brutal attacks on southern racism and his appeals to blacks to move north to escape Jim Crowism in the South the helped earn widespread respect for the *Defender.*

ANDERSON, MARIAN (1897- April 8, 1993) Entertainer, was born in Philadelphia, Pennsylvania whose 1939 concert at the Lincoln Memorial in Washington, DC was a symbolic triumph over racial bigotry. Anderson had first become a national hero of the civil/human rights struggle after the Daughters of the American Revolution (DAR) refused to allow her to perform at their hall in the nation's capital on account of her race. Instead, with the assistance of First Lady Eleanor Roosevelt and others, she gave a stirring concert before the monument to "the great emancipator" on Easter Sunday in March 1939 The Daughters of the American Revolution (DAR) was an organization of women descended from men who fought in the Revolutionary War.

A native of Philadelphia, Pennsylvania, Anderson had a rich, deep voice that Italian conductor Arturo Toscanini described as the kind that appears once in a century. She was born in 1902, and even as a young girl she impressed other members of her church choir with her exceptional talent. At the age of nineteen, she began taking private lessons with Italian voice coach Giuseppe Boghetti. Four years later, Anderson beat 300 other singers in a national music competition for the chance to perform as a soloist with the New York Philharmonic Orchestra. Her appearance there was a success, and soon she was booked for additional concerts.

After spending the early 1930s in Europe studying music and languages and performing to enthusiastic audiences, Anderson returned to the United States. She then toured throughout the country, becoming more and more popular with each passing year. In 1936, President and Mrs. Roosevelt invited her to sing at the White House, making her the first black American singer ever to perform there.

Anderson had just completed yet another successful European tour when the DAR barred her from singing in Washington's Constitution Hall. An outraged Eleanor Roosevelt immediately resigned from the group in protest. The Secretary of Interior then made the Lincoln Memorial available for the Anderson concert, which drew an audience of 75,000 on Easter Sunday of 1939. Later that same year, Eleanor Roosevelt presented the singer with the NAACP's Spingarn Medal in recognition of her musical accomplishments.

Anderson continued her quiet struggle for racial dignity and equality through the remainder of her life. Besides putting to rest the idea that blacks could not ex in the world of opera and classical music, she devoted her time, talent, and money to a variety of causes. In 1958, for example, she was named a U.S. delegate to the United Nations. In this position, she served on a committee that watched over colonies in Africa and the Pacific Ocean area that were in the process of becoming independent countries. She also contributed generously to the NAACP, the Urban League, the YMCA, the International Committee on African Affairs, and Freedom from Hunger Foundation.

In 1963, Anderson received the Medal of Freedom (the U.S. government's highest civilian honor) for her outstanding contributions to the ideals of freedom and democracy. She retired from performing in 1965. As she once wrote in his autobiography, *My*

Lord, What a Morning, "My mission is to leave behind me the kind of impression that will make it easier for those who follow."

BARBER, JESSE MAX (1878-September, 1949) Journalist, was born in Blackstock, South Carolina, to Jesse Max and Susan Barber, former bondspersons. Barber worked his way through school, earning a bachelor's degree from Virginia Union University in Richmond. Following graduation, he moved to Atlanta to help start a new publication, *The Voice of the Negro.* Barber worked his way up from managing editor to principal editor of the publication, which became a respected and popular magazine. As editor, Barber was an outspoken advocate of the early civil rights movement. In 1905 he was one of twenty-nine who answered W.E.B. DuBois's call to form the Niagara Movement, a "radical" group that was the predecessor of the NAACP. When *The Voice* folded in 1907, Barber returned to school, earning a degree in dentistry. He began a professional practice in Philadelphia in 1912. Barber worked with the newly formed NAACP, serving as president of its Philadelphia branch and as a member of its national board of directors for several years. Barber's final public activity was the founding of the John Brown Memorial Association, a group formed to raise funds for a statue honoring the famed abolitionist. The statue was erected in 1935 in North Elba, New York. Barber continued his dental practice until his death in Philadelphia in September 1949.

BARROW, JOE LOUIS (Joe Louis) (1914-1981) Athlete, was born in Lafayette, Alabama. Shortly thereafter his family moved to Detroit, Michigan, where Louis attended Duffield Elementary School for a short time. After leaving school, he worked in an automobile plant and, in his leisure time, boxed.

In 1935, he won an important victory over Primo Carnera at Yankee stadium in New York, Louis then began his boxing career in earnest.

Louis became the heavyweight champion of the world in 1937 and held the title until 1949, interrupting his career to serve in World War II. But a series of unsuccessful marriages and business ventures left Louis nearly penniless after his retirement from the ring.

BARTHE, RICHMOND (1901-March 6, 1989), Sculptor, was born in Bay St. Louis, Mississippi. He was educated at the Art Institute of Chicago. His work was later exhibited at several major American museums, including the Metropolitan Museum of Art. Some of his notable works include *Singing Slave, Maurice Evans and Henry O. Tanner.* His success led to membership in the National Academy of Arts and Letters.

BETHUNE, MARY McLEOD (July 10, 1875-May 18, 1955), Womanist Leader, Civil/Human Rights Leader, Political Leader was born in Mayesville, South Carolina to former bondspersons Samuel and Pastsy McLeod, the fifteenth of seventeen children. The family were farmers. Since there were no schools for African Americans in the area, all of the children worked the cotton fields. When Bethune was nine, she attended a new, one room Presbyterian Church mission school five miles from home. Eager to receive as much book learning as possible, and to become a missionary, at age twelve Bethune received a scholarship to Scotia Seminary, a Presbyterian school in Concord, North Carolina, and for seven years she studied high school and junior college courses, which included the classics, religion, the "culture and refinement" and "industrial education" subjects: sewing, cooking, laundering, and cleaning. She subsequently won a scholarship to the Moody Bible Institute in Chicago and completed her work there in 1895. However, she was "devastated" when she learned that her Church did not permit African Americans to serve as missionaries abroad. Thus, she turned to teaching.

Meanwhile she married Albertus Bethune, who was also a teacher and gave birth to a son. The couple moved several times and taught at various mission schools before Bethune opened her own school in Daytona Beach, Florida in 1904. A gifted orator and a skilled fundraiser, Bethune courted wealthy American businessmen and philanthropists who came to Daytona Beach for vacations and traveled throughout the country selling her school. Beginning, a small frame building, the Daytona Normal and Industrial School for Girls, when merged with Cookman College for boys in 1928, became Bethune-Cookman College, with Mary McCleod Bethune as president. 1904. Albertus Bethune died in 1918 and Bethune never remarried.

Bethune continued to promote her school nationally in the Depression and New Deal years, spoke and wrote widely on educational and racial issues as well as womanist topics By the 1930s, she had become one of the most prominent African American educational, civil/human rights and womanist spokesperson in the country. Her work was recognized by elections to vice presidencies in the National Association for the Advancement of Colored People (NAACP, National Urban League (NUL) and president of the Association for the Study of Negro Life and History (ASNLH). In 1935 she was one of the founders of the National Council of Negro Women (NCNW) and its president until 1949. When she left the leadership of the organization, it had grown to 82 metropolitan affiliates.

Meanwhile, Bethune had attracted the attention of President Franklin D. Roosevelt and his wife Eleanor. She became probably the most prominent member of FDR's "Black Cabinet," a group of select African Americans who advised the president black issues, and in 1936, he appointed her director of Negro affairs for the National Youth Administration, where she supervised the development of recreational facilities and vocational training programs for young African Americans during the New Deal. And, in 1945, she attended the organizing conference of the United Nations as a special representative of the Department of State.

Bethune gave up the presidency in of Bethune Cookman College and continued to commute between Daytona Beach and Washington, DC for her womanist, civil/human rights activities and assignments with the government. Following her death, a few months before her 80th birthday, she was funeralized and memorialized in both Daytona Beach and Washington and buried on the campus of her beloved Bethune Cookman College.

Prior to her death, Bethune left a "last will and testament" to her people that included such thoughts as:

I leave you love; I leave you hope: I leave you the challenge
of developing confidence in one another;
I leave you a thirst for education; I leave you respect
For the use of power; I leave you faith; I leave you
racial dignity; I leave you a desire to live
harmoniously with your fellow man; I leave you
finally a responsibility to our young people.

BOUCHET, EDWARD ALEXANDER (September 15, 1852-
1918), Scientist, was born to Francis and Susan (Cooley)
Bourchet in New Haven, Connecticut. He received an undergraduate degree from Yale College in 1874. In 1876 Yale University bestowed upon him a doctor of philosophy degree-
reportedly, the first ever received by to an African American.
He, then, began a long career teaching chemistry and physics in
high schools and colleges, interrupted in 1904-05, when he became a U. S. Inspector of Customs at the Louisiana Purchase
Exposition. He ended his career on the faculty of Bishop College
(Texas) from 1913-1916.

BROOKS, GWENDOLYN (1917-2000) Author, was born in
Topeka, Kansas, but grew up in Chicago, Illinois. Encouraged by
her parents, she read a lot and began writing poems when she
was very young. Brooks published her first piece of poetry when
she was only thirteen, and after that she regularly contributed
works to the *Chicago Defender*, a major black newspaper. After
graduating from high school, she attended Wilson Junior College
and earned a degree in English in 1936.

Throughout the late 1930s and early 1940s, Brooks gained
more and more recognition for her poetry, first in the Chicago
area and then in other places in the Midwest. In 1945, she published her first collection of poems, *A Street in Bronzeville*. Its
look at everyday lives of ordinary black people greatly impressed several critics. She followed this success with *Annie Allen*, a sequence of poems that told the story of a black woman's
journey to adulthood. On May 1, 1950, she was awarded the Pulitzer Prize for this collection, making her the first African
American writer to receive the honor.

BROWN, CHARLOTTE HAWKINS (1883-1961), Educator was born in Henderson, North Carolina in 1883. During her childhood, the Hawkins family moved to Cambridge, Massachusetts, where Charlotte attended Cambridge English High School and Salem State Normal School. While she was a student at Salem State, the American Missionary Association offered her a teaching position in North Carolina. Because she was dissatisfied with the lack of educational opportunities for African Americans in the South, she accepted. But, at age eighteen, she returned to North Carolina in 1901 to teach rural black children at the Bethany Congregational Church in Sedalia, Guilford County. The school closed after one term, but young Hawkins decided to remain in the community and establish her own school.

In 1902, Hawkins began a fund-raising campaign, principally in New England, in quest of the goal to build a school for North Carolinas blacks. After a successful campaign, she founded the Palmer Memorial Institute in Sedalia, a day and boarding school. The institution was located in a converted blacksmith's shop and was named in memory of Alice Freeman Palmer, a close friend of Hawkins and the school's (Mrs. Palmer had also been the female president of Wellesley College in Massachusetts).

Following her marriage, Charlotte Hawkins Brown was the leading force in making the, Palmer Memorial Institute a nationally recognized and respected preparatory school for African Americans. In its early years, Palmer's curriculum emphasized manual training and industrial education for rural living. But, shortly thereafter Brown expanded the school to over 350 acres of land, including a sizable farm and, by the 1930s, the school began to emphasize academic-classical education. And, under Brown's leadership, Palmer Memorial Institute became fully accredited by the Southern Association of Colleges and Secondary Schools at a time when few black high schools enjoyed this recognition. During her 50 year presidency, over one thousand students graduated. Most of them, true to Brown's philosophy, had gained not only a diploma but also "a firm idea of their own individual worth" and were thought to be "educationally efficient, religiously sincere, and culturally secure".

As the reputation of Brown's work at Palmer spread, she received national recognition in American educational and political circles and a member of the growing leadership class of African Americans. She counted among her close associates Eleanor Roosevelt, W.E.B DuBois, John Hope, Mary McCleod Bethune and Booker T. Washington.

As with many African American institutions and other small American institutions where one person's personality and abilities dominates the institution's existence, Palmer Memorial Institute was hard put in its efforts to survive the death of the founder in 1961. It closed its doors ten years later. However, Brown's memory and that of her school were preserved in a museum established on the Charlotte Hawkins Brown Memorial State Historic Site in 1987.

BRUCE, BLANCHE K. (1841-March 17, 1898) Politician, on March 15, 1875, Mississippi's second black senator, thirty-five-year-old Blanche K. Bruce, took his seat in Congress. He was the only African American to serve a full term in the U.S. Senate until the mid-twentieth century. The native Virginian was born a slave and worked as a body servant for the son of a wealthy planter. When his young master took him to the Confederate Army as a valet, Bruce escaped in Missouri. There he established a school for blacks. Bruce later attended Oberlin College, where he studied for two years. After the Civil War, he became a modestly wealthy Mississippi planter, taught school occasionally, and held minor political offices as a Republican before being elected to the Senate. Bruce's good reputation even won him a few votes from white Democrats in the Mississippi legislature. However, when Bruce's fellow senator (a white) from Mississippi refused to escort him to be sworn in, as was the custom, Senator Roscoe Conkling of New York too Bruce's hand and led him to the front of the chamber. It was a well-publicized event and an historic moment.

On May 19, 1881, President James A. Garfield appointed Bruce Register of the Treasury. After leaving the Senate and the Treasury Bruce became a successful banker.

CARVER, GEORGE WASHINGTON (1864?-1943), Scientist, was born in bondage in Diamond, Missouri. When just an infant, he was kidnapped along with his mother from his enslaver's farm and taken to Arkansas. A man hired by his enslaver was able to track down young George and return him to Missouri, but his mother was never heard from again. So the enslaver and his wife, who were childless, raised the orphaned Carver and his older brother as their own.

Carver went to local schools until he was about thirteen years old. Then he left Missouri and spent his teenage years restlessly wandering back and forth across several Midwestern states. Along the way, he managed to finish high school, doing odd jobs, such as sewing and laundry to support himself. He then enrolled in college and earned his bachelor's and master's degrees in agriculture from Iowa State College.

In 1896 he joined the staff of Tuskegee Institute as director of the department of agricultural research. He retained this position for the rest of his life. At Tuskegee he began researching soil conservation and tried to convince southern farmers to branch out and grow crops other than cotton. His fame as a scientist, in fact, stems largely from the 400 different products he showed could be produced from the peanut, potato and pecan. He also traveled across the South and talked with some of the region's poorest farmers about the problems they faced and offered helpful—and inexpensive—solutions. In addition, he was an excellent teacher who passed along practical knowledge as well as a love of nature to his students.

By the early 1920s, Carver was an international celebrity, hailed by both blacks and whites as the foremost African American scientist of the day. In 1923, he was awarded the NAACP's Spingarn Medal. Additionally, he received the 1939 Roosevelt Medal for distinguished achievement in science. He was also named a fellow of the Royal Academy of England. His last major project was to establish the George Washington Carver Museum and Foundation on the campus of Tuskegee In 1953 his birthplace was made a national historic monument.

COOK, WILL MARION (1869-1944) Entertainer, in 1898- Will Marion Cook directed the sensational musical-comedy sketch *Clorindy, the Origin of the Cakewalk* on Broadway. Disregarding warnings that Broadway audiences would not listen to African Americans singing black opera, Cook composed music to lyrics written by famed black poet Paul Laurence Dunbar and assembled a company of twenty-six black performers. The performances of the first African Americans musical-comedy sketch in New York were held at Casino Roof Garden.

Cook was born in Washington D.C., in 1869. The son of a Howard University law professor, he was sent at age thirteen to the Oberlin Conservatory to study the violin. Cook later studied with violinist Joseph Joachim in Berlin and with John White and Antonin Dvrak at the National Conservatory of Music.

CRUMMELL, ALEXANDER (October 12, 1898-September 10, 1898), Clergy, Civil/Human Rights Leader, was born in New York City to an African prince and a free African American woman. He attended an interracial school in Canaan, New. Hampshire and an institute in Whitesboro, N.Y., which was run by abolitionists, where the curriculum consisted of manual labor as well as the classics. When he was denied admission to the General Theological School of the Episcopal church in 1839 because of his race, Crummell studied theology privately and became an Episcopalian minister in 1844.While still a student, he traveled to England, in 1848, to raise funds from churches for poor blacks and soon thereafter began studying at Queens College in Great Britain. He received an AB degree from Queens in 1853.

After graduation, Crummell went to Liberia as a missionary. He spent the next 20 years there as a parish rector, professor of intellectual and moral science at Liberia College, and participated in public affairs. He became a citizen of the new republic, founded by African American ex-patriots and a strong proponent of Liberian nationalism. Throughout his life he continued to urge" the christianization and civilization of Africa" by skilled, educated blacks from all over the world.

Crummell returned to the United States about 1873 and founded and served as pastor of an Episcopal Church in Washington, D.C. he became a spokesperson for blacks who were looking for greater recognition and respect in the Episcopal church. In 1883, he led the Conference of Church Workers Among Colored People.

After his retirement from the ministry in 1895, Crummell taught at Howard University (1895—97) and founded the American Negro Academy (ANA). The ANA became the leading African American organization promoting scholarly discussion and publications. Its members included W.E.B. DuBois and Paul Laurence Dunbar.

In his early years, Crummell had been a prominent advocate of abolition and after emancipation, he agitated for racial equality, the enfranchisement of African Americans and for the establishment of African American schools. Later in his life, he wrote and lectured widely against Jim Crowism in the post-Reconstruction era and challenged the "talented tenth"—educated African Americans—to provide the necessary leadership in the struggle for equality.

DANDRIDGE, DOROTHY D. (November 9, 1922-September 8, 1965), Entertainer, entered show business at a very young age, entertaining on road tours with her older sister Vivian. Dandridge performed at the Cotton Club when she was sixteen years old. She built a successful career as a nightclub singer while attempting to establish herself as a dramatic film actress. In 1954 Dandridge won the coveted title role in Otto Preminger's black production, *Carmen Jones.* Her performance earned her an Academy Award nomination, the first for an African American woman in a leading role.

Despite this success, Dandridge's film career came to a standstill in the 1950s. Three years before her next film, *Island in the Sun*, was released. The film's theme of interracial romance was repeated in her next projects, *The Deck Ran Red* (1958), *Tamango* (1959), and *Malaga* (1962). Her last great role was Bess in *Porgy and Bess*, another black musical from Otto Preminger. But mainstream roles continued to elude Dandridge, whose race made producers reluctant to cast her opposite a white leading men.

In the early 1960s, Dandridge's life began to unravel personally and professionally. Her stormy marriage to restaurant owner Jack Dennison ended in divorce, and she later filed for bankruptcy and had to forfeit her Hollywood mansion. Dorothy Dandridge died in her apartment on September 8, 1965, apparently the result of an antidepressant drug overdose.

DAVAGE, MATTHEW SIMPSON (1879-1976), Educator, was born in 1879 in Shreveport, Louisiana. He earned a B.A. degree from New Orleans University (now Dillard University) in 1900 and immediately joined the faculty there as an instructor in mathematics. He remained on the faculty until 1905 and, at the same time, pursued graduate studies at the University of Chicago.

Between 1905 and 1915, Davage was business manager of the *Southwestern Christian Advocate*, a Methodist publication. In 1915, he returned to education as president of the George R. Smith College at Sedalia, Missouri. After only one year at Sedalia, he assumed the presidency of the Haven Institute at Meridian, Mississippi, which he quickly left to assume the presidency of Samuel Huston College (now Huston-Tillotson College) in Austin, Texas. In the spring of 1920, Davage was elected president of Rust College in Holly Springs, Mississippi, where he became the first black head to head the fifty-four-year-old historically black institution. In 1924, he became the sixteenth president of Clark University, as it was then called. Davage was the second black person to head the institution, the first having been his predecessor, William Henry Crogman.

During his seventeen-year tenure at Clark, Davage presided over the removal of the institution from southeast Atlanta to its present location near the city's other black institutions of higher education, and he helped to provide new financial strength and vitality for the school, even during the Depression years.

In 1939, Davage became one of the first blacks to speak before the all-white Atlanta Rotary Club. Because of the Jim Crow laws and customs of the time, he could not eat lunch with the

41

Rotarians and had to wait in an adjoining room until the meal was finished. Then he gave a speech entitled, "The Negro's Place in Atlanta's Life." In it, he said, "Some day we may hope, the thinking people of both races will translate that mutual respect and trust into some concrete work. . . . They may meet and work on the same critics trying to say they are seeking to tear down a social order."

DAWSON, WILLIAM (September 26, 1899-May 4, 1971), Politician, for two decades the dean of African American congressmen, was the son of an Alabama barber. He received his education at Fisk University and a Chicago law school. After serving in World War I, Dawson opened a law practice in Chicago and became interested in politics. He began as a precinct worker and soon won favor with the Thompson Republican "machine". He served five terms (1933-43) on the Chicago city council as a Republican before switching to the Democrats after Franklin Roosevelt became president.

During World War II, Dawson became an important member of the Kelly and Daley Democratic machines in Chicago. He served as "ward boss" in five city districts, precinct captain, committeeman, and vice-chairman of the Cook County (Illinois) Democrats. On November 3, 1942, he was elected to the U. S. House of Representatives, where he served for two decades and became "dean of African American congressmen." He was also a vice-chairman of the Democratic National Committee. He retired from politics in 1970 and died a year later.

DEPRIEST, OSCAR (1871-1951), Politician, was born in Florence, Alabama to former bondspersons. His family moved to Kansas in 1878 and he attended public schools in Salina Kansas. He later worked as a painter and decorator. DePriest moved to Chicago, Illinois in 1889, and became a real estate broker, He entered politics in 1904 and was elected to the board of commissioners of Cook County (of which Chicago is the county seat). In 1915, he was elected to the Chicago city council. Twelve years later, he went to Washington as a Republican congressman from Illinois. However, he failed in his bids for reelection in both

1934 and 1936. Thus, he returned to the real estate business. He was the first African American to serve in Congress since George H. White left in 1901.

DETT, NATHANIEL (1882 – 1943), Composer, arranger, and conductor, was awarded the Bowdoin Prize by Harvard University for an essay titled *The Emancipation of Negro Music*. Dett was born in 1882 in the community of Drummondville, Quebec, which had been established by fugitive slaves before the Civil War.

Inspired as a child by black spirituals, Dett studied music at the American Conservatory of Music in Chicago, Columbia University, Harvard University, the Oberlin Conservatory in Lockport, New York, and the University of Pennsylvania. During his early career, Dett performed as a concert pianist while teaching and engaging in further study. Dett taught at Lane College in Texas (1908-1911), Lincoln University in Missouri (1911-1913), Hampton Institute in Virginia (1913-1931), Sam Houston College in Texas (1935-1937), and at Bennett College in North Carolina (1937).

Under the leadership of Dett, the Hampton Institute choir became internationally known, performing at the Library of Congress, New York's Carnegie Hall, and Boston's Symphony Hall. In 1930 the choir toured seven European nations. Meanwhile, Dett took some time off to study with Arthur Foote in Boston and Boulanger at the American Conservatory at Fontainebleau.

Among Dett's notables are *Magnolia* (1912), *Music in the Mine* (1916), *The Chariot Jubilee* (1921), *Enchantment* (1922), and *The Ordering of Moses* (1937). In addition to the Bowdoin Prize, Dett received the Francis Boot Prize for composition, the Palm and Ribbon Award of the Royal Belgian Band, the Harmon Foundation Award, and honorary degrees from Oberlin's Eastman School of Music and Harvard University. Dett died in 1943.

DIXON, WILLIE (d. January 29, 1992, at age 76), Entertainer, was considered one of the greatest traditional bluesmen. Dixon created lusty and sometimes humorous songs full of suggestive images and lyrics. He began recording in 1949 and wrote more than 300 songs, including such blues standards as "Hoochie Coochie Man", "Little Red Rooster", "The Seventh Son" and :Bring it on Home". He also wrote "You Can't Judge a Book by its Cover" and "Wang Dang Doodle".

Although many of Dixon's songs were hits, they were often most closely associated with other musicians. He wrote many of the best pieces for such performers as Howlin' Wolf, Bo Diddley and Muddy Waters. Others were made famous by various rock groups including the Rolling Stones, the Grateful Dead and the Yardbirds.

DORSEY, THOMAS A. (1899-January 30, 1993), Composer, Entertainer, "the father of Gospel Music", was born in Georgia and grew up in a very religious household as the son of a Baptist preacher. By the age of twelve, however, he was playing the piano professionally in bars and bordellos, specializing in the blues and ragtime. He then moved to vaudeville, where he was known as "Georgia Tom" when he toured with stars such as Ma Rainey and Trixie Smith. In partnership with guitarist Tampa Red, Dorsey also wrote and performed a steady stream of suggestive blues tunes during the 1920s, including the million-seller "It's Tight Like That."

But during the same decade, the death of a friend and his own illness as well as a need to find a balance between his Christian upbringing and his love of the blues led Dorsey to begin experimenting with religious music. In 1926 he composed his first religious piece "If You See My Savior, Tell Him You Saw Me." It did not become a hit until it was sung at the National Baptist Convention in 1930. (Later, Mahalia Jackson recorded a version that was very popular.). Even then, it took sometime for Dorsey's energetic blend of blues, ragtime and religious music, which he called "gospel", to be accepted by churches. Many people felt it was scandalous and would have nothing to do with it. But it reached audiences in ways that even the greatest preachers couldn't.

By the early 1930s Dorsey had turned to writing only gospel music. He produced about 1,000 songs over his long career.

Among the most famous were "Sweet Bye and Bye", "Take My Hand, Precious Lord", and "We Shall Walk Through the Valley in Peace". Dorsey's compositions later influenced African American singers including James Cleveland, Aretha Franklin, Edwin Hawkins and the Winans. Some even became popular with white southerners when they were recorded by singers such as country star Red Foley and Elvis Presley.

DREW, CHARLES (June 3,1904-April 1,1950) Physician was born in Washington, DC. He received his medical training at McGill University in Montreal, Quebec in 1933, and Columbia University in 1940. During World War II, his plasma research won wide acceptance both in Europe and the United States. He is also credited with establishing the first blood bank.

After the war, Drew taught at Howard University Medical School. At the time of his death, he was also chief surgeon and chief of staff at Freedman's Hospital in Washington, DC.

Contrary to a popular myth, Drew did not bleed to death after the accident because he was refused treatment at a whites-only hospital. Several African American physicians who were with him at the time always insisted that this story was not true. African American scholars who have studied the circumstances surrounding Drew's death have concluded that he died of his injuries despite receiving excellent care at a Euro-American hospital.

DUBOIS, WILLIAM EDWARD BURGHARDT (W.E.B) (February 23, 1868-August, 1963), Educator, Author, Civil/Human Rights Leader was born in Great Barrington, Massachusetts. He was an early exponent of full equality for African Americans and a cofounder (1905) of the Niagara Movement, which became (1909) the *National Association for the Advancement of Colored People* (NAACP). Unlike Booker T. Washington, who believed that unskilled blacks should focus on economic self-development, and Marcus Garvey, who advocated a "Back to Africa" movement, DuBois demanded that African Americans be given not only economic parity with whites in the United States but full and immediate civil and political equality as well. He also introduced the concept of the "talented tenth," a black elite whose duty it was to better the lives of less fortunate African Americans.

After studying at Fisk University and Harvard College, DuBois received a PhD. Degree from Harvard University in 1896. From 1897 to 1910, he taught economics and history at Atlanta University. Beginning with his doctoral dissertation, "The Suppression of the African Slave Trade to America," DuBois became a prodigious and prolific scholar. Among his major works were *The Philadelphia Negro, Black Reconstruction* (1935) and *The Souls of Black Folk* (1903) in which he suggested that African Americans lived behind a veil of racism, introduced the concept of twoness—a warring soul caught between being a negro and an American—and delivered his harshest criticisms to date of the educational and racial philosophies of Booker T. Washington. In 1910 he became editor of the official and influential NAACP organ, *Crisis,* a position he held until 1934. That year he resigned over the question of voluntary segregation, which he had come to favor over integration, and returned to Atlanta University. (1934–44). His concern for the liberation of people of African descent throughout the world led him to organize the first) of several Pan-African Congresses in Paris in 1919. In 1945, at the Fifth Congress in Manchester, England, he met with the African leaders Kwame *Nkrumah* and Jomo *Kenyatta.*

In 1961, reflecting a growing disenchantment with American racism, he became a member of the American Communist party, and shortly thereafter he renounced his American citizenship and emigrated to Ghana. He spent the last two years of his life as a citizen of Ghana and died there on the eve of the Great March on Washington in August, 1963. He was entombed near the DuBois Institute and Library in Accra.

DUNBAR, PAUL LAURENCE (June 27, 1872-February 9, 1906) Author. The son of a former slave, Dunbar was born in Dayton in 1872. Although he was senior class poet at Dayton's Central High School and editor of the school newspaper and yearbook, Dunbar first worked as an elevator boy. In 1893 he compiled a book of his verse that he sold to passengers on his elevator.

Two years later, Dunbar published *Majors and Minors*. It brought him national black attention after William Dean Howells wrote a very favorable review of the book in *Harper's Weekly*. Dunbar followed up his first success the next year with *Lyrics of Lowly Life*. (Many of his early works were published by airplane inventors Orville and Wilbur Wright, who were experimenting at the time with printing newspapers on a homemade press.) In 1897 Dunbar became an assistant at the Library of Congress, a position he held for only a year.

During the last ten years of his life, Dunbar produced eleven volumes of poetry, three novels, and five collections of short stories. Even though he was from the Midwest, he wrote about the Old South with humor and "a certain tenderness for days gone by".

No black writer before him had been so widely praised by White and Black America. Critics generally agree that his best work was his poetry, especially the ones written in black dialect. William Dean Howells, for example, thought Dunbar was the first African American to have an artist's appreciation for the life of his people that was expressed in verse. Dunbar's biographer, Benjamin Brawley once said that Dunbar "soared above race and touched the heart universal".

DUNN, OSCAR J. (1826-1871), Politician, a freedman, became lieutenant governor of Louisiana in April, 1868, the highest elective office held by an African American up to that time. Dunn was an apprentice to a plasterer and house painter until age fifteen, when he escaped. Born in New Orleans in 1826, Dunn took a job with the Freedman's Bureau there at the close of the Civil War. (he had served as a captain in the Union Army during the war). As a Bureau agent, Dunn checked the employment practices of planters who hired black laborers. He found that the freedmen were often cheated of their minimum $15-a-month earnings and thus reported these and other abuses of the Freedmen's Bureau wage-contract system. Dunn was one of the forty-nine African Americans who attended the Louisiana Constitutional Convention in 1867-68. As lieutenant governor, Dunn presided over the state senate and signed some of the laws emanating from the new state constitution. In 1871, he was named chairman of the Republican State Convention. Since Dunn was a skillful politician, some considered nominating him for governor or U.S. senator before his untimely death in 1871.

FLIPPER, HENRY OSSIAN (March 21, 1856-May 3, 1940) Soldier, was born in bondage in Thomasville, Georgia, the son of Festus and Isabella Flipper.

In 1878 Henry Ossian Flipper finished 50th in a class of 76, becoming West Point's first African American graduate. He was commissioned as a second lieutenant and assigned to the all-black 10th Cavalry Regiment in Texas until 1881 when he was dismissed for allegedly embezzling funds, a charge he vehemently denied for the rest of his life. After his dismissal, Flipper worked as an engineer and a miner. He continued to write, publishing at least three books. He contributed articles to the *Old Santa Fe* and several newspapers.

His knowledge of law was impressive and made him a valuable commodity to employers. Between 1892 and 1903 he worked in the Court of Private Land Claims of the Department of Justice as a special agent. Flipper volunteered his services at the start of the Spanish-American War, and two legislators initiated bills to reinstitute Flipper's military rank. Both bills failed to garner support. In 1919 Flipper moved to Washington to work as a subcommittee translator and interpreter of Spanish. In 1923 he left the government in the wake of the Teapot Dome Scandal (he was not implicated) and worked for an oil company in Venezuela. In 1930 he moved to Atlanta and lived with his brother, Joseph Flipper. He was exonerated posthumously by the military in 1976.

FORTUNE, T. THOMAS (1856-1928), Journalist, founded the *New York Age*. Fortune, born in Florida in 1856 to mulatto parents, was the leading African American journalist until the World War I. After the Civil War, he attended a Freedmen's Bureau school. Fortune's father, a tanner and shoe merchant, served several terms in the Florida legislature during Reconstruction and secured for his son an appointment as page boy in the state senate. The family's political activities and close social contacts with some whites created racial animosity among other whites that eventually forced the family from the capital to Jacksonville, where Fortune's father became town marshal. Fortune himself went to Washington, where he attended Howard University, partly from earnings secured as a special customs agent in Delaware. After leaving Howard, he taught briefly in Florida but soon left for New York.

In 1879, Fortune began his long newspaper career in New York City. He first worked at the *New York Sun*, one of the city's leading newspapers. He published three books-the well-known *Black and White* (1884), a historical essay on land, labor, and politics in the South, as well as *The Negro in Politics* (1885) and *Dreams of Life* (1905). He was active in Republican politics after the Civil War and advocated civil rights for blacks. Fortune closely identified with Booker T. Washington and his ideas, but in later years edited some of Marcus Garvey's black nationalist publications. During World War I, Fortune helped establish the famous 369th black regiment. He died in 1928.

GARNET, HENRY HIGHLAND (1815-1862) Abolitionist, Civil/ Human Rights Leader, was born into bondage near New Market, Kent County, Maryland, on December 23, 1815. In 1816, at the age of eight, he freed himself from enslavement. His father, George Trusty, was the son of a Mandingo warrior prince, taken prisoner in combat. George and Henny (Henrietta) Trusty had one other child, a girl named Mary. George had learned the trade of shoemaking. The Trusty's enslaver William Spencer died in 1824. A few weeks later 11 members of the Trusty family received permission to attend a family funeral. They never returned. Traveling first in a covered market wagon and then on foot for several days, the family group made its way to Wilmington, Delaware. There they separated; seven went to New Jersey, and Garnet's immediate family went to New Hope, Pennsylvania, where Garnet had his first schooling.

In 1825 the Garnets moved to New York City. There, George Trusty gave new names to the family. His wife Henny became Elizabeth, his daughter Mary, Eliza. Although the original first names of George and Henry are unknown, the family name became Garnet. George Garnet found work as a shoemaker and also became a class-leader and exhorter in the Bethel African Methodist Episcopal Church.

Garnet was educated at the African Free School in New York City in 1826. His school mates included Alexander Crummell, an Episcopal priest and a leading black intellectual, who was Garnet's neighbor and close boyhood friend; Samuel Ringgold Ward, a celebrated abolitionist and a cousin of Garnet; James McCune Smith, the first black to earn a medical degree; Ira Aldridge, the celebrated actor; and Charles Reason, the first black college professor in the United States and long-time educator in black schools. Garnet and his classmates formed their own club, the Garrison Literary and Benevolent Association. At the time Garrisonian abolitionism had little mass support among whites, and abolition meetings in New York City had been subjected to mob violence. Thus, the school's authorities feared the use of his name for a club meeting at their school. But, garnet and his friends retained the club's name and moved their activities elsewhere.

While still a boy, Garnet in 1828 made two voyages to Cuba as a cabin boy, and in 1829 he worked as a cook and steward on a schooner from New York to Washington, D.C. On his return from this voyage, he learned that his family had been scattered by the threat of slave catchers. His father reportedly had escaped by leaping from the upper floor of their home–next door to the home of Alexander Crummell. His mother had been sheltered by the family of a neighboring grocer. His sister was taken but successfully maintained a claim that she had always been a resident of New York and therefore no fugitive slave. All of the family's furniture had been stolen or destroyed. Garnet bought a large clasp-knife to defend himself and wandered on Broadway with ideas of vengeance. Friends found him and persuaded him to hide at Jericho on Long Island.

Since Garnet had to support himself, he was bound out to Epenetus Smith of Smithtown, Long Island, as a farm worker. While he was there he was tutored by Smith's son Samuel. In the second year there, when he was 15, Garnet injured his knee playing sports so severely that his indentures were canceled. The leg never properly healed, and he used crutches for the rest of his life. (After 13 years of suffering and illness, the leg was finally amputated at the hip in December 1840.) Garnet subsequently returned to his family, which had reestablished itself in New York. He then continued his schooling, and in 1831 he entered the newly established high school in New York City for African Americans. There he rejoined Alexander Crummell as a fellow student.

Sometime between 1833 and 1835 Garnet affiliated with the First Colored Presbyterian Church in New York City. At the church he became a protégé of the noted minister and abolitionist Theodore Sedgewick Wright, the first black graduate of Princeton's Theological Seminary, who converted Garnet' and then encouraged him to enter the ministry (Garnet later delivered the eulogy at Wright's funeral.) In 1841, the year he was ordained an elder.

In July 1835 Garnet, Alexander Crummell, and Thomas S. Sidney, classmates from New York, went to the newly-established Noyes Academy in Canaan, New Hampshire. Founded by abolitionists, Noyes was open to both blacks and whites and to males as well as females. While in New Hampshire, the students delivered fiery orations at an abolitionist meeting. A vocal minority of local townspeople were determined to close down the school and drive away the 14 blacks enrolled. In August they attached teams of oxen to the schoolhouse, dragged it away, and burned it.

The mob also surrounded the house where Garnet and some of the other blacks were living, and someone fired into the room he was occupying. That evening the mob gathered again but Garnet fired a shot which discouraged them.

There was another institution, Oneida Institute in Whitesboro, New York that welcomed African American students. In early 1836 Garnet joined Crummell and Sidney at Oneida Institute in Whitesboro, New York. Garnet began in the preparatory department while his fellow students were listed as sophomores.

In May 1840 Garnet attended the meeting of the American Anti-Slavery Society in New York and delivered a well-received maiden speech. In September, he graduated from Oneida with honors and settled in Troy, New York.

Even though Garnet was not yet ordained, he had been called as minister to the newly established Liberty Street Presbyterian Church at Troy, New York. Garnet continued to study theology with the noted minister and abolitionist, Nathaniel S. S. Beman, taught school, and worked toward the full establishment of the church whose congregation was black. In 1842 Garnet was licensed to preach and in the following year ordained a minister. He thus became the first pastor of the Liberty Street Presbyterian Church in Troy, where he remained until 1848.

Despite some chronic illnesses, Garnet extended himself beyond the ministry. He assisted in editing *The National Watchman,* an abolitionist paper published in Troy during the latter part of 1842, and later edited *The Clarion,* which combined abolitionist and religious themes. Closely interwoven with Garnet's church work was his work in the Temperance Movement. Garnet was also engaged in politics. He attended black state conventions from 1836 to 1850 he also worked for the extension of black male voting rights in New York state, but a property holding qualification was imposed upon African Americans. He presented several petitions to the legislature on this subject. However, the state property qualification remained the law until the adoption of the Fifteenth Amendment in 1870.

In 1839 the Liberty Party was formed with abolition as one of its major planks. Although its vote in the 1840 elections was minuscule, the party set its sights on the 1844 election. Garnet became an early and enthusiastic supporter of this reform party. He delivered a major address at the party's 1842 meeting in Boston. He was also able to secure the endorsement of the revived National Convention of Colored Men, held in Albany in August 1843 for the party. The year 1844 marked a peak for the party. Then the Free Soil Party and later the Republican Party began to attract reform-minded voters. Garnet later became a somewhat reluctant supporter of the Republican Party.

When Garnet's activism became more militant, he broke with the leading Euro-American abolitionist William Lloyd Garrison, who rejected politics in favor of moral reform. Garnet's impatience with Garrison's position was expressed publicly as early as 1840 when he was one of the eight black founding members of the American and Foreign Anti-Slavery Society which formalized the split in the ranks of abolitionists. Garnet gave further proof of his disaffection in 1843. The August 1843 National Negro Convention in Albany, New York, gathered more than 70 delegates in the first such convention since the early 1830s. Garnet was a prominent member; in particular he was chairman of the nine-member business committee, which was charged with organizing the issues for discussion. He electrified the convention with "An Address to the Slaves of the United States of America," in which he urged bondspersons to take action to gain their own freedom: "You had far better all die—die immediately, than live slaves, and entail your wretchedness upon your posterity. ... However much you and all of us may desire it, there is not much hope of redemption without the shedding of blood. If you must bleed, let it all come at once— rather die freemen, than live to be the slaves." "Let your motto be Resistance! Resistance! Resistance!"

The audience was profoundly moved: some wept, others sat with clenched fists. Frederick Douglass who was not ready to abandon Garrisonian moral suasion, joined with others in opposition to Garnet's position. Douglass spoke for more than an hour against adopting the speech. The rules were suspended to allow Garnet to reply for an hour and a half in a speech, which James McCune Smith said was Garnet's greatest. Unfortunately neither Douglass's speech nor Garnet's reply survive today. The original address was referred to the business committee for moderation and eventually failed to be adopted by one vote.

Garnet also extended his political action into the colonization controversy of the time. He began advocating emigration as a solution for the plight of African Americans in the United States as proposed by the American Colonization Society. Since 1817 most African American leaders condemned the Colonization Society's program and were suspicious of the society's aims and of its creation of the Republic of Liberia, which became independent in 1847. Garnet, however, favored emigration "to any area where there might be hope of being treated justly and with dignity".

In 1848 Garnet moved from Troy, New York to Geneva Switzerland. Then in 1850 he went to Great Britain at the invitation of the Free Labor Movement, an organization opposing the use of products produced by enslaved labor. The following year he was joined by his family and remained in Geneva for two and a half years.

In 1852, the United Presbyterian Church of Scotland sent Garnet to Jamaica as a missionary. Meanwhile, he stepped up his emigrationist activities and founded the African Civilization Society in 1859. As he later explained: We believe that Africa is to be redeemed by Christian civilization and that the great work is to be chiefly achieved by the free and voluntary emigration of enterprising colored people."

In March 1864 Garnet became pastor of the Fifteenth Street Presbyterian Church of Washington. D.C. A year later he became the first African American to deliver a religious message in the U. S House of Representatives Garnet accepted the presidency of Avery College in Pittsburgh in 1868, but returned to Shiloh Church in New York in 1870.

Garnet's friend, Alexander Crummell revealed that Garnet went into a physical and mental decline about 1876 and that "sorrow and discouragement fell upon his soul, and at times the wounded spirit sighed for release." In this mood, in spite of the discouragement of his friends, Garnet actively lobbied for the position of minister to Liberia. Upon his confirmation to the diplomatic post in Liberia, Crummell quoted Garnet as saying: "Please the Lord I can only safely cross the ocean, land on the coast of Africa, look around upon its green fields, tread the soil of my ancestors, live if but a few weeks; then I shall be glad to lie down and be buried beneath its sod."

He preached his farewell sermon at Shiloh on November 6, 1881 and landed in Monrovia on December 28. Less than two months later he was dead. He was given a state funeral by the Liberian government, and Edward Blyden preached the eulogy. Later, during a memorial service in Washington, DC, his life-long friend, Alexander Crummell gave the eulogy and Frederick Douglass and Henry McNeal Turner sat behind him.

GARVEY, MARCUS (August 17,1887- June 10,1940) Black Nationalist Leader, was born in St. Ann's Bay, Jamaica. He migrated to the United States in 1916. On August 1-2, 1920 the national convention of the Universal Negro Improvement Association (UNIA) met in New York City. Marcus Garvey, the founder, spoke to about 25,000 blacks during the rally at Madison Square Garden. Garvey-type black nationalism was reaching its zenith at the time.

Garvey had begun his organization in his native Jamaica in 1914. In 1916 he arrived in the United States to organize a New York chapter of UNIA. By the middle of 1919 thirty branches existed in the United States, principally in the northern ghettos. Garvey founded the newspaper *Negro World* to disseminate his ideas of race pride and to promote his back to Africa stance. His other organizations included the Universal Black Cross Nurses, the Universal African Motor Corps, the Black Star Steamship Line, and the Black Eagle Flying Corps.

In 1921Garvey formally organized the Empire of Africa and appointed himself provisional president. He appealed, unsuccessfully, to the League of Nations for permission to settle a colony in Africa and negotiated towards that end with Liberia. After these failures, he began planning a military expedition to drive the white imperialists out of Africa. This campaign, however, was never launched. In 1923 Garvey was arrested for mail fraud in his attempts to raise money for his steamship line. After being convicted in a U. S. district court, he was sent to the federal peneteniary in Atlanta.

GRIMKE, ARCHIBALD (August 17,1849 – February 25, 1930), Civil Rights Activist, Diplomat, Editor, was a founder of the National Association for the Advancement of Colored People (NAACP). and received its Spingarn Award for his service as the U. S. consul to Santo Domingo.

Grimke was born in Charleston, South Carolina, in 1849. He studied at Lincoln University, and in 1874, he graduated from the Harvard University Law School. Five years later, Grimke married Sarah Stanley, and the couple had one child in 1880.

Beginning in 1883, Grimke edited *The Hub*, a Boston weekly. Grimke was president of the American Negro Academy before becoming the consul to Santo Domingo in 1894.

HALE, WILLIAM JASPER (1874-1944), Educator, was born in Retro, Tennessee. He began his administrative work at a small African American elementary school and worked his way up to the role of principal of the African American St. Elmo secondary school in Chattanooga, Tennessee. In 1911 Hale was appointed principal of the Tennessee Agricultural and Industrial State Normal School, Tennessee's first and only African American state college. He later became its president. His administrative talents helped land the school a fully accredited four-year status in the 1920s. During Hale's thirty-one-year tenure, enrollment grew from 200 to 3,000.

Hale was president of the Conference of the Negro Land Grant Colleges, and he founded and was president of the Tennessee Inter-Racial League. He received the Harmon Foundation Medal in 1930 for advancing black education in the South and was a member of the Nashville Board of Trade and of President Herbert Hoover's Negro Housing Committee.

HANDY, WILLIAM CHRISTOPHER ("W. C.") (November 16, 1873), Entertainer, "the Father of the Blues", was born in Florence, Alabama. He grew up in his grandfather's log cabin, where he very early displayed talents in music. But music, other than religious songs, was frowned upon by his family. Nevertheless, as a teenager, he joined a local band that played secular music.

In 1892, Handy began teaching in Birmingham, but soon abandoned the job because of poor pay. Returning to music, he organized the "Lauzetta Quarter", which had unsuccessful ventures in Chicago and St. Louis before finally finding success in Evansville, Indiana.

In 1896, he joined a minstrel group that toured the midwest, the southwest and the Deep South as well as Cuba. By 1909 Handy and his band had moved their headquarters to Beale Street in Memphis, Tennessee. By this time, Handy was developing a genre of music that incorporated the life and work, the joys and sorrows of ordinary southern blacks. His first composition in the genre was a campaign song for a local mayoral candidate, E. H. Crump. The song, "Mr. Crump", later gained wider popularity as the "Memphis Blues". Following "Memphis Blues" in 1912, two years later Handy composed and performed his most famous work, "the "St. Louis Blues." These compositions sealed "the blues" as an important new musical form in the United States and the fame of W. C. Handy.

After losing his balance and falling from a subway station in 1943, handy lost his sight. However, he continued to compose the blues. In addition, before his blindness, Handy had published *Authors and Composers* (1935) and two other books.

HAYES, ROLAND (1887-1977), Entertainer, was born in Curryville, Georgia, the son of former bondspersons. When he was 13 years old, his family moved to Chattanooga, Tennessee. After arriving in Chattanooga, he became a music student with Arthur Calhoun and later attended Fisk University. While at Fisk, he toured in the United States and abroad with the famed Fisk Jubilee Singers. Later he studied with Arthur Hubbard in Boston, Massachusetts and with George Herschel and Amanda Ira Aldridge (the daughter of Shakespearean actor Ira Aldridge) in England.

Since he had difficulty, as a young African American singer, getting a manager/promoter in the United States, Hayes arranged his own recitals and appeared frequently in most of the country's African American communities. But, these concerts did not bring in much income; hence, by 1920, Hayes went to Europe and attained an international reputation, particularly for his renditions of Negro Spirituals. While in Europe, he also performed before British royalty.

When Hayes returned to the United States following his European tour, he was able to attain a manager/promoter and sang before large audiences, including performances at Boston Symphony Hall. In recognition of his contributions to African Americans and their image, the NAACP awarded Hayes the Spingarn Medal in 1924.

HENSON, MATTHEW ALEXANDER (1866-March, 1955)
Explorer. On April 6, 1909, Henson and Admiral Robert B. Peary
shared in the discovery of the North Pole.

Henson was born in Maryland in 1866, the son of free-born
sharecroppers. Historians believe he was orphaned at an early
age and ran away from home when he was about eleven to escape from a cruel stepmother. Making his way to Washington,
D.C., Henson moved in with an uncle and went to school for a
while. He then worked as a cabin boy on board a merchant ship
and later as a stock boy in a Washington clothing store. There he
met Peary, who hired Henson as his personal servant. Henson
and Peary then went on several expeditions together, including
one to Nicaragua and several to the Arctic in search of the exact
location of the North Pole. Henson proved to be an expert guide
and surveyor.

HOLIDAY, BILLIE (Fagan, Eleanor) (April 7, 1915-July 17,
1959), Entertainer was born in Baltimore, Maryland, the daughter of Clarence Holiday. Her father, who played guitar with the
famed jazz musician Fletcher Henderson, never married her
mother, a domestic worker, who did not prove to be a good parent. Some scholars believe that her dysfunctional childhood had
a lasting, negative effect on Holiday.

As a teenager, Holiday began singing and subsequently developed a unique style in which she used her "small voice" in
"behind-the beat phrasing." By the 1930s, she was heard and
seen by promoter John Hammond while singing in a Harlem
nightclub. In 1933 she recorded with the famous jazz band of
Benny Goodman. Then from 1935 to 1942, she recorded with
Buck Clayton, Lester Young and Teddy Wilson. By this time,
her repertoire included a combination of the sounds of Louis
Armstrong and Bessie Smith. She became nationally known after
1937 when she appeared with the Count Basie's orchestra and
the Artis Shaw orchestra and recorded "Strange Fruit." "Strange
Fruit", which included a monologue on racism, including lynchings, resulted from her personal experiences with bigotry both in
the South and the North.

Following "Strange Fruit", her voice seemed to grow stronger and her performances richer. She signed with Decca records and, in the 1940s, recorded such hits as "Fine and Mellow", "Giod Bless the Child" "Ain't Nobody's Business If I Do" and the bestseller, "Lover Man". But by 1950, drugs and alcohol began to pull Holiday down. Her voice failed and she served time in jail, before collapsing and dying in 1959.

HOPE, JOHN (1868-1936) Educator, Civil/Human Rights Leader (1868-1936), assumed the presidency of Morehouse College (then Atlanta Baptist College) in 1906. One of the most militant of early black educators, Hope was the school's first African American president. He also was the man behind many of the programs that earned the school its reputation for excellence.

Hope was born in 1868 in Augusta, Georgia, to a white father and mother of mixed racial heritage. The family was quite prosperous, and young John's childhood was happy and secure until his father died in 1876. Then the actions of some prejudiced whites and cold-hearted executors (the people in charge of carrying out the terms of a will) caused the family to lose most of their money. Other friends of his father, however, assisted him in receiving an education at Worcester Academy, Augusta Baptist Institute (later Morehouse College) and Brown University, where he received bachelor's and master's degrees. Prior to accepting the presidency of Morehouse, he taught at Roger Williams University in Nashville, Tennessee.

In the same year that young Hope assumed the presidency at Morehouse, he witnessed a violent racial clash in Atlanta. This incident helped solidify his growing militancy. Hope had criticized Booker T. Washington's "Atlanta Compromise" speech and was the only black college president to join the militant Niagara Movement. He was also the only college administrator to attend the founding meeting of the NAACP.

In 1919, Hope co-founded the South's first biracial reform group, the Commission on Interracial Cooperation. (It was the forerunner of the Southern Regional Council.) He served as the group's president beginning in 1932. In 1929, he helped to lead the effort that resulted in a loose affiliation of three black colleges in Atlanta-Atlanta University, Morehouse College and Spelman College. Between 1929 and 1932, he served as president of both Atlanta and Morehouse; then in 1932 he headed Atlanta University alone until his death in 1936. That same year, the NAACP awarded him the Spingarn Medal for his achievements as an educational and civil rights leader.

HOPE, LUGENIA BURNS (February 19,1871-1947), Human Rights Leader, was born in St. Louis, Missouri. As an adolescent she worked for several charitable and settlement organizations. Between 1890 and 1893 she attended the Chicago Art Institute, the Chicago School of Design, and the Chicago Business College. She met John Hope, a future prominent African American educator and civil human rights leader, in 1893. They were married in 1897.

While John Hope taught at the Roger Williams University in Nashville, Tennessee, Hope began a career that would span more than 30 years, in social work and political and civil rights. She continued this work, after 1906 in Atlanta, when John Hope became the first African American president of what was to become Morehouse College. Shortly after arriving in Atlanta, Hope worked with a group that eventually evolved into the Neighborhood Union, the first female-run, social welfare agency for African Americans in Atlanta and one of the first such institution in the nation. From 1908 to 1935 she was chairperson of its Board of Managers of the NU where she oversaw the delivery of medical, recreational, employment, and educational services to Atlanta's African-American neighborhoods. In 1920 Hope received national attention when she led a challenge to the segregation and Euro-American domination in the national YWCA. In response to the recalcitrance of white women on the question of racial equality, Hope offered: "Ignorance is ignorance wherever found, yet the most ignorant white woman may enjoy every privilege that America offers....the ignorant Negro woman should also enjoy them."

At the beginning of World War I, the NU ran the Atlanta YWCA's War Work Councils to serve African-American soldiers, who were barred from the recreational activities available to white soldiers through the base canteens and other USO-related entertainments. As a result of the success of these facilities, she was approached to coordinate a nationwide network of Hostess Houses that eventually provided both African- American and Jewish soldiers, and their families, with a wide variety of services from recreation to relocation counseling.

Hope was also a founding member of the Atlanta Branch of the National Association of Colored Women's Clubs (NACWC) and a pioneer member of other African American womanist organizations including the national Council of Negro Women (NCNW).

Locally, as president of the NU and a vice president of the Atlanta Branch NAACP, she was a leader in the fight for better schooling for African American youth and in the campaign to get access to the ballot for African Americans. Once voting rights seemed assured, she was in the forefront of efforts to teach blacks how to intelligently use their voting rights. One such product was the "citizenship schools" that offered six-week classes on voting, democracy, and the Constitution. Other NAACP chapters around the country soon adopted used these strategic models in the early stages of the modern Civil Rights Movement.

Following the death of John Hope in 1936 Lugenia Burns Hope left Atlanta; returning only in 1947 when her cremated ashes were strewn from the top of the Graves hall dormitory on the Morehouse College campus.

HOUSTON, CHARLES HAMILTON (1895-1950) Attorney, Civil/Human Rights Activist was educated at Amherst College and Harvard University, where he was an editor of the *Harvard Law review*. While teaching at Howard University, he joined the Army during World War I and served in the black unit of the American Expeditionary Forces. After the war, he returned to the faculty of Howard University, where his pupils included Thurgood Marshall. Subsequently, he was a founder of the NAACP Legal Defense and Educational Fund—an effort to consolidate some of the nation's best legal talents in the fight against bias sanctioned by law. In. 1939, The NAACP Legal Defense and Educational Fund, pledged it self to an all-out war on discrimination.

HURSTON, ZORA NEALE (January 7, 1903-January 28, 1960), Author, was born on January 7, 1903 to John and Lucy Anne Hurston in Eatonville, Florida. While attending Howard University, Hurston made a name for herself as one of the emerging writers of the Harlem Renaissance. Lorenzo Turner and Alain Locke served as mentors for Hurston. Her short stories appeared in *Opportunity* and her other works include *Jonah's Gourd Vine* (1934), *Mules and Men* (1935), *Their Eyes Were Watching God* (1937), *Tell My Horse* (1938), *Moses, Man of the Mountain* (1939), and *Seraph on the Suwanee* (1948). Her autobiography, *Dust Tracks on a Road,* was published in 1942.

JOCKEYS, Isaac Murphy, a black jockey riding "Kingman," became the first man to win three Kentucky Derbies. Murphy won his first Derby in 1884 on "Buchanan" and his second in 1890 on "Riley."

Black jockey "Monk" Overton won six straight horse races at the Washington Park racetrack in Chicago. In 1907, another black jockey, Jimmy Lee, also won six straight races at Churchill Downs in Louisville. Pryor to 1907, only two other jockeys had equaled the achievements of Overton and Lee—Englishmen Fred Archer and George Ford ham.

JOHNSON, JAMES WELDON (June 12,1871-June,1938) Author, Civil/Human Rights Leader, was honored on June 10, 1926 in New York City for his careers as an executive secretary of the NAACP, a member of the U.S. Consul, editor, and poet. Johnson was born in Jacksonville, Florida and went to school there. He continued his education at Atlanta University, New York's City College, and Columbia University. He began his professional life in Florida, working as a teacher, journalist, and lawyer before going to New York City to join his brother, J. Rosamond Johnson, as a writer of musical comedies. Johnson is best known for his poetry and prose. His most famous works include *The Autobiography of an Ex-Colored Man* (1912), *The*

Book of American Negro Poetry (1925), God's Trombones (1927), *Black Manhattan* (1930), a novel, and his own autobiography, *Along This Way* (1933). His poem "Lift Every Voice and Sing," which his brother set to music, became known as "the Negro National Anthem."

Johnson's social and professional contacts among blacks and whites in New York, along with his success as a writer and a diplomat and his "moderate" opposition to racial discrimination, made him the ideal choice as the NAACP's first executive secretary. In this position, Johnson led the campaign to outlaw lynching in the United States. His efforts resulted in the Dyer anti lynching bill of 1921, which passed in the House of Representatives but failed in the Senate. Before his death in 1938, Johnson taught for a while at Fisk University in Nashville, Tennessee. He has been called an "American Renaissance Man" in recognition of his many talents and interests.

JOHNSON, JACK (March 31, 1878— June 10, 1946), Athlete, was born Arthur John Johnson in Galveston, Texas, the eldest son of Henry Johnson, a janitor and former bondsman, and Tiny. As a boy, Johnson was involved in many schoolyard fights, usually returning home beaten, bruised, and crying unless his sister came to his defense. Only when his mother, the more s, threatened him with a worse whipping did he begin to fight back. After attending public school for six years, he drifted from one job to another, working variously as a horse trainer, a baker, and a dockworker, usually in the vicinity of his hometown. (1969) and later movie (1970).

Johnson also participated in "battle royals," in which he and eight or more African American youths, often blindfolded, fought each other until the last man standing won the bout and was rewarded with a few cents. But these bouts eventually led him into a professional boxing career.

After several fights in Texas and Chicago, Illinois, against black opponents, most of which he won, Johnson, eventually got an opportunity to face European and Euro-American opponents. After 1901, he defeated several heavyweights from these groups and on December 26, 1908 he scored a fourteenth-round knock out of Tommy Burns in Australia to become the first African American heavyweight champion of the world. Many Euro-Americans, then, began a search for "a great white hope" to defeat Johnson and restore their claim to white athletic as well as intellectual supremacy Finally in 1915, Johnson lost the title in a 26th round knock out by Jess Willard.

During his reign as world heavyweight championship, Johnson flaunted conventional racial norms by dating and marrying white women, showing cockiness in and out of the ring and his ostentatious life style, These activities led to his arrest and conviction in for violating the Mann Act which prohibited carrying women across state lines for "immoral purposes." Following the conviction Johnson went into exile. He returned to the United States in 1920 and spent a year in prison.

Johnson's life has been chronicled in several biographies, in a Pulitzer Prize winning Broadway play and a film. The latter two were entitled "The Great White Hope."

JONES, CASEY On April 30, 1900, the famed steam locomotive driven by John "Casey" Jones collided with another train. Two black men, Wallace Saunders and Sim Webb, were members of the crew. At the time of the collision, Jones ordered Webb to jump to safety while he remained with his train. When Jones's body was recovered, it was discovered that he had kept one hand on the airbrake and the other on the whistle. The incident inspired Saunders to write "Casey Jones," the song that immortalized the noted engineer and his train.

JONES, SISSIERETTA ("Black Patti") (January 5, 1869-June 24, 1933) Entertainer, in 1892, performed for President Benjamin Harrison at the White House. Jones, a soprano, was born in Virginia, spent her childhood in Providence, Rhode Island, and studied at the New England Conservatory. She first attracted the attention of critics in 1892 when she appeared at the Jubilee Spectacle and Cakewalk at Madison Square Garden in New York. One critic called her the "Black Patti," a comparison with the Italian *prima donna* Adelina Patti. According to some authorities, "Black Patti Jones" was sought for roles in *Aida* and

L'Africaine by the Metropolitan Opera, but the project was dropped, reportedly because the "musical world was not ready to accept black prima donnas." Jones toured Europe in 1893. Upon her return to the United States, she organized an all-black company, "Black Patti's Troubadours," in which she was featured soloist.

JOPLIN, SCOTT (November 24, 1868-April 1, 1917), Entertainer, was born in Texas. He showed a talent for music as a child, and by the time he was in his teens, he had already hit the road to play piano in the bars and bordellos of towns along the Mississippi River.

Joplin settled in Missouri in 1894, and there he began studying and composing music. His first hit came in 1899 with "The Maple Leaf Rag." He followed it up with other short ragtime pieces that were also very popular.

He then headed to New York to try his luck at publishing longer and more serious works, including a fully orchestrated folk opera called "Treemonisha." But no one would consider backing a black pianist who had learned his craft in midwestern saloons. Joplin finally had to publish "Treemonisha" himself and even staged an unsuccessful piano version of it in Harlem.

These professional failures and chronic health problems left Joplin battered physically and emotionally. In 1916 he was committed to a mental hospital where he died a year later.

By the time of Joplin's death, most people had lost interest in ragtime music. Joplin, himself, was forgotten by all but a few devoted fans until the early 1970s, when classical music critics raved about a newly released recording of his compositions. Then an African American musical theater group, co-sponsored by Morehouse College, first staged a full-scale production of "Treemonisha" in Atlanta. Finally, in 1974, some of Joplin's ragtime pieces were featured in the popular film "The Sting" and on October 3, at St. Michael's Cemetery in Queens, New York, a bronze plaque was placed on his grave more than fifty years after his death. The plaque was paid for by the American Society of Composers, Authors and Publishers (ASCAP). This commemoration finally acknowledged the contributions of a man who once seemed destined to rest in obscurity.

JUST, ERNEST EVERETT (August 14, 1883-October 27, 1941) Scientist, was born in Charleston, South Carolina to Charles Frazier and Mary Matthews Just. After completing studies at the Kimball Hall Academy in New Hampshire,, he enrolled in Dartmouth College, where, in his freshman year, he received the highest marks in his class in Greek and was the Rufus Choate Scholar for two years. He was the only student to graduate *magna cum laude in 1907. He also received* special honors in botany and history and honors in botany and sociology.

After graduating from Dartmouth, Just began a teaching career at Howard University in Washington, DC. Then, beginning in 1909, he became a research assistant, during the summer months, for Professor Frank Rattray Lillie, the second director of the Marine Biological Laboratory at Woods Hole, Massachusetts, while also studying for advanced degrees,. In 1916, he received the PhD degree,, *magna cum laude* from the university of Chicago in experimental embryology, with a thesis on the mechanics of fertilization.

Just's teaching and research interests were in the physiology of development. His specialties were fertilization, experimental parthenogenesis, hydration, cell division, dehydration in living cells, the effect of ultra violet rays in increasing chromosome number in animals and in altering the organization of the egg with special reference to polarity.

He was one of the authors of *General Cytology,* published in 1924.

In 1924 Just was selected by a group of German biologist to contribute to a monograph on fertilization, one of a series of monographs by specialists working on fundamental problems of the function and structure of the cell. From 1920-1931 Just was the Julius Rosenwald Fellow in Biology of the National Research Council. Under this program he engaged in research as an adjunct researcher at the Kaiser Wilhelm Institute for Biology, Berlin-Dahlarn, working under Professor Max Hartmann. He also worked at the marine biological institute at Woods Hole, Massachusetts. During his career, he published papers over 50 scholarly essays.

Just's importance to zoology might best be summed up by a statement offered by George R. Arthur in *the Crisis*, in 1932:

> If we are to judge his accomplishments by standards set up by men of science, it can be said that Dr. Just is an eminent scientist. If we are to judge his value to Negro education by what he has accomplished in the realm of science, it can be said that to Negro youth especially, he demonstrates the possibility of human achievement regardless of race or color. In the language of Dean Kelly Miller in an appreciation of Dr. Just, What boots it that Euclid was a Greek, Newton an Englishman, Marconi an Italian or Guttenburg a German? Their genius has enriched the blood of mankind regardless of place, time, race or nationality

LANE, ISAAC (1834-1937) Minister, was born in bondage in Tennessee. While a bondsman, he was licensed to preach, but even after emancipation had to supplement his income by raising cotton and selling firewood. He eventually became a bishop and patriarch of the Colored Methodist Episcopal (CME) Church and founded Lane College in Tennessee in as a high school. It became Lane College in 1896 and awarded its first black bachelor's degree in 1899.

LATIMER, LEWIS HOWARD (September 4, 1848-December 11, 1928), Inventor, was born in Chelsea, Massachusetts on September 4, 1848. He learned mechanical drawing in offices of Crosby and Gould, patent attorneys, in Boston, Massachusetts. His first major invention was a toilet system for railroad cars in 1873. He also invented an electric lamp with an inexpensive carbon filament and a threaded wooden socket for light bulbs. He supervised the installation of carbon filament electric lighting in New York City, Philadelphia, Montreal, and London. Additionally, he was responsible for preparing the mechanical drawings for Alexander Graham Bell 's patent application for his telephone design.

Latimer became the first and only African American member of the *Edison Pioneers*, an engineering division of Thomas Edison s Edison Company. He joined the Edison Electric Light Company in 1884 and conducted research on electrical lighting.

In 1890 he published *Incandescent Electric Lighting*, a technical engineering book which became a guide for lighting engineers. For many years preceding his death he served as an expert witness in the court battles over Thomas Edison s patents.

At the time of Latimer s death in 1928, the *Edison Pioneers* attributed his important inventions to a "keen perception of the potential of the electric light and kindred industries." Also, following his death several schools and libraries throughout the country were named for him.

LAVEAU, MARIE (c.1794 or 1796-c. 1879 or 1881) Voodooist, was born free in New Orleans around 1796. She was a beautiful woman of mixed racial heritage who worked as a professional hairdresser in the homes of some of the city's most prominent white women.

Under Laveau's leadership, Louisiana Voodooism blended a distorted form of Catholicism with West Indian beliefs in the magical powers of certain objects. This unusual mixture made the cult very popular and helped it gain acceptance. Laveau 's main source of power was her ability to convince blacks and whites that she could bring them good luck and protect them from evil. She dominated Voodooism in New Orleans for nearly forty years, becoming the most famous and powerful of all the Voodoo queens.

LOCKE, ALAIN (1886 – 1954), Educator, Scholar, a prominent African American intellectual, received a Rhodes Scholarship in 1907; no other African American won this academic honor for more than half a century. Locke was born in Philadelphia in 1886. He obtained his Ph. D. from Harvard University in 1918. As a Rhodes Scholar, Locke studied at England's Oxford University from 1907 to 1910. He continued his studies at the University of Berlin 1910 to 1911, and he became a professor of philosophy at Howard University in 1912, a position he held until his retirement in 1953. Locke published *Race Contacts and Interracial Relations* in 1916. His fame as a literary and art critic and interpreter of black culture rests largely on his anthology, *The New Negro* (1925), a seminal work about the Harlem Renaissance. Locke died in 1954, prior to completing *The Negro in American Culture*. This work was completed by Margaret Just Butcher and published in 1956.

MATZELIGER, JAN E. (1852-1889), Inventor. On March 20, 1883 a Massachusett shoemaker, invented a complicated machine that manufactured an entire shoe. The invention, which was sold to the United Shoe Company, revolutionized the industry. By 1880, machines were able to cut and stitch the leather, but not to shape and attach the upper portion of the shoe to the sole. This had to be done by hand, a slow and tedious process. Working in secret, Matzeliger tackled the "lasting" problem for ten years. In 1883, he received the patent for his perfected product, a "lasting machine," which could hold the shoe on the last, grip and pull the leather down around the heel, set and drive the nails, and discharge the completed shoe.

McQUEEN, THELMA ("Butterfly") (1911-December 22, 1995), Entertainer, was, perhaps, best known for her role as a bondsgirl called Prissy in *Gone With the Wind*. Her lines: "Miss Charlotte, I don't know nuthin' about birthin' babies "became immortal. She subsequently became typecast as a maid. These roles drew criticisms from many blacks who deemed them stereotypical and racist. By the mid-1940s, McQueen left film for theater, but then returned to play several minor roles during the 1970s and 80s. She died in December 1995 as a result of critical burns suffered in a fire in her Augusta, Georgia home.

MCKAY, CLAUDE (September 15, 1890-1948) Author, published two volumes of poetry shortly after his twentieth birthday. In 1913 he came to the United States to study agriculture, but his desire to write poetry prevailed, and he moved to New York City. He began publishing his work in small literary magazines, traveled abroad, and returned to New York to serve under Max Eastman as associate editor of *The Liberator*. In 1922 he completed *Harlem Shadows*, a landmark work of the Harlem renaissance. McKay continued to write novels, poetry and an autobiography until the time of his death.

MICHEAUX, OSCAR (1884-April 1,1951) Author. Although his semiautobiographical stories were considered poor writing by some, Micheaux ensured their success with extensive promotional tours. His third book, *The Homesteader* (1917), attracted the interest of the black, independent Lincoln Motion Picture Company. When Micheaux stubbornly insisted on directing the film version, the company backed out, and Micheaux himself set about financing the film. He found support from the Oklahoma farmers who had funded his novels and thus organized the Oscar Micheaux Corporation in New York City. *The Homesteader* was its first product, released in 1919.

Micheaux went on to produce about thirty more pictures from 1919 to 1937, most suffering from quick production and low budgets. The plots were standard melodrama featuring light-skinned blacks who were often touted as African American versions of Hollywood stars. Micheaux was responsible for the screen debut of Paul Robeson in *Body and Soul* (1924).

MILLER, DORIE (October 12, 1919 – November 24, 1943), Sailor, Navy Cross Recipient, was born on a small farm near Waco, Texas, to sharecropper parents. He enlisted in the navy when he was nineteen and was assigned to sea duty.

On December 7, 1941, Miller was aboard the battleship *Arizona* when it was anchored at Pear Harbor. This ship suffered tremendous damage when the Japanese attacked; Miller was knocked down by the blast. Unlike many crew members, however, Miller stayed aboard the ship and figured out how to fire a gun, a skill he had never been taught.

After moving the mortally wounded captain to safety, Miller successfully fired at four Japanese planes. Three months later, he was awarded the Navy Cross and advanced to mess attendant first class. Miller died while serving aboard the *Liscome Bay* when she was sunk by a Japanese submarine on November 24, 1943.

MITCHELL, NANNIE (d. January 25, 1975 at age eighty-eight) Publisher, was a founder of the *St. Louis Argus* and a veteran business and civic leader. In 1905, Mitchell, along with her late husband William and brother-in-law, J. E. Mitchell, founded the We Shall Rise Insurance Company in St. Louis and began publishing a newsletter to be distributed to black churches in the area. This newsletter eventually became the *Argus,* a newspaper that was published weekly starting in 1915.

PAIGE, LEROY ("SATCHEL") (July 7, 1906-June 8, 1982), Athlete, was born in Mobile, Alabama. A pitcher with a penchant for witticisms, he became a star in the Negro baseball leagues. Despite, his abilities, however, racism prevented him from being elevated to the major leagues, until he was 42 years old (where he became the oldest player to make his major league debut), From 1948 until 1954, he was a major reliever for the Cleveland Indians. His pitching style, where he would raise his leg high and pounce his pitches across the plate, added to his legendary stature. In 1971, Major League Baseball announced that his years in the Negro leagues and the Major leagues were sufficient for him to be given full membership in the Baseball hall of Fame at Cooperstown, New York. Officials had originally planned to honor Paige and other star players from the Negro leagues in a separate division of the Hall of Fame. Baseball fans and others, however, criticized the idea; so officials decided to give Paige full honors. Since Paige, in some of his colloquies, often downplayed his age, many believed that he was older than 42 when he entered the major leagues and older than 71 when he died.

PICKETT, BILL (December 5, 1870-March 23 or April 2, 1932), Rodeo Cowboy, was born in Travis County, Texas, the son of Thomas Jefferson and Mary Virginia Elizabeth Gilbert Pickett. He attended elementary school through the fifth grade.

Pickett became a ranch hand near Taylor, Texas in 1889. By 1888, he had become a professional rodeo and Wild West Show performer; principally with the with the 101 Ranch and Wild West Show after 1905. He remained with 101 Ranch and Wild

West until 1930. Between 1905 and 1927, while not working for 101 Ranch and Wild West, he worked as a hand on the 101 Ranch in Ponca City, Oklahoma.

Pickett achieved fame in the rodeo world after 1900 for inventing a process by which dogs weighing less than fifty pounds could bring half ton steers to their knees by biting the steers' lips and hanging on. The process became known as "bulldogging". At first the practice was used to control animals that were being herded for shipment to slaughterhouse. Later however, Pickett and others used "bulldogging" during rodeo performances at county fairs and elsewhere.

Cowboys and rodeos remained a part of systemic racism in the United States and White America was slow to recognize Pickett as a hero of the Old West. After 1905, however, "the Dusky Demon", as he came to be called, was introduced to the owners of the101Ranch by Will Rogers. Eventually he appeared with 101 Ranch shows in such places as Madison Square Garden in New York, the Boston Garden and the Chicago Coliseum. He often shared billings with Will Rogers and Tom Mix, who went on to become movie stars. But Pickett was better received in Europe, as he even performed before members of the English royal family.

In the early 1920s Pickett decreased his active participation in rodeos and worked mostly as a hand on ranches. Although, he remained healthy and spry for his age, his 101 Ranch fell on hard financial hands. Pickett died in 1932 after being kicked by a horse.

The absence of Pickett from the folklore of the early history of the western frontier is, of course, largely attributable to white racism. Although, as Cecil Johnson, one of Pickett's biographers informs" "Many insist that [Pickett] was without debate the greatest all-around work and show business cowboy ever to straddle a horse...[and] the quintessence of the American cowboy, he was not inducted into the national Cowboy Hall of fame during his lifetime. The honor only came posthumously in 1971.

PINCHBACK, PBS (May 10, 1837-December 21,1921) Politician, a former Union officer and lieutenant governor of Louisiana, was named temporary governor of the state on December 11, 1872, becoming the first African American to serve as a state governor. He served for forty-three days as incumbent Henry C. Warmoth was impeached. Pinchback was the son of a white Mississippi planter and army officer and a mulatto woman who bore nine other children. His father moved his children north for manumission. Young Pinchback was tutored at home and then formal schooled in Cincinnati, Ohio. After his father's death, he worked on Mississippi river boats.

During the Civil War, Pinchback organized a company of Union volunteers at New Orleans and became their captain. He held many political offices during the Reconstruction of Louisiana, including U.S. senator. Pinchback earned a reputation as a shrewd, aggressive politician. The U.S. senate, following three years of debate and controversy, refused to seat P.B.S. Pinchback of Louisiana.

In the fall of 1872, Pinchback was elected to the U.S. House of Representatives and later to the U.S. Senate in the winter of 1873. During the long debate over Pinchback's case, including nearly an entire extra session of Congress, the affable Pinchback became a national political figure as well as a prominent name in Washington society. Opponents of Pinchback argued that he had not been properly elected and was not qualified; others insisted that the opposition to Pinchback supposedly stemmed from senators' wives being against social intercourse with Pinchback's wife, thereby resulting in their husbands' negative votes.

With support from the nation's first black governor, P.B.S. Pinchback, Louisiana legislators passed provisions for a school for blacks. Southern University was established as a result of this legislation, opening its door to 12 students in 1881. Five years later the state appropriated $14,000 for new facilities for the school. An agricultural and mechanical department was added in 1890 and within a year Southern became a land-grant institution.

PLESSY, HOMER ADOLF (March 17 1862-March 11, 1925) Plaintiff, on June 7, 1892, purchased a first-class ticket from New Orleans to Covington on the East Louisiana Railway. Plessy, who is believed to have been a carpenter born in New Orleans, was seven-eighths Caucasian and one-eighth African. He boarded the train and took a seat in the coach reserved for whites. When the conductor ordered him to move to the coach reserved for blacks, Plessy refused. An officer removed Plessy from the train and took him to the parish jail of New Orleans where he was charged with criminally violating an 1890 Louisiana statute that required separate accommodations for blacks and whites. The U.S. Supreme Court upheld separate but equal public facilities for blacks in the case of *Plessy v. Ferguson*, a case that stemmed from a dispute over transportation facilities in Louisiana. The plaintiff, Homer Adolf Plessy, contended that the 1890 Louisiana statute that required separate accommodations be used by blacks and whites violated the Thirteenth and Fourteenth Amendments. Plessy, who was seven-eighths Caucasian and one-eighth African, also argued that, because the "colored blood" in him was not detectable, he should have the same rights and privileges as white citizens. The Comite des Citoyens, an organization of blacks in New Orleans, aided Plessy and his lawyers. The Court majority, however, ruled that the Louisiana statute did not, in fact, violate either amendment. The segregation of the races thus won the sanction of the highest national tribunal. Justice John Harlan, in a prophetic dissent, asserted that segregation laws fostered ideas of racial inferiority and would increase attacks against the rights of blacks.

RAINEY, JOSEPH H. (June 21, 1832-August 2, 1887) Politician, of Georgetown, South Carolina was seated in the U.S. House of Representative on December 12, 1879. Rainey was born to enslaved parents. His own freedom was purchased before the Civil War by his father, a barber. A well-educated mulatto, Rainey himself became a barber in Charleston. Even though he was a respected member of the Charleston black community, he was called to work on fortification by the Confederates during the Civil War. Rainey refused and exiled himself in the West Indies, where he remained until the end of the Civil War. During Reconstruction, he returned to South Carolina and served as a delegate to the Constitutional Convention of 1868. In 1870 he was elected to the state senate, but soon resigned to accept the House seat vacated by B. Franklin Whittimore, Rainey was then elected to the four succeeding congresses. As a house member, he frequently spoke in favor of education and other social advances for African Americans. The House's first black member was also a consultant to President Rutherford B. Hayes and once received the president's personal commendation for sobriety and attention to duty. After returning from Congress in 1879, Rainey served as an Internal Revenue Service (IRS) agent in South Carolina, then entered business in Washington, D.C. He returned to Georgetown in 1886 and died there a year later.

REVELS, HIRAM R. (d. January 16, 1901) Politician. A former barber and preacher, was a reluctant politician. But it is reported that his fervent prayer before the Mississippi legislature in 1870 persuaded many to vote for him. Many Democrats opposed his selection to the Senate and argued vainly that he could not legally be seated, not having been a citizen before the Civil War. (Constitutionally, senators must be U.S. citizens for at least nine years). He ironically, took the seat of former Senator and Confederate president Jefferson Davis and became the only African American in the U. S. Congress. After retiring from politics, leaving an undistinguished legislative record behind, Revels became president of Alcorn College for Negroes in Mississippi.

RILLIEUX, NORBERT (March 17, 1806-October 8, 1894), Inventor, was born in New Orleans, Louisiana, the son of Vincent Rillieux, Jr., a wealthy engineer of French descent and Constance Vivant, the daughter of a wealthy free African American family. By 1830 young Rillieux had traveled to France and was an instructor in the Ecole Centrale in Paris. He apparently published articles on steam power while at the school.

In 1831, Rillieux successfully attacked the problem of sugar refining. Traditionally, sugar had been produced by reducing sugarcane juice through a process known as "the Jamaica Train." But the "Jamaica Train" required several bondspersons, using long ladles, to skim the boiling sugar juice from one open kettle to the next. It was a long, tedious and dangerous process. However, Rillieux developed an apparatus, in which condensing coils that used the vapor from one vacuum chamber to evaporate the juice from a second chamber. The invention increased the speed of sugar refining and made it more efficient, less expensive and safer for the bondspersons who were employed in the process. Although it was a boon to the sugar industry in Louisiana and elsewhere, it did little to decrease the demand for bondspersons on the sugar plantations.

Since French planters were apparently not interested, at the time, in Rillieux's invention, he returned to New Orleans by 1833 and constructed the device on several large Louisiana plantations. On August 26, 1843 Rillieux received a patent from the U. S. Patent Office for a double-effect evaporator and in 1846 for a triple-effect evaporator.

The significance of Rillieux's invention for the sugar industry has been compared to the effects of Eli Whitney's gin for the cotton industry. In a larger sense, it was one of the most important scientific inventions in ante-bellum America.

SCHOMBURG, ARTURO ALFONSO (January 24-1874-June 8, 1938), Bibliophile, curator, author was born to Carlos and Maria Schomburg in San Juan, Puerto Rico. He attended public schools in San Juan and graduated from the Instituto de Instruccion and the Instituo de Ensenanza Popular. Schomburg attended St. Thomas College in the Virgin Islands and began to collect books and photographs about Puerto Ricans of African descent. (The passion for collecting material sprang from an incident in grade school-a teacher asked him to write an essay on his heritage and he was unable to find any material.)

Schomburg expands his collection to include all people of African descent-by 1926 his collection included over 5,000 books, 3,000 manuscripts, 2,000 etchings, and several thousand pamphlets. In April 1891, he went to New York City and became a member of the Puerto Rico Revolutionary Party. He became a mason a year later. Schomburg wrote *Racial Integrity: A Plea for the Establishment of a Chair of Negro History in Our Schools, Colleges, etc.,* and magazine articles and brochures on masonry. In 1927, he received the William E. Harmon Award for his outstanding work.

SCOTT, EMMETT (February 13-1873-1957), Educator, Political Leader was a former secretary to Booker T. Washington. He was appointed special assistant to the Secretary of War on November 5, 1917. Specifically, Scott worked for nondiscriminatory application of the Selective Service Act; to formulate plans to build up morale among blacks, soldiers, and civilians; and to investigate complaints of unfair treatment of blacks. He also disseminated news concerning black soldiers on the home front. In June of 1918, Scott called a conference of about thirty black newspaper publishers who pledged their support of the American war effort but denounced anti-black violence and discrimination at home. The coalition called for the recruitment of black Red Cross nurses and asked for the appointment of a black war correspondent.

SCOTTSBORO BOYS Famous civil rights case involving discrimination in the American criminal justice system.

In 1931 nine African American youths were indicted at Scottsboro, Ala., on charges of having raped two white women in a freight car passing through Alabama. In a series of trials the youths were found guilty and sentenced to death or to prison terms of 75 to 99 years. The U.S. Supreme Court subsequently reversed the convictions twice on procedural grounds (that the youths' right to counsel had been infringed and that no blacks had served on the grand or trial jury).

At a second trial one of the women recanted her previous testimony. The Alabama trial judge set aside the guilty verdict as contrary to the weight of the evidence and ordered a new trial. In 1937 charges against five of the men were dropped and the state agreed to consider parole for the others. Two were paroled in 1944, one in 1951.

When the fourth escaped (1948) to Michigan, the state refused to return him to Alabama. In 1976, Alabama pardoned Clarence Norris, who had broken parole and fled the state in 1946. The widely held belief that the case against the "Scottsboro boys" was unproved and that the verdicts were the result of racism caused 1930s liberals and radicals to come to the defense of the youths. The fact that Communists used the case for propaganda alienated the NAACP, which had earlier sought to assist the boys, as well as many Euro-American liberals.

STANLEY, FRANK L. (1906-1974), Publisher, was the son of a Chicago, Illinois butcher. At the age of six, his family moved to Louisville, Kentucky. He attended Atlanta University, where he was an all-American quarterback and captain of the football and basketball teams, and the University of Cincinnati. He received honorary doctorate degrees from several universities, including the University of Kentucky. In 1933, Stanley went to work for the *Louisville Defender* as a reporter. Three years later he became editor, general manager, and a part owner. During the years that he published the *Defender*, it received more than thirty-five awards in journalism, including the President's Special Service Award of the National Newspaper Publishers' Association (NNPA) in 1970 and the coveted Russwurm Award in 1974. He was a co-founder of the NNPA and was elected its president on five separate occasions.

Stanley drafted the legislation which led to the desegregation of state universities in Kentucky by its General Assembly in 1950. Ten years later he wrote the bill that created the Kentucky Commission on Human Rights, and was one of the original members of that body. His influence on race relations in Kentucky was noted by the *Louisville Courier Journal* on the occasion of the 25th anniversary of the *Defender* in 1950. "Much of the credit," the newspaper said editorially, "for the even and amiable pace Kentucky has maintained in its working out of race relations problems must be given to the *Defender.*" Stanley was the force behind the *Defender's* role in that achievement.

TANNER, HENRY OSSAWA (June 21, 1859-May 25, 1937), Painter. Tanner was born the eldest of seven children of Benjamin Tucker and Sarah Elizabeth Tanner on June 21, 1859, in Pittsburgh, Pennsylvania. He married a white singer, Jessie Maculey Olssen, on December 14, 1899. The couple had one son. Jesse Tanner died on May 25, 1937. The Musical Lesson, painted by Henry Ossawa Tanner (1859-1937) was accepted by the Societe des Artists for exhibition. Tanner originally from Pennsylvania, had moved to Paris in 1891 to escape racism and study art after several failed attempts to make a name for himself in the states. In 1896 Tanner turned to painting biblical themes. His *Daniel in the Lion's Den* was the first, followed by *The Raising of Lazarus*, which was purchased by the French government after winning a medal at the Paris Exhibition of 1897. His other biblical works included *Christ and Nicodemus*, which won a Lippincott prize, *Wise and Foolish Virgins,* and *The Two Disciples at the Tomb,* which won a Harris prize.

Tanner was awarded a gold medal at the Panama Pacific Exposition (1915); silver medals at the Exposition Universelle in Paris (1900), the Pan-American Exposition in Buffalo (1901), and the St. Louis Exposition (1904); and a bronze medal at the National Arts Club exhibition (1927). In 1905, Tanner became the first black artist to have work included in the Carnegie Institute's exhibition. The French government named Tanner the chevalier of the Legion of Honor in 1923.

TERRELL, MARY CHURCH (September 23,1863-July 24, 1954) Womanist Leader, Civil/Human Rights Leader was born to enslaved parents in Memphis Tennessee. Although born in bondage, her parents eventually became well educated and wealthy through business and real estate dealings and provided their daughter with the best education available to women at that time. She attended Oberlin College in Ohio, earning a bachelor's degree in 1884 and a master's degree in 1888. She probably would have become a teacher, but her father considered the occupation beneath her. After a two-year tour of Europe, Church settled in Washington, DC, and became active in the suffragist movement, founding the Colored Women's League in 1892. In 1896 this club merged with the National Federation of Afro-American Women to become the National Association of Colored Women, and Church Terrell was elected its first president Church inherited a substantial fortune from her parents and married Robert Terrell a prominent Washington, DC educator, attorney and jurist. .

In 1895 she became the first African American woman appointed to the District of Columbia Board of Education. A charter member of the NAACP, she was a vociferous advocate for equal rights for women and African Americans. She also served as a delegate at various international women's rights congresses. She remained wedded to the goal of racial integration and was a leader in the movement to desegregate restaurants in Washington, DC in the 1950s,

TERRELL, ROBERT HERBERTON (1857-1925), Jurist, Civil Rights Activist, was born to Harris and Louisa Ann Terrell in Charlottesville, Virginia. He attended a District of Columbia school and the Groton Academy at Groton, Massachusetts for his early education. In June of 1884 he graduated magna cum laude from Harvard College and Howard University Law School granted him a LL.B degree in 1889. Terrell married Mary E. Church in 1891. In January of 1910, President William Taft nominated him to be a judge of the Municipal Court of the District of Columbia. With the help of Booker T. Washington, Terrell was able to secure the position even though the Senate protested the appointment of a black to the post. Nine years earlier, Washington had been instrumental in Terrell's appointment as justice of the peace in the District of Columbia. But Terrell was not a wholehearted follower of Washington. He openly criticized Washington's condemnation of the dishonorable discharge, in 1906, of the 25th black infantry after the Brownsville, Texas, riot. Terrell was also a grand master of the Grand United Order of Old Fellows of the District of Columbia, of which he was the grand master. Terrell and others established a chapter of the Sigma Pi Phi fraternity in the District of Columbia.

TROTTER, WILLIAM MONROE (1872-1934), Journalist, Civil/Human Rights Leader, a Phi Beta Kappa graduate of Harvard University, founded the *Boston Guardian*, a black newspaper that demanded full equality for blacks and spoke out against Booker T. Washington's policies on grounds that they were too accommodating. Trotter opened the *Guardian* offices in the same building where William Lloyd Garrison had published *The Liberator*, and where Harriet Beecher Stowe's *Uncle Tom's Cabin* was printed. In editing the *Guardian*, Trotter abandoned a career as an insurance executive because, he said, "the conviction grew upon me that pursuit of business, money, civic, literary position was like building a house upon sands; if race prejudice and persecution and public discrimination for mere color was to spread up from the South and result in a fixed caste of color...every colored American would be really a civil outcast, forever an alien, in the public life."

Trotter confronted Booker T. Washington to voice his differing views on July 30, 1903, at the Columbus Avenue African Zion Church in Boston. Trotter and his followers were arrested for heckling Washington; Trotter was sentenced to thirty days in jail. He explained that he had resorted to a public confrontation with Washington because the "Tuskegee kingpin" held a monopoly on the American media and opposing views could not be heard. The treatment of Trotter in Boston inspired W.E.B. DuBois to become more active in the opposition to Washington. Trotter collaborated with DuBois in the organization of the Niagara Movement, but declined a position of leadership in the NAACP because of his distrust of whites. Yet Trotter continued his career as a civil rights activist. In 1906 he protested President Theodore Roosevelt's discharge of the black soldiers involved in the Brownsville, Texas riot. In 1910 Trotter led a demonstration against a Boston performance of *The Clansman*, an anti-black play. In 1913 he accused President Woodrow Wilson of lying after Wilson had denied responsibility for segregation in the government cafeterias of Washington, D.C. Two years later, Trotter landed in jail for picketing the showing of the anti-black film *Birth of A Nation*.

In 1919, when the Paris Peace Conference convened, Trotter applied for a passport. He wanted to attend this world forum to present grievances of American blacks. When the United States government denied his visa, Trotter obtained a job as a cook on a transatlantic ship and managed to reach Europe anyway. As a representative for the National Equal Rights League and for the Race Petitioners, Trotter supported the Japanese motion to include a prohibition against discrimination in the Covenant of the League of Nations. The Western Allies, which included the United States, opposed such a provision. Trotter had been born in Boston in 1872. After earning a bachelor of arts degree from Harvard University he returned for his master's, which he received in 1895. In his final years, his money and energy dwindling, Trotter continued to agitate for equal rights.

In 1934, he fell or was pushed from a balcony and died.

TRUTH, SOJOURNER (1797-November 26, 1883) Abolitionist, Womanist Leader was born in 1797 as a bondswoman, with the name Isabella, in Hurley, New York. The mother of five children, she was separated from her husband prior to gaining her freedom in 1827. After her statutory emancipation in New York in 1827, Truth went to work for a "religious fanatic" named Pierson in New York City. By 1843, she had become disillusioned with Pierson and left, proclaiming that her name was no longer Isabella, but Sojourner. She said that "the Lord gave Truth, because [she] was to declare the truth to the people." She became a legendary "sojourner," as she traveled about espousing abolition, women's rights, and other reforms. She held steadfastly to the belief that she was a chosen messenger of God. Though illiterate, Truth made a substantial impression upon her audiences. On one occasion, when Frederick Douglass was speaking at Faneuil Hall in Boston, he said that blacks could not hope to find justice in America. Truth countered this pessimism by asking "Frederick, is God dead?" Truth also played a prominent role in the Second National Women's Suffrage Convention in Akron, Ohio, in1852. During the Civil War, she supported the arming of slaves and helped care for wounded soldiers and freedmen. During the Reconstruction era and until the end of her life, she urged property ownership and education as keys to black advancement.

TURNER, HENRY McNEAL (1833-May 18, 1915) Minister, Soldier, Politician, Civil/Human Rights Leader, Pan Africanist, Educator was born free in Abbeville, South Carolina. At an early age he was hired out to work in the field with bondspersons. His first education came from white playmates. Making his way to Baltimore, Maryland, at the age of fifteen, Turner worked as a messenger and a handyman at a medical school, where he had access to books and magazines. He continued his self-education until an Episcopal bishop agreed to teach him. This was one of the influences that led Turner to become an AME minister.

During the American Civil War, President Lincoln appointed Turner chaplain of the 54th Massachusetts black regiment. After the war, he worked with the Freedmen's Bureau in Georgia and became actively involved in Republican politics. He served in the Georgia constitutional convention of 1868 and was elected to the state legislature, where he strongly opposed the successful attempt of Euro-American lawmakers to expel the black reconstruction legislators.

These and other experiences eventually convinced Turner that the black man had no future in the United States. He became a colonizationist and Pan-Africanist, or a supporter of the rights of native Africans and their descendants all over the world. In 1878, he was among the backers of a failed expedition involving about 200 blacks who went to Liberia hoping to settle there.

In addition to these activities, Turner served the AME Church in various ways. He was director of the AME publishing house and editor of the church's periodicals, for example, and was head of Moms Brown College, an AME school in Atlanta, Georgia.

UNCLE TOM Paternalistic, derisive racial term. It was based on *Uncle Tom's Cabin,* a novel by a northern white woman named Harriet Beecher Stowe, that was published in Boston, Massachusetts on March 20, 1832. With its dramatic exaggeration of the cruelties of slavery, it created sympathy for blacks in the North and greatly angered southerners. However, in the era of Jim Crow, it was used to denigrate and castigate African Americans who appeared to accommodate themselves to segregation and discrimination. After his "Atlanta Compromise" address in 1895, in which he endorsed separation of the races, Booker T. Washington was labeled by many as the nation's leading Uncle Tom. In the Civil Rights era, those who seemed accommodating or timid in the quest for equality were also mocked by more militant activists as Uncle Toms.

WALKER, MADAME C. J. (SARAH BREEDLOVE McWILLIAMS WALKER) (December 23,1867-May 25, 1919) Businesswoman, Inventor, was born to Minerva and Owen Breedlove in northeast Louisiana. Her parents, both ex-bondspersons, were sharecroppers. She was orphaned at age seven. Her mother died first. Her father remarried and apparently died before she was eight years old. Because of her economic circumstances, she attended school for only a short period. In order to improve her financial and social status, she married a Mr. McWilliams at age fourteen, and had a daughter, A'Lelia, in 1885. Widowed at twenty in 1887, she and her daughter moved from Vicksburg to St. Louis, Missouri. For eighteen years, from 1887-1905, she supported herself and her daughter by working as a washerwoman.

While in St. Louis in 1905, Walker came up with the idea of beginning a cosmetics business. The formula that she developed for hair care did not straighten hair. It was designed to heal scalp disease through more frequent shampooing, massage and the application of an ointment consisting of petroleum and a medicinal sulfur. Walker did use a hot comb, but contrary to some reports she did not invent it. Indeed such a system had been used elsewhere earlier, including in Europe. The principal elements of Madame Walker's System and a key to her success were a shampoo, a pomade "hair-grower", vigorous brushing, and the application of heated iron combs to the hair. The "method" transformed stubborn, lusterless hair into shining smoothness. The Madame C. J. Walker Manufacturing Company employed principally women who had formerly done their hair treatments to the home. Known as "Walker Agents," they became familiar figures throughout the United States and the Caribbean where they made their "house calls", always dressed in the characteristic white shirtwaists tucked into long black skirts and carrying the black satchels, containing preparations and combing apparatus necessary for dressing hair. Sales of the Pomade and a collection of sixteen other beauty products, many packaged decoratively in tin containers with a portrait of Madame Walker, accompanied by heavy advertising in African American newspapers and magazines and her own frequent instructional tours, made Madame Walker one of the best known African American women in the country by the 1920's. Her fame even spread to Europe, where the Walker System coiffure of dancer Josephine Baker so fascinated Parisians in the 1920's that a French company produced a comparable pomade, calling it "Baker-Fix"

Walker left St. Louis in 1905 and relocated her business to Denver, Colorado. However, she soon left the establishment in the care of her daughter, Lelia, while she traveled to other parts of the country, particularly in the South, promoting her products. She gave demonstrations and lectures bout the products to all who would listen, but particularly to clubs and churches.

As the business continued to prosper, Walker opened a second establishment in Pittsburgh, Pennsylvania in 1908, which was managed by her daughter A'Lelia. In 1910 she transferred operations from both the Denver and Pittsburgh offices to a new headquarters in Indianapolis, where a hair care plant was constructed as the central unit of the new Walker Enterprises. This enterprise included the Walker College of Hair Culture and Walker Manufacturing. By this time she had also developed a mail order business. This branch of the company was placed in the hands of her daughter A'leila Bundles who used Pittsburgh as the home base for the operations, as well as Walker College which trained. "hair culturists".

The parent Madame C.J. Walker Manufacturing Company, headquartered in Indianapolis, Indiana, provided employment for some three thousand persons. Her sales force, scattered throughout the country, had, according to Madame's estimates, more than 20,000 agent in 1919.

Reflective of the increasing wealth of the family, Walker's daughter purchased a townhouse in Harlem in 1913 and Madame Walker, herself, moved to New York in 1916. Madame also became a noted philanthropist—donating generously to African American organizations, including churches, the NAACP, the YM and YWCA and the National association of Colored Women. Indeed her donation to the latter group enabled it to purchase the home of Frederick Douglass in Washington, DC. Although, with little formal education herself, she also provided college scholarships, especially to young black women.

WASHINGTON, BOOKER TALIAFERRO (Booker T. Washington) (April 5,1856— November 4, 1915) Educator, Political Leader was born in. Franklin County, Virginia. His mother was a mulatto bondswoman on a plantation, his father a white man. After the Civil War, he worked in salt furnaces and coal mines in Maiden, W.Va., and attended school part time, until he was able to enter the Hampton Institute (Va.). A friend of the principal paid his tuition, and he worked as a janitor to earn his room and board. After three years (1872—75) at Hampton he taught at a school for African-American children in Mallen, then studied at Wayland Seminary, Washington, D.C. Appointed (1879) an instructor at Hampton Institute (now Hampton University), he was given charge of the training of 75 Native Americans, under the guidance of Gen. Samuel Chapman Armstrong. He later developed the night school.

In 1881 he was chosen to organize a normal and industrial school for African Americans at Tuskegee, Alabama. Under his direction, Tuskegee Institute (now Tuskegee University.) became one of the leading African-American educational institutions in the United States. Its programs emphasized agricultural-industrial training as a means to self-respect and economic independence for black people.

Washington gave many speeches in the explaining his philosophy and work at Tuskegee and raising funds, both in the United States and in Europe, and was considered one of the best public speakers of the time.

In September 1895 at the Cotton States International Exposition in asked for economic and political progress for blacks aided by whites while playing down political power and social equality. His speech pleased many whites and gained financial support for his school. The *Atlanta Constitution* called it "the greatest speech ever delivered in the South." President Grover Cleveland sent Washington a congratulatory telegram. Some African Americans, including W.E.B DuBois, congratulated Washington. Others were vehemently opposed to the racial agenda that Washington outlined in the address. They feared that it would harm the cause of black equality in the nation. Foremost among the early African American critics were John Hope, president of Atlanta Baptist College (later Morehouse College), the Boston publisher William Monroe Trotter, and AME Bishop Henry McNeal Turner. After a noisy confrontation between Trotter and Washington in Boston in 1903, W.E.B DuBois became the most vocal opponent of Washington's racial philosophy.

In June 1896, Booker T. Washington received an honorary master of arts degree from Harvard University. He also received an honorary degree from Dartmouth College as well as a number of African American institutions. Upon visiting Alabama's Tuskegee Institute, President William McKinley paid tribute to the institution's success and to its founder, Booker T. Washington. The students and faculty welcomed the presidential party with a display of floats that illustrated the phases of the school and its teachings throughout its seventeen years of existence. In his speech, McKinley said, "An evidence of the soundness of the purposes of this institution is that those in charge of its management evidently don't believe in attempting the unattainable, and their instruction in self-reliance and practical industry is most valuable."

On August 23-24, 1900, the National Negro Business League, sponsored by Booker T. Washington, formed in Boston. More than four hundred delegates from thirty-four states had answered Washington's call to stimulate black businesses. Washington himself was elected the first president of the organization, and after only one year of the League's existence, he reported a large number of new black businesses. By 1907 the national organization had 320 branches. Though service-oriented businesses were the most numerous, black engaged in various types and sizes of business enterprises. The North Carolina Mutual Insurance Company, founded in 1898, became the largest black-owned firm.

On October 16, 1901, Booker T. Washington dined with President Theodore Roosevelt at the White House. But the meet-

ing was bitterly criticized by many whites, especially southerners, as a departure from racial etiquette. The previous year,
Washington's autobiography, *Up from Slavery*, had been hailed
by southern and northern whites for its nonvindictive attitude
toward the South and its previous slave system. The book has
become a classic in American letters, primarily because of
Washington's prominence.

WHITE, GEORGE H. (December 18, 1852-December 28, 1918)
Politician, was born in bondage in Rosendale, North Carolina
Representative George H. White left Congress. White had begun
his work in the House of Representatives on March 15, 1897, after North Carolina had elected him in 1896. His state reelected
him in 1898. In a moving valedictory address, White attacked
Jim Crowism and predicted that the African American would return to the United States Congress. But more than twenty years
passed before another African American served in Congress.

WRIGHT, JONATHAN JASPER (1840-1885) Jurist, a well-
educated Pennsylvanian, became associate justice of the South
Carolina Supreme Court on February 2, 1870. Wright served for
seven years as the highest black judicial officer in the nation. Although Wright was one of only three members of the court, he
exercised no influence on behalf of African American rights. Yet
white Democratic leaders sought constantly to have him removed on charges of corruption. Wright left the bench in 1877 as
black reconstruction toppled in the state.

WHITE, WALTER FRANCIS (-March 21,1955), Civil/Human
Rights Leader, was born in Atlanta Georgia. After graduating
from Atlanta University, he worked for a local insurance company
in his native city and became active in the local NAACP. Although White had blond hair and blue eyes, he was of African descent and identified with the black race, especially after he
witnessed the 1906 Atlanta race riot.

White joined the national NAACP as an assistant secretary
in 1918 and, upon the retirement of James Weldon Johnson, was
elevated to executive secretary in 1931.

In 1937 White was honored by the NAACP for his work as the organization's executive secretary, his investigations into lynchings, and his lobbying for a federal anti-lynching law. White was successful in getting anti-lynching measures introduced in the Congress in 1935 and 1940, but both attempts died in the Senate. But, during his tenure as NAACP executive secretary, he led the NAACP during most of its judicial triumphs of the 1940s and 1950s, culminating with the landmark school desegregation case, Brown v Board of Education just before his death.

White was also among the notable authors of the Harlem Renaissance, producing several works, including two novels, *Fire in the Flint* and *Flight*.

WILLIAMS, DANIEL HALE (1856-August 4-1932) Physician was born in 1856 in Philadelphia, Pennsylvania, to a black woman and a white man. His father died when he was eleven, and his mother deserted him not long after that. For the next few years he supported himself by working on board a lake steamer and then as a barber.

Thanks to the generosity of a former surgeon on General Ulysses S. Grant's staff, Williams was eventually able to attend the Chicago Medical College. But he graduated at a time when black doctors were not allowed to practice in Chicago hospitals. So in 1891, he founded Provident Hospital and opened it to doctors and patients of all races.

It was at Provident in 1893 that Williams performed ground-breaking surgery on a man who had been stabbed in an artery very close to his heart. The man survived the delicate operation, but when Williams announced the news, many people doubted that a black doctor could have had anything to do with such an important event.

Squabbles among staff members at Provident eventually caused Williams to leave the hospital he had started. He then became the only black doctor on the staff of Chicago's St. Luke Hospital, and in 1913 he was named the first black member of the American College of Surgeons.

In addition to practicing medicine, Williams was an active

member of the NAACP. He also promoted the building of hospitals and training schools for black doctors and nurses. Toward the end of his life, however, Williams was the target of harsh criticism from fellow blacks for leaving Provident and marrying a white woman. By the time of his death in 1931, he was a bitter and frustrated man.

WOODS, GRANVILLE T. (1896-1920) Inventor, received his first patient for a steam boiler furnace on January 3, 1884. The invention, which used a more efficient method of combustion and therefore economized fuel, was the first of about thirty-five that he patented throughout his life. Though Woods dealt mainly with electricity as it pertained to telephone communications and telegraphy, he invented other items such as the incubator and an apparatus consisting of a series of tracks for amusement park rides. Woods retained about one-third of his patents for himself and sold or assigned the others to companies such as General Electric, American Engineering, and Westinghouse Electric and Manufacturing. Woods gained experience with machines at the age of ten when he worked in a machine shop and received instruction in the evenings. At 16 he worked as a fireman and engineer on a Missouri railroad.

WOODSON, CARTER G. (1875- 1950) Author, Association Executive, was born in New Canton, Virginia. Woodson, the son of former bondspersons, held a doctorate degree from Harvard University. He edited a number of publications of the ASNLH, including the highly respected *Journal of Negro History* and became known as "the father of Negro History".

As a young man; Woodson worked as a coal miner in West Virginia and put himself through high school. He graduated from Berea College in Kentucky in 1903. Following graduation, he was hired to teach English in the Philippines. Woodson studied Romance languages through correspondence courses. After returning to the U.S., he began teaching at Dunbar High School in Washington, DC. In 1912 he earned a Ph.D. in history from Harvard University. He was the second African American to earn a Harvard doctorate. He founded the Association for the Study of

Negro Life and History, the *Journal of Negro History*, the Associated Publishers, and *Negro History Bulletin*. In 1926, he began promoting Negro History Week during the second week of February to celebrate the birthdays of Abraham Lincoln and Frederick Douglass. In the 1960s it became Black History Month.

YOUNG, CHARLES (1864- January 8, 1922) Soldier, was the son of a former bondsperson in the Union Army was born in Kentucky. He studied at the west point academy in 1884 and served with distinction in Cuba, Haiti and Mexico, but he always labored under the burdens of racial discrimination. Most of the black outfits had been activated shortly after the end of the Civil War for action against native Americans in the West. During the Spanish-American War, blacks, like many of their white counterparts, were ill prepared in terms of experience, equipment, and training for combat in a tropical zone. Yet in the end, the blacks won the praises of almost all their officers. At the beginning of the Spanish-American War, there was only one black commissioned officer, Captain Charles Young. At the close of the war there were more than one hundred black officers, including Young, now a Brevet Major and commander of the Ninth Ohio regiment.

During World War I, Young was called for a physical examination and made to retire because of poor health. This action was an apparent subterfuge to prevent Young's promotion to general. After protests from blacks, Young was recalled, but he was assigned to relatively obscure duty in Illinois and Liberia.

III. AN ERA OF CIVIL RIGHTS

ABERNATHY, RALPH DAVID (March 11, 1926-April 17, 1990), Civil/Human Rights Leader, was born on March 11, 1926, on his family's farm in Linden, Alabama, to William L. and Louivery Valentine (Bell) Abernathy. He was the tenth of twelve children. At a young age, Abernathy was strongly influenced by his parents' Christian beliefs, which gave him aspirations to become a minister.

Once Abernathy graduated from Linden Academy, a local black high school, he was drafted into the United States Army where he served during the final months of World War II. After his army stint was over, he returned to Alabama and enrolled in Alabama State College where he gained invaluable experience as a leader and organizer of student protests against the school's mistreatment of students. Following his graduation, with a degree in mathematics in 1950, he served shortly as the school's dean of men. Meanwhile, he had been ordained as a Baptist minister.

Abernathy earned a M.A. degree in sociology in 1951 from Atlanta University. While in Atlanta, he heard a young Martin Luther King, Jr. preach a sermon at Ebenezer Baptist Church. Impressed with King's dynamic preaching ability, he introduced himself to King for the first time.

After earning his Masters degree, Abernathy returned to Alabama and worked as a part-time minister for the Easter Star Baptist Church in Demopolis, Alabama. In 1951, at the age of 26, he became the minister of First Baptist, one of Montgomery's most prestigious black churches. He would hold this position for ten years. In 1954 Martin Luther King, Jr. was named the minister to Montgomery's Dexter Avenue Baptist Church, and he and his family and the Abernathy family became close personal friends.

In 1955 when Montgomery blacks conceived a plan to boycott the city's buses in retaliation for Rosa Parks being arrested for sitting in the front of a bus, Abernathy and King helped rally blacks and form the Montgomery Improvement Association (MIA) to organize and conduct the boycott. While King served as MIA's president, Abernathy served as its program chief and was responsible for maintaining the nonviolent boycott's momentum.

Enduring white bigots' racially-charged death threats and terrorist actions, Abernathy and King managed to maintain the boycott until 1956 when the U.S. Supreme Court upheld an injunction against the bus company's discriminatory policies. Building on the momentum of their victory, Abernathy and King went to Atlanta in January of 1957 and, with other black ministers, from throughout the South, formed the Southern Christian Leadership Conference (SCLC), an organization of church and grass roots groups, to fight against discrimination in the South. While in Atlanta Abernathy's home and church were bombed by segregationist hoods; but Abernathy's family escaped injury. Martin Luther King, Jr. moved from Montgomery to Atlanta in 1960, to take full leadership of SCLC. In 1961, Abernathy, at King's request, also moved to Atlanta and became the minister of West Hunter Street Baptist Church. In 1965, King promoted Abernathy as the vice-president of SCLC operations. For the next few years, Abernathy and King vigorously led nonviolent desegregation protests and marches throughout the South as well as the North. Perhaps the most prominent victories they achieved were the passage of the 1964 Civil Rights Act and the 1965 Voting Rights Act as results of their protests in Birmingham and Selma, Alabama, respectively. During the period between 1955 and 1968, Abernathy and King were jailed together a total of seventeen times.

In 1968 while organizing a city sanitation worker's strike in Memphis, Tennessee, King was shot by James Earl Ray and died at Abernathy's side. The SCLC board named Abernathy as the organization's new president. Overcoming his grief of losing his closest friend, Abernathy continued to lead demonstrations against racial and social injustices, including a disappointing

1968 Poor People's Campaign march on Washington, D.C. to protest the manner in which the United States treated its poor.

After resigning from SCLC in 1977, Abernathy unsuccessfully ran for the Georgia Fifth District U.S. Congressional seat. Undaunted by his electoral defeat, he would later form the Foundation for Economic Enterprises Development (FEED) to help train blacks for better jobs as well as continue his ministerial work at West Hunter Street Baptist Church.

In 1989, Abernathy published his controversial autobiography, *And the Walls Came Tumbling Down*, which many black leaders criticized for its uncompromising look at King's alleged extra-marital activities. By this time, declining health forced Abernathy to limit many of his activities.

ADDERLEY, JULIAN "CANNONBALL" (1928-August 8, 1975), Entertainer, called a "prophet of contemporary jazz, Adderley was born in Tampa, Florida, the son of a jazz cornetist. Known primarily as an alto saxophonist, Adderley also played tenor sax, trumpet, clarinet, and flute. He studied brass and reed instruments in Tallahassee, Florida, high school from 1944 until 1948 and formed his first jazz group there with the school's band director as advisor. Because of his hearty appetite, fellow students nicknamed him "Canninbal," which later became "Cannonball." From 1948 until 1956, Adderley was music director at the Dillard High School in Fort Lauderdale, Florida. At the same time, he directed his own jazz group in southern Florida. He served for three years as a member of the 36th Army Dance Band and later studied at the Naval School of Music in Washington D.C. Adderley's first big break came in New York in 1955 when he appeared with Oscar Pettiford. The next year he signed his first recording contract with EmArcy Records. Adderley later recorded for Capitol Records and other companies and became famous for such albums as *Black Messiah, Country Preacher, Fiddler on the Roof, Walk Tall,* and *Quiet Nights.* His last album was *Phoenix.* Until 1957, Adderley toured with his brother, Nat, a cornetist. In 1957, he joined the Miles Davis group. After a tour with George Shearing, he formed his own quintet, including his brother Nat, in 1959. Charles Suber, publisher of *Down Beat* magazine, which named Adderley New Alto Star of the Year in 1959, described the "Cannonball" as "a helluva musician. . . . He was one of the best alto players in recent years." During his eulogy of Adderley before 2,000 mourners in Tallahassee, Florida, the Reverend Jesse Jackson, director of People United to Save Humanity (PUSH), said the "Cannonball" had "his greatness and his fame, but he did not use it, abuse it, or lose it. He expanded it. . . . When he blew his saxophone you felt a little ease in the troubled world and the savage beast had to hold his peace."

ARMSTRONG, LOUIS (July 4,1900-July 6, 1971, Entertainer was born and grew up in New Orleans, the son of a factory worker and a domestic worker. After his parents separated, he and his mother went to live with his grandmother. During this time, he shot a gun in a New Year's Eve celebration and was sent to a Boy's Home. Here, he joined the Home's band as a bugle and cornet player. Following his release from incarceration, Armstrong played in local "honky tonks" in the evening after working days on coal and milk wagons.

During World War I, Armstrong began to play with the noted jazz bands of King Oliver and Kid Ory and in 1922 joined Oliver in Chicago. He later went to New York where he formed his own band and played trumpet. As he developed his talents, he came to anticipate almost all of the innovations that are now standard in modern jazz.

By the 1930s, the Louis Armstrong Orchestra was one of the major "Big Bands" of the era. Armstrong, himself, also began singing and further developed a unique style known as "scat"—where he slurred or scatted words in a seemingly nonsensical fashion. Among his major hits were "Blueberry Hill" and "Hello Dolly". From the period of the Second World War until the time of his death, Armstrong also had roles in several movies—usually as a jazz musician.

During his long and successful career, he reshaped the development of American music by introducing the sounds of black folk music from New Orleans into the mainstream culture. A run-in with the law when he was thirteen landed him in a juvenile home, where he learned to play the cornet and discovered his talent for imitating the popular songs of the day just by listening to them. He was also a very innovative musician who could add surprising twists and turns to a melody as he played it.

As his reputation grew, Armstrong not only became one of the most popular entertainers in the United States but toured Asia, Africa, and Europe as well, where he often performed before several thousand persons. This international notoriety led the U. S. State department to name him a Goodwill Ambassador. Yet, at home, Armstrong still faced the vestiges of bondage and Jim Crow; and although he came to oppose segregated performances, he rarely spoke publicly against racism. A notable exception was during the Little Rock school desegregation crisis of 1957 when he scolded President Dwight Eisenhower's lack of forceful action against a defiant governor, Orval Faubus, and white mobs. Under pressures of public opinion and some congresspersons, Eisenhower later sent federal troops into Little Rock.

BAKER, ELLA JO (December 13, 1903-December 13, 1986), Civil/Human Rights Activist, was born to Blake and Georgianna Baker in Norfolk, Virginia. When Ella was seven years old, the family moved to Littleton, North Carolina. She attended both high school and college at Shaw University (North Carolina), from which she received a Bachelors degree in 1927. Following graduation, she moved to New York City, where she lived with a cousin, while working as a waitress and, later, in a factory.

While in New York, she became active in several civic and social organizations. In 1932, while working as an office manager for the *Negro National News*, she was named the national director of the Young Negroes Cooperative League. By 1938, she had become a southern field secretary for the NAACP. Five years later she was promoted to National Director of Branches for the civil rights organization. Although Baker never married, she left the NAACP in 1946 in order to care for a niece. But she was not out of civil rights activity for long; by 1954 she had returned to the NAACP and became president of its New York City branch.

The new Civil Rights Movement of the 1950s and 1960s drew Baker South again to work with Martin Luther King, Jr. and his Southern Christian Leadership Conference (SCLC). At SCLC, she helped organize the Nonviolent Resistance to Segregation Leadership Conference that met in Raleigh, North Carolina in 1960, in order to coordinate the activities of students involved in lunch counter sit-ins to protest racial discrimination. More than 300 student leaders attended the meeting, which resulted in the formation of the Student Non-Violent Coordinating Committee (SNCC). After playing a major role in the founding of this new, "militant" civil rights group, Baker left SCLC and became a consultant with the Southern Conference Educational Fund (SCEF), a subsidiary of a white "liberal" social and political group known as the Southern Conference for Human Welfare (SCHW). The SCEF was one of the few majority white organizations to support black civil rights activities during the 1950s and 1960s. While working with the SCEF, Baker helped Fannie Lou Hamer and others establish the Mississippi Freedom Democratic Party [MFDP], a bi-racial alternative to the regular all-white Mississippi Democratic Party, and delivered the principal address at the MFDP's first convention in Jackson, Mississippi in 1964.

Before her death in 1986, Baker returned to New York where she continued, "in retirement," to advise and counsel social and political groups dedicated to human welfare. The story of her life was first seen by national audiences in the film "Fundi: The Story of Ella Baker," which was released in the late 1970s.

BALDWIN, JAMES A. (August 2, 1924-December 1, 1987), Author, civil/human rights activist, was born in the Harlem section of New York City, the son of David, a clergyman, and Berdie Emma (Jones) Baldwin. As a teenager, Baldwin, himself, became a Pentecostal preacher. But, while in high school, he also edited a literary magazine. After graduating from high school he took a job in a defense plant, where he faced severe racial discrimination. Thus, after his father died, in 1943, he moved to the Greenwich Village in New York. While working odd jobs in

New York City, he became a frequently published author of essays and reviews.

After encouragement from the author Richard Wright, Baldwin began a novel, which he finished after arriving in Paris in 1948. This book, *Go Tell It on the Mountain* (1958) was a partly, autobiographical portrayal of storefront religion in Harlem. His next novel, *Notes of a Native Son* (1955) was a collection of essays, inspired by Richard Wright's 1939 novel. Other works also dealt with race and homosexuality, until Baldwin returned to America, as the Civil Rights Movement was unfolding.

He immediately immersed himself in the Movement, sometimes as an activist, but more often as a prolific interpreter of the meaning of race in America. He first produced the polemical, *Nobody Knows My Name* in 1961, and, then, the highly acclaimed, *The Fire Next Time* in 1964. It was in *The Fire Next Time* that Baldwin predicted the coming of the ghetto riots of the late 1960s. His play, *Blues for Mister Charles* and a collection of short stories, *Going to Meet the Man* (1965) also treated racial themes.

Yet, Baldwin's writing and lecturing on race was not without criticism. Black Panther leader Eldridge Cleaver once accused him of "fawning on whites" and hating blacks, and members of the Black Arts Movement believed that he should be writing only for and about blacks. Still, Baldwin insisted that he was an American, not a black, writer who was "concerned with the issues of his multiracial country." Baldwin, himself, became so disillusioned with American racism that he returned to exile in Paris in the early 1970s and remained there until his death in 1987. At the time of his death, Baldwin was working on a book about Martin Luther King, Jr. Baldwin was one of the most successful writers in addressing issues of race, class, and gender. As far as black writers, Orde Coombs once said: "It is not too much to say that this man saved our lives, or at least gave us the necessary ammunition to face what we knew would continue to be a hostile and condescending world."

Baldwin was a member of the national advisory board of the Congress of Racial Equality (CORE) and a member of the National Institute of Arts and Letters. He was the recipient of Sax

(1945), Rosenwald (1948), and Guggenheim (1954) fellowships.

BLAKELY, ART (d. October 16, 1990), Entertainer, was a drummer and jazz band leader. He was a powerful and influential jazz talent who had a lifelong knack for identifying and nurturing gifted musicians. In 1954, along with Horace Silver, he founded the constantly changing band known as Jazz Messengers. The group served as a virtual school for up-and-coming musicians, including Freddie Hubbard, Wayne Shorter, Branford and Wynon Marsalis, Donald Byrd and McCoy Tyner. Among the older "graduates" of the Jazz Messengers were such notable musicians as Keith Jarrett, Chuck Mangione, Chick Corea, Terrence Blanchard, Jackie McLean and Donald Harrison.

BERRY, LEONIDAS HARRIS (July 20, 1902-December 4, 1995), Foreign Service Official, civil/human rights activist, physician, was born in Woodsdale, Person County, North Carolina and raised in Norfolk, Virginia, the son of Reverend Llewellyn L. Berry, an African American Methodist Episcopal minister, and Beulah (Harris) Berry, a school teacher. His father pastored small churches in Virginia and North Carolina and served for 21 years as Secretary of Home and Foreign Missions of the A.M.E. Church. Leonidas Berry received a B.S. degree from Wilberforce University (Ohio) in 1924, and an S.B. degree from the University of Chicago in 1925. Five years later, Rush Medical College of the University of Chicago bestowed upon him the M.D. degree. He then launched a successful and prosperous medical career that spanned over six decades and eventually led to Berry's recognition as one of America's foremost authorities on gastrointestinal disease.

Berry's achievements defined him not only as a trailblazer for African Americans in the medical field, but as a pioneer in medical research. In 1946, he became the first black physician admitted to the staff of Michael Reese Hospital in Chicago, and, in the same year, became the first black internist at Chicago's Cook County Hospital. While at Cook County, Berry utilized the fiber-optic gastro camera to view inside the digestive tract, marking the first time an American physician had successfully performed the procedure. In 1955, Berry created a unique device designed to obtain tissue samples from the stomach for direct examination, an instrument that would become known as the Eder-Berry Biopsy Gastro scope. As an expert in gastroenterology, he served as an officer in both the American Gastroscopic Society and the American College of Gastroenterology. In 1965, he was elected president of the National Medical Association, and later became chair of the gastroenterology division of Provident Hospital.

During the 1960s, Berry served as a foreign cultural exchange lecturer with the U.S. State Department, traveling to countries in East and West Africa, Japan, Korea, and France. Also during this time, Berry was active in the United Front, a black civil rights group in Cairo, Illinois that raised and contributed funds for education, legal defense, and other needs for the small southern Illinois community. In 1970, the Flying Black Medics, an organization Berry founded to provide medical relief to underprivileged areas, flew medical supplies, doctors, nurses, and paramedics from Chicago to Cairo. Berry also served over black communities in Illinois, as well as in Alabama, which were in dire need of medical attention; in some cases, these communities were seeing doctors for the first time as a result of his efforts. In 1975, Berry retired as chief of endoscope services and Senior Attending Physician at Cook County Hospital, having trained approximately 500 postgraduate residents. He published extensively in journals on medicine and co-authored, *Gastrointestinal PanEndoscopy*, which is considered a definitive work on the subject.

Berry received numerous awards and honors for his achievements, including the Rudolph Schindler Award from the American Society of Gastrointestinal Endoscopy and the Clinical Achievement Award from the American College of Gastroenterology. In 1980, a group of physicians formed the Leonidas H. Berry Society for Digestive Disease, and in 1989, the National Medical Association inaugurated the Leonidas H. Berry Lecture Series. Berry's extensive involvement in civic organizations included a term as president of the Chicago Center of the NAACP. In 1989, the chapter honored him with the Freedom Award for

Public Service.

Berry also held an interest in genealogical research and in 1982 published the book, *I Wouldn't Take Nothin' For My Journey Now: Two Centuries of an Afro-American Minister's Family*, a project which chronicled six generations of his family's history.

BLACK PANTHER PARTY Black Nationalist Group. The Black Panther Party was founded in Oakland, California. The two principal founders were Huey P. Newton, a native of Grove Louisiana, and Bobby Seale of Dallas, Texas. Newton and Seale grew up in California and met in 1960 at Merritt Junior College in Oakland. Inspired by police brutality and other forms of racism, as well as the teachings of Malcolm X, the duo was active in the college's African American student association. They eventually withdrew and organized the Black Panther Party.

The Black Panther Party adopted a ten-point program demanding: full employment, restitution for past exploitation and oppression, education relevant to black needs and aspirations, release of all black political prisoners, decent housing, exemptions from military service, trial of blacks by all-black juries, an end to police brutality, and black political and economic power. The Panthers insisted on "power to the people." They advocated self-defense, called for a socialistic economy, provided food and educational programs for young children, and published their own newspaper. They drew wide admiration, if not a large following, from young blacks in the northeast and West Coast.

BOLDEN, DOROTHY LEE (1923-2005), Labor Leader, Civil Rights Activist, was born in Atlanta, Georgia to Raymond Bolden, a chauffeur, and Georgia Mae Patterson, a cook. Her education ended at the secondary school level. After a fall at age three, Bolden was blinded, but she regained her sight a few years later and by her teens was working, after school as a diaper washer for $1.25 a week. For the rest of her life, Bolden had a career in domestic service that was frequently punctuated with other unskilled employment at bus stations, delivery companies and department stores. She once offered that she took jobs outside of domestic work in order to build up some Social Security benefits.

Always one of an independent mind, Bolden was once arrested for allegedly" talking back" to an employer. And, as she rode buses from her home in northwest Atlanta to places of employment in Atlanta's affluent white suburbs, she became a popular figure among fellow domestic workers. These attitudes and practices led her into the Civil Rights Movement in Atlanta in the 1960s and eventually into labor organizing. In 1964, she gained some notoriety as one of the leaders of a protest against the Atlanta Board of Education. The group demanded equal educational facilities in their neighborhood. Then, in 1968, encouraged by fellow domestic workers and her neighbor, Martin Luther King, Jr, Bolden organized the National Domestic Workers Union.

Under Bolden's leadership the Domestic Workers Union was able to increase the average daily wage for domestic workers from $3.50 to $5.00 a day to $13,50 to $15.00 per day, an, in places like Atlanta, an additional amount for transportation fares.

By 1970, Bolden had drawn the attention of local, state and federal officials. She served on the Georgia Commission on the Status of Women and was consulted by the White House during the administrations of presidents Richard Nixon, Gerald Ford and Jimmy Carter. Then after "retiring" in the 1980s, Bolden became "a political gadfly" as she, in her characteristic "plain speaking" and often brusque style, chided and cajoled local lawmakers "to do the right thing" for the poor.

BRAGG, JANET HARMON (d. April 11, 1993 at age 86), Pilot, was the first African American woman in the United States to earn a full commercial pilot's license. A native of the state of Georgia, she graduated from Spelman College in Atlanta and did graduate work at Loyola University in Illinois and the University of Chicago. She developed her interest in flying in 1930 while she was dating one of the country's first black flight instructors. She then took flying lessons and in 1933 bought the first of three airplanes she eventually owned. Two years later she was one of the first nine African Americans admitted to the Curtiss Wright

Aeronautical University to study aircraft mechanics. After being denied the opportunity to try out for a commercial pilot's license in Alabama on account of her race, she headed north to Illinois where she was able to take and pass the test. Bragg later formed the black Challenger Air Pilots Association and helped train Ethiopian soldiers during World War II. She continued to fly as a hobby from the 1950s through the 1970s.

BRANTON, WILEY AUSTIN (December 13, 1923-December 15, 1988), Attorney, civil/human rights activist, was born in Pine Bluff, Arkansas, the son of Leo Andrew, a taxicab company owner, and Lucille (McKee) Branton. He received his Bachelors degree from Arkansas A&M University (1950) and was one of the first African Americans to graduate from the University of Arkansas Law School in 1953. During World War II he served in the U.S. Army in the Pacific (1943-1946).

After law school, Branton opened a practice in Little Rock. He received international attention in the 1950s as the NAACP's chief attorney representing the nine black children who were trying to enter Little Rock's Central High School. He also made significant contributions in the voting rights arena as both a public officer and private citizen. In 1962, he was selected the first Executive Director of the Southern Regional Council's Voter Education Project (VEP), based in Atlanta, Georgia. The project was a cooperative effort that successfully registered over 600,000 black voters in 11 states and helped create the momentum for the 1965 Voting Rights Act. And, during the early 1960s, Branton represented "freedom riders" in Mississippi where blacks engaged in voter registration drives throughout the South.

After gaining considerable notoriety in Little Rock, Branton moved to Washington, D.C. in 1960, where he first served as a consultant to U.S. Attorney General Nicholas Katzenback, then as executive director of the President's Council on Equal Opportunity. He also assisted President Lyndon B. Johnson in the development of his administration's civil rights program.

Following these appointments, Branton established his own law firm, directed one of Washington's anti-poverty programs, headed a non-partisan fund to support voter registration activities, was Dean of the Howard University Law School (1978-1983) and ended his career as a partner in a major D.C. law firm.

Toward the end of his life, Branton was a leader in the civil rights community's drive to prevent Robert Bork, a judicial "conservative" from being appointed to the U.S. Supreme Court. He also continued to work on a campaign to improve accreditation processes for minorities in the American Bar Association (ABA). He was honored, posthumously, by the National Bar Association (NBA) with the establishment of the Wiley A. Branton symposium in 1997.

BUNCHE, RALPH JOHNSON (August 7, 1904-December 9, 1971), UN Ambassador, was born in Detroit, Michigan, to Fred Bunche an itinerant barber and Olive Agnes Johnson, an amateur pianist. Orphaned at 12 years old, Ralph Bunche and his sister moved to Los Angeles, California, to be raised by their maternal grandmother, Lucy Johnson. Despite this early trial, Bunche continued to excel in education. He graduated valedictorian of both his Jefferson High School and University of California-Los Angeles (UCLA), classes, in 1923 and 1927 respectively. In 1928 and 1934, Bunche, respectively, earned his Masters and Doctoral degrees in political science from Harvard University. Also in 1934, Bunche became the first African American to receive a doctorate in political science.

Bunche expressed interest in world affairs and peace for all humankind while pursuing his international studies degree at UCLA. He also expressed his optimism and goodwill in a 1925 academic paper, in which he rejected Thomas Hobbes' theory that humans are naturally brutish, self-serving, and egotistical. As cited in the *New Yorker*, Bunche stated: "It is true that man has these qualities in him, but I contend that these base characteristics are in part counteracted by good ones. I have a deep-set conviction that man must have an inherent notion of right and wrong, a fundamental moral structure and a simple sense of individual obligation, whether he be in a natural state or in a society.

Although Bunche gained international prominence as a diplomat, he gained his initial recognition as a scholar. From 1936 to 1938, Bunche completed his postdoctoral studies at Northwestern University, London School of Economics, and University of Capetown. In addition to his own studies, Bunche was influential in establishing the political science department at Howard University, Washington, D.C., where he served as an instructor, assistant and associate professor in the same department. Also in 1936, he became co-director of the Institute of Race Relations at Swarthmore College. Finally, he assisted Gunnar Myrdal on *An American Dilemma*, a seminal study of race relations and prejudice in America.

In his continued efforts in support of the "goodness of man," Bunche left academia to join the fight against those negative aspects of man in World War II. However, he was not able to physically fight because of an earlier sports injury. Therefore, he joined the National Defense Program's Office of the Coordinator of Information, later known as the Office of Strategic Services. Bunche served in this capacity as the senior analyst of Africa and the Far East. In addition to becoming the chief of the office's Africa section, he also worked for the U.S. State Department where he wrote sections of the United Nations' (UN), charter regarding the administration of former colonies of countries defeated in World War II. Among many firsts, Bunche, in 1946, became the first and was the only African American to serve on the U.S. delegation to the first General Assembly of the UN. In 1955, he rose to the highest U.S. official at the UN, undersecretary-general. He was the first black American to achieve this milestone.

During his tenure at the UN, Bunche was able to substantiate his earlier pronouncement in the goodness of man. One of several historical peace missions he negotiated was that of the Arab-Israeli conflict over the partitioning of Palestine for a Jewish state. In 1949, he succeeded in negotiating an end to the conflict. For his efforts, in 1950, Bunche became the first black to receive the Nobel Peace Prize. Some of his other assignments were the 1956 Suez crisis, where Egyptian conflict was about to go to war, and his 1960 peace keeping mission in Congo, (Zaire), where he prevented total disarray. Due to his many accomplishments, President Harry Truman offered Bunche a position as the assistant secretary of state. He promptly declined in protest to Jim Crow segregation in Washington.

Bunche was not only concerned with humankind globally, for he also participated in the Civil Rights Movement. In 1937, he picketed with the National Association for the Advancement of Colored People (NAACP). In 1963, he participated in the March on Washington. Additionally, he marched on Selma and Montgomery, Alabama in 1965.

Among Bunche's many awards in 1949, the Spingarn Medal, the highest award given by the NAACP; Theodore Roosevelt Association Medal of Honor in 1954; Franklin D. Roosevelt Four Freedoms Award and Presidential Medal of Freedom in 1963; had a public elementary school named for him in Atlanta, Georgia; and was inducted into the African American Hall of Fame in 1991.

CARMICHAEL, STOKELEY (KWAME TURÈ) (June 29, 1941-November 16, 1998), Civil/Human Rights Leader, Black Nationalist Leader, was born in Port of Spain Trinidad, West Indies, the son of Adolphus, a carpenter and taxi driver, and Mabel F. Carmichael, a maid. He was brought to the Harlem section of New York City at the age of eleven, and almost immediately found himself in trouble as a marijuana smoking gang member. When the family moved from Harlem to an all-white neighborhood in the Bronx, Carmichael joined an all-white gang, bent on stealing cars. He, however, soon changed his direction and entered the Bronx High School of Science, a school for gifted students. When the sit-in movement began in the 1960s, Carmichael, although still a high school senior, joined a group of youth, sponsored by the Congress of Racial Equality (CORE) in picketing a Woolworth Department Store in New York City.

Once out of high school, Carmichael was offered scholarships to attend major, predominately white universities, but he decided to enroll in the largely black, Howard University, instead. He received a Bachelors degree in Philosophy from Howard in 1964. But, even while in college, he continued his civil rights activism. He joined a Freedom Ride to Mississippi, participated in the Mississippi Freedom Summer of 1964, and joined civil rights protests in Cambridge, Maryland. He was often arrested, and sometimes beaten.

After graduating from college, Carmichael became a senior field secretary for the Student Non-Violent Coordinating Committee (SNCC). While in Alabama, in the mid 1960s, he helped organize the Lowdnes County Freedom Organization as an independent and separate political party. Units of the party soon spread to other nearby counties in the Alabama Black Belt. The party used a black panther as its symbol.

In May 1966, SNCC elected Carmichael as its chairman. The organization then took on a more "radical" character than it had under the previous leader, the more "moderate" John Lewis. Barely a month after Carmichael assumed leadership of the group, SNCC members joined James Meredith, the first known black student enrolled at the University of Mississippi, on a "march against fear" through Mississippi. During the march, Carmichael led other in speeches and chants of "Black Power." The slogan symbolized a more separatist and nationalist path toward black equality than that previously espoused by major civil rights actions, including SNCC.

Within a year after his election as SNCC chairman, Carmichael resigned the position to return to his post as field secretary. He was succeeded by another member of the "radical wing" of the group, H. Rap Brown. Carmichael himself, also became Prime Minister of the newly formed Black Panther Party (BPP), a separatist, third party created in 1968 by two young Californians, Huey Newton and Bobby Seale. While in its embryonic stage, Carmichael organized an alliance with BPP and SNCC, but the alliance soon fell apart and Carmichael was expelled from SNCC in July 1968. Meanwhile, he organized the All African Peoples Revolutionary Party.

Carmichael left the Black Panther Party in 1969 and moved to Guinea, with his new bride, South African singer Miriam Makeba. From Guinea, he continued to espouse the Pan-African ideology of a cultural unity of Africans and the African Diaspora which he had detailed in his book, *Stokely Speaks: Black Power Back to Pan Africanism* (1971). He returned to the United States

107

occasionally, after 1972, for lectures on his ideology. But with this new stance and his permanent residence in Guinea, for all practical purposes, Carmichael's role as an American civil rights leader had ended.

In addition to *Stokely Speaks*, Carmichael is the co-author, with Charles Hamilton of *Black Power: The Politics of Liberation in America* (1967). He is the recipient of an honorary LL.D. degree from Shaw University (North Carolina) and a posthumous award of distinction from his alma mater, Howard University.

CHERRY, GWENDOLYN SAWYER (August 27, 1923-February 7, 1979), Politician, was born in Miami, Florida, the daughter of Dr. William and Alberta Sawyer. Her father was the first black physician in Dade County, Florida. Cherry earned a B.A. degree from Florida A&M University in 1946. After receiving her baccalaureate she left Florida to pursue an M.A. degree in Human Relations at New York University, which she received in 1950. Cherry finished her formal education in 1965 when she earned a J.D. from Florida A&M.

Cherry was a teacher for 17 years. In 1962 she co-authored the book, *Portraits in Color: The Lives of Colorful Negro Women*. After receiving her law degree, Cherry became the first black woman lawyer in Dade County. As a practicing attorney she served as a legal assistant to the Coast Guard.

In 1970, Cherry was elected to the Florida State Legislature from the 106th District in Miami. She was the first black woman to become a state representative in Florida. As a representative, Cherry was active in women's and health issues. She was the first Florida legislator to propose passage of the Equal Rights Amendment. Reflecting her interest in health issues, Cherry pushed legislation that called for the testing of newborn infants for sickle cell anemia. In addition to local concerns Cherry successfully expanded her political interests and achievements into the state and national scene.

She was a past president of the National Women's Political Caucus and founder of the Florida chapter of that organization. She was also a member of the National Organization for Women

(NOW), American Association of University Women and the National Association of Women Lawyers. Cherry's last political accomplishment occurred in January of 1979 when she was elected Vice-President of the National Order of Women Legislators, just months before she would perish in an automobile accident in Tallahassee, Florida.

COLES, NATHANIEL ADAM (NAT "KING" COLE)

(March 17, 1915 or 1917 or 1919-February 15, 1965), Entertainer, was born in Montgomery, Alabama, the son of a butcher and a deacon in the Baptist church and a church organist. His family moved to Chicago, Illinois while he was still a child. There, his father became a minister and his mother remained an organist and a music teacher. One of her pupils was young Nat. Indeed she was the only piano teacher he ever had. In his first performance, at age 4, he played "Yes, We Have No Bananas". He learned not only jazz and gospel music, but classical as well, performing, as he later said, everything "from Bach to Rachmaninoff". The family lived in the Bronzeville neighborhood of Chicago, which was famous in the late-1920s for its nightlife and jazz clubs. Nat would sneak out of the house and hang outside the clubs, listening to artists like Louis Armstrong, Earl Hines, and Jimmie Noone. He also participated in Walter Dyett's renowned music program at DuSable High School.

Nat was inspired by the music of Earl "Fatha" Hines, and began his performing career in the mid-1930s while he was still a teenager, and adopted the name Nat Cole (losing the "s" from his last name). His older brother, Eddie Coles, a bassist, soon joined Nat's band and they first recorded in 1936. They had some success as a local band in and around Chicago and recorded for black music companies. They became regular performers at local night clubs. During this time, Nat got his nickname "King" while performing at one jazz club. Cole was also a pianist in a national touring revival of ragtime and Broadway legend Eubie Blaker's review, *Shuffle Along*. When the review suddenly failed in Long Beach, California, Cole decided to remain on the west coast.

In Los Angeles, Cole and three other musicians formed the

"King Cole Swingers" in Long Beach and played in a number of local bars before getting a" gig" on the Long Beach Pike for $90 per week. Throughout the late 1930s the group recorded several tapes for radio broadcasts and Cole became known as a leading jazz pianist, with appearances even in Philharmonic concerts.

Cole's repertoire of piano, bass, and guitar in the era of big bands became very popular and was considered by some as "revolutionary." for a jazz trio. It was soon emulated by many musicians, including Tommy Flangan Art Tatum, Ahmad Jamal, and Oscar Peterson, as well as blues pianists Charles Brown and Ray Charles. He also performed as a pianist on "jam sessions" with Lester Young, Red Garland, and Lionel Hampton. But Cole did not achieve national and international notoriety until "Sweet Lorraine" in 1940. Although he sang ballads with the trio, he was shy about his gravel voice. He prided himself on his diction, but he never considered himself a strong singer. His subdued style, however, contrasted well with the belting approach of most jazz singers.

In the early 1940s The King Cole Trio signed with the fledgling Capitol Records and Cole stayed with that recording company for the rest of his career. By the 1950s, Cole's popularity was so great that the Capitol Records building, on Hollywood and Vine Streets in Los Angeles, was sometimes referred to as "The House that Nat and Frank (Sinatra) Built."

Cole's first vocal hit was "Straighten Up and Fly Right", based on an African American folk tale that his father had used as a theme for a sermon. The song's success proved that an audience for folk-based material existed. Furthermore, the tune was considered a predecessor to the first rock and roll records. Indeed, Bo Diddley, who performed similar transformations of folk material, counted Cole as an influence.

In a move that was quite unique at the time, Cole also reached out to Euro-American audiences with the hit "Mona Lisa", which became a best-seller in 1950. This began a new phase in his career, which had been primarily as a pop balladeer: though he never totally ignored his roots in jazz. As late as 1956, he recorded an all-jazz album, *After Midnight*. Reflective of his growing fame, Cole became the first African American to have his own radio program. He repeated that success in the late-1950s with the first truly national television show starring an African-American. In both cases, the programs were ultimately cancelled because of Euro-American backlashes, especially in the South that prompted to cancellation of the programs. Cole, an integrationist, had always refused to perform before segregated audiences and had white guests on his shows. Then, in 1956, he was attacked on stage in Birmingham, Alabama by members of the White Citizens' Council who apparently hated him for his integrationist positions. Cole was slightly injured in the melee, but completed the show, and vowed never to perform in the South again.

But Cole's brushes with racism were not confined to the South. In 1948, he purchased a home in the all-white Hancock Park neighborhood in Los Angeles, California. The Property Owners Association told Cole they didn't want any undesirables moving in their neighborhood To which. Cole retorted :"Neither do I. And if I see anybody undesirable coming in here, I'll be the first to complain."

In addition to radio and television, Cole also appeared in film, including a role as W. C. Handy in Saint Louis Blues and the Nat King Cole Story. Indeed, his final cinema appearance in *Cat Ballou*, was first seen a few months after his death in 1965.

COLLINS, GEORGE W. (March 5, 1925-December 8, 1972), Politician, was born in Chicago, Illinois. After graduating from high school, he served in the U.S. Army, with an engineering company in the South Pacific, attaining the rank of sergeant (1943-1946). He graduated from the Central YMCA College in Chicago in 1954, and became a clerk with the Chicago Municipal Court while earning a degree in business law from Northwestern University in 1957.

From 1958 to 1961 he was deputy sheriff of Cook County and served as secretary to Alderman Benjamin Lewis of the 24th Ward, and as an administrative assistant to the Chicago Board of Health. After Lewis' death in 1963 Collins succeeded him as 24th Ward alderman and remained in that office until his election to Congress. When Sixth District Representative Daniel J. Ronan died in August 1969, Collins was elected to fill out Ronan's un-expired term in the 91st Congress and for a full term in the 92nd Congress. He began his service on November 3, 1970.

In the Congress, Collins was a member of the Public Works and Government Operations Committees. He supported, "in principle," the Nixon administration's proposals to provide a minimum federal payment to low-income families with children and to share federal tax revenues with states and localities, but criticized the plans' funding levels as inadequate. He sought to increase funding for the Elementary and Secondary Education Act and advocated passage of federal highway legislation that addressed the needs of mass transit programs and of urban resi-dents removed from their neighborhoods by road construction. Collins also introduced a bill requiring the Treasury Department to provide free tax preparation service to low and moderate-income taxpayers. He joined in efforts to reform the Federal Housing Administration, after hearings conducted by the Gov-ernment Operations' Subcommittee on Legal and Monetary Af-fairs revealed that low-income homeowners had been defrauded by speculators, real estate brokers, and home repair companies. A month after his reelection to a second term, Collins was killed in an airplane crash while traveling to Chicago to help purchase toys for the 24th Ward's annual children's Christmas party.

COLTRANE, JOHN (September 23, 1926-1967) Entertainer, was born in North Carolina. Coltrane's music, which defied categorization and was a subject of controversy in its day, was instrumental in the development of modern jazz. The famed saxophonist was born on September 23, 1926, in North Carolina. By the late 1940s he had joined Dizzy Gillespie's orchestra, which he played for four years with, and was already beginning to experiment with technical innovation and composition.

In the 1950s modern jazz became a tremendously virile id-iom, and, playing with the likes of Miles Davis and Thelonious Monk, Coltrane learned to deepen control of his instrument through tricks of phrasing and harmony. Exhausting every possi-bility for his horn in the course of a song, Coltrane's technique of exploring all the avenues relied on rapid runs in which individual notes were virtually indistinguishable, a stylistic element that became known as "sheets of sound."

In 1960, with McCoy Tyner on piano, Elvin Jones on drums, and Jimmy Garrison on bass, Coltrane formed his own quartet. His most celebrated theme-and-variations piece, *My Favorite Things,* was produced during this period that was marked by experimentation with triple meter, pentatonic scales, and modal foundations. Coltrane's ever-increasingly complex ametric and improvisational experimentation made him one of the most famous living jazz legends by the mid-1960s, and he enjoyed celebrity that extended to Europe and Japan.

CROCKETT, GEORGE WILLIAM, JR. (August 10, 1909-September 15, 1977), Politician, was born in Jacksonville, Florida on August 10, 1909 to George William and Minnie A. (Jenkins) Crockett. He attended the public schools of Jacksonville, then earned a B.A. degree from Morehouse College (Georgia) in 1931 and a J.D. degree from the University of Michigan in 1934. Following graduation, he returned to Jacksonville and began a private practice of law.

In 1939, Crockett became the first African American attorney employed by the U.S. Department of Labor. In 1943, President Franklin D. Roosevelt appointed him a hearing examiner with the newly formed Fair Employment Practices Commission (FEPC). A year later, he moved to Detroit, Michigan to become director of the Fair Employment Practices Commission (FEPC). A year later, he moved to Detroit, Michigan to become director of the Fair Employment Practices office of the United Auto Workers (UAW). After his return to private practice in 1946, Crockett remained active in the defense of labor unions and civil rights activists. In this regard, he represented clients before the House UnAmerican Activities Committee (HUAC) and the U.S. Supreme Court.

Crockett served as a judge of the Recorders Court in Detroit from 1966 to 1978 and in 1974 was elected presiding judge of that court. He also served as a visiting judge on the Michigan Court of Appeals and as corporation counsel for the City of Detroit. He became a well known leader in Detroit's Black Community, when, in 1990, he declared his candidacy for the congressional seat left vacant by the resignation in Charles Diggs in 1980. He was elected to fill that vacancy on November 4, 1980, and at the same time was elected for a full term in the Ninety-seventh Congress. He was sworn in on November 12, 1980.

In the House of Representatives, Crockett served as a member of the Committee on Foreign Affairs, the Committee on the Judiciary and the Select Committee on Aging. He was chairman of the Foreign Affairs Subcommittee on Western Hemisphere Affairs which oversees U.S. policy in Latin America and the Caribbean. He has used his position on Foreign Affairs to voice opposition to the South African government's policy of apartheid. In 1984 he was one of several anti-apartheid protestors who were arrested outside the South African Embassy in Washington. He spent a night in jail.

In 1990, Crockett, expressing a desire "to slow down a little," retired from the Congress. Reacting to the retirement, the *Detroit Free Press* said it hoped that Crockett's successor would share "his passion for human rights and social justice...."

DAVIS, BENJAMIN JEFFERSON JR. (September 8, 1903-August 22, 1964), Politician, was born in Dawson, Georgia. His father Benjamin Davis, Sr. moved the family to Atlanta in 1909 and was the founder and editor of the *Atlanta Independent*, one of the leading African American political publications of the time. A stable middle class household, the Davis family were residents of the same community and friends of the familial progenitors of Martin Luther King, Jr. Growing up in a politically charged household, the young Benjamin Davis developed an early interest for debating and attended the Morehouse College Academy, where he graduated with honors in 1920. Davis went on to earn his B.A. from Amherst College in Massachusetts in 1925 and his law degree from Harvard in 1929.

Deciding to launch his law career in Atlanta, Davis, in 1932, decided to take on an explosive case of a young black man that was arrested while leading a protest for the rights of poor people in the city. Angelo Herndon, a militant communist that fought for equal rights of all people, was a target of the Georgia government not only because of his open support for communist ideology, but because he was beginning to be successful in building an unheard of interracial coalition against poverty in a time where integration was far from the norm. During his defense of Herndon, Davis became more and more sympathetic with the communist cause. Facing the death penalty under an 1861 law enacted by the Georgia Legislature to prevent slave insurrections, Herndon was singled out because of the communist literature that he was distributing during the protest. With an all-white jury, a judge that often read a newspaper during the trial, and repeated references to Herndon as "nigger," the jury quickly found the client of Benjamin Davis guilty, but decided to hand out a "merciful" sentence of eighteen years in prison. Impacted so much by the trial, Davis gave up his law practice in Atlanta and moved to Harlem, New York to join the American Communist Party (ACP). There he became a lead attorney for the International Labor Defense team and took the case of Herndon all the way to the Supreme Court, where the conviction was overturned and Herndon set free.

In the ACP, Davis became editor of *Liberation*, the party's periodical directed at blacks. Later in 1936, he became a writer and music critic for the *Daily Worker,* the party's official organ. Widely embraced as a viable political alternative, communism, in Harlem, especially after the Great Depression when unemployment hit a high of 85%, was a thriving political movement free of the stigma attached to it throughout the country. As a leader in the ACP, Davis was respected and well-liked amongst Harlem celebrities and aristocrats, and equally admired amongst the masses of struggling families. While working at the party's national headquarters, Davis entered into politics. First he ran for Congress in 1942, but lost in an at-large election. But when the Reverend Adam Clayton Powell won the congressional seat from Harlem, Davis ran for and won Powell's City Council seat in 1943 as a candidate from the ACP. During his campaign, celebrities like Cab Calloway, Joe Louis, Paul Robeson, Billie Holiday, Art Tatum, Ella Fitzgerald, Duke Ellington, and Count Basie publicly supported the dapper and well-groomed Davis. Loved and admired by his constituency he was reelected in 1945.

Council terms were extended to four years and Davis came up for a third term in 1949. Prior to that year, however the federal government brought the communist councilman before the House Un-American Activities Committee and indicted him under the Smith Act on July 21, 1948. Hence, Davis lost his bid to another black politician, Earl Brown, who had Democratic, Republican and liberal backing.

Subsequently, Davis went to federal prison and was released in 1952 alongside ten others that were convicted and known as the Communist Eleven. Bound by legal restrictions to not speak publicly for four years after his release, Davis was finally able to speak before a packed ballroom of over 1000 supporters at the Theresa Hotel in Harlem in 1956. Two years later, Davis attempted again to run for the New York State Senate, but was unable to get his campaign off of the ground. Until his passing in 1964, Davis was arrested often for his communist views and outspoken ways, but he never ceased being active in the fight for the rights of oppressed people.

DAVIS, BENJAMIN O., Sr. (1877-1970), Soldier, was born in Washington, DC, the son of Louis and Henrietta Davis, former bondspersons, and studied at Howard University there. He entered the U. S. Army as a first lieutenant in 1898 and served with the 8th Infantry during the Spanish-American War. Prior to World War II, Davis served in the Phillipines, Liberia, and in Wyoming. He also taught military science at Wilberforce University and at Tuskegee Institute. During World War II he served in the European Theater of Operations as an advisor on the problems of black servicemen, and he helped implement the desegregation of armed forces facilities in Europe. When he retired in 1948, Davis was named an assistant to the inspector general in Washington, DC. His awards and decorations included the Distinguished Service Medal, the Bronze Star, the *Croix de Guerre* with Palm, and an honorary degree from Atlanta University. He was the father of General Benjamin Davis, Jr. who also had a distinguished military career.

DAVIS, BENJAMIN O., JR. (1912-2002), Soldier, was com-

116

mander of the 15th Air Force bombers in their attacks on Romanian oil fields during World War II, became the first black general in the U.S. Air Force. Davis, son of the Army's General Benjamin O. Davis, Sr., was born in Washington D.C., in 1912. He was educated at Western Reserve University, the University of Chicago, and the U.S. Military Academy at West Point. In 1936 Davis became the fourth black to graduate from West Point. He received his wings from the Tuskegee Advanced Flying School in 1942 and became commander of the 99th Fighter Squadron at the Army Air Field at Tuskegee. He was ordered to North Africa in 1943. During and after World War II, Davis served in Italy, Japan, Formosa, Germany, and Korea, where he served as commander of the 51st Fighter-Interceptor Wing. Davis's awards and decorations include the Distinguished Service Medal, the Silver Star, the Legion of Merit, and the Distinguished Flying Cross.

DAVIS, SAMMY JR (December 8, 1925-May 16, 1990), Entertainer, Civil/Human Rights Activist was born in the Harlem section of New York City. His father, Sammy, Sr. was a noted musician in the Will Mastin Trio. Davis, himself, began performing with the Mastin group, a vaudeville performance, at the age of three. In his adult years, Davis became a singer, dancer and actor who was featured on stage, in film, on television and in nightclubs. He made his Broadway debut in 1956 in the musical "Mr. Wonderful" and later won a Tony nomination for his starring role as a cosmopolitan boxer in "Golden Boy."

Davis' major recordings included "The Way You Look Tonight" (1946), "Hey There" (1954), "That Old Black Magic" (1955), "I've Got to Be Me" (1969) and "The candy Man" (1972).

In his recordings and films, Davis often teamed with the Euro-American illuminaries Dean Martin and Frank Sinatra. His first role in movies was as a child in "Rufus Jones for President" (1933), which starred singer Ethel waters. He also had major roles in Anna Lucasta (19580, Porgy and Bess (1959), "Oceans Eleven" (1960), "Robin and the Seven Hoods" (1964) and "Sweet Charity" (1969. His last appearance was in "Tap" with

Gregory Hines in 1989.

Between 1956 and 1990, Davis appeared on almost every comedy series and variety show on television. In 1966, he starred briefly in his own show—one of the first ever hosted by an African American.

During the Civil Rights Movement of the 1960s Davis supported the efforts led by Martin Luther King Jr. by marching and performing at fundraisers. He was, for example, was one of several stars who entertained the marchers who reached Montgomery, Alabama from Selma during the voting rights demonstrations in March, 1965. He also helped raise money for the defense of African American radical Angela Davis after she was imprisoned for conspiracy to commit murder in the late 1960s.

Although Davis' popularity as a performer and an American patriot helped him to transcend race in many respects, his marriage to the Swedish actress Mai Britt was a subject of controversy. Indeed, he was "disinvited" to an inaugural activity for President John F. Kennedy because it was feared that his presence with his blonde wife might "inflame southerners." Davis as also involved in another controversy of a racial nature in 1972. While attending a function for President Richard M. Nixon during the Republican National Convention that year, he startled the president when he came up behind Nixon and gave him a big hug while flashing a wide, "catfish" grin. Some African Americans, particularly, decried the act as "stereotypical" and "Uncle Tomish."

Davis chronicled his quixotic rise from vaudeville to the pinnacles of American entertainment in two autobiographies *Yes I Can* in 1965 and *Why Me i*n 1989. On the occasion of his death in 1990, Benjamin Hooks, executive director of the NAACP, lauded Davis as "an American treasure that the whole world loved."

ELLINGTON, EDWARD KENNEDY (Duke) (April 29, 1899-May 24,1974), Entertainer, was born in Washington, DC and grew up there. Gifted from childhood with a talent for music, he began playing the piano at age seven. He especially liked to experiment with unusual chords and sounds, which finally led his frustrated teacher to give up on him.

But Ellington kept playing on his own and learned to imitate and memorize pieces he heard other people play. He composed his first song at seventeen and began playing professionally at eighteen. By then, he was already known as "Duke" thanks to a friend who thought it suited his stylish clothes, sophisticated manners, and elegant way of talking.

In 1922, after establishing a reputation as an outstanding jazz pianist around the Washington area, Ellington headed north to New York City with a few of his band mates. There they played in Harlem's best-known nightspot, the Cotton Club, where their performances were carried live on radio and broadcast from coast to coast. By the end of the decade, the Duke Ellington band was famous all over the country.

During the 1930s and early 1940s, Ellington and his orchestra were the most popular black jazz band in the United states. After the 1940s, when jazz declined in popularity, his orchestra was one of the few that survived. In fact, in themed-to-late 1950s, a new generation of fans "discovered" Ellington, and for the rest of his like he remained at or near the top of the jazz world.

Besides being a popular and respected musician, Ellington was a noted composer. He wrote most of the material his orchestra recorded and he also sold other pieces to music publishers. Over the course of his entire career, Ellington wrote or co-wrote more than 2,000 compositions, including "Mood Indigo", "Take the A' Train", "Don't Get Around Much Anymore". "Satin Doll" and "Caravan". In later years he composed several orchestral works, tone poems, jazz masses, operas, and scores for film, ballets, and television.

Among Ellington's numerous awards were the NAACP's Spingarn Medal, the French Legion of Merit (France's highest honor) and the United States' highest civilian honor, the Medal of Freedom, which he received in 1970.

On the occasion of his death in 1974, a spokesperson for the NAACP noted: "Few composers have attained the greatness that was the Duke's....He was indomitable."

EVERS, MEDGAR WILEY (July 12, 1925-June 11,1963), Civil/Human Rights Leader, was born in Decatur, Mississippi. He dropped out of high school at age 17 and joined the U. S Army in World War II. Upon his return to Mississippi, he finished high school and earned a degree from Alcorn A&M College in his native state. Following college, he took a job with the Magnolia Mutual Insurance company. In the meantime, he was attracted to the unfolding modern Civil Rights Movement in the South and subsequently became field secretary for the Mississippi NAACP, working out of Jackson.

Bold and courageous, Evers challenged discrimination in all facets of Mississippi life in the midst of jailings, bombings and threats on his life and that of his family. Then, on the night of June 11, 1963, he was fatally gunned down by a sniper in Jackson, making him the latest victim of assassination resulting from civil rights activity. The man accused of the crime, a white segregationist named Byron de la Beckwith, was eventually acquitted when a jury could not reach a verdict in the case. More than 30 years later, through the dogged insistence of Evers' wife, Myrlie, de la Beckwith was retried and found guilty.

FARMER, JAMES LEONARD, JR. (January 12, 1920-July 9, 1999), Civil/Human Rights Leader, was born in Marshall, Texas to James Leonard, a professor at Wiley College, and Pearl Marion (Houston) Farmer. Young Farmer grew up on the campus of Wiley and received his B.S. degree in chemistry there at the age of 18. He first thought of a career in medicine but, then turned to religion. He earned a Bachelor of Divinity degree from the School of Religion at Howard University in 1941, and was prepared to enter the Methodist ministry. He declined, however, to be ordained because the Methodist Church was still a segregated one. Instead, he turned his attention to social activism.

Beginning in 1941, Farmer served as race relations secretary for the Fellowship of Reconciliation, a pacifist group. He left the Fellowship in 1945 to become an organizer for the Upholsterers Union and later an international representative for the State, County, and Municipal Employees Union.

Farmer entered the Civil Rights Movement in 1942, when

he helped a group of students at the University of Chicago organize the Congress of Racial Equality (CORE). Within a year of its founding, CORE conducted a successful sit-in at a restaurant in Chicago's Loop. CORE, then, launched its stand-in protests at theaters and other places of accommodation, often forcing these facilities to admit blacks. At this time, CORE was always supported by an interracial corps of volunteers. Such a group began a challenge to this segregation in the Upper South as early as 1947.

Meanwhile Farmer had become national chairman of CORE. But, from 1942 to 1956, the heart of the organization was its core of local, autonomous chapters, and the national offices, including the chairman's, were staffed by volunteers. Farmer, then, sought other avenues by which to make a living. Between 1959 and 1961, he was a program director for the national NAACP. But when the NAACP refused to endorse a Freedom Ride into the Deep South in 1961 (which was to be patterned after CORE's "Journey of Reconciliation" through the upper South 14 years earlier), Farmer left that civil rights organization.

Fortunately, CORE was now able to offer him a position as full-time executive director. In May, Farmer and a bi-racial team of 13 young persons began their ride into the Deep South. The brutal, racist violence that they encountered, particularly in Alabama and Mississippi, disturbed much of the nation. And, as CORE continued its direct action resistance to segregation, it became, alongside the NAACP and SCLC, a major organization in the Civil Rights Movement. Farmer, himself, was elevated to the top ranks of civil rights leadership, accompanying the SCLC's Martin Luther King, Jr., the NAACP's Roy Wilkins, and the National Urban League's Whitney Young.

Farmer left CORE, which fell increasingly into the school of Black Power organizations, like SNCC, in 1966 to head a national job training and literacy program. When this project failed, he took a position on the faculty at Lincoln University in Pennsylvania, as a professor of social work. But he quickly returned to the public arena, moving hastily back to New York to unsuccessfully challenge Shirley Chisholm for a seat in Congress. After being defeated by Chisholm, the first black woman to serve in the U.S. Congress, President Richard Nixon in 1969, named Farmer an assistant secretary of the Department of Health, Education, and Welfare. He left this position after only one year of service.

After retiring from the Civil Rights Movement and federal service, Farmer was variously president of the Council on Minority Planning and Strategy (1973), executive director of the Coalition of American Public Employees (1977), and a university lecturer.

FRANKLIN, C. L. (-July 17, 1984), Minister, Entertainer, Civil Rights/Human Rights Activist, was pastor of the New Bethel Baptist Church in Detroit, Michigan for thirty-eight years. He also recorded more than twenty albums of his sermons, including the most popular one *The Eagle Stirred Its Nest*. On some of the recordings, he was joined by the New Bethel Baptist church choir and his daughter, the famed soul singer, Aretha Franklin.

In 1963, a few months before the great March on Washington, Franklin led a protest march in Detroit that included several thousand people. In 1979, Franklin was seriously wounded by robbers and remained in a coma for five years. After his death, in 1984, civil rights leader Jesse Jackson eulogized Franklin as "the high priest of soul preaching."

FRAZIER, E. FRANKLIN (September 24, 1894-May 17, 1962) Educator, Author, was born in Baltimore, Maryland, on September 24, 1894, was a Howard University graduate. He received his Ph.D. from the University of Chicago in 1931 but returned to Howard three years later to begin a twenty-five-year affiliation with their sociology department. Eventually he was appointed chairman of the department. Before his retirement from Howard in 1959, he interrupted his tenure to teach at Columbia University and New York University, among others. He had traveled to Brazil and the West Indies as a Guggenheim fellow in the early 1940s, and he was made president of the American Sociological Society in 1948. For the United Nations Educational, Scientific and Cultural Organization (UNESCO), Frazier served as chairman of the committee of experts on race and chief of the organization's Applied Science Division in Parris.

A recognized authority on the black family, Frazier wrote *The Negro Family in* Chicago, The *Negro Family in the United States, The Negro in the United States, The Negro Church in America and Black Bourgeoisie.* Several of his works were controversial, but, perhaps, none more than *Black Bourgeoisie* that argued that middle class blacks were islolating themselves from poverty stricken African Americans.

FULLER, SAMUEL (S. B.) (June 4, 1903-October 24, 1988), Corporate Executive, was born in Monroe, Louisiana, in the parish of Ouachita Paris. Little is known of Fuller's parents, except they were sharecroppers and his mother died when he was 17 years old. He dropped out of school after the sixth grade. By the age of nine, Fuller was selling "Cloverine Salve" on the streets of Monroe, Louisiana. In 1928, he and his wife hitchhiked to Chicago, where Fuller found work in a coal yard. Later, Fuller worked as an insurance representative for Commonwealth Burial Association. After four years, he was promoted to a managerial position.

Assisted by his wife, Fuller invested in a soap that he peddled from door-to-door. This venture was so successful that he incorporated the business, Fuller Products Company in 1929. By 1939, Fuller's company had become an empire with a value of over several million dollars. In a secret transaction in 1947, he acquired Boyer International Laboratories. Throughout the 1950s, Fuller was known as a master salesman and his companies produced face creams, lotions, perfumes, and a complete line of household products. While cosmetics remained the core of his trade, he also owned shares in newspapers, the *New York Age* and *Pittsburgh Courier* (where he chaired the Board of Directors in 1960). Also, Fuller owned department stores, Chicago's Regal Theater, agricultural interests, and invested in real estate trusts in New York City. He was considered one of the wealthiest black men in the United States and was affectionately known as "the Godfather" of black business. By the early 1960s, Fuller's business interests were worth ten million dollars, with a

60 percent interracial clientele.

During the late 1960s, Fuller's business investments began to decline. Because of the racial tension of the 1960s, Southern White Citizens' Councils tried to destroy the company by boycotting sales throughout the South. White storeowners removed Fuller's products from their shelves and since much of his business came from whites, they devastated Fuller Products Company.

In 1964, the Securities and Exchange Commission (SEC) charged Fuller with selling unregistered high interest promissory notes on his business and placed him on probation. By 1968, Fuller had lost his publishing and retail stores and Fuller Products Company declared bankruptcy in 1969. At the same time he suffered from a backlash in the African American community, because of his negative statements toward blacks in business. He was alleged to have said: "Negroes lack initiative, courage, integrity, loyalty and wisdom."

In the 1970s, Fuller revived his business under federal bankruptcy laws. Because he had done so much to promote black entrepreneurship, particularly in Chicago, in 1975, a group of businesspeople, led by entrepreneur George Johnson and Johnson Publishing Company executive John H. Johnson, cosponsored a testimonial dinner for Fuller. Illinois Governor Danie Walker declared June 4, 1975, S. B. Fuller Day in his honor as well. At the Chicago event, Fuller was presented with $70,000 and 2,000 shares of stock, valued at $50,000, to help save his company from financial collapse.

By 1962, Fuller had obtained a license to preach and later became an assistant pastor of the St. Andrew Temple of Faith, Truth and Love Baptist Church. He was once the head of the South Side chapter of the NAACP and the first African American member of the National Association of Manufacturers. During the administration of President Dwight D. Eisenhower, he raised money for the Republican National Committee. He was also a generous contributor to numerous charities, institutions, and scholarship funds.

GASTON, ARTHUR G. ("A.G.") (July 4, 1892-January 19,

1996), Businessman, was born in Demopolis, Alabama. He moved to Birmingham in 1905. After service in the Army during World War I, Gaston returned to Alabama and worked in a coal mine in Fairfield. While working in the Fairfield mines, he came up with the idea to sell lunches to his fellow workers. Using his income from this venture, he later began loaning money to the workers between paydays, with a 25% interest rate. He, subsequently, combined this venture with a burial insurance enterprise that extended beyond the mine into the neighboring African American communities. Then in 1920, he and his father-in-law opened the Smith and Gaston mortuary. But, in the 1930s, the father-in-law got into political quarrels with the mayor of Fairfield and the funeral parlor was forced out of the city. It, then, relocated to Birmingham.

In Birmingham, Gaston developed a financial empire that included the funeral home, a savings and loan association, concert promotions, and a motel. During the Civil Rights Movement, Martin Luther King, Jr and his associates were frequent guests at the Gaston motel. On May 12, 1963 while King and his chief lieutenant, Ralph Abernathy were registered at the motel, a bomb tore into part of the facility. During the melee which followed, Alabama state troopers beat some of the other guests as they tried to escape. At the time of the bombing Gaston was at the White House attending one of President John F Kennedy's state dinner. He returned home to find that bigots had also thrown firebombs at his lavish home. Interestingly and ironically, while Gaston allowed leaders of the Birmingham protests of 1963 to live at his motel and to plot their strategies there, he was not entirely supportive of direct action protests. He, especially, opposed the participation of students. His positions led the Reverend Fred Shuttlesworth, the premiere civil rights leader in Birmingham, to once refer to Gaston as a "Super Uncle Tom".

GAYE, MARVIN (April 2, 1939-April 1, 1984) Entertainer, was born in Washington, DC. He began his singing career with Motown Records as a solo artist. At first, Gaye did background instrumentals for various Motown performers, including Smokey Robinson. But soon he was one of the company's hottest vocalists. His pop-soul hits from the 1960s—including "Can I Get a Witness," "How Sweet It Is to Be Loved by You," and "I Heard It through the Grapevine"— are considered classics. He and Tammi Terrell also topped the charts during those years with a number of romantic ballads such as "You're All I Need to Get By" and "Ain't Nothin' Like the Real Thing." Terrell's death from a brain tumor in 1970 had a profound effect on Gaye, who left the music business briefly. He returned in 1971 with an album entitled *What's Going On* that was very different from his previous Motown recordings. The songs

Gaye wrote, sang, and played for this ground-breaking album dealt with social issues such as pollution, the Vietnam War, drug addiction, and "ghetto life." The title song and two others, "Mercy, Mercy Me" and "Inner City Blues," all made it into the top ten on the pop charts.

Gaye followed this up with more romantic music, this time more seductively sexual than the glossy soul hits Motown was famous for during the 1960s. But by the mid 1970s he had become heavily involved with cocaine, and his career went downhill.

In 1982, Gaye began a promising comeback with an album called *Midnight Love* that featured the hit song, "Sexual Healing." It won two Grammy Awards in 1983 and prompted the singer to go on his first concert tour in seven years. He still had not been able to overcome his cocaine habit, however. It contributed to the problems between father and son that left Gaye dead just one day before his forty- fifth birthday.

GIBSON, ALTHEA (August 25,1927-2003) Athlete, African American tennis star was born in Silver, South Carolina but grew up in the Harlem district of New York City. She was a "tough and undisciplined youngster" who often skipped school to hang out in the street or go to the movies. But as a teenager she displayed a talent for paddleball (a form of tennis) that caught the eye of a city recreation department worker named Buddy Walker. Thinking that Gibson might do well at regular tennis, Walker bought her a racket and arranged for her to play against professional Fred Johnson at an interracial New York club. Johnson was equally impressed, as were other club members who saw that the teenager's skills were definitely above average. They paid for her to take lessons from Johnson, who taught her the basics of the game and helped her improve her overall technique. Within a year after she had begun working at tennis, Gibson was on her way to success. She won the girls' singles title in the New York State Open Championship in 1942 and again in 1944 and 1945. She began playing on the women's circuit in 1946, and even though she failed in her attempt to win the singles title, she attracted the attention of Hubert Eaton and Robert W. Johnson. These two black physicians had made a second career out of helping promising young black tennis players, and they felt Gibson had a great deal of potential. So they both saw to it that she received further training and that she finished high school and went on to college.

Gibson was a standout performer in women's tennis for the next ten years, from the late 1940s through the late 1950s. Because tennis had always been a game of well -to-do white people, she broke down many barriers in the process as the first black to play in major lawn tennis tournaments. In 1950, for example, she was the first black to compete at prestigious Forest Hills on New York's Long Island. After that, many other clubs in the United States and overseas opened their courts to her, too. In 1957, Gibson became the first black woman to play and win at Forest Hills and Wimbledon in singles and doubles competition. She triumphed again at both championships In 1958, she then retired from tennis at a time when she was ranked as the best female player in the world. Since then, she tried her hand at many things, including professional golf. Toward the end of her life she was a recreational consultant and planner. In 1971 she was elected to the National Lawn Tennis Hall of Fame.

GILLESPIE, JOHN BIRKS (DIZZY GILLESPIE) (October 21,1917-January 6, 1993), Entertainer, was born in Cheraw, South Carolina. He fell in love with the trumpet when he was in the third grade and began to play publicly by age 15. He later studied harmony and theory at the Laurinburg Institute in North Carolina. Starting out with the bands of Cab Calloway

and Billy Eckstine, he, then, helped to create the revolutionary bebop style as well as Afro-Cuban jazz. His trademark bulging cheeks, bent horn, and fun-loving showmanship entertained audiences throughout the world for over fifty years.

GRANGER, SHELTON B. (February 21, 1921-September 21, 1991), Educator, Association Executive, was born in Harrisburg, Pennsylvania, the son of late Dr. and Mrs. A. T. Granger. Granger received his A.B. from Howard University in 1942 and his M.S. from Columbia University in 1947. He had an illustrious career in social planning, administration, education, and consulting capacities. Granger served in the U.S. Army from 1942 through 1946 as a first Lieutenant.

Throughout his professional career, various Urban League branches employed Granger. He worked for the Cleveland Urban League and was director of Industrial Relations from 1947-1951. He served as the executive director of the Minnesota Urban League from 1951-1958 and the executive director of the Cleveland Urban League from 1958-1962. Equally noteworthy is his government employment. Granger served as director of the Youth Development Division, Children's Bureau, and Department of Health Education & Welfare (HEW) from 1962-1963. He worked as the director in the Human Resources Development Division of the Latin America Bureau for International Development from 1963-1965. From 1965-1966, Granger served as the Deputy Assistant Secretary for the department of HEW and the Deputy Assistant Secretary of International Affairs in the department of HEW from 1966-1969. He served as the executive director of HEW from 1972-1977 and as a consultant for the Business and Government Council beginning in 1979.

Granger taught at many educational institutions during his career. He was a guest lecturer at Minnesota University and at Maryland School of Social Work. Granger served as a field instructor at the School of Applied Social Science at Case-Western Reserve University. He also served as a field instructor at Atlanta and Minnesota University's School of Social Work. Granger became an associate professor at the University of Pennsylvania. His major publication was *The Urban Crisis –*

Challenge for the Century published by Paul S. Amidon & Associates in Minneapolis, Minnesota in 1970.

HALE, CLARA (April 1, 1905-December 18, 1992), Human Rights Leader, was born in Philadelphia, Pennsylvania. After her husband died in 1932, she supported her three children by cleaning other people's homes during the day and theaters at night. This arrangement, however, often forced her to leave her own children at home alone. Thus, she developed an idea of taking care of her own children as well as others in a day care arrangement. She became an official licensed foster mother in 1941.

In 1968, at the age of 63, Hale wanted to retire, but she was introduced to a young woman, a heroin addict, who had a two-month old baby. Hale took in the baby. Word of this deed spread quickly, and within two months, 22 babies had been deposited in Hale's apartment in New York City. Eventually, the city of New York provided some financial assistance to aid "Mother Hale" in her childcare project. In 1975, the city provided her with a five-story building – named Hale House. Private donors, including rock star John Lennon, also came forward with help. And after his assassination in 1979, his widow, Yoko Ono set up a foundation to contribute $20,000 annually to the Hale House.

Hale House children ranged in age from ten days to four years. Many of them suffered from drug withdrawal. Very few of them were ever put up for adoption as Hale hoped, someday, to return them to their parents, after they recovered from drug addiction. "Mother Hale's" children were black and white, male and female, who were referred by individuals, clergy, hospitals, police, social workers, and others.

In 1985, President Ronald Reagan invited "Mother Hale" to his State of the Union Address, and publicly recognized her as a "true American hero." The Salvation Army also bestowed upon her its highest honor, the Booth Community Service Award and the John Jay College of Criminal Justice Award (New York) awarded her an honorary degree. In response to all of these accolades, "Mother Hale" once said: "I love children and I love caring for them…. That is what the Lord meant me to do."

HALEY, ALEX (August 11, 1921-February 10, 1972), Author, was born in Hemming, Tennessee. In 1976 Haley became the first African American to win literary fame for depicting his family's history, in the book entitled *Roots*. *Roots* traced Haley's family history from its West African origins to bondage and freedom in America. The book was a product of several years of genealogical research on three continents.

Roots won a Pulitzer Prize. Subsequently, it became the basis of one of television's most popular miniseries. The story of Haley's family, presented in eight parts, was viewed by approximately 130 million people. It was lauded for providing a frank depiction of the nation's formative years, including the period of African American bondage. Several analysts and critics of the miniseries noted the moral challenges to the nation that were explicit in the telecasts.

Haley's fame resulting from *Roots* was tarnished, however, in 1977 when African American author Margaret walker claimed that the book had been plagiarized from her novel, *Jubilee*. Later, author Harold Courlander also charged that the work plagiarized his book, *The African*. In his defense, Haley asserted that his research assistants had given hi materials without properly citing the source. On the other hand, Haley achieved a reputation for his extensive research and attention to detail in *Roots* as well as *The Autobiography of Malcolm X*.

HAMER, FANNIE LOU (TOWNSEND) (October 6, 1917-March 14, 1977), Civil/Human Rights Leader, was born in Montgomery County, Mississippi, the youngest of 20 children of Joe and Lou Ella Townsend, rural sharecroppers. When Fannie was two years old, the family moved to Sunflower County. Before she was six years old she joined her parents and siblings on a white landowner's farm as a cotton picker.

After Townsend had saved enough money to purchase his own farming equipment and livestock, the family abandoned sharecropping and rented their own farmland. But resentful whites soon ended this venture in independence by poisoning all of the family's animals. Fannie returned with her family to farm laboring for whites. Amid her "sun up to sun down" farm work,

Fannie tried to attend school at least four months during each year, but abandoned this venture at age 12.

A few years after Fannie's father died in 1937, she married Perry "Pap" Hamer and secured a job as a sharecropper and timekeeper on a Sunflower County plantation. She held these jobs for 18 years, until 1962 when she was fired for attempting to register to vote.

Hamer's interest in voting rights was influenced by a civil rights rally she attended at a Ruleville, Mississippi church in August 1962. She was so inspired by the speeches of the Reverend James Bevel of the Southern Christian Leadership Conference (SCLC), James Forman of the Student Non-Violent Coordinating Committee (SNCC), and others that she signed a list promising to attempt to register at the county courthouse in Indianola the following Friday. She also assumed leadership of the group of 17 other would-be voters.

On August 31, 1962, Fannie Lou Hamer and her group of black activists were given a day-long test on the Mississippi State Constitution at the Indianola courthouse (the test wasn't given to white persons) and sent home without knowing whether they had qualified to vote. On the way back to Ruleville, police stopped their bus and ordered them back to Indianola, where the driver was fined $100 for operating an illegally colored or painted bus. A judge released him after the group paid $30.

It was not until almost six months later, on January 10, 1963, that Hamer passed the Mississippi literacy test on her third attempt, and qualified as one of only a handful of registered voters among her county's 30,000 blacks. By this time she had become very active in the Civil Rights Movement, participating in SCLC, CORE, the NAACP and COFO (the Council of Federated Organizations). She obtained names on petitions to aid needy black families and sharpened her organizing skills at various SCLC workshops both within and outside of the state. She became a SNCC field secretary and focused on voter registration and welfare programs. Meanwhile, in order to support herself, she got a job in a Ruleville cotton gin in the spring of 1963, but was dismissed the next year.

Hamer's home was first attacked by gunmen in the late

summer of 1962, shortly after her first attempts to register to vote. By the end of 1963, as a result of her increased civil rights activity, she was often jailed and even severely beaten while incarcerated; once she almost lost the use of a kidney and an eye. After one such beating in 1964, she was left without medical attention until civil rights leaders Bevel and Andrew Young of SCLC managed to secure her release. She was then sent first to Greenwood, Mississippi and, next, to Atlanta, Georgia for treatment of her wounds.

Despite the jailings and "brushes with death," Hamer continued both her civil rights and political activities in the heart of rural Mississippi. After being shunned by the regular white Democratic Party of Mississippi, Hamer and other black activists formed the bi-racial Mississippi Freedom Democratic Party (MFDP) in 1964. In August of that year, with Hamer as vice-chairman, the MFDP challenged the regular Mississippi Democrats for seats at the National Democratic Convention in Atlantic City, New Jersey. Although the Convention agreed to allow two members of the bi-racial MFDP delegation to be seated along with the regular Democrats, the MFDP rejected the offer and left the floor. But Fannie Lou Hamer gained national attention with her eloquent portrayal of the horrors of attempting to exercise civil rights in Mississippi.

During that same year, 1964, Hamer sought election to Congress from the majority black Second District of Mississippi. But even though blacks comprised 59 percent of the area's 300,000 residents, they accounted for only 6,616 registered voters. And many of these were intimidated and frightened away from the polls. Hamer lost the election in a "landslide". The next year, however, she was at the national capitol, challenging the seating of five of Mississippi's congressmen. On the floor of the U.S. House of Representatives she told the nation that the Mississippi lawmakers were, because of voter discrimination, elected illegally and that it was not "just Mississippi's problem," it was "America's problem." The House ended its investigation of Hamer's charges on September 17, 1965 without unseating the congressmen. Although the MFDP did not win seats in the elections of 1964, and list its challenge in 1965, it did win several positions in the state in 1968 and 1972.

After her national public appearances in 1964 and 1965, Hamer became a widely sought-after speaker and lecturer before church, civic, and educational organizations. She was an invited guest of the governments of Ghana, Guinea, and Nigeria. In Guinea she was personally received by President Sekou Toure.

In 1969, only seven years after she failed her first literacy test for voting in Mississippi, Hamer was honored by two of the most prestigious black colleges in America. Tougaloo College (Mississippi) awarded her an honorary Doctor of Humane Letters degree and Morehouse College, the alma mater of Martin Luther King, Jr. conferred upon her a certificate of distinguished service.

In 1976, a single Democratic Party, with integrated factions, represented the state of Mississippi. One year later, at the time of her death, Hamer remained Vice Chairperson of the MFDP.

Hamer also founded the Freedom Farm Cooperative, a garment factory that provided jobs for residents of Ruleville, Mississippi. She worked and attained not only jobs, but housing, new security and new dignity for many in Mississippi.

Although Hamer continued her involvement in grassroots activism for uplifting her people until her death and despite being a victim of savage, white brutality, she remained committed to racial integration and harmony and refused to hate whites. She once said: "Ain't no such thing as I can hate anybody and hope to see God's face."

HANSBERRY, LORRAINE (May 19,1930-January 12, 1965) Playwright. Lorraine Hansberry's play *A Raisin in the Sun* opened on Broadway on March 11, 1959. The story of a black family's frustrating efforts to move out of the ghetto and into a white neighborhood, it was the first play by a black woman to appear on the New York stage. (It was also produced, directed, and acted by blacks.)-Later that year, Hansberry became the first black to win the New York Drama Critics Circle Award for the best play of 1959. A native of Chicago, Illinois, Hansberry was born in 1930. After graduating from high school, she briefly studied art at the Chicago Art Institute, the University of Wisconsin, and in Mexico. It was while she was still at the University of Wisconsin that she walked in on a play rehearsal one day and was so fascinated by what she saw that she decided to try to do some writing for the stage.

.

HARRIS, PATRICIA ROBERTS (May 31, 1924-March 23, 1985), Federal Official, U.S. Ambassador, corporate lawyer, was born in Matton, Illinois, on May 31, 1924 to Bert and Hildren C. Roberts. Raised by her mother, Harris lived in a small town where there were only a few black families, where she soon became familiar with racism and began participating in civil rights activities at an early age,

Harris attended Howard University in Washington, D.C. and earned an A.B. (summa cum laude) degree from there in 1945. During her stay at Howard, she served as campus branch vice-chairman for the National Association for the Advancement of Colored People (NAACP) and participated in several nonviolent demonstrations against racial injustices, including one of the first student sit-ins to desegregate a local cafeteria.

In 1945, Harris returned to Illinois and started taking industrial relations courses at the University of Chicago. She also became an active member of the Young Women's Christian Association (YWCA). In 1949, she returned to Washington, D.C. to pursue graduate studies at American University. During this period, she also became the assistant director of the American Council of Human Rights.

From 1953 to 1959, Harris served as the executive director of Delta Sigma Theta, a black sorority. Deciding that being a lawyer could fulfill her many interests and goals, she enrolled in George Washington University Law School in 1957 and graduated at the top of her class in 1960.

After graduation, Harris worked for the criminal division of the United States Department of Justice for about a year. Then in 1961, she joined the faculty of the Howard University Law School and remained there until she accepted an ambassador to Luxembourg position from the Johnson administration in 1965. At the end of her diplomatic service in September of 1967, she returned to Howard and became the first black woman to serve as the dean of its law school, in 1969. Abdicating this position within a month due to faculty and student strife, Harris joined a Washington, D.C. based law firm where she worked as a corporate lawyer until she accepted President Jimmy Carter's appointment to U.S. Secretary of Housing and Urban Development in 1977.

Two years later, in 1979, Harris switched positions and became the U.S. Secretary of Health, Education and Welfare, a position that she held until 1982. These two cabinet positions enabled Harris to battle entrenched racism and address social issues, such as housing discrimination that plagued the black community.

After leaving the Cabinet, in 1982, Harris unsuccessfully ran for mayor of Washington, D.C. against Marion Barry. In 1983, she joined the George Washington University faculty before dying of lung cancer on March 23, 1985.

HASTIE, WILLIAM HENRY (November 17, 1904-April 14, 1977), Attorney, Politician, Jurist, was born in Knoxville, Tennessee, received a BA from Amherst College, where he finished first in his class, and then received a law degree (1930) from Harvard, becoming the second African American to serve on the Harvard Law Review. He then taught at Howard University Law School, where he worked with his friend, Charles Hamilton Houston, and his student, Thurgood Marshall, among others, to develop legal challenges to segregation. In private practice, as part of the law firm Houston, Houston, and Hastie, he argued a number of civil rights cases.

In 1933, Hastie was appointed Assistant Solicitor in the Department of the Interior by President Franklin Roosevelt, and in 1937 Roosevelt appointed him judge of the Federal District Court in the Virgin Islands, making him the country's first African-American federal magistrate. He left that position in 1939 to become Dean of Howard's Law School. In 1941 Hastie became an aide to Secretary of War Henry L. Stimson, and worked to reform the military's segregationist policies. But Hastie resigned from that position in 1943 to protest the military's entrenched "reactionary policies and discriminatory practices."

In 1946, Hastie became the first African-American governor of the Virgin Islands, and in 1949 President Harry Truman appointed him judge of the Third United States Circuit Court of Appeals, making him the first African American to be appointed as a federal circuit judge.

Hastie entered government service during the early years of President Franklin Roosevelt's New Deal as an assistant solicitor, or lawyer, in the U.S. Department of the Interior, His historic nomination for a District Court judgeship was approved by the U.S. Senate despite strong opposition from some southerners. They considered him a "leftist," mostly because he supported civil rights activities. Among those who favored his nomination, however, were the NAACP (which later awarded him the Spingarn Medal for his "distinguished career as jurist and an uncompromising champion of equal justice") and influential whites at the Harvard Law School.

After completing his two-year term in the Virgin Islands, Hastie headed the Howard University Law School from 1939 until 1946. During part of this same period, he also served in President Franklin Roosevelt's "Black Cabinet" as a civilian aide to the Secretary of War. He eventually resigned from this job in protest against the War Department's failure to act against segregation in the Air Force.

HAYES, CHARLES ARTHUR (February 17, 1918-April 8, 1997), Labor Leader, Politician, was born in Cairo, Illinois. He graduated from Cairo's Sumner School in 1935. While working in Cairo as a machine operator, he helped organize Local 1424 of the United Brotherhood of Carpenters and Joiners of America.

Hayes became an important labor leader after being elected president of Carpenters Local 1424 in 1940. After leaving this position in 1942, he became chairman of the grievance committee for the United Packinghouse Workers of America UPWA (1943-1949); then field representative (1949-1954), and finally district director, District No. 1, UPWA (1954-1968). In 1968, he was elected International Vice President of the Amalgamated Meat Cutters Union. From 1979 until his retirement in 1983, he was also vice president and director of Region 12 of the United

Food and Commercial Workers International Union. Hayes also became an international vice president of the Illinois State AFL-CIO, a vice president of Operation PUSH and a member of the executive board of the Chicago Urban League.

After Harold Washington resigned from the House in April 1983, to run for mayor of Chicago, Hayes defeated 14 opponents in a special primary and then went on in August to win the general election for the right to represent Illinois' first Congressional District (which covers much of south central Chicago). After being sworn into office on September 12, 1983, he was appointed to the Education and Labor and the Small Business Committees.

Hayes' interests in the Congress included economic security and education. In the 100th Congress (1988), he introduced an omnibus Economic Bill of Rights for all Americans that was designed to improve the nation's quality of life. In addition, he supported measures to assist educational agencies to fight school drop-out problems.

As a member of the House Minimum Wage Task Force, Hayes was instrumental in the passage of a bill that would raise the minimum wage from $3.35 per hour to $5.05 by 1991. President George Bush, however, opposed the proposed large increase in the minimum wage. Nevertheless Hayes was the only member of Congress to attain "a 100% lifetime voting record on issues important to labor."

After Hayes' almost four terms in the House, Chicago voters turned to a younger, more "liberal" candidate, former Black Panther and city Alderman Bobby Rush, who defeated the incumbent Congressman in 1991.

HENRY, AARON (July 2, 1922-May 19, 1997), Civil/Human Rights Leader, state legislator, was born in Dublin, Mississippi, to Edd, a sharecropper, and Mattie Logan Henry. He earned a B.A. degree from Xavier University (Louisiana). After leaving college, Henry opened a pharmacy in Clarksdale, Mississippi in 1950. Four years later, he began his civil rights career as a member of the NAACP.

As the Civil Rights Movement spread in the 1950s, Henry founded the Council of Federated Organizations (COFO), a coordinating group for the various civil rights organizations in Mississippi. Five years later he was elected President of the Mississippi State NAACP. In this capacity, he was arrested as a Freedom Rider in 1961; organized a racial boycott of merchants in Clarksdale, Mississippi the same year; and helped found the Mississippi Freedom Democratic Party (MFDP) in 1964. The year before when COFO staged a mock election, since so many blacks were denied the right to participate in the official political process of the state, Henry was elected "governor of Mississippi." Almost 80,000 blacks, nearly three times as many as were officially registered, at the time, participated in the mock election.

When the MFDP challenged the regular Mississippi delegation at the 1964 Democratic National Convention, Henry, as an "at large delegate," was a leader of the challenging group. Then, in 1965, he helped to found the Loyalist Democratic Party of Mississippi and chaired its delegation to the National Democratic Conventions in 1968 and 1972. Once the rival Mississippi delegations were united, as a bi-racial group in 1976, Henry was the co-chair of the state's delegates. He capped his political career with elections to the Mississippi House of Representatives, first in 1982, and subsequently until 1996. This feat was made possible only after Henry filed a lawsuit which resulted in redistricting of state legislative districts, which enhanced the chances for election of black candidates.

HENDERSON, VIVIAN (February 10, 1923-January 28, 1976), Educator, a native of Bristol, Virginia, was born on February 10, 1923. He received a bachelor's degree from North Carolina College in Durham (later North Carolina Central University), and M.A. and Ph.D. degrees in economics from the University of Iowa. In 1948, Henderson began his teaching career in Texas at Prairie View A & M College, but returned to his alma mater, North Carolina College, the following year as a professor of economics. In 1952, Henderson moved to a similar position at Fisk University in Tennessee where he eventually became chairman of the Department of Economics. Henderson was named president of Clark College in 1965.

In addition to his roles as a teacher and an administrator, Henderson achieved distinction as one of the nation's most foremost African-American scholars in economics. He was the author of *The Economic Status of Negroes* (1963), co-author of *The Advancing South: Manpower Prospects and Problems* (1959), and contributing author of *Principles of Economics* (1959). He also contributed to *Race, Regions and Jobs*, edited by Arthur Ross and Herbert Hill in 1967. His work, according to the *Atlanta Journal*, "is considered to have had an important impact in convincing industry and business of the buying power of the black American community."

Outside the academic world, Henderson was a member of the boards of directors of the Atlanta Community Chest (later the United Way), the Atlanta chapter of the American Civil Liberties Union, the Atlanta Urban League, the Ford Foundation, the National Sharecroppers Fund, the Institute for Services to Education, the Martin Luther King, Jr. Center for Non-Violent Social Change, and the Voter Education, and the Voter Education Project (VEP), among others. He was also chairman of the board of the Southern Regional Council (SRC) and chairman of the Georgia advisory committee of the U.S. Commission on Civil Rights (CCR).

Henderson's governmental activities included serving as a member of the advisory committee of the Atlanta Charter Commission, co-chairman for education of the Georgia Goals Commission, advisor to former President Lyndon Johnson, and member of the Manpower Advisory Committee of the U.S. Department of Labor.

Former Atlanta Mayor Ivan Allen, Jr., called Henderson's death in 1976 "a great loss to the city. . . . He left a vital and lasting impact. . . ." Atlanta Mayor Maynard H. Jackson added that the educator was a man "never too busy to accept the call to serve."

HOLLOWELL, DONALD LEE (December 19, 1917-December 27, 2004), Attorney, government official, civil/human rights activist, was born in Wichita, Kansas. He was the son of Harrison Hannibal and Ocenie Bernice (Davis) Hollowell. He received the

B.A. degree magna cum laude in Sociology and English from Lane College (Jackson, Tennessee) in 1947. He entered Loyola University Law School (Chicago) and received the J.D. degree in 1951. In 1942 he was married to Louise Evangeline Thornton. Attorney Hollowell was admitted to the Georgia Bar in 1952 and practiced law in Atlanta from 1952 to 1966. His career had been one of remarkable accomplishments and achievements in spite of an initial life of poverty during the Depression. As a boy growing up in Kansas he had worked since the age of five to help his family. Because of the poverty he experienced during the Depression, Hollowell dropped out of high school to join the Army. While in the Army he was stationed in the South and was exposed to the injustices of segregation. This experience served as an incentive for him to return to the region as a lawyer prepared to fight civil rights. Hollowell once stated, that he "...felt the need for there to be lawyers who were able to work at the elimination of segregation," and "I knew the South could be a fine section of the country in which to live if it could eliminate the vestiges of segregation."

Hollowell became known as "Mr. Civil Rights" in Atlanta because of his valiant fight to end the "vestiges of segregation." In the early 1950s Hollowell was the attorney in the unsuccessful suit of Horace Ward to enter the University of Georgia Law School. Horace Ward eventually became a judge of a United States District Court. Hollowell also represented Martin Luther King, Jr. after his arrests during the civil rights movement in the early 1960s and was chief counsel in the Atlanta city bus desegregation case in 1959. He was a participating attorney in the suits that desegregated the Atlanta Airport in 1957 and the Fulton County Courthouse in 1961.

In 1963, President John F. Kennedy invited attorney Hollowell and two other black lawyers from Atlanta, along with a group of national bar leaders, to meet with him at the White House to discuss the nation's civil rights problems. During this time President Kennedy had asked for an end to racial demonstrations that could provoke violence while civil rights legislation was under consideration by Congress. In recognition of his many outstanding contributions in the area of civil rights, Hollowell was appointed to head the Atlanta regional office of the Equal Employment Opportunity Commission (EEOC) in 1966 by President Lyndon B. Johnson.

In addition to his work as a civil rights attorney and activist, Hollowell had served the community in many capacities and had received awards for his service. He was a member of the boards of trustees of Spelman College, of the Interdenominational Theological Center, and of the Atlanta University Center. He had served as Chairman of the Fulton County (GA) Democratic Clubs and a member of the executive committee of the National Conference of Christians and Jews. He was also a member of the national and Atlanta Bar associations, Gate City Bar Association, State Bar of Georgia and the Federal Bar Association.

Among the many prestigious awards Hollowell received during his lifetime were Lawyer of the Year, NAACP, 1965; Civil Rights Award, Council on Human Relations, 1966; Civil Liberties Award, A.C.L.U., 1967; 750 Award, WSB Radio, 1967 and 1970; Equal Opportunity Day Award Atlanta Urban League, 1969; Unsung Hero Award, S.E. Region NAACP, 1973; Charles Houston Alumni Award, Harvard Law School, 1974; and he was decorated with the Bronze Star while serving in the United States military.

In 1986 Hollowell was selected as one of three Black Georgians of the Year by the State Committee on the Life and History of Black Georgians. In 1993 the Black Law Students Association of Loyola University Chicago School of Law established the Donald L. Hollowell Distinguished Service Award to honor African American alumni who had demonstrated excellence in the practice of law and a commitment to community service.

And for his lifetime of achievement and dedication to civil rights, the Emory University Law School established a professorship in his name and the city of Atlanta named a street after him. After his death Hollowell's undergraduate alma mater, Lane College, announced plans to name its library in his honor.

HOLMAN, M. CARL (June 27, 1919-August 9, 1988), Educator, civil/human rights leader, was born in Minta City, Mississippi, the son of Moses and Mamie (Durham) Holman. He graduated magna cum laude from Lincoln University in 1942; received an M.A. from the University of Chicago in 1944 and an M.F.A. degree from Yale University in 1954.

Holman was on the faculty in English at Clark College (Georgia) when he became chairman of the press and public city committee for the Atlanta NAACP (1955-1960). In 1960, when students began demonstrations at lunch counters and other public facilities in Atlanta, Holman became one of their principal advisors and a liaison with black adult community leaders. He was also a founder and editor of the Atlanta *Inquirer* newspaper which was established as the voice "of the student sit-in movement."

In 1967, Holman became vice president for programs of the National Urban Coalition, a Washington, D.C. based organization dedicated to welding together alliances of "forces to free up the economic and social potential" of Americans who live in towns and cities. Four years later, he became president of the Coalition and is generally credited with making the group a nationally recognized entity in the civil and human rights movements.

Holman had a special interest in promoting the educational progress of disadvantaged youth. A major facet of the Coalition's program was his "Say Yes to a Youngster's Future" concept. He advocated "dual literacy," which equated the importance of educating minority and female youth in mathematics, science, and technology with reading and writing. He became convinced that America's future competitiveness and productivity in the world would eventually rest in the hands of its urban minorities, and that they must be prepared for their responsibilities in the 21st Century.

Holman was also a member of the executive committee of the D.C. Board of Higher Education (1968-1972), a member of the President's Commission on White House Fellows, and a founder of TransAfrica, a Pan-Africanist political lobby. He won the Belvins Davis Playwriting Award from Yale University in 1954 and was a John Hay Whitney fellow in 1952. In 1977, he received a citation for Public Service from the University of Chicago Alumni Association, and in 1981 was the recipient of Equal

Opportunity Day Award from the National Urban League and a Distinguished Service Award from the National Conference of Social Welfare.

HUGHES, (JAMES) LANGSTON (February 1, 1902 -May 22, 1967), Author, columnist, was born in Joplin, Missouri, the son of James Nathaniel and Carrie Mercer (Langston) Hughes. His maternal grandfather was Charles Langston, an Ohio abolitionist, and half brother of Reconstruction congressman John Mercer Langston. After Hughes' birth his family was constantly on the move, stopping in such places as Buffalo, New York; Cleveland, Ohio; Colorado Springs, Colorado; and Kansas City, Lawrence, and Topeka, Kansas. By 1914, the parents had separated and Langston soon settled with his mother and stepfather in Lincoln, Illinois. He read his first poem, as "class poet," at the graduation exercises for the Lincoln grammar school in 1916; after which the family moved back to Cleveland. Hughes graduated from Central High School in Cleveland as editor of the class yearbook.

In 1921, Hughes accompanied his stepfather, Homer Clarke, to Mexico, and while there taught English in two Mexican schools; published a piece of prose, "Mexican Games," in the *Brownies Book*, as well as his classic, "The Negro Speaks of Rivers" in *The Crisis*. After returning to the United States, in the same year, he enrolled at Columbia University, but remained there for only one year.

He left Columbia to work and to travel. As a mess steward he was able to travel to Africa, the Azores, the Canary Islands, Genoa, and Paris. Meanwhile, he continued to write prize-winning poetry. In 1926, after returning to the United States, he entered Lincoln University of Pennsylvania, and published his first volume of poems, *The Weary Blues,* the same year.

In the 1930s, Hughes traveled extensively in the American South and West, and abroad to Haiti, the Soviet Union, and Spain. In 1937 he reported on the Spanish Civil War for the Baltimore *Afro-American.*

It was also in the 1930s that Hughes' political views became more radical, as he witnessed the effects of the Great Depression on so many people. Like many other intellectuals of the era, he came to see the Soviet Union as a symbol of hope for disadvantaged people and a model for human rights activists. While he never officially joined the American Communist Party, he did associate with various other "left-wing" groups, publications, and causes. But as his writings "took on a more radical tone," he found increasing difficulty getting his works published. Thus, after returning from Spain, in 1938, he realized that he would have to "tone down" his militancy in order to make a satisfactory living as a writer.

In 1943, Hughes began his famous "Simple" column for the *Chicago Defender*. Through "Simple" Hughes showed both the follies and pathos of black life and added often penetrating philosophical thought. He went to the South in 1947 to spend a year as visiting professor at Atlanta University; then returned to Chicago for a one-year appointment as poet-in-residence at the Laboratory School of the University of Chicago.

Although he was investigated by Senator Joseph McCarthy's Committee on Un-American Activities (HUAC) in the 1950s for "alleged leftist activities and writings," he was not charged and eventually lectured in Europe for the U.S. Information Agency, in 1965.

Hughes' poetry extended chronologically from the Harlem Renaissance of the 1920s to the Black Revolution of the 1960s. Because he wrote so prolifically about Harlem and its people he became known as the "Poet Laureate of Harlem." Perhaps, his best work, exemplary of his role as a social and protest commentator, called *Montage of a Dream Deferred* (1951) depicted Harlem on the verge of a violent, racial explosion.

Hughes has won many awards and honors for his writing, particularly his works on race relations, including the Spingarn Medal in 1960. The next year he was elected to the Natural Institute of Arts and Letters. The poet, who never married, died of congestive heart failure in New York.

HURLEY, RUBY (1909-1980), Civil/Human Rights Leader, a native of Washington, D.C., joined the NAACP after heading a committee "that sought to establish singer Marian Anderson's right to sing" at Constitution Hall in the capital in 1939. Because of white opposition, the famed opera star had to perform her concert at the Lincoln Memorial instead. In 1943, Hurley joined the NAACP as national youth director. In her eight years as youth director, the NAACP's membership tripled to 92 college chapters and 178 youth councils, enrolling 25,000 members.

Following her success in the youth division, Hurley was sent into the Deep South to coordinate membership campaigns and reactivate dormant branches. Out of these activities, the southeastern regional office, embracing the states of Alabama, Florida, Georgia, Mississippi, North Carolina, South Carolina, and Tennessee, was established. It became the largest region of the entire NAACP.

Hurley began her work in the South in 1951, the same year that a Christmas night bomb killed Harry T. Moore, the NAACP's Florida coordinator, and his wife, Harriett. Hate and violence, then, became her constant companions for the next twenty-seven years.

In an interview with the *Atlanta Constitution* on May 30, 1978, Hurley, who said she "never found time to sit down and worry about the obscene telephone calls, threats against her life, and 'never say die' pro-segregation politicians," recalled her life's work and commented on present and future trends. For example, Hurley recalled her attempts to gather information about the murder of black teenager Emmett Till in 1955 by posing as a field hand at several Mississippi plantations:" I must have been crazy. Young people talk about what they would have done if they were living during those times. . . . But they wouldn't have done anything. They couldn't have done any more than their elders. . . .

"I started worrying about black young people when I heard them saying they're black and they're proud. But just being black is no reason to be proud. . . . May feeling is that if you're going to be proud, you ought to have some knowledge (about the history of the black race) to build a basis to the proud. You won't have to go bragging that you're black and proud. . . .

"As long as there are black people and white people, there will be conflicts". . . .

"There is still a lot of work to be done, and I'm too old to do it. I can't keep up with the pace and maintain sanity anymore. I'll leave that to someone else."

On June 3, 1978 several hundred people gathered at a hotel in Atlanta to pay tribute to Hurley, on the occasion of her retirement after more than three decades of service to the nation's "oldest, largest, and most respected" civil rights organization.

JAMES, DANIEL "CHAPPIE", JR. (February 11, 1920- February 25, 1978), Airman, was born in Pensacola, Florida. He was the son of Daniel James, Sr., a lamp lighter, and Lillie Anna (Brown) James. His mother ran a private elementary and junior high school which enabled her to pay for James' college education. James earned a degree in physical education at the Tuskegee Institute in Tuskegee, Alabama in 1942. While at Tuskegee, he enrolled in a government program for black pilots and practiced stunt-flying in his spare time.

In 1943, James was commissioned into the U.S. Army Air Force and fought in the Pacific during World War II. He advanced through the ranks to flight leader of the 12th Fighter Bomber Squad in the Philippines in 1949. From 1950 to 1955, he was a fighter pilot at Otis Air Force Base in Korea. He became the commander of the 60th Fighter Interceptor Squad from 1955 to 1956. In 1956, he became a staff officer at the Office of Deputy Chief of Staff Operation Air Defense Division, a position that he served at until 1960.

From 1960 to 1964, he served as an assistant director of Operations, 81st Fighter Wing RAF; then as a departmental wing commander at Bentqaters, England. He became the director of Operations Training and departmental commander of Operations at Davis-Monthan Air Force Base in Arizona from 1964 to 1966. In 1966, he became the department commander of Operations at Ubon Royal Thai Air Base in Thailand. In 1967, he became the vice commander of the 33rd Tactical Fighter Wing. Two years later, he became commander of the 727th Flying Training Wing at Wheelus Air Base in Libya. On January 30, 1970, James was appointed Brigadier General in the U.S. Air Force. From 1970 to 1975, he served as the departmental spokesman for the Secretary of Defense, Public Affairs Division.

James became the vice commander of Military Airlift Command at Scott Air Force Base in Illinois from 1974 to 1975. On September 1, 1975, he became the first black man in the armed forces to receive a four star ranking. At the same time, he left the Pentagon job to assume the job of commander of North American Air Defense Command. In this role, he assumed operational control of all United States and Canadian air space defense forces, which included over 63,000 men around the world.

In 1977, Wallace and Wallace Enterprises built the General Daniel "Chappie" James Airmen and Industrial Museum in Tuskegee, Alabama, in his honor. James retired from the Air Force on February 1, 1978, after experiencing a heart attack in the fall of 1977. In the 1980s The General Daniel "Chappie" James Center for Aerospace Science and Health Education was built on Tuskegee Institute campus in Alabama in his honor. James will be remembered for not only his accomplishments, which included flying over 179 combat missions during the Korean and Vietnam wars, but also for his endeavors to help blacks in the military, which included an arrest, along with several black pilots, for staging a "sit-in" in an all-white club at Freeman Field in Seymour, Indiana.

JENKINS, ESAU (July 3, 1910-October 30, 1972), Civil/Human Rights Activist, educator, was born on Johns Island (Sea Islands), South Carolina. He left grammar school after the fourth grade, partially because his father needed him in the fields. He also left, because, in his words the schools were "not encouraging to go to". Shortly after this he went to Charleston, South Carolina and started working on a boat. Yet was still determined to get his education because he knew he could not do much on a fourth grade education. He would later attend four more years of school.

In 1930 Jenkins returned to Johns Island and begin farming for himself. He purchased a truck and began transporting his crop to the market in Charleston. Most of the vegetable stores were owned by Greeks. As a result, Jenkins attended school for two years to study the Greek language. As his trucking business grew, he began to invest in other business endeavors. He invested in a fruit store, a motel (J. and P. Motel), and in 1950 he opened the Atlantic Beach Business.

During the 1940s the Sea Islanders were characterized by sub-standard housing and bad health conditions. Many people suffered from diseases associated with malnutrition and poverty. Education was highly inadequate and as a result, residents were unable to vote because South Carolina law required that registered voters be able to read and understand the Constitution.

Confronted with these problems, Jenkins decided to start his own programs designed to improve the lives of his fellow blacks. His first project consisted of buying a 1945 bus to transport children to the city to attend school. He also began organizing a drive for a black high school. As a result of this effort, in 1953, the Haut Gap High School was opened on the Sea Island. In 1948, he bought busses to transport blacks that commuted to Charleston to work. While on these busses Jenkins, and others, would begin teaching adults how to read the part of the Constitution they would have to read before becoming registered voters.

In an effort to pay bail for blacks who were jailed for insignificant charges, Jenkins organized the Progressive Club which met in the Moving Star Hall every third Sunday at a cost of 25 cents. The Progressive Club was later moved to a larger building and called the Sea Island Center to serve the people of James and Wadmalaw as well as Johns Island. In the mid-1950s, the Progressive Club would become the basis for citizenship schools and voter registration campaigns.

In 1954, Septima Clark and Anna Kelly, local civil and human rights leaders, urged Jenkins to attend the Highlander Folk School's United Nations Workshop on race relations. After attending the workshop, Jenkins returned home and in 1957 founded the Sea Island School for the purpose of teaching adults to read and become citizens. As a result of this effort, between the years of 1956 and 1960, voter registration more than tripled on the Sea Islands. In 1956, in an effort to show blacks they could run for public office, Jenkins ran for Trustee of the County School board. He finished third in the balloting. He later stated that he did not run because he expected to win, but he ran because he wanted blacks to know that they could run for any office their qualifications permitted.

During the 1960s, Jenkins continued to develop programs in the areas of his deepest concerns: voter education, health care, and improving the general social and economic conditions of his people. In 1966 he founded a Credit Union that was designed to loan money to black people at low interest rates.

In the late 1950s and early 1960s Jenkins also organized programs designed to alleviate some of the misery associated with migrant families in the Sea Islands. He helped create the Rural Mission, an organization that provided daycare and health programs for migrant families. At the time of his death in 1972, Jenkins and the Rural Mission began the planning stages for what became the Sea Island Comprehensive Health Center, a Nursing Home and a low-income housing project. The present day Sea Island Comprehensive Center is a living monument to the life's work of Esau Jenkins.

JOHNSON, CHARLES SPURGEON (1893-1956) Educator, author, was born in Bristol, Tennessee and educated at Virginia Union University and the University of Chicago. On September 1, 1947, Charles Spurgeon Johnson began his administration as president of Fisk University, becoming the first black man to head the Nashville institution. 1893 and was. From 1917 to 1919 he directed the division of research for the Chicago Urban League while also investigating black migration for the Carnegie Foundation. Johnson served on the Chicago Committee on Race Relations from 1923 to 1929. When Johnson assumed the presidency of Fisk University, he had already become a sociologist and writer. He founded and edited the National Urban League's house organ, *Opportunity* magazine, in 1923 and sponsored literary contests for young black writers during the Harlem Renaissance. Johnson's major published works include *Shadow of the Plantation* (1934), *The Collapse of Cotton Tenancy* (1934), *The Negro College Graduate* (1938), and *Growing Up in the Black Belt* (1941).

JOHNSON, JOHN HAROLD (January 19, 1918-2005), Publisher, was born in Arkansas City, Arkansas, the son of Leroy, a sawmill worker, and Gertrude Jenkins Johnson, a domestic worker. Young John's father was killed in a mill accident when he was only six years of age. His mother, subsequently, married another mill worker. When John was 15, his mother took him to the Chicago World's Fair and the family decided to remain in the city. The immigrants had to go on welfare for more than a year during the Great Depression of the 1930s, while both stepfather and son sought work. Both were hired by New Deal work relief programs. Nevertheless, Johnson became an honors student at DuSable High School as well as a debater, editor of both the school newspaper and yearbook, and both class and student body president.

During his senior year in high school, Johnson spoke at a banquet honoring black seniors which was sponsored annually by the Chicago Urban League. One of the persons who heard him speak was Harry Pace, president of the great Supreme Liberty Life Insurance Company of Chicago, one of the nation's largest black businesses, at the time. Pace, who had given the principal address at the dinner, was so impressed by the performance of young Johnson that he hired him as a part-time office boy, and assisted his part-time enrollment at the University of Chicago. After being promoted to Pace's assistant in 1938, Johnson completed his studies at night, at the School of Commerce of Northwestern University's Chicago branch.

Since, in college, Johnson had majored in both business and journalism, one of his duties at Supreme Liberty was the preparation of a daily digest of news about black Americans. After he noted interest, even outside of the company, in his news summary, Johnson struck upon an idea. With his mother's furniture as collateral, he borrowed $500, in 1942, and produced the first edition of his new magazine, *Negro Digest,* in November of that year. The monthly periodical quickly moved from a race digest to features, and within a year had grown from 5,000 subscribers to 10,000 the next year.

On the heels of this success, in November 1945, Johnson began a new venture, a picture magazine called *Ebony.* This publication was, for the most part, an imitation of the popular, mainstream *Life* magazine, but featured black life and history, rather than white ones. *Ebony* served as the first introduction to the lifestyles of middle class Black America for many whites as well as blacks. The magazine was an overnight success, selling 25,000 copies on its first run. Within two decades, it became one of the nation's leading popular periodicals, with more than one million copies in circulation each year, and annual advertising revenues in excess of $7 million.

Following *Ebony,* Johnson published other periodicals, including the popular pocket-sized news magazine, *Jet.* He also opened a publishing wing of the company. Building upon these successes, Johnson acquired other business interests including a controlling one in the Supreme Life Insurance Company. He also became chairman of the company's board of directors.

In 1995, *Ebony* South Africa. By this time, Johnson was one of the nation's wealthiest and most influential African American businessmen.

Johnson's recognitions include the Russwunn Award from the National Newspaper Publishers Association (1966); the NAACP's Spingam Medal (1966); Columbia University Journalism Award (1974); and the Chicago Business Hall of Fame (1983), among others. Several American colleges and universities have awarded him honorary degrees, including Benedict College (South Carolina), Morehouse College (Georgia); Northwestern University and Syracuse University.

JOHNSON, MORDECAI WYATT (January 12, 1890- September 10, 1976) Educator, was born in Paris, Tennessee. He was educated at Morehouse College, the University of Chicago, the Rochester Theological Seminary, and Howard University. Upon receipt of a Master of Sacred Theology degree from Harvard in 1923, Johnson attracted national attention for a speech titled *"The Faith of the American Negro."* After teaching at Morehouse and Howard, he took post as the first black president of Howard.

When Johnson assumed the presidency, in 1926, Howard consisted of a cluster of unaccredited departments, a situation that Johnson sought to improve. In 1928 Johnson secured a congressional allocation of annual appropriations for the support and development of Howard University. When Johnson retired, Howard had ten schools and colleges; had an enrollment of more than six thousand students; and its School of Medicine was producing about half of the black doctors in the United States. Johnson was succeeded by law professor and civil rights attorney James M. Nabrit, Jr.

JULIAN, PERCY LAVON (April 11, 1899-April 19, 1975), Scientist, was born in Montgomery, Alabama Percy Julian, black research chemist in the area of human reproduction, was honored in New York by the NAACP. Julian, the son of a Montgomery, Alabama, railway clerk, graduated from DePauw University and was a researcher at Harvard University and the University of Vienna. He taught at Howard and DePauw before becoming an industrial chemist in Chicago. He later established his own company, Julian Laboratories, which manufactured soya products, hormones, and pharmaceuticals.

In 1935 Julian developed physostigmine, a drug that is used in the treatment of glaucoma. While working for the Glidden Company, Julian worked with the soya bean, developing a protein that helped to develop AeroFoam a fire extinguisher used by the Navy. After leaving Glidden, he synthesized the female hormone progesterone, and the male hormone testosterone by extracting sterols from soybean oil. His most famous exploit however, is his synthesis of cortisone which is used to treat arthritis and other inflammatory diseases.

KENNY, BILL (d. March 24, 1978) Entertainer. Bill Kenny, whose tenor voice helped make the original Ink Spots one of the world's best known singing groups in the 1940s.

Kenny, together with Charles Fuqua, Orville Jones, and Ivory Watson, formed the Ink Spots in 1939. He was the last survivor of the group and continued performing almost up to his death.

KING, ALBERTA WILLIAMS (d.1974), Churchwoman, Civil

Human Rights Activist (Mrs. Martin Luther King, Sr)., was born Alberta Williams, the daughter of the Reverend Adam Daniel Williams, one of the founders of the historic Ebenezer Baptist Church. Her husband, a powerful religious and political figure in Atlanta for more than twenty-five years, succeeded Williams as pastor of the church. Dr. Martin Luther King, Jr., was serving as co-pastor of the church at the time of his assassination in April 1968. Another son, the Reverend A. D. Williams King, drowned in 1969.While "Mother King" was seen in only a few of her son's most prominent civil rights protests, she provided significant support and family stability "behind the scenes."

On June 30, 1974 a young black man interrupted the worship services at Ebenezer Baptist Church in Atlanta with gunfire, killing church deacon Edward Boykin and Alberta King, mother of slain civil rights leader Martin Luther King, Jr. Another worshipper, Mrs. Jimmie Mitchel, was wounded. The alleged gunman, identified as Marcus Chenault of Dayton, Ohio, was subdued by other worshippers, including Derek King, grandson of the slain woman. Chenault told Atlanta police that he had orders from "his god" to go to Atlanta and kill the Reverend Martin Luther King, Sr., father of the Nobel Prize-winning civil rights leader. Instead, he allegedly fired upon Mrs. King and others as the sixty-nine-year-old matriarch of the King family played "The Lord's Prayer" on a church organ.

The accused slayer was described as an Ohio State University dropout who became deeply involved in a small religious cult that claimed that blacks were descendants of the original Jews. Chenault was said to have taken the name "Servant Jacob" and discarded his original name. The cult reportedly believed that black Christian ministers deceived African Americans and hence were the cause of many of the social and economic woes of blacks.

Reacting to the tragedy, Atlanta Mayor Maynard H. Jackson compared the deaths in the King family to those of the family of the late President John F. Kennedy, stating: "Never have I seen a family suffer so much for so long and yet give such brilliant leadership."

KING, MARTIN LUTHER, SR (December 19, 1899- November 11, 1984), Clergyman, Civil/Human Rights Leader, was born Michael Luther King to a sharecropper and cleaning woman in Stockhridge. Georgia. (He changed his name in 1934 to honor the famous German religious scholar Martin Luther.) At age seventeen, he moved to Atlanta and became a minister. He also attended Morehouse College. King later succeeded his father-in-law. Adam Daniel Williams as pastor of the Ebenezer Baptist Church, one of Atlanta's largest black churches. He remained as pastor or co-pastor of the church until 1975.

Even before King became pastor of Ebenezer Baptist Church, he had become active in civic, political, and racial affairs in Atlanta. In 1924, for example, he was one of the black leaders who successfully lobbied for the construction of the Booker T. Washington High School, the first secondary school for blacks in the city. In 1936, King was a leader in a voting rights march to Atlanta's City Hall. And in 1961, he participated in protests against segregated cafeterias in the city and helped negotiate an agreement for their desegregation. King was also a director of Citizens Trust Company, the city's leading black bank.

He served as a member of the board of directors or trustees of SCLC, Morehouse College. The Morehouse School of Religion, and the Carrie Steele-Pitts Orphans Home. In 1972, the Atlanta chapter of the National Conference of Christians and Jews named him "Clergyman of the Year." Although King lost his famous son to an assassin's bullet in 1968 and his wife to another assassin in 1974. He continued to insist, "I don't hate. There is no time for that, and no reason either. Nothing that a man does takes him lower than when he allows himself to fall so low as to hate anyone."

KING, MARTIN LUTHER, JR. (January 15, 1929-April 4, 1968), Civil/Human Rights Leader, organization executive, minister, was born Michael Luther King, Jr. in Atlanta, Georgia, the son of Michael (Martin) Luther, Sr. and Alberta (Williams) King. He received the B.A. degree in Sociology from Morehouse College (Georgia) in 1948. He then entered Crozier Theological

Seminary in Chester, Pennsylvania, where he was awarded the Masters degree in 1951. After completing his dissertation in 1955, while serving as the pastor of the Dexter Avenue Baptist Church in Montgomery, Alabama, King received the Ph.D. degree from Boston University in that same year.

King, Jr. was "called" to the ministry in 1947 while still a student at Morehouse College. He accepted the pastorate of the Dexter Avenue Baptist Church in 1954; and in 1955, when Mrs. Rosa Parks' refusal to relinquish her seat on a Montgomery bus to a white man escalated the indigenous Civil Rights Movement in that southern Alabama city, King emerged as the leader of the struggle there. By the end of 1956, when the buses in Montgomery were desegregated, the Movement changed to a larger arena. King and other Christian leaders organized the Southern Christian Leadership Conference (SCLC) with headquarters in Atlanta.

From 1957 until his assassination in 1968, King was also the co-pastor of the Ebenezer Baptist Church in Atlanta, where his father was the senior pastor. As the civil rights movements across the South intensified and were aggregated into a national movement, so did King's fame spread and his influence increase. While in a Harlem department store to promote his first book, *Stride Toward Freedom*, in October 1958, he was stabbed by a demented black woman. King recovered from his injuries and continued his crusade for justice and dignity for African Americans.

Also, in 1964, Congress passed the first major Civil Rights Bill of this century. The bill was signed into law by President Lyndon B. Johnson in July of that year. Then, in the spring of 1965, King led a march from Selma to Montgomery (the capital city of Alabama) to protest the disenfranchisement of African Americans. On their first attempt to march to Montgomery, when King was absent, the protestors were brutally driven back by Alabama state police, as they attempted to cross the Edmund Pettus Bridge in Selma. After federal intervention, with the National Guard, the March took place from March 21-25, 1965. At the conclusion of the March, King gave a rousing speech on the steps of the statehouse.

After 1965 King attempted to take his nonviolent brand of activism to the urban centers of the North, but was not always well received. He was stoned while participating in civil rights demonstrations in the Chicago campaign.

In April 1967 King publicly expressed his opposition to the War in Vietnam and was criticized by government officials and many of his supporters. On April 4, 1968, while in Memphis, Tennessee to support striking garbage workers, Martin Luther King, Jr. was assassinated on a balcony of the Lorraine Motel.

LA FONTANT-MANKARIOUS, JEWEL STRADFORD (December 3, 1922-May 31, 1994), United Nations Representative, Political Leader, was born in Chicago, Illinois, the daughter of Attorney C. Francis and Adda (Carter) Stradford. Attorney La Fontant-Mankarious was an active, second generation Republican, who was influential in the struggles for equality and justice in Chicago and in Illinois.

La Fontant-Mankarious received her B.A. degree from Oberlin College (Ohio) in 1943. She, then, entered the University of Chicago Law School, where she was awarded the J.D. degree in 1946.

La Fontant-Mankarious served as a member of the United States delegation to the 27th session (1972) of the United Nations. She was Deputy Solicitor General of the U.S. Department of Justice (1973-1975) and chaired the Federal Women's Program for the Department under Solicitor General, Robert C. Bork. She was a very active and influential member of the Republican Party at the city, state, and national levels. La Fontant-Mankarious was also an ambassador-at-large for the U.S. State Department, and she is also U.S. Coordinator for Refugee Affairs.

La Fontant-Mankarious was a Senior Partner in Vedder, Price, Kaufman, Klammholz. She served on a number of Corporate boards: Jewel Co., Inc.; Hanes, Inc.; Foote, Cone and Belding; TWC-TWA; Continental Illinois Bank and Trust Co.; Pantry Pride, Inc.; Bendix Corporation; and the Revlon Group. She is a member of the Alumni Board of the University of Chicago Law School. She has also served as Secretary of the National Bar Association (1956-1961), the Chicago Bar Association (1962-1964), and is a Trustee of Lake Forest College (Illinois).

La Fontant-Mankarious' honors include an honorary Doctor of Laws degree from Roosevelt College (Illinois), 1990; an honorary Doctor of Humane Letters from Central State University (Ohio), 1990; and a Citation for Public Service from the University of Chicago, 1990.

LITTLE, MALCOLM (MALCOLM X; EL-HAJI MALIK EL-SHABAZZ) (May 19, 1925-February 21, 1965), Nationalist Leader, clergyman, was born in Omaha, Nebraska, the seventh of 11 children of the Reverend Earl Little, who was both a Baptist minister and an organizer for Marcus Garvey's Universal Negro Improvement Association (UNIA) and Louise (Norton) Little. The Reverend Mr. Little was allegedly murdered by Ku Klux Klansmen in Lansing, Michigan when Malcolm was only six years of age. Previously the family had been driven out of Omaha by "white terrorists," because of the Reverend Little's racial and nationalistic activities. With his family in disarray, young Malcolm dropped out of high school and drifted first to Boston, then to Harlem. He supported himself through numerous "hustles," including burglary, the illicit lottery, "pimping" and drug running. In 1946, he was apprehended and sentenced to eight to ten years in prison for burglary and larceny. He completed more than six years in a Massachusetts prison before being paroled in 1952.

While in prison, with his younger brother, Reginald, Malcolm converted to a sect, popular among young black inmates at the time, called the Lost-Found Nation of Islam. This sect, which was also known as the Black Muslims, led by Elijah Muhammad out of Chicago, Illinois, emerged as the principal rival to Martin Luther King, Jr.'s philosophy of racial leadership during the Civil Rights Movement of the 1960s. Whereas King espoused the principles of love for white oppressors and nonviolent resistance to racial oppression, Muhammad and the Muslims poured vitriolic hatred upon "white devils," renounced racial integration, and insisted on the right to self-defense.

Before his release from prison Little renounced his "slave"

surname, and substituted "X" in place of it. Shortly after his release, he became a Muslim minister. For almost a dozen years, because of his fiery oratory and charismatic appearance, he became the best known of all of the Black Muslim leaders in the country. Although he headed a Harlem mosque, he spoke to and organized temples all across the country. He is credited with increasing the national Muslim membership from under 500 converts to more than 10,000. He also spoke to many more thousands of Muslim sympathizers, college students, and other groups in the United States, the Middle East, and Africa.

Partially as a result of Malcolm's great popularity, divisions erupted between him and Muhammad. So when Malcolm publicly referred to the assassination of President John F. Kennedy in November 1963 as an example of "chickens coming home to roost," the Muslim leader took the occasion to suspend him. After three months of suspension, Malcolm left the Nation of Islam in March 1964.

After leaving the Black Muslims, Malcolm founded two groups of his own, a church, the Muslim Mosque of Harlem, and a political unit, the Organization of Afro-American Unity (OAU). The OAU had chapters in several American cities as well as Africa and Europe. One of Malcolm's goals for the OAU was to move the American Civil Rights Movement from a national protest to an international issue. He tried to get mainstream leaders of the Movement, with whom he often clashed, and African political leaders to embrace the concept that the United States had violated the "human rights" of black Americans and, hence, should be held accountable in the United Nations. Neither group, however, endorsed Malcolm's goals.

Indeed, toward the end of his life, Malcolm seemed isolated from the left, the middle, and the right. He was bitterly denounced as "an apostle of hate and violence" by U.S. and state government officials, the press, and mainstream black leaders; and he was allegedly threatened by white racists, as well as supporters of Elijah Muhammad. On February 21, 1965, while he was addressing a rally in the Audubon Ballroom in New York City, he was shot to death. Three men, identified as Black Muslims, were convicted of the murder in March 1966.

Although Malcolm seldom received public acclaim in his lifetime, several schools and colleges, including a public institution in Harlem, were named for him after his death. And his wife Betty and his six daughters have since won respect among national civil rights leaders, including the widow of Martin Luther King, Jr., Coretta Scott.

LITTLE ROCK NINE On September 24-25, after unsuccessfully trying to persuade Arkansas governor Orval Faubus to give up his efforts to block desegregation of Central High School in Little Rock, President Dwight Eisenhower ordered federal troops into the city to stop people from interfering with federal court orders. The Little Rock incident was the most serious clash between a state government and the federal government in modern times. Faubus and a mob of whites backed down in the face of military power and finally allowed nine black children to begin attending a desegregated high school on September 25. "The Little Rock Nine" were Minnijean Brown,Elizabeth Eckford, Ernest Green, Calotta Walls, Gloria Ray, Thelma Mothershed, Melba Patillo, Terrence Roberts, and Jefferson Thomas.

LOOBY, Z. ALEXANDER (-March 24, 1972) Civil/Human Rights Leader, a NAACP attorney, was one of the first African Americans elected to the Nashville, Tennessee city council and served on that body between 1951 and 1971. On April 19, 1960, his Nashville home was destroyed by a dynamite bomb. Looby and his family escaped injury, but the bomb damaged several other homes in the neighborhood. It also blew out hundreds of windows at the nearby Meharry Medical College (a black school), where several students were injured by flying glass. Looby had served as the attorney for more than 100 college students arrested in Nashville sit-ins since demonstrations had begun in February, 1960. After the bombing, more than 2,000 blacks marched on the Nashville City Hall protesting the police's failure to stop the racial violence.

LYKE, JAMES PATTERSON (February 18, 1939-December

159

27, 1992), Clergyman, was born in Chicago, Illinois, the son of Ora Sneed Lyke. The family lived in a housing project in an impoverished area. His mother, a Baptist, sent him to a Catholic school after the fourth grade in order "to keep him out of trouble." After attending seminary, he taught at a Catholic high school in Ohio in 1968. Following the assassination of Martin Luther King, Jr. in 1968, Lyke asked to be sent to Memphis, Tennessee. Once assigned to Memphis, he became the first black Catholic priest regularly assigned to the state of Tennessee. He became deeply involved in civil rights activities in the area and introduced African American elements into the worship services of his largely black parish. Following a brief service in Memphis, his desire to return to an educational setting was rewarded with an appointment to serve as pastor and director of the Newman Center at Grambling State University in Louisiana. Lyke spent only two years in Grambling before Pope John Paul II appointed him auxiliary bishop of Cleveland, Ohio and vicar of the region.

Lyke had met Martin Luther King, Jr. before his death and warmly embraced King's campaigns for social justice. In Cleveland, he worked with the local unit of the Southern Christian Leadership Conference's (SCLC) Operation Breadbasket. He also coordinated efforts to have the diverse ethnic groups in the city to "live together and form communities together."

Bishop Lyke's compassionate and effective leadership style won him considerable respect from the Catholic hierarchy, generally, and black Catholics in particular. He was elected president of the national Black Catholic Caucus, where he coordinated the publication of *Lead me, Guide me*, the first African American Catholic hymnal. This project was a part of the effort, begun in the 1960s, to "blend black cultural elements and the Mass." Lyke wrote an introduction for the hymnal on "inculturation." While in Cleveland, he published a pastoral address entitled "Say Not I am Too Young" as a means of motivating area youth to service. He also helped to spearhead the creation of a Black Liturgy Subcommittee of the national Bishops' committee on the Liturgy and was a member of the administrative committee and the administrative board of the Committee for Pro-

Life Activities and director of the Sister Thea Bowman Foundation. Outside of the Church, Lyke was a member of the NAACP and the Southern Poverty Law Center. In May 1990, following a sexual scandal which drove Eugene A. Marino from his position as the first black Archbishop of Atlanta and the highest ranking clergyman in the Catholic Church in the United States, Lyke was selected to go to Atlanta with the title of apostolic administrator. All understood that he was to try to heal the wounds left in the wake of the Marino resignation.

After publicly forgiving Marino, Lyke proceeded "to restore morale, to heal, and to bring leadership" to the Archdiocese. Then after only a few weeks as administrator, the Pope elevated Lyke to the position of Archbishop of Atlanta. But fate, again, seemed to deal an ill hand to the quest to have a black Archbishop in Atlanta and to promote the Church's image among African Americans; for after only a few months in office, Lyke was diagnosed with terminal cancer.

LYLE, GEORGE, JR. (March 20, 1912-June 29, 1977), Journalist, was born in St. Louis, Missouri, but grew up in Philadelphia where he attended the public schools. He was the only son of George and Ethel (Hedgemon) Lyle, Sr. Family sources state that George, Sr. was the first black principal in Philadelphia and a charter member of Alpha Phi Alpha fraternity; Ethel Lyle was the first black English teacher in Philadelphia and a founder of Alpha Kappa Alpha sorority. George Lyle, Jr., received his B.S. from Hampton Institute in 1933 and did postgraduate study at the University of Pennsylvania, 1933-1934. In 1932 he competed in the Olympic Track and Field Tryouts, running in the 200 and 100-yard events against eventual Olympic medalist Eddie Tolan.

After a brief period teaching school in Shelby, North Carolina, Lyle began his journalistic career when he accepted a position with the *Afro-American Newspaper* in Baltimore, Maryland, 1934-1936. He then became managing editor of the *Philadelphia Tribune*, 1936-1942. During World War II Lyle enlisted in the U.S. Coast Guard. After the war he was a sportswriter for the *Philadelphia Record*, 1945-1947. When that paper folded, he moved to the *Philadelphia Inquirer*, 1947-1949. He was the first black to be on the staff of the *Philadelphia Bulletin*. In the late 1940s Lyle began to broadcast on radio. He did baseball games for the Philadelphia Stars of Black National League and interviewed Jackie Robinson the day after he signed with the Brooklyn Dodgers. Lyle worked for WDAS Radio and hosted a jazz program at WJMJ Radio, 1949-1950.

Lyle was a groundbreaker for blacks in sports journalism. His career marked a number of "firsts." He became the first black ring announcer for the Pennsylvania Athletic Commission when he announced the nationally televised fight between Kid Gavilan and Tiger Jones, an event he noted as a career highlight. In 1950 Lyle began a 20-year affiliation with WCAU Radio where his chief responsibility was as producer of the Philadelphia Eagles Football games. He was the first black to broadcast University of Pennsylvania games. Another career high mark for Lyle was producing those broadcasts in 1960 when the Eagles won the championship. Lyle was also the first black to broadcast for WHAT-FM, where he was sports director, 1959-1967. For a number of years Lyle was secretary of the Philadelphia Sports Writers Association.

In 1971 George Lyle went to Lincoln University as its Public Relations Director. He and Athletic Director Manny Rivero instituted the Lincoln University Scholastic Basketball Tournament for high school boys' teams. Lincoln students later presented him with a plaque for his leadership in communications. Lyle was described as creative, courtly, a "gentleman" and possessed of a ready wit. He died one day prior to his retirement in 1977.

MARSHALL, THURGOOD (July 2, 1902-January 24, 1993), Jurist, was born in Baltimore, Maryland to William C., a country club steward, and Norma A., a school teacher, Marshall. He received a B.A. degree from Lincoln University (Pennsylvania). After having been denied admission to the law school of the University of Maryland because of his race, he attended the Howard University Law School and became a protégé of the brilliant law professor, Charles Houston. Following his graduation in 1933, Marshall teamed with Houston and successfully sued the University of Maryland for discrimination against black students.

Marshall, then, moved to New York City and began his long career with the National Association for the Advancement of Colored People (NAACP), in 1936. Beginning as legal counsel, he worked his way up to chief counsel by 1940. In a career with the NAACP that spanned a quarter of a century, Marshall joined and then led a cadre of talented, mostly black, constitutional lawyers who crusaded against the legal underpinnings of segregation and discrimination in American life. They challenged and eventually overturned state sanctioned bias in schools, recreation, transportation, employment, and public accommodations. Their efforts reached their zenith in the early 1950s when they went before the United States Supreme Court with three cases challenging segregation in the public schools.

In preparing their arguments, the Marshall-led team used not only legal precedent, but sociological and psychological data to bolster their arguments that segregated education, even where physical facilities might be equal (as they rarely were) was unconstitutional. On May 17, 1954, after the Supreme Court consolidated the cases, under the title, *Brown v Board of Education* (of Topeka, Kansas), the High Court agreed that segregated schools "affected the hearts and minds" of black children "in a way unlikely ever to be undone." The *Brown* decision was the impetus for a widening attack on racial discrimination in America, which went beyond the courts into the streets, as direct action campaigns of civil disobedience, boycotts, marches, and other protests became commonplace, North as well as South. The actions and results were so profound that they constituted a new epoch in American history –the Era of Civil Rights.

With the *Brown* victory and many, many more achieved, Marshall agreed to accept an appointment from President John F. Kennedy to the U.S. Court of Appeals for the Second Circuit in 1961. Four years later, President Lyndon B. Johnson named him Solicitor General of the United States and, then, in 1969 elevated him to the United States Supreme Court –the first African American ever to sit on the nation's highest tribunal.

Marshall soon became a leader of what was, at first, a liberal to moderate majority on the Court. But, over the years, with the death or retirement of several justices and the appointment of more conservative jurists by Republican presidents, his view became an increasingly minority one. Yet he remained consistent in his championing of individual liberties and a staunch, even passionate, opposition to discrimination of any kind. He was also one of the judiciary's strongest supporters of affirmative action. Although, in deteriorating health for several years, Marshall remained on the Court, until 1991, trying to preserve the views and opinions that he had espoused since he was a law student at Howard University. But, saying that his body was "just falling apart" because of old age, he surrendered the seat two years before his death.

MAYS, BENJAMIN ELIJAH (August 1, 1894-March 28, 1984), Educator, Civil/Human Rights Leader, was born August 1, 1894, in Epworth, South Carolina. His parents were former slaves and tenant farmers. In 1928, Mays graduated with honors from Bates College in Lewiston, Maine. While attending graduate school at the University of Chicago, he held a variety of teaching jobs and also served as a Baptist minister. He received his doctorate degree from the University of Chicago in 1935.

Mays was dean of the School of Religion at Howard University from 1934 until 1940, at which time he became president of Morehouse College in Atlanta. The highly respected school was then facing some serious problems that threatened its future. The Depression had left it in financial trouble, and student enrollment had dropped after many young men decided to look for work in the booming wartime economy instead.

But through his skills as a speechmaker and fundraiser, May was eventually able to restore Morehouse's vitality and prestige. He expanded the programs that former president John Hope had begun, which enabled the college to produce an outstanding group of black business and professional men as well as civil rights leaders such as Martin Luther King, Jr.

Also like John Hope, Mays became known as a militant civil rights advocate. As he explained years later: "I was born a little stubborn on the race issue... I felt that no man had a right to look down on another man. Every man, whether he's on the right of you, the left of you, certainly in back of you—it makes no difference—is still a man." At the historic March on Washington in 1963, Mays led the opening prayer and gave a speech. Five years later, in an emotional eulogy at the funeral of Martin Luther King, Jr., he praised the slain civil rights leader and blamed his death on America's racist society.

Mays served on the NAACP board of directors and wrote hundreds of essays in magazines, newspapers, and scholarly journals condemning segregation and discrimination and pleading for racial justice and harmony. He wrote several books on the subject, too, including *A Gospel for Social Awakening* (1950), *Seeking to BE a Christian in Race Relations* (1957), *Disturbed About Man* (1969), and his autobiography, *Born to Rebel* (1971).

In 1969, two years after his retirement from Morehouse, Mays won a seat on the Atlanta Board of Education. The next year he was elected the group's first black president. He was re-elected to the position six times over the next twelve years.

In 1984, Mays was inducted into the South Carolina Hall of fame, at age eighty-nine. Since, at the time, Mays was hospitalized with pneumonia, the plaque recognizing his induction was presented to him in Atlanta by former president Jimmy carter. Carter, a longtime friend, called Mays "a credit to Georgia and South Carolina, he's a credit to the Southland and he's a credit to the Unites States of America and to the world." After receiving the award, Mays, himself, observed: "I was born a little stubborn on the race issue....I felt that no man had a right to look down on another man. Every man, whether he's on the right of you, the left of you, certainly in back of you—it makes no difference—is still a man."

In commenting on Mays's death in 1984, Charlie Moreland, president of the Morehouse College Alumni Association, remembered one of Mays's favorite quotations: "It must be born in mind that reaching your goal is not tragic. The tragedy lies in not having a goal to reach."

MCKISSICK, FLOYD B. (March 9, 1922-April 28, 1991),

Civil/Human Rights Leader, Jurist, was born in Asheville, North Carolina on March 9, 1922 to Ernest Boyce and Magnolia Ester (Thompson) McKissick. His concern with civil rights spanned his entire lifetime.

Ernest Boyce McKissick was a bellman at the Vanderbilt Hotel in Asheville. He emphasized education and said that there would only be one servant in the family and that was he. Floyd McKissick attended Morehouse College (Georgia), after having served in the U.S. Army during World War II, and graduated from North Carolina College in 1951. Then, he became the first black to graduate from the University of North Carolina at Chapel Hill Law School with an LL.B. degree, after NAACP lawyer Thurgood Marshall filed suit on his behalf.

Upon completion of his studies, McKissick filed suit in 1958 to get his daughter, Jocelyn, into an all-white school in Durham. He subsequently filed suit to get each of his four children into other area schools.

He later became legal counsel for the Congress of Racial Equality (CORE). In 1963, he was elected chairman, and in 1966, director of the organization. He was noted for stepping up CORE's program of civil disobedience. He was an advocate of Black Power and once described his philosophy as follows: "It is a movement dedicated to the exercise of American democracy in its highest tradition…to remove the basic causes of alienation, frustration, despair, low self-esteem, and hopelessness."

After his tenure with CORE, McKissick undertook a Ford Foundation project to help blacks attain positions of responsibility in the cities where they were approaching a majority of the population. Then he took a controversial position as a vocal supporter of President Richard Nixon's reelection effort in 1972. He defended his position claiming that African Americans had been taken for granted by the Democratic Party and that the Republican Party was becoming more mainstream. He later said he took this stance in part to get support for his Soul City Project.

In 1974, McKissick formed the Soul City Corporation. His aim was to create a community in which African Americans would control political and economic life. Unfortunately, federal funding was reduced and the city was not able to attract enough business to become self-sufficient. It was projected that the city would have 400,000 inhabitants by the year 2000, but in 1991 the population was only 400.

McKissick, however, remained busy. He had a successful law practice with his son in Durham, North Carolina. In addition, in 1990, Governor Jim Martin appointed him a District Court Judge for North Carolina's Ninth District.

McNAIR, RONALD (1951-January 28, 1986), Astronaut, was one of seven members of the crew of the space ship, *Challenger* who died when the vessel exploded in the skies on January 28, 1986. The space ship had just lifted off from Cape Canaveral, Florida. McNair, a physicist, was the nation's second African American astronaut.

In one of the eulogies for McNair, the famed African American actress Cycely Tyson observed: "Ron and his crewmates touched...us....They touched the other side of the sky for us."

McPHERSON, ALAN, JR. (d. Apr. 17, 1978) Author, was awarded a Pulitzer Prize in fiction for his volume of short stories, *Elbow Room* on April 17, 1978. The book characterized "various aspects of the black experience."

McPherson, a thirty-four year old native of Savannah, Georgia received a bachelor's degree from Morris Brown College in 1965, and an LL.B. degree from the Harvard University Law School in 1968. A year later he earned a master's of fine arts degree from the University of Iowa. McPherson taught writing in the college of law at Iowa before joining the faculty at the University of California at Santa Cruz from 1969 until 1970.

The new Pulitzer Prize winner had also been a contributing editor of *Atlantic Monthly* magazine and a contributor to *Black Insights, Cutting Edges*, and *New Black Voices*. He also wrote *Hue and Cry*, a collection of short stories and edited *Railroad: Trains and Train People in American Culture* in 1969 and 1976, respectively.

In 1970, McPherson won the National Institute of Arts and Letters literature prize, and in 1972 and 1973 he was awarded

Guggenheim fellowships.

At the time of his receipt of the Pulitzer Prize, McPherson was an associate professor of English at the University of Virginia.

The Pulitzer Prize, considered by many "the most prestigious award that can be bestowed in the literary arts and journalism," carried a stipend of $1,000 and was administered by the trustees of Columbia University.

METCALFE, RALPH HAROLD (May 29, 1910-October 10, 1978), Politician, Athlete, was born in Chicago, Illinois, the son of Major Clarence and Mayme Metcalfe (Attaway). He received his Ph.D. degree from Marquette University (Milwaukee, Wisconsin) in 1936 and an M.A. degree in Physical Education from the University of Southern California in 1939.

Metcalfe was a member of the United States Olympic track team in 1932 and 1936, where he won gold medals. In the 1936 Olympic Games, in Berlin, Germany, he ran on the winning 400-meter relay team with Jesse Owens. Later, he taught political science, while also coaching the track team. He served the United States Army's Transportation Corps from 1942 until 1945, where he rose to the rank of first lieutenant. In the same year as his discharge from military service, he became director of the Civil Rights Department of the Chicago Commission on Human Relations. He was also Illinois State Athletic Commissioner from 1949 to 1952.

Metcalfe left the Athletic Commission in 1952 to seek elective office. In 1952, he won a position as Third Ward Democratic Committeeman in Chicago and a seat on the Chicago City Council in 1955. When veteran Democratic Congressman William L. Dawson announced his retirement from the House in 1970, Metcalfe decided to seek the First District Congressional seat. Dawson, a long-time leader in Chicago's Democratic machine and one of the most powerful blacks in Illinois, threw his support to Metcalfe. Thus, the former Olympic champion easily won the election for Dawson's seat. Ironically, Dawson, himself, died a few days later. When Metcalfe entered the House of Representatives on January 3, 1971, he was assigned to the Merchant

Marine and Fisheries and the Interstate and Foreign Commerce committees.

In the Congress, Metcalfe worked to expand the availability of home improvement loans and federal housing programs, particularly ones to improve the safety of residents in public housing projects. He was also a leader in efforts to eliminate the practice of "redlining"—the withholding of home loans and insurance from low-income neighborhoods.

While chairman of the Merchant Marine and Fisheries Subcommittee on the Panama Canal, Metcalfe pushed for increased opportunities for education, housing and jobs in the Panama Canal Zone, and supported the Panama Canal treaty, which was ratified in 1978. Domestically, he also sought to offer minority companies access to work on projects to revitalize the nation's railroads and he held well publicized hearings on airline safety, preventive medical care for school children and prison administration.

But Metcalfe broke with Chicago's powerful Democratic political machine in 1972, over the question of police brutality against blacks in the city. He conducted public hearings, where victims and witnesses testified. A citizens lobby group was also organized which sought reforms. He even went so far as to support independent, "anti-machine" candidates and refused to endorse the venerable Mayor Richard J. Daley for reelection in 1975.

Mayor Daley quickly retaliated. He stripped Metcalfe of his Third Ward "patronage" and recruited and supported a challenger for the Congressional seat in the 1976 Democratic primary. But, Metcalfe not only defeated the Daley candidate, Edwina France, he ran unopposed for the party's nomination two years later. He died on October 10, 1978, only a month before his widely predicted victory for a fifth term, in the November general elections.

Metcalfe was the founder of the Ralph H. Metcalfe (Youth) Foundation; a member of the American Veterans Committee; American Legion; the Chicago Urban League; the NAACP; the U.S. Olympians, Midwest Chapter; the Board of the Illinois Federal Savings and Loan Association; and the Chicago Planning

Committee.

MITCHELL, ARTHUR L. W, (December 22, 1883-May 9, 1968) Politician, was born near Lafayette, Alabama to former bondspersons. He received an education at Tuskegee Institute, where he was Booker T. Washington's office boy, and at Talladega College in Alabama. Mitchell taught school in rural Alabama and served as an assistant law clerk in Washington, DC before moving to Chicago, Illinois. When he first arrived in Chicago, he became involved in Republican ward politics but soon joined the Democrats with the shifting African American political party in the Depression years. In November of 1934, he defeated Republican congressman Oscar dePriest to become the first African American member of his party in the U. S. House of Representatives. In the Congress, Mitchell professed to be a moderate, thus drawing the ire of the African American press and the NAACP. He did, however, sponsor a long and costly suit that ended on April 28, 1941 when the United States Supreme Court ruled that separate railroad car facilities "must be substantially equal." Mitchell served four terms in the Congress.

NIXON, EDGAR DANIEL (E. D. Nixon) (July 12, 1899-February 26, 1987), Civil/Human Rights Leader was born on July 12, 1899 in Montgomery. He received only about sixteen months of formal education. Between 1923 and 1964, he worked as a Pullman porter on a Birmingham—to—Cincinnati train and was a longtime member of the Brotherhood of Sleeping Car Porters, In 1949, Nixon was elected president of the Alabama state NAACP.

Six years later, he was still active in the state and local NAACP when he received a call from Rosa Parks after she was arrested for refusing to give up her seat on a segregated Montgomery bus to a white man, When the local police refused to tell him anything about the situation because he was an "unauthorized person," Nixon contacted Clifford Durr, a white Montgomery lawyer sympathetic to blacks. Durr was able to find out the specific charge against Parks (failing to obey a bus driver) and urged Nixon to seek the services of NAACP lawyer Fred Gray to challenge the constitutionality of the state law requiring segregation on city buses,

In addition to contacting Durr and Gray immediately after Parks's arrest, Nixon is also credited with posting her hail, informing Martin Luther King, Jr. of the incident, and proposing the Montgomery bus boycott He also helped choose King as president of the Montgomery Improvement Association (MIA), the group that directed the successful 381-day boycott.

Nixon is also known as the man who publicly scolded fearful and stubborn blacks into taking action in Montgomery. After some black ministers urged that the bust boycott be kept secret. Nixon asked, what the heck you talking about? How you going to have a mass meeting, going to boycott a city bus line, without the white folk knowing it? You ought to make up your mind right now that you either admit you are a grown man or concede to the fact that you are a bunch of scared boys."

He also told a crowd at a mass meeting. "Before you brothers and sisters get her comfortable in your seats, I want to say if anybody here is afraid, he better take his hat and go home. We've worn aprons long enough. It's time for us to take them off."

Nixon's home, which was the target of a bomb (luring the height of the protests, is now an Alabama state historical landmark. Nixon himself was honored at a testimonial dinner in Atlanta. Georgia. in 1985. At that time, he remarked: "Fifty thousand people rose up and rocked the cradle of the Confederacy until we could sit where we wanted to on a bus. A whole lot of things came about because we rocked the cradle. "

MOORE, HARRY T. (November 18, 1905-December 25, 1951), Civil/Human Rights Leader, was born in Houston, Florida, the son of Johnny and Rosa Moore. After Johnny Moore died in 1914, Rosa struggled to care for herself and her only child, Harry. The next year, she sent him to Daytona Beach to live with one of her sisters. The next year, young Moore moved to Jacksonville where he lived with three of his aunts. After three years in Jacksonville, Moore returned to his hometown. In 1919, he enrolled in the high school program of Florida Memorial College. He graduated from Florida Memorial in 1925 with a "normal degree." He then went to work as a teacher in Cocoa, Florida, where he taught the fourth grade at a black elementary school. Following his marriage to a fellow school teacher, Harriette Vyda Simms, Moore became a teacher and principal at the Titusville Colored School. Meanwhile, acutely aware of discrimination against blacks, generally and employment discrimination against black teachers particularly, he organized a chapter of the NAACP in Brevard County. The group became one of the most successful branches of the NAACP in Florida.

In 1937, supported by the all-black Florida State Teachers Association and NAACP attorney Thurgood Marshall, Moore spearheaded a suit to equalize the salaries of white and black teachers in Florida. This was the first such action filed in the Deep South. Although this case was lost in state court, it served as an encouragement and model for similar actions that were eventually successful in federal courts in Florida.

Encouraged by these efforts, Moore plunged more deeply into civil rights work. In 1943, he organized the Florida State Conference of the NAACP and became its unpaid executive secretary. In this capacity he wrote letters and published flyers and broadsides protesting against discrimination in employment, segregated schools, and the disfranchisement of black voters. Within two years of its founding, the Florida State Conference of the NAACP enrolled 10,000 members in 63 branches. But, in January 1949, the national NAACP raised membership dues from one to two dollars annually. Memberships plummeted throughout the country. In Florida, within a year of the increase in dues, membership dropped to 3,000.

Moore, undaunted by the reductions in NAACP memberships, continued his fight against disfranchisement and opened a new campaign against lynching. After the U.S. Supreme Court outlawed the "White Primary" in the case of *Smith vs. Allwright* (1944), Moore organized the Progressive Voters League in the state. This group succeeded in registering over 116,000 black voters over the next six years. This represented 31% of all eligible black voters in the state, "a figure that was 51% higher than any other Southern state."

Despite these successes, however, Moore and the national NAACP began to have increasing disagreements over his tactics, his political activities and his status as a full-time paid employee of the civil rights organization.

Meanwhile, Moore had involved himself into one of the most notorious incidents of racial injustice in United States history. The case began in July 1949 when four young African American men were accused of raping a white woman in Groveland, Florida. An incensed white mob launched a rampage of violence in Groveland's black community, which led to the call up of the Florida National Guard to restore order. But, Moore soon learned that the black defendants in the rape case had been brutally beaten while in custody. Moore pointed to Lake County Sheriff Willis McCall as the principal villain. With McCall still in office, three of the accused blacks were convicted. Two of them were sentenced to death. In April 1951, however, the U.S. Supreme Court overturned their convictions. But, Lake County opted to try the blacks again. Then, on November 6, 1951, while driving two of the defendants to court for a pre-trial hearing, Sheriff McCall allegedly shot the two blacks, killing one of them and critically wounding the other one. McCall claimed that the prisoners, who were handcuffed, had attacked him while trying to escape. The surviving prisoner, Walter Irvin, countered that McCall had "yanked them" out of the car and started firing. Moore demanded McCall's suspension and an indictment for murder.

About six weeks after the McCall incident, on Christmas Day in 1951, a bomb exploded beneath Moore's home in the area where he and his wife were sleeping. Moore was pronounced dead on arrival at the local hospital. His wife died nine days later. The Moore murders shocked the nation and protests reached as far as the White House, where Harry S. Truman served as President. He ordered an FBI investigation that lasted for several months. Nevertheless, no one was ever brought to justice.

Harry T. Moore was the first NAACP official killed during the modern Civil Rights Movement and he and his wife, Harriette, remain the only husband and wife "to give their lives to the movement." In a speech at Bethune-Cookman College in Daytona Beach, Florida on February 11, 2002, Juanita Evangeline Moore, daughter of Harry and Harriette Moore, said of her father: "This is a man who devoted his entire life . . . around his activities with the NAACP and the Progressive Voter's League . . . It saddens me to see the legacy of my father overlooked by so many people. It is a slap in the face to see many of us not registered to vote – the very right that my father and other great civil rights leaders gave their lives for."

MUHAMMAD, ELIJAH (October 10, 1897-February 25, 1975) Clergy, Black Nationalist Leader, was born Elijah Poole in Sandersville, Georgia, in 1897. His father was a Baptist preacher, sawmill worker, and tenant farmer. As a young man, Elijah was deeply religious and very race conscious. He was working as a laborer in Georgia in 1923 when his white employer cursed him. Angered by the insult, Elijah decided to leave the South for what he hoped would be a better life up north. Settling in Detroit, Michigan, with his family, he worked at several different jobs until the Depression hit and the Pooles were forced to go on relief.

About this same time, Elijah came under the influence of W.D. Fard or Wallace Fard Muhammad, a mysterious black silk peddler. Fard had been telling blacks that they were members of a superior race that was descended from Muslims of Afro-Asia. Claiming to be a messenger from Allah, or "white devils" who had made their lives so miserable. Christianity, he insisted, was a false religion used by white people to keep blacks enslaved. Elijah Poole soon became Fard's closest associate. When Fard mysteriously disappeared in 1934, Poole—known by then as Elijah Muhammad—took control of the group as "The Messenger of Allah to the Lost Found Nation of Islam in the Wilderness of North America."

During World War II, Muhammad and his Black Muslim followers created an uproar when they refused to fight for the United States and sided with Japan instead. Muhammad himself was convicted of encouraging resistance to the draft and served time in a federal prison. He was released in 1946.

Meanwhile, Muslim membership dropped from a high of about 8,000 under Fard's leadership to 1,000. But during the 1950s and especially the l960s, the Black Muslims saw their numbers increase. Even the bitter conflict between Muhammad and his most famous follower, Malcolm X, did not destroy the Nation of Islam. It has remained an important religious, political, and economic influence among urban blacks in particular.

On July 31, 1960, Elijah Muhammad, leader of the Black Muslims, called for the establishment of an all black state. The idea of creating such a state (or group of states) later became a symbol and rallying cry for new supporters of black nationalism, a movement that favors separate political, social, economic, and cultural actions and institutions for black people.

MURRAY, ANNA (PAULI) (November 20, 1910-July 1, 1985), Civil/Human Rights Leader was born in Baltimore, Maryland. Her mother, Agnes Murray, died in 1914. Her father, William Murray, was a graduate of Howard University and taught in a local high school. Anna and her five brothers and sisters were raised by relatives in Baltimore. Eventually she went to live with her aunt, Pauline Fitzgerald, a school teacher. After graduating from Hillside High School at the head of her class, she moved to New York City. Murray attended Hunter College and financed her studies with various jobs. However, after the Stock Market Crash in 1929, she was unable to find work and was forced to abandon her education.

In the 1930s Murray worked for the Works Projects Administration (WPA) and as a teacher in the New York City Remedial Reading Project. She also published articles and poems in various magazines. They included her novel, *Angel of the Desert,* that was serialized in the *Carolina Times.*

In 1938, she became involved in the Civil Rights Movement. By attempting to enroll in the all-white University of North Carolina. With the support of the National Association for the Advancement of Colored People (NAACP) Murray's case received national publicity. But she was unable to gain admission on account of her race. As a member of the Fellowship of Reconciliation (FOR), Murray also became involved in attempts to end segregation in public transportation which resulted in her arrest and imprisonment in March 1940 for refusing to sit at the back of a bus in Virginia. In 1941 Murray enrolled at the Howard University law school with the intention of becoming a civil rights lawyer. The following year she joined with George Houser, James Farmer and Bayard Rustin, to form the Congress of Racial Equality (CORE). In this connection, in 1943, Murray published two significant essays on civil rights, *Negroes Are Fed Up* in *Common Sense* and an article about the Harlem race riot in the socialist newspaper, *New York Call.* Her most famous poem on race relations, *Dark Testament,* was also written in that year.

After Murray graduated from Howard University in 1944 she went to Harvard University on a Rosenwald Fellowship. However, after the award had been announced, Harvard Law School rejected her because of her gender. Murray then enrolled in the University of California where she received a degree in law. Her master's thesis was *The Right to Equal Opportunity in Employment.* After her matriculation in California Murray moved to New York City and provided support to the growing civil rights movement. Her book, *States' Laws on Race and Color,* was published in 1951. Thurgood Marshall, chief counsel for the NAACP,, described the book as the Bible for civil rights lawyers.

In the early 1950s Murray became increasingly involved in civil rights activism. As a result, in 1952 she lost a position at Cornell University because some of the individuals who provided references for her, including Eleanor Roosevelt, Thurgood Marshall and A. Philip Randolph, were considered to be "too radical". She was told in a letter that they decided to give "one hundred per cent protection" to the university "in view of the troublous times in which we live".

In 1956 Murray published *Proud Shoes: The Story of an American Family,* a biography of her grandparents, and their struggle with racial prejudice. In 1960 she traveled to Ghana to explore her African cultural roots. When she returned President John F. Kennedy appointed her to his Committee on Civil and Political Rights.

Although Murray continued her civil rights activism into the

1960s, she became increasingly critical of the civil rights leadership because she felt that males dominated the top positions. In August, 1963,, at the time of the great March on Washington, she wrote to A. Philip Randolph that she had: "been increasingly perturbed over the blatant disparity between the major role which Negro women have played and are playing in the crucial grass-roots levels of our struggle and the minor role of leadership they have been assigned in the national policy-making decisions." Next to civil rights activism, Murray's principal devotion was to the Episcopal Church. In 1977, she became the first African American woman to be ordained as a priest in that church. This experience and her racial activism were documented in her autobiography, *Song in a Weary Throat: An American Pilgrimage*, which was published posthumously in 1987.

NIX, ROBERT NELSON CORNELIUS, SR. (August 9, 1908-June 22,1987), Politician was born in Orangeburg, South Carolina, the son of Nelson Cornelius and Sylvia (Benjamin) Nix. He received a B.A. Degree from Lincoln University of Pennsylvania 1921 and a LL.B. from the University of Pennsylvania in 1924. Before going to Congress, in 1958, Nix was a deputy attorney general in Pennsylvania (1934-1938). Once elected to Congress, Nix won reelection handily for the next two decades, despite his opponents' charges of absenteeism and "blind allegiance" to Philadelphia's "Democratic machine." He went on to become the second most senior black representative in the House.

In the Congress, Nix became a member of the Foreign Affairs, Post Office and Civil Service, Veterans Affairs, and Merchant Marine and Fisheries Committees. He was named chairman of the Post Office Committee in 1971.

Although Nix was loyal to the Democratic administrations of Presidents John F. Kennedy and Lyndon Johnson; worked behind the scenes to prevent the House from denying Harlem Congressman Adam Clayton Powell, Jr. his seat amid charges of corruption; supported the 1963 Civil Rights March on Washington; and worked for passage of civil rights legislation; he rarely spoke publicly on racial or social issues. He once said that the

National Advisory Commission on Civil Disorders (the Kerner Commission) was wrong when it concluded, in 1967, that the nation was moving toward two societies, one white, one black, separate and unequal. He refused to characterize police conduct in black ghettoes as "repression" and offered that police and ghetto residents were arriving at "some understanding between them." He also refused to be categorized as "a ghetto congressman" or "a black congressman," preferring, instead, simply to be known as "a congressman who represents his entire district." Yet, Nix consistently voted in favor of civil rights, education, labor, and urban development legislation while a congressman "for all the people."

Perhaps, however, because of the view, which some held, that he was one of the most "conservative" members of the Congressional Black Caucus (CBC), Nix barely survived a challenge from Philadelphia minister, William H. Gray III in 1976. Two years later, he lost his effort for an 11th term to Gray. But, Nix remained in politics as a leader of Philadelphia's 32nd ward until his death.

OWENS, JAMES CLEVELAND "JESSE" (September 12, 1913-March 31, 1981), Athlete, goodwill ambassador, was born in Danville, Alabama to Henry, a tenant farmer, and Emma (Alexander) Owens. He was called "J. C." by his family, but a teacher misunderstood his shy mumbling of his name in school. She recorded his name as "Jesse," and Owens was too fearful to correct the error; hence "J. C." Owens became "Jesse." By the time Owens was 11 years old, his family had moved to Cleveland, Ohio. There he attended the Fairmount Junior High School and the East Technical High School, where he became a world-class track star, and president of the Student Council.

In track, Owens performed impressively in the 100 and 200-yard dashes as well as the broad jump. In high school, one of his few losses was to Ralph Metcalfe, another great black sprinter, in the 1932 Olympic tryouts in Los Angeles. But Owens continued his winning ways when he entered Ohio State University in 1933. He set world records in the 100-yard dash, 220-yard low hurdles, as well as the broad jump. Indeed his jump of 26 feet, 8

¼ inches stood as a record from May 25, 1933 until it was broken by Ralph Boston in 1961.

Owens ran and jumped his way onto the pages of history during the 1936 Olympics in Berlin, Germany. He won four gold medals in the 100 meters, the 200 meters, the broad jump, and as anchor for the 400 meter American relay team. He was the first athlete ever to win four gold medals in one Olympic competition. These feats, with the Nazi tyrant Adolph Hitler in attendance, were another dramatic blow to the notion of Aryan racial supremacy.

After Berlin, Owens became a businessman and traveled extensively throughout the world, not only as a role model for youth, but as a goodwill ambassador for the United States. He was also an official for the Works Progress Administration (WPA) during the Great Depression and national director of the Office of Civilian Defense's Physical Education for Black Americans programs from 1942-1946. His quiet demeanor and patriotism were, in many ways, similar to those of Joe Louis.

Ten years after Owens' death, at the behest of Ohio Congressman Louis Stokes, President George Walker Herbert Bush presented to his widow, Ruth, a posthumous Congressional Gold Medal. On that occasion, Bush said that Owens was "an Olympic hero and an American hero every day of his life."

PARSONS, JAMES BENTON (August 13, 1913-June 19, 1993) Jurist, was born in Kansas City, Missouri, the son of James B. and Maggie Virginia (Mason) Parsons. He received a B.A. degree from James, Milliken University in 1934, a M.A. from the University of Chicago in 1946, and an LL.D. degree from Chicago in 1949. Parsons began working as a field agent at Lincoln University of Missouri in 1934, and by 1940 had served as an instructor of political science, head of the music department, and assistant to the dean of men. In 1940, he left Lincoln to teach in the public schools of Greensboro, North Carolina.

By 1949, Parsons had moved to Chicago and had begun the private practice of law, while also teaching at the John Marshall Law School. He also entered city government in that same year as an assistant corporate counsel. From 1951 to 1960, he was an assistant U.S. Attorney in Chicago. He left this post in 1960 to serve on the bench of the Superior Court in Cook County, Illinois (for which Chicago is the county seat and largest city). After only one year on the Superior Court, President Kennedy appointed him to the U.S. District Court for the Northern District of Illinois. By 1979, he had become the court's chief judge.

On the bench, Parsons achieved public notice for his rulings against traffic controllers in their 1970 strike, for a 1987 ruling upholding the Tenant's Bill of Rights in Chicago and for a 1988 decision allowing the Daley Center in Chicago to publicly display nativity scenes. Off the bench, he remained outspoken, declaring on one occasion that blacks had neither the background nor the education to commit "white man's crimes," such as counterfeiting, embezzling, mail fraud, and jewel theft, with "any degree of skill...because the society has prevented [them] from getting into that world." He also once said: Blacks "must be accepted in every facet of life – not merely with a pretense toward equality – but with a feeling of identity." Parsons retired from the bench in 1992, one year before his death.

In addition to his judicial duties, Parsons has been chairman of the Chicago Conference on Race and Religion and a trustee of the Chicago Urban League and the National Conference of Christians and Jews.

PAYNE, ETHEL LOIS (August 14, 1911-May 28, 1991), Journalist, civil/human rights activist, was born in Chicago, Illinois to William, a Pullman Porter, and Bessie (Austin) Payne, a high school teacher. She studied at Crane Junior College and the Medill School of Journalism, both in Chicago. In the early 1950s she began a career as a reporter for the black newspaper, the *Chicago Defender.*

In a journalistic career that expanded over more than a quarter of a century, Payne covered a broad spectrum of events and issues, both domestic and international, with particular emphasis on the modern Civil Rights Movement. In 1952, she won the "best news story award" from the Illinois Press Association. Shortly thereafter she became a White House correspondent.

At the White House, Payne earned a reputation as a dogged

reporter who demanded nothing less than all of the facts. At the same time that she was gaining a reputation as a first rate national correspondent, Payne also traveled to Africa and reported on revolutionary and independence movements on that continent. She covered the Asian-African Conference in Bandung, Indonesia in 1955. In 1957, she accompanied Vice President Richard Nixon to independence ceremonies in Ghana. Then, in 1966 and 1967, she interviewed and reported the activities of African American soldiers in Vietnam.

In 1972, Payne appeared as a commentator on the CBS radio and television program "Spectrum," thus becoming the first African American woman to be employed in such a position by a major national network.

In the early 1980s, she was a leader in the campaign for the release of South African leader Nelson Mandela from prison.

Among Payne's honors and awards were the Capitol Press Club Award for her Vietnam reporting in 1967; the Africare Distinguished Service Award in 1983; and the Trans Africa African Freedom Award in 1987. In 2002, the "First Lady of the Black Press," was honored with the issue of a postage stamp as part of the U.S. Postal Service's "Women in Journalism" series.

PENDLETON, CLARENCE MCLANE (November 10, 1930-June 5, 1989), Federal Official, was born in Louisville, Kentucky to Clarence McLane Pendleton, Sr. and Edna Marie Ramsaur. He grew up in Washington, D.C., where his father was a swimming coach at Howard University.

Pendleton attended Dunbar High School in Washington and earned a B.S. degree from Howard University in 1954. He worked briefly at the Washington Recreation Department before joining the United States Army, where he eventually rose to the rank of medical specialist third class. After leaving the military in 1957, he returned to Howard and obtained a Masters degree in education. He, then, became Howard's swimming coach and led a team that won ten championships in eleven years.

In 1968, Pendleton left Howard and became a recreation coordinator with the Model Cities Program in Baltimore, Maryland. Two years later, he returned to Washington and took a position as director of the Urban Affairs Department of the National Recreation and Parks Association. His job called for him to increase community involvement in establishing recreation programs as well as persuading the federal government to invest in these programs for an extended period of time.

In 1972, San Diego, California mayor Pete Wilson hired Pendleton to direct that city's Model Cities Program. After three and a half years in this post, he became executive director of the San Diego Urban League, where, among other things, he helped package loans for small businesses. While working in San Diego, Pendleton changed his political philosophy from what he called a "bleeding heart liberal" to that of a Republican, who strongly believed in black self-reliance instead of reliance on the federal government. He, then openly endorsed former California governor Ronald Reagan's 1980 presidential campaign; he was the only member of the San Diego Urban League to do so.

On November 16, 1981, now President Ronald Reagan appointed Pendleton to the position of chairman of the United States Commission on Civil Rights (USCCR). After his confirmation by the Senate in early 1982, Pendleton stunned and alienated many civil rights and political leaders as well as some of the commission's own members when he announced his controversial "color blind" approach to civil rights. He labeled affirmative action "a bankrupt policy." He also opposed busing to achieve school desegregation.

While Pendleton's firm support of President Reagan drew the ire of civil rights leaders, he occasionally broke with the administration. For example Pendleton, as well as the rest of the USCCR differed with the President and his administration's advocacy of the 1994 Supreme Court decision in *Grove City College vs. Bell*, where the high tribunal ruled that federal laws which prohibit sexual discrimination by schools receiving federal funds should apply only to the individual departments or units where the bias occurred and not apply to the school as a whole.

In 1986, the Congress cut the budget of the Civil Rights Commission from $11.6 million to $7.5 million. These budget reductions forced the Commission to substantially reduce its staff and its activities. Nevertheless, Pendleton continued to work for the commission, and he also remained active in business and public affairs in San Diego, until his sudden death from a heart attack on June 5, 1988.

PERRY, LINCOLN THEODORE ANDREW ("Stepin Fetchit") (1902-November 19, 1985) Entertainer, was born in Key West Florida. He began an acting career in the 1930s, appearing in such films as *Steamboat Round the Bend*. He was, perhaps, best known for his roles as "a shuffling, head-scratching" servant. He took his stage name from a race horse on which he had won some money in Oklahoma before leaving for Hollywood in the 1920s. Perry was the fist African American performer to appear on film with such luminaries as Will Rogers and Shirley temple.

Perry's film characters were criticized by many African Americans for what was seen as negative stereotypes of their race. Perry, however, defended his roles and asserted that they were "contributions." He once offered: "...when I came into motion pictures, it was as an individual....I had no manager, and no one had the idea of making a Negro a star....I became the first Negro entertainer to become a millionaire....All the things that Bill Cosby and Sidney Poitier have done wouldn't be possible if I hadn't broken the law [the race barrier]. I set up thrones for them to come and sit on."

Nevertheless, in 1960, a CBS-TV documentary, "Of Black America" characterized Perry as a "stupid, lazy, eye-rolling stereotype." Perry then sued the network for three million dollars, alleging that he had been subjected "to hatred, contempt [and] ridicule." In 1974 a federal judge dismissed the suit.

POWELL, ADAM CLAYTON, JR. (November 29, 1908—April 4, 1972), Politician, clergyman, was born in New Haven, Connecticut to Adam Clayton Powell Sr., a wealthy and influential minister and civil rights leader, and Mallie (Fletcher) Powell. When Adam, Jr. was six months old, the family moved to New York City. Powell received a BA degree from the City College of New York in 1930 and a MA degree in religious education from Columbia University in 1031.

Also, in 1930, he became the assistant manager of Harlem's Abyssinian Baptist Church, where his father pastored, and helped organize mass meetings and picket lines at Harlem Hospital, which had dismissed five black doctors from its staff because of their race. Then in 1932, he began a church-sponsored program to provide food, clothing, and temporary jobs to area residents during the Great Depression.

Meanwhile, he continued his civil rights leadership throughout the decade. He organized rallies, boycotts, and rent strikes that forced bus lines, utilities, and retail stores to hire and/or promote black employees. In 1939, he even persuaded the New York World's Fair to hire and promote African Americans.

In 1936, Powell succeeded his father as pastor of Abyssinian Baptist Church. Although, he soon began a long political career and continued his flamboyant and risqué' life style, his parishioners remained awed by his charisma and forceful leadership kept him as pastor for most of the rest of his life.

Powell first won elective office in New York City as a Councilman in 1941. From 1942 to 1944, he was a member of the New York State Office of Price Administration (OPA). Meanwhile, he also published a crusading, weekly newspaper, *The People's Voice*. In 1945, he was first elected to the U.S. Congress.

Powell served in the Congress for two and one half decades, gaining so much seniority that, by 1961, he had become chairman of one of the most powerful committees in the House – Education and Labor. Under Powell's leadership, the Congress passed some of the most important social legislation of the 20th Century, including increases in minimum wages, education and training for the deaf, new school lunch and student loan programs, aid to elementary and secondary schools and public libraries as well as vocational training, among others. Most of the social legislation that comprised the "New Frontiers Agenda" of President John F. Kennedy and "the Great Society" agenda of President Lyndon B. Johnson emerged from Powell's committee. During the same time, he sought unsuccessfully to attach riders to much of this legislation to prevent it from being used for segregated schools, particularly. Although "the Powell Amendment" never won the full approval of a heavily southern and heavily "conservative" Congress, it served notice on southern communities of what might come in the future and, indeed, was a precursor to the Civil Rights Act of 1964.

Amid his influence in the Congress and his popularity in Black America, Powell continued his flamboyant lifestyle, which led to excessive absenteeism from his Congressional duties as well as from his district and his church, alleged mismanagement of his committee's budget and foreign travels at public expense. The absences from his congressional district were exacerbated when he sought to avoid a judgment for slander of a "Harlem bag woman." Finally, on January 9, 1967, the House Democratic Caucus removed Powell as chair of the Education and Labor Committee. The full House, then, ordered an investigation of his conduct by the Judiciary Committee and suspended him from his seat in the meanwhile.

The Judiciary Committee soon recommended that Powell be censured, fined, and deprived of his seniority, but the full House rejected these recommendations, by a vote of 307 to 116 on March 1, 1967, and, instead directed that he be stripped of his Congressional seat in the 90th Congress. Undaunted, Powell ran for and recaptured his seat in a special election on April 11, 1967. Powell, however, did not immediately take his seat. Instead he waited until the regular elections in November 1968, where he, again, offered for and won reelection. The House, however, stipulated that he would have to return without his seniority. Powell refused to accept these restrictions and refused to take a seat in the 91st Congress in January 1969. Six months later, the U.S. Supreme Court overturned Powell's original exclusion from the House, but let the removal of his 22 years of seniority stand. This decision took some of the fight and fire out of Powell, but did little to slow his "fast track" lifestyle, which included foreign travels and "womanizing." But he did offer for another new term in the primary and general elections, where he ran as an Independent, of 1970. But in a bitterly fought campaign, he went down to defeat at the hands of Harlem politician, Charles Rangel. Powell, one of America's most colorful political personalities, then, returned to the pastorate of his Harlem church, where he remained, while not traveling, until his death on April 4, 1972.

RANDOLPH, ASA PHILIP (A. PHILIP RANDOLPH) (April 15, 1889-), Labor Leader, Civil/Human Rights Leader, was born in Crescent City, Florida was born in Crescent City, Florida. The son of a Methodist minister, he was educated locally before moving to New York where he studied economics and philosophy at the City College.

While in New York he worked as an elevator operator, a porter and a waiter. In 1917 Randolph founded *The Messenger* (later the *Black Worker),* which campaigned for black civil rights. During the First World War he was arrested for violating the Espionage Act. He and his co-editor, Chandler Owen, were accused of treason after opposing African Americans joining the army.

After the war Randolph lectured at the Rand School of Social Science. A member of the Socialist Party, he made several unsuccessful attempts to be elected to political office in New York. During this same period, he was involved in organizing black workers in laundries, clothes factories and cinemas and in 1929 became president of the Brotherhood of Sleeping Car Porters (BSCP). Over the next few years he built it into the first successful black trade union. The BSCP were members of the American Federation of Labor (AFL) but in protest against its failure to fight discrimination in its ranks, Randolph took his union into the Congress of Industrial Organizations (CIOO).

After threatening to organize a March on Washington in June, 1941, President Franklin D. Roosevelt issued Executive Order 8802 on 25th June, 1941, barring discrimination in defense industries and federal bureaus (the Fair Employment Act).

After the Second World War Randolph led a campaign in favor of racial equality in the military. This resulted in Harry S. Truman issuing executive order 9981 on 26th July, 1948, banning segregation in the armed forces.

When the AFL merged with the CIO, Randolph became vice president of the new organization. He also became president of the Negro American Labor Council (1960-66).

In 1963 Randolph helped organize the March on Washington for Jobs and Freedom, which drew a bi-racial crowd of more than 250,000 people..

In his final years Randolph worked closely with Bayard Rustin in the A. Philip Randolph Institute, which was supported by the AFL-CIO.

ROBINSON, JOHN ROOSEVELT ("JACKIE") (January 31, 1919-October 24, 1972), Athlete, civil/human rights activist, was the son of Jerry, a sharecropper, and Mallie Robinson, a domestic worker. He was born in Cairo, Georgia, but after his father abandoned the family when Jackie was only a baby, his mother carried her five children to Pasadena, California, where her brother lived. While his mother supported the family as a domestic worker, Jackie, the youngest child, helped out by working odd jobs, including caddie, newsboy, and shoe shine boy. But he also attended the John Muir Technical High School in Pasadena, where he starred in baseball, basketball, football, and track and field. He graduated from high school in 1937 and two years later entered the University of California at Los Angeles (UCLA). At UCLA, he became a star running back on the football team, a star forward on the basketball team, a star base stealer on the baseball team, and the 1940 National Collegiate Athletic Association (NCAA) broad jump champion. The next year he dropped out of college, only a few months from graduation, to help his poverty-stricken family. But he did not lose his love for sports, and the sports world did not lose its interest in him.

Scouts from the Los Angeles Bulldogs professional football team had seen Robinson star in the 1941 College All-Star game. They quickly signed him to a contract. But the next year Robinson was drafted into the Army. He was admitted to Officers Candidate School after he protested that all black applications in his camp were being rejected.

After leaving the army as a first lieutenant in 1944, Robinson was a basketball coach at the all-black Sam Houston College in Austin, Texas, but quit, because of the low pay, to play for the

Kansas City Monarchs of the national black baseball league. Although he became a star player with the Monarchs, and the Boston Red Sox, a major league baseball team, gave him a tryout, the major leagues were not yet ready to sign Robinson or any other black player.

Yet, Robinson continued to impress all who saw him including scouts, managers, and owners of Big League baseball teams. He regularly batted over .300, as a good shortstop and an excellent base stealer. By the fall of 1945, Branch Rickey, president of the Brooklyn Dodgers of the National Baseball League, could wait no longer. He had felt for some time that the major leagues should be desegregated. He was now convinced that Jackie Robinson, because of his ability, character, and intelligence, was the man to do it.

Robinson went first to the Dodgers' top farm team, the Montreal Royals of the AAA International League, where he batted .349, stole 40 bases, and helped the team win the league and Little World Series championships in 1946. He was good enough to move up to the Dodgers in the next season. When he donned a Dodgers uniform, at first base, in the spring of 1947, he became the first black person to play major league baseball in modern times. During his first year, Robinson, despite racist insults on and off the field, performed so well that he was voted "Rookie of the Year" in the National League. He continued this excellent caliber of play until he retired at the end of the 1956 baseball season. In 1962 he was elected to baseball's coveted Hall of Fame.

In order to accomplish his historic feat as a pioneer in desegregating professional sports in America, Robinson was forced to inhibit his aggressive personality and his fervent disdain for racism. But the dignity with which he endured abuse, together with the excellence of his performance, won him respect, sometimes grudgingly, from even some of his fiercest opponents. In the world of sports, he stands alongside Joe Louis, Jesse Owens, Althea Gibson, and others as outstanding role models and powerful spiritual symbols for the aspiration of all African Americans.

Following retirement, Robinson served as vice president of the Chuck Full O'Nuts restaurant chain in New York City and as a political aide and ally of Republican Governor Nelson A. Rockefeller of New York.

ROBINSON, MAX (1937-December 20, 1988), Journalist, was the first African American news anchorperson on a national network television program. After working for several years at WTPO-TV in Washington, DC, he became a co-anchor with Peter Jennings and Frank Reynolds on the ABC-TV Network's "Evening News" in 1978. However, Carl Bernstein, the chief of the ABC News bureau in Chicago later admitted that Robinson was "deliberately excluded from any decision-making related to the newscast." In a speech at Smith College in February 1981, Robinson, himself, accused ABC of racism. Two years later, following the death of Reynolds, Jennings was named sole anchor of the "Evening News" and Robinson was relegated to weekend anchor positions and "news briefs." The next year he left ABC and joined the news staff of WMAQ-TV in Chicago, Illinois. In June 1985, Robinson was admitted a hospital, diagnosed with "emotional and physical exhaustion. He never returned to full-time news reporting.

Following Robinson's death in 1988, Roone Arledge, president of ABC News offered: "He made an important contribution to ABC News for which we will always be grateful."

RUSTIN, BAYARD (March 17, 1912-August 24, 1987), Civil/Human Rights Leader, was born in West Chester, Pennsylvania, the son of Janifer and Julia (Davis) Rustin. While singing with Josh White and "Leadbelly," he earned money for tuition to attend Cheyney State Normal School (Pennsylvania), and the City College of New York. Also while a student there in the late 1930s, Rustin joined the Young Communist League and became an organizer. He left this position in 1941 and became a member of the Fellowship of Reconciliation, "a nondenominational religious group that sought social justice" and the Congress of Racial Equality (CORE), "a nonviolent direct-action organization dedicated to improving race relations and ending racial discrimination" in the United States. Both groups were bi-racial.

While working with the Fellowship of Reconciliation and

CORE, Rustin became acquainted with A. Philip Randolph, the black labor and civil rights leader. He came to admire both the philosophies and character of Randolph and joined him in planning a March on Washington in 1941. The proposed March was designed to protest racial discrimination in the defense industry. The March was cancelled after President Franklin D. Roosevelt was persuaded to issue an executive order prohibiting such discrimination in industries that supported military efforts in World War II. During the war, Rustin, himself, registered as a "conscientious objector." But, he refused an assignment to hospital work and was sentenced to a federal penitentiary at Lewisburg, Pennsylvania, where he remained for the remainder of the war.

Following the war, Rustin spearheaded the planning for a "Journey of Reconciliation." During 1947, blacks and whites sat together as they rode on public transportation. This movement is often cited as a model for "Freedom Rides" which took place in several southern states during the 1960s.

In the 1940s, Rustin was often accused of being a socialist and a communist and was arrested for his protest activities on several occasions. On one occasion, he spent three weeks on a North Carolina "chain gang," after participating in a "freedom ride."

During the infancy of the modern Civil Rights Movement in the 1950s, Rustin was introduced to Martin Luther King, Jr. Sharing King's ideas of non-violent, direct action, he soon became an advisor to King and aided in the founding of the Southern Christian Leadership Conference (SCLC). As the Civil Rights Movement gained momentum and the idea of a new March on Washington "for jobs and justice" blossomed, Rustin was appointed "organizational coordinator" for the proposed national protest. He is often credited with playing the major "behind the scenes" role for the successful March, which brought 250,000 people to the steps of the Lincoln Memorial in August 1963. It was there that Martin Luther King, Jr. rose to the height of his oratory and leadership with the famous "I Have a Dream" speech.

During the next year after the March on Washington, Rustin organized a boycott of schools in New York City to "protest the system's racial injustices and reluctance to integrate the schools." Approximately 444,000 students participated in the boycott. Then, in 1964, Rustin became executive director and president of the A. Philip Randolph Institute. This organization, named in honor of Rustin's mentor in protest, was dedicated to promoting civil and workers' rights. Rustin led this group from 1964 until his death in 1987. Rustin was the highest known gay leader in the Civil Rights Movement.

SAMPSON, EDITH SPURLOCK (October 13, 1901-October 8, 1979), United Nations Delegate and Jurist, was born in Pittsburgh, Pennsylvania, to Louis Spurlock, a cleaning shop employee and Elizabeth A. McGruder. Although public education was not compulsory, Edith Sampson excelled in school. In the early 1920s, she attended the New York School of Social Work. Departing from New York, Sampson moved to Chicago where she enrolled in night classes at the Marshall Law School. While working in the daytime, she earned her Bachelors degree in 1925. And in 1927, she received her Master of Laws degree from Loyola University Law School. With this achievement, Sampson became the first black woman to receive that degree from Loyola.

Upon graduation, Sampson began her legal career. From 1925 to 1942, she was a probation officer and referee with the Juvenile Court of Cook County, Illinois. Also during this period she began a private practice with her second husband, Joseph E. Clayton. In 1947, she was appointed assistant state attorney of Cook County.

Two years later, Sampson's popularity and career blossomed. In 1949, the National Council of Negro Women selected Sampson to represent the organization in the "World Town Hall of the Air," a global tour which propagandized American democracy during the height of the Cold War. One questioner asked Sampson about the African American plight in America. Sampson replied: "You ask, do we get fair treatment? My answer is no. Just the same, I'd rather be a Negro in America than a citizen of any other country. In the past century we have made more progress than dark-skinned people anywhere else in the world." Upon the tour's return to America, in 1950, it became permanent and Sampson was elected its president.

With increased notoriety, the tour served as a launch pad for Sampson's career. In 1950, President Truman appointed Sampson as an alternate delegate to the United Nations. She became the first African American female to be an official American representative to the United Nations. In addition, "she served with Eleanor Roosevelt on the Social, Humanitarian, and Cultural Committee, and she was reelected in 1952." Also in 1952, Sampson was re-appointed alternate delegate. Furthermore, during the Eisenhower administration she was a member-at-large of the U.S. Commission for UNESCO. In 1962, Sampson became the first black woman elected associate judge in America. From 1962 to 1978, Edith Sampson was reelected Cook County Circuit Judge.

Sampson received both favorable and negative publicity. She was known to be a fair and sensitive judge. Since the majority of her cases involved the working class poor, Sampson rarely delayed her cases. However, many militants criticized her for being too moderate. William Worthy, *Crisis* contributor, criticized her for moderate characterizations of the black plight in America. Sampson considered herself a step in the process of social change. In 1978, she retired and one year later died.

SIMMONS, ALTHEA T. L. (April 17, 1924-September 13, 1990), Civil/Human Rights Activist, was born in Shreveport, Louisiana, the daughter of M. M., a high school principal and Lillian Simmons, a teacher, who instilled in their children a zeal for an education. She therefore, received a B.S. degree in Business Education from Southern University (Louisiana) in 1945, a Masters degree in Marketing from the University of Illinois in 1951 and a J.D. degree from Howard University in 1956.

After completing 26 years of field service as a grassroots mobilizer for the NAACP, Simmons in 1979, became the association's Washington Bureau Director. She first served within that organization as a voter registration coordinator but became its Legislative Advisor and Field Director (1969-1974), National Education Director (1974-1977), and Associate Director (1977-

1979). Simmons also served on the National Manpower Advisory Commission on Private Philanthropy and Public Needs (1973-1975); the National Organization for Women (NOW) Legal Defense and Educational Fund Inc., (1974-1977); the National Advisory Council, Hogg Foundation for Mental Health, (1973-1976); the U.S. Census Advisory on Black Populations for the 1980 Census (1975-1980); the Office of Federal Contract Compliance of the National Advisory Council and the board of trustees, Teachers' College United Seamen's Service, (1976).

In 1979 Simmons was appointed by NAACP Executive Director Benjamin Hooks to succeed Clarence Mitchell, Jr. as the NAACP's chief Washington lobbyist. Although comparisons were made of her to the late Mr. Mitchell, this did not distract her from taking charge in her quiet behind the scenes way. Admittedly a workaholic, she was well respected by her staff as well as political adversaries for her assertive method of communicating support for progressive legislation.

Of the many causes she supported toward economic and social equality Simmons prioritized the extension of the 1964 Voting Rights Act, the national holiday honoring the Reverend Dr. Martin Luther King Jr., and the bill imposing sanctions against South African racial policies as the most significant. The "negative conservatism" pervasive throughout the administration of President Ronald Reagan only stimulated her to expand protections and benefits for women, blacks, Hispanics, the handicapped and other minorities. However, she was also respected by such adversaries as Senator Orin G. Hatch, Republican of Utah and Melvin Bradley, Special Assistant to President Reagan.

Armed with her overstuffed briefcase, which always included a directory of civil rights organizations and a book she affectionately called her bible, *The Mandate for Leadership: Policy Management in a Conservative Administration*, Simmons monitored the schedules of Congressional committees that handled civil rights matters. Frequently social affairs on Capitol Hill were also attended, if only briefly, when she decided that the NAACP should have a presence. Simmons reportedly worked a reception crowd effectively in 30 minutes in her effort to complete the unfinished agenda of civil rights, especially by preventing the erosion of gains made over the past 25 years.

Her "hardnosed lobbying" also helped bring about passage of the Fair Housing Act of 1968. Furthermore, she played a pivotal role in the fight in Congress to deny Robert Bork's appointment to the United States Supreme Court and facilitated the work of the Resolutions Committee at NAACP conventions by planning summits, conferences, marches, and various protests and demonstrations.

She received several awards for her professional and community service, including a Leadership Award from the National Association for Equal Opportunity in Education (NAPEO) (1988) and the National Bar Association's Gertrude E. Rush Award in 1990.

Toward the end of her life, Simmons was ill for several months, but still set up an office in her hospital room at Howard University. She said she wanted to continue her work rather than rest. She said: "The job must go on. There is little time to rest."

SMITH, ANTONIO MACEO (April 16, 1903-December 19, 1977), Federal Official, educator, was born in Texarkana, Texas, the son of Frank and Winnie (Jones) Smith. He received an A.B. degree from Fisk University (Nashville, Tennessee) in 1924. He then entered New York University where he was awarded the M.B.A. degree in 1928.

Smith began his professional career as a teacher in the Dallas Public Schools. After only a short while in this position, he left to accept an appointment as Assistant to the Regular Administrator of Equal Opportunity in the U. S. Department of Housing and Urban Development's [HUD] Fort Worth, Texas office. He was later promoted to the position of Administrator of the National Housing Authority, which investigated and recommended remedial action for victims in the Kansas flood of 1951.

In later years Smith was selected by the Justice Department to study Juvenile Crime and Youth Delinquency in the District of Columbia and represented Dallas, Texas in a Washington, D.C. conference on problems of desegregating public facilities.

As a businessman, for over forty years, Smith organized the Western Mutual Life Insurance Company in Dallas, Texas; was

Executive Vice-President, Sterling Enterprises; Proprietor, A. Maceo Smith and Associates; Co-proprietor of Harlem Advertising Agency, New York City; Oklahoma State Manager of Universal Life Insurance Company; Co-owner of Smith and Daniels Realty Co., Texarkana, Texas; and Publisher of the Dallas Express Newspaper, Dallas, Texas.

Among other positions Smith held were Executive Director, Dallas Negro Chamber of Commerce; Vice-President, National Negro Business League; President, Dallas Urban League; Co-Founder, Texas Conference of NAACP Branches; and Co-Founder, National Association of Real Estate Brokers. He was also a former president, Southwest Area YMCA board member; board member, Greater Dallas Council of Churches; trustee of Bishop College and a member of the National Conference of Christians and Jews Board. He also served as a board member of the Texas Association of Developing Colleges, a member of the Texas Commission on Human Relations and a member of the Dallas Rotary Club.

Smith's honors and awards included a Fisk University Alumni citation; Distinguished Service Award, Texas Conference, NAACP; Southwest Area Council, YMCA Award; Award for Distinguished Service in Housing, Prairie View A&M College; Special Service Award, Fort Worth Federal Business Association; Certificate of Merit Award HUD, and Distinguished Service Award, Dallas County Home Builders Association.

SPAULDING, CHARLES CLINTON, JR. (November 19, 1907-September 10, 1987), Corporate Executive, attorney, was born in Durham, North Carolina to Charles Clinton Spaulding, Sr. and Fannie (Jones) Spaulding. His father was the third president of the North Carolina Mutual Insurance Company.

Spaulding received an A.B. degree from Clark University (Massachusetts) in June 1930. In 1935, St. John's University School of Law (Brooklyn, New York) conferred upon him the LL.B. degree. Later, he was awarded a J.D. degree in 1960 by the New York University Law School.

While serving as vice president and general counsel of North Carolina Mutual Insurance Company, for approximately

40 years, Spaulding also served in a number of other company-linked positions. These included the chairmanship of the Real Estate and Mortgage Committee and the By-Laws Committee of the Board of Directors, and member of the Finance and Executive Committees. Aside from these company-linked positions, he was a member of the Board of Directors of Mechanics and Farmers Bank and the Mutual Savings and Loan Association of Durham.

During his lifetime, Spaulding served in a number of positions that enabled him to impact public policy at both the regional and national levels. These included the position of treasurer and member of the Executive Committee of the National Bar Association, and membership in the Insurance, Taxation, Corporation, and Family Law Sections of the American Bar Association and a member of the Criminal Code Commission of the State of North Carolina for three years. This Commission, appointed by the Attorney General of North Carolina spent three years revising the General Statutes of the State of North Carolina. Community-based affiliations included the Chairmanship of the Citizens' Advisory Committee of the City of Durham, North Carolina, and Chairman of the Durham Chapter of the American Cancer Society.

After retiring from the North Carolina Mutual Insurance Company in 1973, Spaulding joined the law firm of Pearson, Malone, Johnson, DeJarmon and Spaulding. On October 1, 1981, he opened a private practice of law.

The National Bar Association recognized Spaulding's outstanding service as a member of its Executive Committee in 1973 when he was presented the C. Francis Stratford Award for excellence in leadership.

STEWART, BENNETT McVEY (August 6, 1912-April 26, 1998), Politician, was born in Huntsville, Alabama. He attended public schools in Huntsville and received a B.A. degree from Miles College (Alabama) in 1936. From 1936 to 1938, he was an assistant principal of the Irondale High School in Birmingham. In 1938, Stewart returned to Miles College as an associate professor of sociology. He left this position in 1940 to become an executive in an insurance company.

In 1950 Stewart became the Illinois state director for the company, a position he held for 18 years. He, then, left the insurance business to become an inspector with the city of Chicago's building department and a rehabilitation specialist with the Chicago Department of Urban Renewal, where he advised property owners on the financing of renovations. In 1971, he was elected to the Chicago City Council from the 21st Ward, and was elected Democratic committeeman for the same ward in 1972. He held both of these offices until 1978.

After Congressman Ralph H. Metcalfe died in October 1979, Stewart offered as a candidate to fill this vacancy. In the general elections in November, he defeated former Chicago Alderman A. A. Rayner and was sworn into the 96th Congress on January 3, 1979.

In the Congress, Stewart was a member of the powerful Appropriations Committee. He supported federal loan guarantees for the financially troubled Chrysler Motor Corporation, which employed more than 1,500 workers in his district. And he advocated and tried to extend the time low-income persons could spend in public service employment programs.

After allegations of mismanagement in the Chicago Housing Authority surfaced, Stewart requested and received a General Accounting Office (GAO) review of the agency, in 1980. The investigation revealed that the agency's mismanagement had led it to the verge of bankruptcy. Stewart also carried on the tradition of Ralph Metcalfe and reintroduced resolutions calling for the celebration of Black History Month in February of each year. He often spoke out against proposed constitutional amendments to prohibit busing to achieve desegregation in public schools. He attacked the proposals as a "subversion" of the 14th Amendment and an attempt to reestablish segregation in the country.

In 1980, Stewart sought reelection for a full term in the House, but was defeated by a more charismatic candidate, Harold Washington. Stewart, then, returned to Chicago as interim director of the Chicago Department of Inter-Governmental Affairs (1981-1983). After 1983, he retired from public life.

TAYLOR, HOBART, JR. (December 17, 1920-April 2, 1981), Federal Official, attorney, was born in Texarkana, Texas, the son of Hobart, Sr. and Charlotte (Wallace) Taylor. Hobart Taylor, Sr. later moved the family to Houston where he became a businessman and a civil rights leader and retired as a millionaire.

Taylor, Jr. received an A.B. degree in Political Science from Prairie View A&M College (Prairie View, Texas) in 1939. He, then, entered Howard University where he was awarded an A.M. degree in Political Science and Government in 1941; he was awarded a J.D. degree by the University of Michigan in 1943. A former editor of the Michigan *Law Review*, he was admitted to the Michigan Bar in 1944. He also served as research assistant to the Chief Justice of Michigan, and Assistant Prosecuting Attorney and Corporation Counsel for Michigan's Wayne County.

Hobart Taylor, Jr. entered federal service in 1961 as a Special Counsel to President John F. Kennedy Although Taylor's legal acumen spoke for itself, a personal friend of his father from Texas, then Vice President Lyndon B. Johnson requested his presence in the White House. Taylor helped to craft the language of the Civil Rights Act of 1964 and went on to serve as Assistant Special Counsel to President Johnson after the assassination of President Kennedy, a member of the Commission on Postal Service and the President's Commission on Executive Exchange during the presidential administration of Jimmy Carter. He once remarked: "Seeing the Civil Rights Act of 1964 passed was one of the most satisfying experiences of my life." Following the passage of the Act, he was named by Johnson to serve as Executive Vice President and Director of Staff for the newly formed U.S. Equal Employment Opportunity Commission (EEOC) Taylor became the driving force in the early stages of the EEOC and helped to insure its initial stability. He was also one of the first officials to use the term "affirmative action", which began as a policy under the EEOC to prevent further discrimination.

After leaving the EEOC, he served as Director, Export-Import Bank of the United States, and was on the Boards of Directors of Aetna Life Insurance; A and P Food Stores; Standard Oil of Ohio, Westinghouse; Eastern Airlines; and the Burroughs Corporation. He was also the President of Beneficial Life Insurance Society of Detroit and a junior partner in Bledsoe and Taylor; then senior member, Taylor, Patrick, Bailer and Lee; and a partner in Dawson, Quinn, Riddell, Taylor and Davis, of Washington, D.C.

Taylor was a member of the Democratic National Committee and the NAACP as well as a board member and/or trustee of Dillard, Howard, and Michigan universities and the Loomis Institute.

Taylor's honors include alumni awards from his three alma maters and the National Urban League, National Association for the Advancement of Colored People, National Business League, Jewish Federation Council of Los Angeles, Chicago Committee of 100, U.S. Departments of Labor and the U.S. Navy. He was also designated a *Commandeur de l'ordre, National de la Republique de Cote D'Ivoire* by the Republic of the Ivory Coast.

VAUGHN, SARAH (1934-April 4, 1990) Entertainer, affectionately nicknamed "the Divine One", was born in Newark, New Jersey. As a youth, she had been called "Sassie". Vaughn studied piano and organ and sang in her church choir. In 1942, she was a winner at one of the amateur contests held at the famous Apollo Theater in Harlem. Subsequently, she performed with Earl "Fatha" Hines, Billy Eckstine, Dizzy Gillespie, John Kirby and Charlie Parker.

By 1947, she had become a jazz soloist and won very favorable critical accolades for her alto pitch which ranged from "honeyed to harsh." Among her more notable works were "Misty", "Lover Man", and "It's Magic." By the 1950s, she was performing annually in Europe as well as in all parts of the United States.

WALDEN, AUSTIN THOMAS (A.T.) (April 12, 1885-1965), Attorney, Civil/Human Rights Leader, was born to former bondspersons Jennie Tomirn and Jeff Walden. He attended Fort Valley High and Industrial School and was the lone graduate of the class of 1902. He received a bachelors degree from Atlanta University in 1907 and a law degree from the Unrvers6y of Michigan Law School in 1911.

Walden began practicing law in Macon in 1912, In June 1917 he joined the US army and daring World War 1 served as a captain and assistant judge advocate. He received an honorable discharge from the military in February 1919 and in that same year moved hrs law practice to Atlanta.

In 1948 Walden was a founding president of the Gate City Bar Association, a professional group of African American attorneys. He was also a member of the American Bar Association (ABA). As an attorney Walden appeared before courts in Georgia and other areas of the South as well as the United States Supreme Court. He began as a defender of often indigent blacks and faced often hostile judges and juries.

In addition to his legal practice, Walden became a member and/or officer in almost all of the major African American social welfare and political organizations in Atlanta and the nation. These included the NAACP, the Urban League and the YMCA. After acquiring some degree of wealth, he also became an investor in Atlanta's black banks and served on their boards of directors. He later built his own office building near historic Auburn Avenue in Atlanta, which housed his own law firm's offices. Among his clients was the National Baptist Convention, the largest black organization in the United States. He also became a member of the NAACP Legal defense Fund during the Civil Rights Era.

Beginning in the 1930s, Walden and other African American leaders in Atlanta drew national attention when they began organizing blacks to register and vote. Following the fall of the White Primary in Georgia in 1946, as a result of these efforts African Americans in Atlanta were poised to play a major role in shaping black politics and race relations in Atlanta. Through an organization known as the Atlanta Negro Voters League (ANVL), the Walden-led cadre of leaders traded black votes for as favorable climate of race relations as well as, infra-structural, educational, recreational improvements for Black Atlanta. As a result of his" wheeling-dealing" in the councils of White Power, Walden emerged as a genuine "political boss" in the New South.

Yet he did not abandon the practice of law. Indeed, he became one of the most prominent civil rights attorneys in the nation. After failing to win admission for a protégé, Horace ward to the University of Georgia, he and his team were successful in breaking down barriers at that university in 1961. He also played a prominent role in the successful attacks on bias at Georgia state University, in the Atlanta public schools and in public transportation in Atlanta.

Although Walden was not successful in obtaining a major political office in Georgia—he did serve on the Democratic executive committees for Atlanta and Georgia—he achieved a substantial milestone in 1964 when he was named an ad hoc judge for the Municipal Court of Atlanta—the highest judicial post held by an African American in Georgia at that time. However, he held the office for only a few months before his death the next year. Upon the occasion of his death, the *Atlanta Constitution* eulogized him as a "great southerner."

WALKER, JAMES ("Walker") (1926-October 30, 1992), Entertainer, was born in Mileston, Mississippi. In 1854, after being discharged from the U. S. Navy, he joined "the Dixie Hummingbirds" quartet. Walker soon became the lead singer and one of "the Hummingbirds" most powerful singers as well as a composer, writing more than seventy songs for his group. Under his leadership, "The Hummingbirds" became one of the nation's best known gospel quartets.

WASHINGTON, HAROLD LEE (April 15, 1922-November 25, 1987), Politician, was born in Chicago, Illinois, the son of Roy Lee, a Methodist minister as well as a Democratic precinct captain and Bertha Jones Washington. He attended DuSable High School in Chicago, where he was a track star. However, he left school in February 1943 in order to enlist in the U. S. Army. In the military, Washington rose to the rank of first Sergeant in an Engineer Aviation Battalion which received a Meritorious service Award for building a bomber landing strip on the Pacific island of Anguar in only twenty days.

Washington was discharged from the Army in 1946 and returned to Chicago to complete high school and begin collegiate studies. He received a BA degree from Roosevelt University (Illinois) in 1949 and a JD degree from the Northwestern University School of Law in 1952. He first became involved in local politics in 1954, when he succeeded his father as a Democratic precinct captain. Meanwhile, he also entered the practice of law and served as a corporation counsel (prosecutor) in Chicago from 1954 to 1958 and an arbitrator for the Illinois Industrial Commission from 1960 to 1964.

Washington entered elective politics in 1965 and won election to the Illinois House of Representatives. In 1976 he was elected to the state senate. Washington, however, ran into legal and political troubles in 1970 after being accused of accepting retainers from five clients for whom he failed to provide services. Thus, his license to practice law was suspended for one year. But during the course of this suspension, it was revealed that he had allegedly filed no tax returns for nineteen years. He was convicted in a U. S. District Court in 1972 for failing to file returns for four years. He was sentenced to two years in prison, but a federal judge suspended all but forty days of the penalty. Then, in 1975, the state supreme court lifted the suspension of his law license.

After winning only eleven percent of the vote in the Chicago mayoral election of 1977, Washington made a successful bid for a seat in the U. S. House of Representatives from the First District of Illinois in 1980. He defeated the candidate of the Democratic Party "machine" and then went on to win a landslide victory over his Republican opponent in the general elections. Washington garnered more than ninety percent of the votes cast. In the Congress, he championed social causes and services and led the fight to extend the provisions of the 1965 Voting Rights Act. He vigorously opposed most of the conservative policies, including increased military spending, of President Ronald Reagan. His popularity in his district continued to grow and when he offered for reelection in 1982, he increased his percentage of the votes cast to ninety-seven. Although Washington had committed himself to a long career in the Congress, black Chicagoans had different plans for him. During his second term in the House, Washington decided to enter the race for mayor of Chicago.

By the 1980s, many blacks in Chicago had become disillusioned with the politics of the "political machine" identified with Chicago's long serving mayor, Richard J. Daley. And although large numbers of them had supported Jane Byrne, an opponent of the Daley Machine and the first woman elected mayor of the city, they were not entirely satisfied with her policies toward them either. At any rate, a yearning for a black mayor of the nation's fourth largest city had developed.

As blacks energized and mobilized for the campaign to elect Washington, subtle, as well as overt, racial overtones were injected into the campaign by Washington's opponents. Nevertheless, on the strength of the black, Hispanic and liberal white vote, Washington defeated both Byrne and Richard M. Daley, son of the former mayor, in the Democratic Primary, with thirty-six percent of the ballots cast, and then went on, despite continued injections of race into the campaigns, to defeat his Republican challenger Bernard Epton with fifty-two percent of the vote. In his inaugural address on April 29, 1983, the new mayor credited his victory to "the greatest grass roots effort in the history of the city of Chicago." He asked for help from all of the citizens of the city and promised that "we are going to do some great deeds here together."

Despite Washington's victory with a majority of the votes cast, his political opponents still did not embrace the black mayor. A group of aldermen, entrenched in Chicago's ethnic and ward politics, set out to undercut his authority and to block his proposed reforms. The group of twenty-nine, led by alderman Edward R. Vrydolyak, were pitted against a pro-Washington group of twenty-one aldermen. The stormy relationship between the mayor and the Vrydolyak subsided only toward the end of the mayor's first term.

After fighting his way to some accomplishments, including the creation of an ethics commission, ward redistricting (increasing representation for African Americans and Hispanics), increasing the number of city contracts awarded to minorities, and improved public services, Washington offered for reelection in February of 1987. He turned back a comeback bid by former mayor Byrne in the Democratic Primary, garnering fifty-three percent of the votes cast and, then, retained his fifty-three percent of the vote margin against Vrrydolyak and Donald Halder in the General Elections. Tragically, however, within six months after his reelection and the promise of even greater reforms for the citizens of Chicago, Washington collapsed and died of a heart attack, at his desk, on November 25, 1987. In one of the many eulogies of Washington, Governor James Thompson said the mayor "knew the joy of politics as well as the tragedy. He was ferocious in political combat. But, most important, he determined that his election would mean something for people and this great city."

WASHINGTON, WALTER EDWARD (April 15, 1915-October 27, 2003) Politician, was born in Dawson, Georgia. His family later moved to Jamestown, New York, an industrial city that was relatively hospitable to its small Black Community. His father worked as a hotel bellhop, shoeshine man and ball bearing polisher. When his mother died, while Walter was in grade school, he went to live with a Miss Evelyn Andrews, a close friend of the family and later received notoriety in high school as a track star. After moving to Washington, D. C., Washington earned bachelor's and law degrees from Howard University there in 1938 and 1948, respectively. At Howard, he became a member of the student council and played football. One of his instructors, Ralph Bunche, advised Washington to pursue a career in public administration.

From 1941 to 1945 Washington served as a housing manager for the National Capital Housing Authority. Then, from 1945 to 1961, he served in various other executive positions with the Authority. In 1966, he became head of the New York City Housing Authority. But after only one year in this position, President Lyndon B. Johnson named him to the new position of mayor-commissioner of Washington, D. C., in a reorganized triumvirate commission system that governed the city. He was reappointed for two additional terms by President Richard M. Nixon.

Washington had been on the job for a mere six months when rioting broke out in Washington in the wake of the assassination of Martin Luther King, Jr. The mayor-commissioner won high marks for his dispassionate handling of the violence and for restoring order quickly. He, personally, walked through the city urging calm and resisted calls to have looters shot.

In 1973 the U. S. Congress approved home rule for the District of Columbia. In the city's first mayoral elections, in 1974, Washington was elected the city's first mayor. However, the city was still responsible to a southern-dominated Congress in several respects, particularly for much of its budget. Washington once complained that he was "unique. I have a great deal more responsibility than I have authority." As mayor, Washington won praise from federal officials and others for his careful, moderate approaches to his job and in his infrequent public pronouncements and for his frugal management of government. However, the city's black neighborhoods continued to be plagued by poor housing, drug infestation and crime. True to his low-key approach, Washington approached these problems slow and cautiously. Thus, when he ran for re-election in 1978, a more passionate and fiery candidate, running on a platform of community-based issues, Marion Barry easily defeated Washington.

One of the principal tributes to Washington's leadership, at least in the view of federal officials, was that he left a forty million dollar surplus in the city's budget. After leaving public service, Washington became a partner in a Washington law firm. He also devoted much time to an effort to establish a National Museum of Art and a city museum in the District of Columbia.

Following Washington's death, D. C. congressional delegate Eleanor Holmes Norton eulogized him for the "legendary. . . way which he dealt with the president and the Congress."

During his long career in public service, Washington served as vice chairman of the Human Resources Development Commission of the National League of Cities; was on the advisory board of the U. S. Conference of Mayors and a trustee of the John F. Kennedy Center for Performing Arts. He was given awards and citations by the NAACP (1969), the National Jewish Hospitality Committee (1973) the Capital Press Club (1974) and the Howard University Law Alumni Association (1974)

WATERS, ETHEL (October 31, 1900-August 1, 1977), Entertainer, was born in Chester, Pennsylvania. She first appeared on stage at age seventeen and later toured with jazz groups where she became "a leading theater and café personality." But after a religious conversion, Waters gave up singing in nightclubs and turned to spirituals.

After her talents were more widely recognized, Waters made her Broadway debut in Plantation Review of 1924. In this production, she scored one of the greatest song hits ever when she introduced the piece "Dinah." From Broadway she began making motion pictures and was cast in As Thousands Cheer, At Home Abroad, and Rhapsody in Black. In 1950, Waters was nominated for an Academy Award for her role in Pinky. Her last motion picture was The Sound and the Fury in 1958. By this time, however, Waters began appearing on such television programs as "The Tennessee Ernie Ford Show," "Daniel Boone," and "Route 66."

In her later life, Waters turned increasingly to singing, becoming noted particularly for blues renditions of "Am I Blue" and "Stormy Weather" as well as black spirituals. She was, according to an article in *the Atlanta Constitution*, "the first woman ever to sing 'St Louis Blues'" and thrilled millions around the world with her rendition of "His Eye Is on the Sparrow" with the Billy Graham Evangelical Crusade. She had been singing with the Crusade for fifteen years at the time of her death. Waters'; *His Eye Is on the Sparrow*, was published in 1951 and became a best seller.

In the 1960s, stricken with diabetes and heart problems, it was revealed that Waters had lost much of her wealth and was subsisting on social security. She admitted her financial difficulties but she said "if half the people that owed me money paid it back, I'd be a rich woman." Yet she refused to make television commercials in order to earn more money. Instead, she exclaimed "I couldn't be happier because I'm at peace with the Lord."

In an editorial published after Waters's death, *the Atlanta Constitution* commented that "few American entertainment figures have had careers as varied and memorable as Ethel Waters."

WILKINS, ROY (August 30, 1901-September 8, 1981), Civil/ Human Rights Leader, was born in St. Louis, Missouri, to William D., a minister, and Mayfield (Edmondson) Wilkins. His mother died when he was only three years of age. Young Wilkins was reared by an aunt and uncle in St. Paul, Minnesota. He attended high school there and was editor of his school's student magazine. In 1923, Wilkins received a Bachelors degree in sociology from the University of Minnesota.

While in college, Wilkins also studied journalism and was the night editor of his campus newspaper, the Minnesota *Daily*, and editor of the St. Paul *Appeal*, a black weekly. Also, as an undergraduate, he became involved in civil rights activity. He was secretary of the St. Paul chapter of the NAACP. Following a brutal lynching of blacks in Duluth, Minnesota, he delivered a stirring anti-lynching speech that won him a first prize at the University of Minnesota oratorical contest.

After graduation, Wilkins began a long journalistic career with a black weekly newspaper, the Kansas City *Call*. He progressed from reporter to managing editor over a period of seven years. He fought Jim Crow both through his newspaper columns and as secretary of the Kansas City Missouri Chapter of the NAACP. In 1930, even the national officers of the organization noticed his vigorous campaign to oust a segregationist in Kansas from the United States Senate.

The next year the new NAACP Executive Secretary, Walter White, called Wilkins to New York to serve as the civil rights group's assistant secretary. Wilkins quickly showed his ability, devotion, and courage. The NAACP had received complaints that black workers at the Army Engineer Mississippi River flood project were being discriminated against. The complaints included a charge that black laborers, who constructed flood prevention levees, were being paid only an average of ten cents an hour, much less than white workers, and that they were forced to buy all of their supplies from commissaries at exorbitant prices. Furthermore, there were reports that some black workers who had protested the biased conditions had been beaten or murdered. In 1932 Wilkins and a fellow journalist, George Schuyler, disguised as day laborers, set out to investigate the reports of bias and misdeeds on the Mississippi project. Police quickly arrested Schuyler at a Vicksburg, Mississippi boarding house, seized his pen, notebook, and money, and ordered him out of the state. Wilkins, who was living elsewhere, escaped unmolested. Neither, however, left the state. They moved to northwestern Mississippi and continued their investigation. The NAACP used their information to secure a Congressional probe of the Mississippi project, which resulted in ameliorating legislation. In 1934, Wilkins did manage to get himself arrested while picketing the office of the U.S. Attorney General in Washington, D.C. The protesters accused the Justice Department of failing to include lynching on the agenda of a national conference on crime.

Wilkins got a new opportunity to use his journalistic training and experience beginning in 1934, when he succeeded W. E. B. DuBois as editor of *The Crisis*, the NAACP's official organ. While editor of *The Crisis* he also spoke and wrote widely on behalf of the NAACP and the issues that it espoused. On one occasion, in 1943, he represented the NAACP in an effort to save the jobs of black transit workers in Philadelphia that were threatened by a strike of white motormen. The whites had objected to a recent promotion of eight blacks. As the NAACP's representative, Wilkins helped mediate the dispute, which ended after six days with the blacks still in their jobs.

In 1945, Wilkins joined DuBois and Walter White as a consultant to the American delegation at the founding meeting of the United Nations in San Francisco. And when White went on a one-year's leave of absence in 1949, Wilkins was elevated to acting executive secretary of the NAACP. During this time he also served as chairman of the National Emergency Civil Rights Mobilization that met in Washington, D.C. in January 1950, to press the federal government for fair employment and civil rights.

After Walter White returned from leave in the early summer of 1950, the NAACP underwent a managerial reorganization. Wilkins became internal administrator, with the responsibility of directing the national office, while White devoted himself to external affairs.

Within a year after the historic *Brown* vs. *Board of Education* school desegregation decision, Walter White, who had done so much to help produce that event, died of a heart attack. The NAACP Board of Directors quickly and unanimously elected Roy Wilkins as his successor.

As NAACP Executive Secretary from 1955 until 1977, Wilkins guided the civil rights organization into a more activist role. Congruent with the spirit of the times, the group abandoned its exclusive emphasis on school desegregation, housing bias, job discrimination, and voting rights, and took to the streets in direct action campaigns aimed at overturning discrimination in public accommodations. Wilkins, himself, was one of the leaders of the historic March on Washington in August 1963, and he marched with Martin Luther King, Jr. for voting rights in Selma, Alabama in 1965, and in the Meredith March Against Fear in Mississippi in 1966.

But since the NAACP, even under Wilkins, still focused its resources more on legal action, lobbying, and public relations than demonstrations, it was still seen as one of the more "conservative" of the organizations in the Civil Rights Movement. At the same time, however, NAACP lawyers and NAACP dollars were often used to extricate direct action demonstrators, some of them critics of the organization, from southern jails. And Wilkins was always included among those consulted within and without the Movement on direction, purpose, and strategy.

Much of the personal criticism of Wilkins stemmed from his outspoken opposition to the concept of "Black Power." Although he joined the Meredith March in Mississippi in 1966, where student cries of "Black Power" were first heard in the Movement, he broke sharply and openly with the advocates of the phrase.

Wilkins' recognitions included the Spingarn Medal of the NAACP in 1964, a Presidential Medal of Freedom in 1969, and the Freedom Award of Freedom House, also in 1969.

After retirement, Wilkins remained relatively inactive, because of declining health. Nevertheless, he could not escape further controversy. In a 1978 article, the *Atlanta Daily World* reported that Wilkins was suspected of working as an undercover agent for the FBI in an effort to discredit Martin Luther King, Jr. But King's close associate, SCLC President Joseph Lowery branded the accusation "a vicious effort on the part of the FBI to weaken the Civil Rights Movement." When Wilkins died on September 8, 1981, President Ronald Reagan ordered American flags flown at half-mast on all federal government buildings and installations.

WILLIAMS, PAUL REVERE (February 18, 1894-January 23, 1980), Architect, author, was born in Los Angeles, California to Chester and Lila Williams. Due to the death of his parents, he was orphaned at age four. Orphaned, Paul was raised by Mr. and Mrs. Clarkson. From 1912-1916 he attended the Los Angeles School of Art and the Beaux Arts School of Design Atelier. He attended the University of Southern California, from 1916-1919. Williams earned a Ph.D. degree from Howard University (Washington, D.C.).

Williams began his career working in architectural firms before earning his license to practice architecture in 1921. In 1922, he established his own architectural firm, Paul Revere Williams and Associates. In 1937, he wrote an autobiography entitled *I Am A Negro*. Williams designed many private and public facilities, including the homes of Frank Sinatra, William "Bojangles" Robinson, and Lucille Ball. Some of the public facilities he designed were the Los Angeles International Airport, U.S. Naval Station in Long Beach, and Wilson High School, Los Angeles' first high-rise educational building. During his busy schedule he found time to write two books entitled: *Small Homes of Tomorrow* (1945) and *New Homes of Today* (1946).

Williams received many appointments and accolades during his illustrious architectural career: in 1926, he became the first black member of the American Institute of Architects; was named Consulting Architect for the Southern California Division of Bank America and Associate Architect for the Federal Customs Building in Los Angeles; in 1953, he won the Spingarn Medal, the highest medal awarded by the NAACP, as well as the Los Angeles Chamber of Commerce's Award for Creative Planning in 1955. Williams was appointed by President Dwight Eisenhower to the President's Advisory Committee on Housing; by President Calvin Coolidge to the National Monument Commission; by Governor Earl Warren to the State Redevelopment Commission; by Governor Goodwin Knight to the State Housing Commission of California; and by Governor Patrick Brown to the California Beautiful Commission.

Despite receiving recognition from the majority culture, Williams, an active Republican, remained loyal to his heritage. He faced the stumbling blocks of racism. In his essay, "Tomorrow," he wrote about a counselor who told him to study to be a doctor instead of an architect because the counselor said, "I never heard of a Negro architect." An example of his profound insight on the topic of race relations, Williams said, "of course, I know that I cannot be accepted socially by whites. I have no desire to be, for I firmly believe that the Negro, in order to break down the racial barriers which affect his business success, should be ever careful in preserving the social barriers that set him apart."

Williams was determined to defeat prejudice by showing white Americans that African Americans can be successful in all competitive arenas. Williams said that, "White Americans have a reasonable basis for their prejudice against the Negro race, and if that prejudice is ever to be overcome it must be through the efforts of individual Negroes to rise above the average cultural level of their kind. Therefore, I owe it to myself and to my people to accept this challenge."

WILLIAMS, ROBERT F. (February 26, 1925-October 15, 1995), Civil/Human Rights Leader, was born in Monroe, North Carolina, the son of John Lemuel and Emma (Carter) Williams. Between 1942 and 1953, he attended Elizabeth City State Teachers College and Johnson C. Smith University in North Carolina as well as West Virginia State College, but apparently never received a baccalaureate degree.

Williams' activism began in 1942, when he was only 17 years old. Working as a machinist in a National Youth Administration (NYA) training program in North Carolina, he supported a brief strike of workers. Shortly thereafter he moved to Michigan and became an autoworker. Although he attended some of the meetings of the Communist Party in Detroit, he did not join the organization. In 1943, he found himself embroiled in the Detroit Riot, where blacks sought to fight off roaming white mobs. He soon relocated to San Francisco and worked briefly in a Navy Yard, before returning to his native Monroe. From there, he was drafted into the U.S. Army. While at Camp Crowder in Missouri, following World War II, he joined a protest against the racist acts of white officers and was sent to the camp stockade for insubordination. After leaving confinement at Camp Crowder, he was transferred to Fort Lewis Washington. After only six months there, he received an honorable discharge "without a good conduct medal."

Back in Monroe, Williams earned his high school diploma and wrote poetry, but earned little income. In search of livable wages, he worked briefly in New York and Los Angeles, before enlisting in the Marine Corps in 1954. He signed up for training as an information specialist, but instead was assigned to special combat training. As an expression of his resentment, Williams refused to salute the American flag at a parade ceremony, which resulted in a sentence of 180 days in the brig at Camp Pendleton, California. After his release, Williams underwent combat training for a possible assignment in Korea, but was discharged from the service before his unit embarked for the Asian peninsula.

Back in Monroe, again, Williams joined a predominately white interfaith Human Relations Group and the local NAACP. In 1955, the NAACP chapter in Monroe had only six active members. Williams took over the leadership of the organization and began a membership drive, focusing on laborers and the unemployed. The chapter's membership soon grew to almost 100 persons.

During this period, it was not uncommon for local Ku Kluxers, joined by others from neighboring South Carolina to drive through black neighborhoods, shooting them up. Blacks appealed for help to North Carolina Governor Luther Hodges, but received little relief. Williams and the local NAACP branch then formed a chapter of the National Rifle Association (NRA) and began training its members in the use of firearms. In the summer of 1957, a motorcade of Klansmen attacked the home of Dr. Albert E. Perry, a NAACP member. A black "armed defense squad" drove them away. Suddenly, this type of Klan activity ended in Monroe. Although, white controlled media generally suppressed news of the event, it was widely reported in the nation's black press.

In the fall of 1958, two young black boys were arrested and charged with rape after a seven-year old white girl kissed one of them on the cheek. The boys, aged seven and nine, were convicted and sentenced to 14 years in the state reformatory. Williams organized local protests, which were soon followed by others as far away as Europe. The state subsequently released the two boys.

As the Monroe Branch's reputation for militancy, including the advocacy of violent self-defense, spread, the National NAACP suspended Williams for two months. Williams, however, remained active in the Civil Rights Movement and began publishing a newspaper, *The Crusader*, to further disseminate his views.

Williams, then, continued to be a thorn in the side of local and state officials in North Carolina. They allegedly offered him bribes to tone down his rhetoric and his activities. When these failed, they allegedly tried to kill him. In June of 1961, a local automobile dealer was accused of trying to "run Williams off the road." Then in August, A. A. Mauney, Monroe's police chief told Williams that within "thirty minutes you'll be hanging in the courthouse square." The chief's comments came amid new racial violence aimed at local blacks as well as "Freedom Riders" from the North who were in the area protesting segregation on interstate buses.

During the melees a white couple, with alleged Klan sympathies, drove through a black community. Williams personally intervened to protect them from angry blacks. However, local authorities claimed that instead of protecting the whites, Williams had actually kidnapped them. The FBI joined local authorities in attempting to arrest Williams on the kidnapping charges. However, he escaped to the North and eventually went into exile in Cuba.

In Cuba, Williams won the support of the revolutionary government of Fidel Castro. He was allowed to continue his anti-racist activities through a medium known as "Radio Free Dixie" whose broadcasts reached the southern part of the United States. He later traveled to China, where he convinced Mao Tsetung to issue a statement of support for the African American freedom struggle.

Williams returned to the United States in 1969. He joined the Peoples Association for Human Rights and the New Afrika Movement. He was subsequently elected the first president of the Republic of New Afrika. Interestingly enough, after his return from exile, a New York Times article portrayed Williams as an opponent of the Cuban Revolution. While in Cuba, Williams had forged close relationships with noted revolutionaries, including Che Guevara. But, he did express concerns about the American Communists' positions on the black struggle for freedom in the United States. He claimed that they tended to "marginalize the African American community." These statements did not set well with American as well as Soviet Communist Party leaders and led to restrictions on "Radio Free Dixie."

Whether through writings or speeches, Williams, having settled in Michigan, remained an active and controversial person for the rest of his life. Before his own death in 1965, Malcolm X had said Williams "was just a couple of years ahead of his time; but he laid a good groundwork, and he will be given credit in history for the stand that he took."

WILLIAMSON, QUINTON VIRGIL (Q. V.) (December 25, 1918-August 4, 1985), Politician, businessman, the fifth of 13 children, was born in Atlanta, Georgia to Bertha and Noah Williamson. Q. V. attended Morehouse College (Georgia) where he took a B.A. degree in Business Administration in 1940.

Williamson has been referred to as a "trailblazer" in both politics and business, laying the foundation for other blacks to follow. Approximately three years after graduating from Morehouse, he founded Q.V. Williamson Real Estate Company, which ultimately became one of the largest real estate firms in Atlanta. In its heyday, the firm has had as many as 30 employees.

In the capacity of realtor, Q. V. formed the National Development Company, a corporation that sought to alleviate the critical housing shortage among blacks. The company purchased some 200 acres of land and built houses that led to the development of the Collier Heights subdivision, one of the leading black upper income housing developments at the time. And, as President and Chairman of the National Real Estate Brokers (a predominantly black group), he testified before congressional committees in the 1960s on civil rights and fair housing laws.

In the political arena, in 1965, Williamson became the first black since Reconstruction to be elected, citywide, to the Atlanta City Council, then called the Board of Aldermen. In 1969 this body unanimously elected Williamson as vice-president of its group. He also served on numerous committees of the City Council, including chairman of the Finance Committee. Colleagues said that Q. V. "displayed a knack for playing the white man's game of power politics... and he was considered a hero in the black community." Thus he attempted to increase black employment in all city departments. In 1965 there were only 60 black policemen, by 1969, the number increased to 175; there were 30 black firemen in 1965 but by 1969 there were 110.

Williamson, a leading black Republican, was an alternate delegate to the 1964 Republican National Convention and was one of 12 blacks appointed by the Republican National Committee to an advisory committee designed to find ways to strengthen Republican support among blacks.

Though exhibiting exemplary leadership skills in both business and politics, Williamson's life was not without controversy. His record was tainted with manipulation, conflict of interest and personal aggrandizement; at times he was unable to separate his political activity from his business interest. Thus Atlanta's Board of Ethics charged Williamson with violating the city's "conflict of interest rules" for voting to give a construction job to a firm that had promised to employ him. His realtor company also had been accused of housing violations. Nevertheless, at his death, Williamson was praised by black and white politicians and business persons for the influence and impact he had on public policies at both the regional and nation level.

Williamson was active in many professional and community organizations. He was chairman of the Board of Atlanta Mortgage Brokerage Company, chairman of the Executive Committee of Empire Real Estate Board, president of the Atlanta Currency Exchange, co-chair of the Atlanta Summit Leadership Conference, co-chair of the Atlanta Negro Voters League, member of the Butler Street YMCA Board of Directors, and member of the Mayor's Committee on Equal Job Opportunities.

WRIGHT, RICHARD (September 4, 1908-November 30, 1960), Author, civil/human rights activist, was born to Nathan Wright, a sharecropper, and Ella (Wilson) Wright in Natchez, Mississippi. His father deserted the family when Richard was only five years of age. After his mother, a rural schoolteacher and housemaid, suffered a series of paralyzing strokes, Wright's grandparents cared for him. However, the strain of attending the stricken mother and rearing her two sons often proved too much to bear. Thus, Wright suffered hunger and despair, and even spent a brief period in an orphanage. But his maternal grandparents continued to strive to support the family, and Wright was able to spend most of his youth with them in their Jackson, Mississippi home.

Wright's grandmother was a moralist who attended the Seventh-Day Adventist Church, but Richard, himself, refused to be baptized and disdained any organized religion. Yet, the grandmother endeavored to have him educated in the rigidly segregated schools of Mississippi. Wright, however, left school after completing the ninth grade and headed for what he thought was a better life, first in Memphis, in 1925, and then the North. But both racism and the Great Depression shattered his dreams of a "promised land" in Chicago. After several jobs, including dishwasher, porter, and insurance salesman, he joined the unemployment lines. And, his disillusionment also led him into Garveyism, then Marxism, and the Communist party, which he joined in 1933.

Wright's first publications as a novelist and essayist were in leftist publications such as *International Literature and New Masses*. But by the late 1930s he was a prize-winning author in mainstream publications, and had authored two of his most notable works, *Uncle Tom's Children* and *Native Son* (1939). Both of these books were powerful portrayals of white racism in America. *Uncle Tom's Children* was set in the rural South while *Native Son* had as its focus a northern urban ghetto. Both books showed the reactions of individual blacks to racist oppression, and suggested the need for resistance to overcome it. Since, however, Wright saw American capitalism as a principal villain in his stories and collective action as a potential remedy, many Americans dismissed the work as communist propaganda. More tolerant persons, however, applauded the literary genius in these works of social commentary. *Native Son* became a Book-of-the-Month and propelled Wright into the national spotlight. He also acquired a degree of wealth, and, in the same year, 1939, married Dinah Meadman.

Wright followed the success of *Native Son*, with his autobiography *Black Boy* in 1943. *Black Boy* was another Book-of-the-Month and, even, surpassed *Native Son* in sales. In *Black Boy*, Wright used his coming-of-age in Mississippi to show some of racism's devastating effects on southern blacks.

But Wright did not confine his social protest to written pages, he championed the cause of civil and human rights in the Communist Party and other interracial organizations. However, he broke with the communists in 1942, after realizing that they "used the Negro cause more than they served it." Yet, he supported with some reluctance, the party's call for unconditional participation on the part of American blacks in the war against Nazi Germany. He completed his break with the communists, however, after they refused to protest the discrimination against donors in Red Cross blood banks.

In 1947, after returning from an extended visit to France, Wright encountered a new incidence of racism in the Greenwich Village, New York neighborhood in which he lived. By this time he could no longer tolerate any racial limitations. He, thus, removed himself from American life and retreated to a "freer" existence in Paris, where he lived and wrote until his death. Wright was a 1941 Spingarn medalist.

YERBY, FRANK (1916-1991) Author, earned a master's degree from Fisk University in 1938. He taught college-level English for several years in Florida and Louisiana before heading north in 1941 to take a wartime factory job in Detroit, Michigan. During this same period, Yerby also began writing. His first published short story, "Health Card," was a bitter tale of racial injustice. It won a special O.Henry Memorial Award in 1944. Yerby then turned to producing historical fiction. In 1946, he published his first novel, *The Foxes of Harrow,* which took place on a southern plantation before the Civil War. (A year later, it was made into a hit movie starring Rex Harrison and Maureen O'Hara.) He returned again and again to this setting for many of his later stories and novels, which proved to be enormously popular with readers. Some of his other best-selling works were *The Golden Hawk, A Woman Called Fancy,* and *The Saracen Blade.* Yerby was often the target of criticism for his choice of subject matter. Black reviewers condemned him for not addressing the problems of his African American race. Reviewers who did not know he was black accused him of wasting his writing talent on cardboard characters and overdone plots. As the child of a racially mixed couple, Yerby responded by declaring: "I don't think a writer's output should be dictated by a biological accident. It happens there are many things I know far better than the race problem." Pointing out that his background was a mix of Scotch-Irish, Native American, and black, he explained, "I simply insist on remaining a member of the human race." His own solution to the racial discrimination he experienced in the United States was to leave the country. Yerby spent the second half of his life in Europe, living first in France before settling permanently in Spain.

YOUNG, WHITNEY MOORE, JR. (July 31, 1921 -March 11, 1971), Civil/Human Rights Leader, Organization Executive, was born in Lincoln Ridge, Kentucky to Whitney M. Sr., headmaster of a preparatory school, and Laura (Ray) Young, a teacher. He attended Lincoln Institute, a private school for blacks in Louisville, where his father was president. At Kentucky State College, Young was a basketball player and president of the senior class. He graduated from Kentucky State in 1941 and took a job as a teacher at the Rosenwald High School in Madisonville, Kentucky. He left this position, where he also served as coach and assistant principal, and entered the United States Army.

After his discharge from the Army, Young decided on a career in social work. To prepare himself, he earned a M.A. degree from the University of Minnesota in 1947. He wrote a history of the Urban League of St. Paul, Minnesota for his Masters' thesis. Following graduation, this same organization hired him as its director of industrial relations and vocational guidance. In this position, he was instrumental in securing jobs for local blacks in previously all-white positions, including clerks in department stores and motormen. In 1950, Young moved to Omaha, Nebraska to become executive secretary of the Omaha Urban League. While there, he also taught social work at the University of Nebraska and at Creighton University in Omaha. In 1954, he went south to Atlanta, to become the new dean of the School of Social Work at Atlanta University.

In Atlanta, he not only built an excellent reputation as an educational administrator by increasing both his school's enrollment and budget, but became a leader in local civil rights activities. He was elected vice president of the Atlanta branch of the NAACP. After leaving Atlanta in 1960 to take a Rockefeller Foundation special grant for study at Howard University, he was chosen, on August, 1961, Executive Director of the National Urban League (NUL).

Young was the fourth of a series of strong and able NUL Executive Directors, who included George Haynes (1911-1914), Eugene Knuckle Jones (1914-1941), and Lester Granger (1941-1961). He continued the tradition of efficiency and effectiveness of his predecessors by tightening the loose structure of the organization with greater centralization. He established five regional offices as well as a Washington lobbying facility. These changes and other NUL activities were supported by huge budget increases; from $325,000 annually when Young took over to more than $6,000,000, just a few years later.

Since the NUL's focus was on economic and social conditions among blacks, Young worked closely with major corporate executives in the country and the U.S. Labor Department. He impressed them as an intelligent, patriotic capitalist, who championed "green power" (money) over "Black Power." He, thus, won substantial support both from the public and private sectors for his programs. While his "Marshall Plan" at home for blacks, which envisioned expenditures of $100 billion to help overcome inequities, was never adopted, other ideas were. For example, his proposals that business actively recruit and train unskilled blacks became a core feature in the programs of the National Alliance for Business (NAB), founded under the direction of automaker, Henry Ford II.

Although Young was often placed in the "conservative" category of black leaders during the Civil Rights Movement, he often spoke and wrote forcefully for equality. In *To Be Equal* (1964) for example, he harshly criticized government and industry for the dismal economic plight of black Americans and called urgently for relief. And he brought the NUL into the activist ranks of the Civil Rights Movement as a leader of the 1963 March on Washington. Young, himself, often joined Martin Luther King, Jr. in marches and picketing at Selma and Montgomery, Alabama and elsewhere.

In 1969 Young was one of 20 Americans who were presented the Medal of Freedom, the nation's highest civilian award, by President Lyndon B. Johnson. He drowned while vacationing in the Gulf of Guinea, near Lagos, Nigeria in 1971.

IV. THE SEARCH FOR A BLACK AGENDA: TRADITIONS AND NEW CONTOURS

AILEY, ALVIN (January 5-1931-December 1, 1989), Entertainer, was born in Rogers, Texas. He founded the Alvin Ailey American Dance Theater in 1958 and choreographed seventy-nine ballets. In 1961, Ailey created his best known work "Revelations", which was based on his childhood experiences in black Baptist churches. The dance became his company's signature piece.

Ailey was also known for honoring the works of others whom he admired or with whose causes he supported. For example, "For Bird with Love" was a tribute to jazz saxophonist Charlie "Bird" Parker, who had been a victim of drug abuse. He refused to allow his company to perform in South Africa during that country's apartheid regime.

ASHE, ARTHUR (July 10, 1943-February 6,1993), Athlete, was born in Richmond, Virginia. He first played tennis when he was only seven years old, using a borrowed racket and practicing with it on the segregated courts near his home. Noticing that Ashe had talent, a playground instructor arranged for him to spend some time with Robert W. Johnson, a physician from Lynchburg, Virginia, who had made a second career out of training young black tennis players (The African American tennis star Althea Gibson had once been his student).

Over the course of several summers, Johnson helped Ashe work on his game. He also taught the youngster how to handle the pressures of competition without showing anger or frustration. Years later, Ashe put those lessons to the test time and time again. On the court, he displayed a sense of dignity, quiet determination, and an almost "superhuman calmness" that amazed—and sometimes annoyed his opponents. As the only African American athlete in a sport dominated by wealthy Euro-Americans, he changed many people's ideas about black athletes.

Ashe's rise up the amateur ranks continued throughout the 1960s. In 1963, for example, he was the first black named to the U. S. Davis Cup team. At the time, he was attending the University of California at Los Angeles (UCLA) on a tennis scholarship. There he trained under Pancho Gonzalez and J. D. Morgan. After graduating in

After undergoing open-heart surgery during the early 1980s, Ashe apparently contracted AIDS from a blood transfusion He confirmed the fact in April, 1992. Despite the debilitating disease, he continued his schedule of speeches, participated in anti apartheid protests, denounced racism in sports as well as the U. S. government's policies towards Haitian refugees.

BAILEY, PEARL (March 29, 1918-August 17, 1990), Entertainer, was born to African American and Creek parents in Newport News, Virginia. She began her professional career in vaudeville, singing in small clubs in Pennsylvania and Washington, DC. She then became a features singer with several big bands, including Count Basie's. After touring with the USO during World War II, Bailey made her first appearance on a New York stage in a play called "St. Louis Woman". She received national notoriety when she starred with Cab Calloway in the all-black version of the Broadway hit "Hello Dolly". Bailey's success as an entertainer has been partially attributed to the fact that she adeptly used her talents to transcend the racial stereotypes that stifled many other African American performers of her generation. She won such popularity among all groups in the United States that she was affectionately called "Pearlie Mae" and an "Ambassador of Love." Much of this renown stemmed from the distinctive witticisms she injected into her performances. She once offered: "If I just sang a song, it would mean nothing."

BASIE, WILLIAM ("Count") (August 21,1905-April 26, 1994), Entertainer, grew up in Red Bank, New Jersey and began taking twenty-five cent music lessons at the age of eight. Despite his protests, Basie's mother insisted that he was "going to learn how to play the piano if it kills you."

Basie began his professional career with Walter Page's Blue Devils group in the late 1920a, and later joined Benny Moten's band in 1929. When Moten died six years later, Basie took over and began the Count Basie Band. The group first achieved performance in 1935 when John Hammond, a jazz impresario who had brought Billie Holiday to prominence saw Basie's band in Kansas City. He was so impressed that he urged Basie to increase the size of the group from ten members and booked its first national tour.

It was also in Kansas City that Basie acquired the famous nickname "Count". A radio announcer while discussing the "royal family" of jazz, which included "Duke of Ellington" and "King of Oliver" he struck upon the idea of a "Count of Basie." But Basie never really liked the royal title. He once offered: "I wanted to be called Buck or Hoot or even Arkansas fats"—silent film heroes.

By 1936 Basie and his band had gained a national reputation and traveled widely throughout the country, although it was in residency at the Roseland Ballroom in New York City. During this period, the band "delivered several seminal improvisers to the world of jazz." Most notable were Buck Clayton, Herschel Evans and Lester Young, "whose logical flow of melody became the standard for horn players of subsequent generations."

The Basie band began recording in 1937 with such numbers as "One O'Clock Jump" which became "studies in call and response phrasing in which the saxophones often trade simple blues riffs with the brass." The group's early albums also included "Basie's Back in Town", "Blues by Basie" and "Super Chief".

During the 1950s the Basie band was pared down and began collaborating with blues singer "Big "Joe Williams in what "was widely considered a creative peak" for both Basie and Williams. Basie's last performance was on March 19, 1984 at the Hollywood Palladium in California on the fiftieth anniversary of his professional career.

Basie, who was perhaps most influenced by the legendary "Fats" Waller was a musician, according to jazz critic Whitney Balliett, who piloted "his ship from the keyboard with an occasional raised finger, an almost imperceptible nod, a sudden widely opened eye, a left-hand chord, a lifted chin, a smile, and plays background and solo piano that is the quintessence of swinging and taste and good cheer, even when almost nothing happens around it."

Following Basie's death in 1984, Joe Williams observed: "...we have just lost a national treasure but the happiness that his music gave will live."

BATES, DAISY (c. 1914-November 4, 1999), Civil/Human Rights Leader, association executive, was born in Huttig, Arkansas. She never knew her birth parents. Her adoptive parents were Orlee and Susie Smith. When she was only 15 years old, Daisy met her future husband, Lucius Christopher Bates. After they married in 1941, the two settled in Little Rock and used his savings from a job as an insurance salesman to begin one of Arkansas' largest and most successful black owned newspapers, *The Arkansas State Press. The Press* fought for better social and economic conditions for black Arkansans and fought alleged police brutality. It was credited with helping to achieve black policemen for black neighborhoods in Little Rock and for improving race relations there, and in other areas of the state, generally.

After the U.S. Supreme Court outlawed school segregation in *Brown* vs. *Board of Education*, in 1954, Bates, as president of the Arkansas Conference of the NAACP, became prominent in the effort to desegregate schools in her state. Although the superintendent of Little Rock's schools had announced the intent to proceed with "gradual integration" shortly after the *Brown* decision, nothing was accomplished immediately. Bates and others, then, concluded that local officials were "foot dragging" and, thus, began efforts on their own to achieve desegregation. Eventually nine black children agreed to become plaintiffs in a suit to force desegregation. In 1956, a federal judge ordered the desegregation of the Little Rock schools to begin in September 1957.

Sporadic acts of violence, including a rock thrown through the front window of the Bates' home, broke out prior to the opening of schools in Little Rock in the fall of 1957. On August 29, a federal judge issued an injunction delaying the scheduled desegregation, citing reports and rumors of violence and potential violence. Once this decision was overturned on appeal, the school board asked black students to voluntarily stay away from the school and Governor Orval Faubus ordered the Arkansas National Guard to Little Rock's Central High School to prevent "violence." Faubus, previously described as a "moderate" on racial issues, also made a decision to prevent the black children from entering the school. After initial attempts by black pupils to enroll on September 3 and September 23, 1957 were thwarted by violence, President Dwight D. Eisenhower, who had generally favored a "States' Rights," gradual approach to the desegregation of the nation's schools, ordered the Arkansas National Guard federalized and the Secretary of Defense to take appropriate means to enforce the desegregation orders of the courts.

On September 25, 1957, Daisy Bates escorted the black children, "the Little Rock Nine," into Central High School, under the protection of federal troops. A month later, Bates and several other NAACP officials were arrested and charged with violating a recently enacted city ordinance that required organizations "to supply the city clerk's office with information regarding its membership, contributors, and expenditures." Amid widespread denunciations of this action across the country, Bates refused to comply and was subsequently fined $100.

Still, the desegregation of Central High did not go smoothly, there were continued sporadic violence, taunts, Daisy Bates, were continuously harassed and the school and threats. The black children and their parents, as well as Reverend Llewellyn L. Berry, an African American Methodist Episcopal minister, and Beulah (Harris) Berry, a school teacher. His father pastored small churches in Virginia and North Carolina and served for 21 years as Secretary of Home and Foreign Missions of the A.M.E. Church.

BEARDEN, HAROLD IRVIN (May 8, 1910-March 19, 1990), Minister, Civil /Human Rights Leader, was born in Atlanta, Georgia, the son of Lloyd and Mary Da Costa Bearden. He received an AB degree at Morris Brown College and a BD degree from Turner Theological Seminary (both in Georgia). Bearden was ordained a deacon in the African Methodist Episcopal Church (AME) in 1930 and an elder in 1931. He pastured the Big Bethel AME Church, one of the oldest and largest African American congregations in Atlanta, from 1951 to 1964.

From 1960 to 1962, Bearden was an acting presiding elder of the AME Church and in 1964, he was consecrated a bishop in Cincinnati, Ohio. After elevation to the bishopric, Bearden was assigned to Central and West Africa. While there he was elected president of the board of trustees of Monrovia College in Liberia. Upon his return to the United States, Bearden had district assignments in Ohio and Texas before being named bishop of the Sixth Episcopal District in his native Georgia in 1976. Between 1973 and 1974 he was president of the AME Council of Bishops.

Bearden served as bishop of the Sixth Episcopal District of Georgia until 1980, but continued to serve on special assignments for his church until his retirement in 1984.

Bearden served as president of the Atlanta chapter of the NAACP in 1958-59. During his tenure, a suit was filed to desegregate the Atlanta public schools and the city's buses. Prior to the filing of the bus suit, Bearden was one of the 100 black ministers who participated in a demonstration that defied Georgia's bus desegregation laws. Two years later a federal court ordered the buses desegregated. Meanwhile he continued to use his Sunday radio broadcasts to chide both segregationists and black accommodationists about Jim Crow practices in Atlanta and the nation, and he was one of the first major adult leaders to support student sit-in demonstrations in Atlanta in the 1960s.

Bearden was also a director of the Atlanta University Center consortium of black colleges and was a chairman of the boards of trustees of both of his alma maters—Morris Brown College and Turner Theological Seminary. In 1978 the state senate of Georgia named him an "outstanding citizen."

In one of the eulogies for Bearden, after his death in 1990,

Jesse Hill, president of the Atlanta Life Insurance Company and a trustee of the Big Bethel Church, offered that: "When the history of the turbulent '60s and the bi-racial progress of Atlanta is written, the name of bishop Harold I. Bearden, then the dynamic, fearless pastor of Big Bethel AME Church, has to be placed up front." And John Hurst Adams, a senior bishop of the AME's Sixth Episcopal district, remembered Bearden as "a major influence in the life of the community. He was active in community development, the civil rights movement, and all aspects in the advancement of the community and especially aspects of African American community unity."

BLACKWELL, LUCIEN E. (August 1, 1931-January 24, 2003), Politician, labor official, was born in Whitset, Pennsylvania. He attended West Philadelphia High School, but left before obtaining his diploma. Blackwell lacked formal higher education, but he persevered through the "school of hard knocks." He first found employment working on the waterfront of Philadelphia. He began as an unskilled laborer and gradually moved up to be a foreman, a trustee, vice president, business agent and eventually, in 1973, he became the president of Local 1332, International Longshoreman's Association of the AFL-CIO. He served in this capacity until 1991. Blackwell also served in the United States Armed Forces during the Korean War, and received the National Defense Service Medal with two Bronze Service Stars, a Meritorious Unit Commendation, and the Good Conduct Medal.

Before becoming a state representative in 1973, Blackwell was the Chairman of the Philadelphia Gas Commission. He used his insight as a labor official to regulate utility prices. Accordingly, he made history by rejecting three requests by the Philadelphia Gas Works to increase gas rates that resulted in the streamlining of management operations for the first time in the history of the Philadelphia utility.

In 1973 Blackwell emerged as an astute politician. During his term as a state representative (1973-1975), he sponsored Resolution 67 that was aimed at countering the gang problem infesting Philadelphia. The resolution brought a legislative panel to Philadelphia to investigate the city's gang war problem and to recommend solutions to this negative vice in the community. As a result of his leadership, the Crisis Intervention Network, "which received nationwide acclaim for its anti-crime activities," came into fruition.

In 1975 Blackwell began his sixteen-year tenure as a member of Philadelphia's City Council. As a city councilman he remained committed to the common people. The exhaustive list of his accomplishments as a city councilman partially include leading the way in appropriating funds for turning graffiti-marred walls of Philadelphia into artistic opportunities for the youth of the city and "protesting the closing of the Philadelphia General Hospital, and initiating action that resulted in the allocation of the first expenditures of the more than $50 million for a homeless program which was the first in the nation." The latter endeavor by Blackwell was accompanied by his fast for six weeks as a means of protest of the deplorable maintenance of housing projects by the Philadelphia Housing Authority. During this tenure Blackwell also ran for mayor twice, in 1979 and 1991, but was defeated on both occasions.

Blackwell was presented an opportunity to enter the United States House of Representatives when William H. Gray III of Pennsylvania's 2nd Congressional District resigned to become president of the United Negro College Fund in September of 1991. Blackwell won a special House election on November 5, 1991 and pronounced that he would "not become a big shot" and he "hoped God will rip out my eyes and pull out my tongue and throw it to the four winds" if he ever failed to adhere to the people's needs. This style of candid leadership of the "small people" of the nation helped Congressman Blackwell take a "remarkable leap in seniority", the fastest in 44 years.

In the Congress, Blackwell sat on the Public Works and Transportation and the Merchant Marine and Fisheries Committee and the Sub-committee on Economic Development, where he was vice chairman. Blackwell was also appointed to a special task force to deal with the "crisis of hopelessness" in the national health care reform. Of the latter, he once stated: "The spiraling cost of routine care, preventive care, prescription drugs and long-term care has forced many families to choose between buying food and seeing a doctor or between caring for themselves and paying rent." He concluded by saying that "clearly change is needed."

BOWMAN, THEA (1948-March 30, 1989), Clergy, Educator, was the only African American member of the Franciscan Sisters of Perpetual Adoration. She also served as director of intercultural awareness for its Jackson, Mississippi diocese and was a member of the faculty of the Institute of Black catholic Studies at Xavier University in New Orleans (the only historically black Catholic-related institution of higher education in the United States).

In 1988, Bowman recorded an album, *Sister Thea: Songs of My People*, which consisted of fifteen African American spirituals. The recording led to nationwide popularity for the sister and she was sought for appearances and performances on college campuses and at several national conventions. In that same year, she appeared on the CBS-TV news program. "60 Minutes" which led to discussions about a possible movie based on her life and work.

Because of her pioneering efforts to encourage black Catholics "to express their cultural roots inside the church" as well as other aspects of her educational work, Bowman received many awards and recognitions. In 1989 she received the U.S. Catholic Award from *U. S. Catholic Magazine* "for furthering the cause of women in the Roman Catholic Church." And in the same year, the Sister Thea Bowman Black Catholic Educational Foundation was established in order to "provide financial support for black students in Catholic primary and secondary schools and in Catholic colleges and universities.

Upon the occasion of her death in 1990, bishop Joseph Houck, of the diocese of Jackson, offered: "She was an outstanding woman. She was proud of her heritage and totally dedicated to the vision of Jesus Christ for love and growth of all people."

BRADLEY, THOMAS (December 29, 1917-September 29, 1998), Politician, was born in Calvert, Texas, to Lee Thomas and

Crenner (Hawkins) Bradley. In 1937, Bradley entered the University of California – Los Angeles. However, in 1940, he withdrew to become a Los Angeles police officer. Although Bradley interrupted his education for approximately twenty years, he earned his law degree from Southwestern University in 1956.

Bradley enjoyed an illustrious career as a police officer. During his 22 years as a police officer; he rose from a juvenile officer and detective to the first black lieutenant. After his final five years as a police officer, Bradley began his private legal practice. However, he did not remain out of government for long. In 1963, Bradley became the first elected African American Los Angeles City Councilman. He served Los Angeles in this capacity for the next decade. In 1969, Bradley initiated his first campaign for the highest position in the city, mayor. Not to be denied twice, in 1973, he became Los Angeles' first black mayor. Bradley continued to achieve milestone after milestone. He became Los Angeles' mayor for an unprecedented five consecutive terms.

During his tenure as mayor, Bradley supervised the city's phenomenal growth. Under his guidance, Los Angeles built a rapid transit system and its budget increased from $623 million to approximately $4 billion. Mayor Thomas Bradley successfully courted the 1984 Summer Olympic Games. Hence the city earned the name "Gateway to the Pacific Realm." Furthermore, under Bradley's leadership, downtown Los Angeles grew five times its 1973 size.

However, he was not able to accomplish the aforementioned milestones without experiencing some setbacks. Bradley had to struggle with the rise in inner-city crime, drug abuse, racial tensions, and the Los Angeles Police Department's (LAPD) reputation of police brutality. The 1991 videotape beating of black motorist, Rodney King, by several white LAPD officers served as the precursor to the impending crisis. However, the officers' acquittal sparked several days of rebellion. Bradley, limited by the City Council's power, asked for LAPD Chief Daryl Gates' resignation.

Constantly striving for higher goals, Bradley set his sights on becoming California's governor. In 1982 and 1986, he campaigned and narrowly lost the general election. The attempt was significant because it marked the first time that a black candidate received the "primarily white statewide support of the Democratic Party." Additionally, if he had been elected, Bradley would have become the first African American governor.

BRANSON, HERMAN (August 14, 1914-June 7, 1995), Educator, was born in Pocahontas, Virginia. He was educated at Virginia State College, *summa cum laude*, 1936, and the University of Cincinnati, where he received a PhD in Physics, 1939.

Branson began a teaching career at Howard University in 1941 and was named Director of the ESMWT (Experimental Science and Mathematics W Technology) Program in Physics at Howard (1942-44) and Director of ASTRP courses in Physics at Howard University. In 1944, he was promoted to professor of Physics and Chairman of the Department of Physics. In 1947, Branson was named the Director of the Office of Naval Research and Atomic Energy Commission Projects in Physics at Howard and from 1946 to 1950 he was Director of the Research Corporation Project there..

In 1968, Herman Branson was selected as President of Central State University. After only two years in this position, he left Central State to become president of Lincoln University (PA) and served in that capacity until his retirement in 1985.

Branson's teaching and research interests were in mathematical biology and protein structure. He was an AAAS Fellow (1936-1939); a member of Sigma Xi, the honor society or the American Chemical Society and Sigma Pi Sigma, the society for the American Physics Association; a Rosenwald Fellow and a senior fellow at the National Research Council; a member of the American Chemical Society, American Physical Society, Washington Academy of Science, Philosophical Society of Washington, Carver Research Foundation, National Science Teachers Association, the National Medical Fellowships (1971), and National Research Council (1972 to the time of his death).

BROWN, RONALD HARMON (August 1, 1941-April 3, 1996) Political Leader, Federal Officer, was born in Washington,

D.C., the son of William H., a hotel manager, and Gloria Osborne Carter Brown. Brown received his B. A. degree at Middlebury College in Vermont in 1962. After serving as the only black officer at his U. S. Army post in West Germany, he returned home to earn his law degree from St. John's University School of Law in 1970.

After law school, Brown built a successful career as a lobbyist and a social worker for the National Urban League in Washington, D.C., from 1968-79. While serving as the first African-American attorney at a major Washington law firm, he also served as deputy campaign manager for Senator Edward Kennedy from 1979-80. Brown also served as chief counsel for U. S. Senate Committee on the Judiciary in 1980 and general counsel and staff director for Senator Edward Kennedy in 1981. From 1981-85, he served as the Democratic National Committee deputy chairperson and chief counsel and became the chair from 1989 through 1992. Brown was successful in helping Democrats win important elections. He helped elect the first black governor in Virginia and a black mayor in New York City. Also, Democrats won four congressional seats in special elections, including former vice-president Dan Quayle's seat in heavily Republican Indiana. Between his duties on the Democratic National Committee, Brown served as campaign manager for Jesse Jackson at the 1988 Democratic National Convention.

During the 1990s, Brown's greatest challenge was redefining the image of the Democratic Party. By nudging the party toward the center of the political spectrum, he threw the party's support behind an emerging Democratic figure, Arkansas governor Bill Clinton. During the 1992 campaign, Brown helped calm the voices of dissent in the Democratic Party and created unity for the party's candidate. His behind-the-scenes maneuverings were key to the first Democratic presidential victory since 1976.

In appreciation for his work, Clinton named Brown the Secretary of Commerce. The U. S. Senate in 1993 confirmed him as the nation's first African-American Secretary of Commerce. Brown was a key spokesperson for the administration's economic and trade policies, helping U. S. firms win contracts in developing and newly industrialized nations.

Brown's life was cut short, on April 3, 1996, in a plane crash during a trade mission to Bosnia. During his lifetime, Brown received American Jurisprudence awards for outstanding achievement and outstanding scholastic achievement in poverty law. He was also the recipient of several honorary degrees. The Ron Brown Scholars program, established in his honor, has emerged as one of the nation's most lucrative scholarship for black students.

CALLOWAY, CAB (December 25, 1907 or 1908-November 18, 1994), Entertainer, first achieved notoriety as a band leader and scat singer at the famed Cotton Club in Harlem, New York, where he often filled in for Duke Ellington. He was one of the first performers to use scat—singing randomly with non-sensical syllables. The sound was widely applauded by audiences in New York and elsewhere. One of his most notable compositions, "Minnie the Moocher", with the refrain—hi de hi de hi de ho— invited the audience to sing along in a call and response style.

Calloway also appeared in several films in the 1930s and 1950s. He was introduced to younger generations when he appeared in a 1980 film, *The Blues Brothers*, where he performed "Minnie the Moocher."

CAMPANELLA, ROY (November 19, 1921-June 26, 1993), Athlete, was born in Philadelphia, Pennsylvania to a black mother and a father of Italian descent. He began playing professional baseball at the age of fifteen and joined the Negro Leagues as a member of the Elite Giants out of Baltimore, Maryland. He became a Brooklyn Dodger in 1948, the year after Jackie Robinson broke the color barrier in major league baseball. (Twenty-one years later, he followed Robinson again, this time as the second black player elected to the Hall of Fame.)

Campanella spent the next ten years as a Dodger. A powerful hitter with exceptional fielding skills and a natural ability to lead, he quickly became one of the game's best all-around catchers. He picked up Most Valuable Player awards in 1951, 1953, and 1955 and was a major force behind the Dodgers' success during the 1950s, which included five pennants and, in 1955, a

World Series victory. Always friendly and cheerful, he was also one of the game's most popular stars.

Campanella's dazzling career was cut short one icy night in 1958 when his car skidded off a road on Long Island, New York. The vehicle then overturned, leaving him paralyzed from the chest down. On May 7, 1959, a benefit game between the Dodgers and the Yankees was held in the Los Angeles Coliseum to help pay for the costs of his medical care. In attendance were 93,103 fans, and thousands more were turned away. It was—and still is—the largest crowd ever to attend a major league baseball game.

Despite his disability, Campanella remained active with the Dodgers organization for the rest of his life. In 1977, he began serving as a special instructor of promising young catchers during the spring training season.

CHISHOLM, SHIRLEY ANITA (ST. HILL) (November 30, 1924-January 1, 2005), Politician, educator, was born on November 30, 1924, in Brooklyn, New York, to Charles and Ruby St. Hill, who were both from Barbados. Despite their low incomes, Chisholm's parents provided her with a stable family life as well as black pride. Her high academic credentials in high school earned her scholarship offers from Oberlin and Vassar colleges; however she enrolled at Brooklyn College for financial reasons. At Brooklyn College, Chisholm pursued a teaching career. In 1946, she graduated *cum laude* with a B.A. degree in education. She, then, enrolled at Columbia University where she pursued a Masters degree in early childhood education.

During the 1950s, Chisholm entered politics for the first time when she helped Lewis S. Flagg, Jr., a black lawyer, campaign for a district court judgeship in New York. In 1960, she helped form the Unity Democratic Club which was designed to cultivate and elect candidates for New York State's 17th District. In 1964, Chisholm ran for the 17th Assembly District seat and won. During her four years as a representative, she was instrumental in helping to introduce several bills to help disadvantaged students and domestic employees.

Then in 1968, Chisholm was elected U.S. Congresswoman

from New York's 12th District—the first African-American female ever elected to the House of Representatives. She served seven terms, from 1968 to 1982. In Congress, Chisholm served on the Veteran's Affairs Committee, the House Rules Committee, and the Education and Labor Committee and introduced bills to aid the less fortunate. She was an early proponent of increased day care programs and an ardent champion of a guaranteed annual income.

In 1972, Chisholm, hoping to encourage other minorities to run, ran for the Democratic presidential nomination. She entered primaries in 12 states, won 28 delegates and received 152 first ballot votes at the Democratic National Convention.

Following her unsuccessful attempt to gain the Democratic Party's presidential nomination, Chisholm returned to the House and helped lead an impassioned campaign to oppose President Richard Nixon's plans to dismantle the Office of Economic Opportunity. She also played a leading role in the effort to expand the coverage of the minimum wage so as to include domestic workers.

Under succeeding Republican presidential administrations, including those of Gerald Ford and Ronald Reagan, Chisholm continued to be a strident voice for the poor, the dispossessed, minorities and women and a fervent, often eloquent, opponent of "conservative" political policies and actions.

In 1982, because of the "increasingly conservative political atmosphere" and the serious illness of her husband, Chisholm retired from the Congress. Even though she remained out of politics, she endorsed Jesse Jackson's 1984 and 1988 U.S. Presidential bids and often spoke on political issues at colleges and universities across America. From 1983 to 1987, she was a distinguished professor at Mount Holyoke College in Massachusetts. She also wrote two autobiographies on her life, *Unbought and Unbossed* in 1970 and *The Good Fight* in 1973.

CLARK, SEPTIMA POINSETTA (1898-December 15, 1987), Civil/Human Rights Leader, was born to former bondspersons in Charleston, South Carolina. She earned a bachelors degree from Benedict College in her native state and a master's degree from

Hampton Institute in Virginia. Clark became a teacher on John's Island in South Carolina in 1916. Two years later she moved to the Avery Institute in Charleston. During that same year, she began major political activities by organizing a drive to collect 20,000 signatures on a petition to have African American teachers hired in the Charleston County School District. In 1920, the law prohibiting the employment of black teachers was repealed. In 1927, Clark moved to Columbia, South Carolina and immediately aided a campaign to equalize salaries for black and white teachers.

After residing for several years in Columbia, Clark returned to Charleston and resumed teaching. However, in 1955 she was dismissed from her teaching position for being a member of the NAACP. Meanwhile, she worked at the Highlander Folk School in Tennessee where she developed a program to teach illiterate African Americans how to pass literacy tests and qualify to vote. She later became a director at Highlander and a supervisor of teacher training for the Southern Christian Leadership Conference (SCLC).

CLEAGE, ALBERT BUFORD (JARAMOGI ABEBE AGYEMAN) (June 3, 1911-February 20, 2000), Clergyman, was born in Indianapolis, Indiana, the son of Albert Buford (a physician) and Pearl (Reed) Cleage. After attending Wayne State University in Michigan (1929-1931) and Fisk University (Tennessee) (1931-1932), he received a B.A. degree from Wayne State in 1937. In 1934, he attained a Bachelor of Divinity degree from the Oberlin College Graduate School of Theology. Cleage also studied briefly at the University of Southern California Film School in the 1940s. Between 1936 and 1938, Cleage was a social worker for the Detroit, Michigan Department of Public Health. During this period, he was also a minister in the Union Congregational Church in Painesville, Ohio. Continuing in the ministry, he served variously at the Chandler Memorial Congregational Church in Lexington, Kentucky (1942-1943); the St. John's Congregational Church in Springfield, Massachusetts (1946-1951); the Church for the Fellowship of All Peoples in San Francisco, California (1943-1944); and the St. Mark's

Community Presbyterian Church of Detroit (1951-1953). In 1953 he founded the Central Congregational Church in Detroit. Four years later, he founded the Black Christian Nationalist Movement that led to the establishment of the Shrine of the Black Madonna and the Pan African Orthodox Christian Church denomination in the 1960s and 1970s, respectively.

Beginning with his tenure at the St. John's Church, Cleage became active in the Civil Rights Movement and other political and social causes. He was a leader of the local NAACP branch in Springfield, Massachusetts and championed equal employment opportunities, especially. In June of 1963, Cleage joined the Reverend Martin Luther King, Jr. in a "Walk to Freedom" through the streets of Detroit. Soon thereafter, however, Cleage began an intensive study of earlier black religious movements and concluded that the teachings of Malcolm X and the Nation of Islam held a good deal of attraction for him. Malcolm's philosophies were at odds with the integrationist tenets of King and other leaders of the Civil Rights Movement.

Cleage took another major step toward the Separatist philosophy espoused by Malcolm X in March of 1967, when he installed an 18-foot painting that featured a black Madonna and the infant Jesus. When the work was dedicated on Easter Sunday, Cleage revealed his ideas for a separate Christian denomination for African Americans – a denomination which would worship a savior who, he claimed, the Bible suggested was of African heritage. This dedication signaled the birth of the Black Christian Nationalist Movement. Although, based upon Christian doctrine, as interpreted by Cleage, the Movement also adopted aspects of the political and social philosophies of Black Nationalist Marcus Garvey and the religious and political doctrines of Elijah Muhammed and Malcolm X of the Nation of Islam.

The Black Christian Nationalist Movement (BCNM) soon won hundreds of converts in Detroit and by the 1990s had spread as far as Houston, Texas in the southwest and Atlanta, Georgia in the southeast. By that time, however, as the Civil Rights Movement continued to wane, attendance at the "mother" Shrine Church in Detroit had declined considerably. The BCNM, nevertheless, remained a distinctive element of African American religious life in the United States. It was, like the Nation of Islam, one of the first major challenges to traditional black worship in African American history. And, it was bolstered by codifications of doctrine from Cleage's own speeches and writings as well as his disciples. The novel concept of Jesus as a black revolutionary, one who led "a non-white people struggling for national liberation against the rule of a white nation" was, and is, an attractive alternative to blacks disaffected with the tenets and practices of "a white Christian nation" – the United States of America.

Following Cleage's death in February 2000, Detroit's Congresswoman Carolyn Cheeks Kilpatrick said that he "was an articulate spokesman for the advancement of the black struggle against injustice, racism and inequality. Through his many books and publications, he articulated a vision for Black America that included the use of religion as a system of liberation instead of oppression."

CLEAVER, ELDRIDGE LEROY (June 5, 1935-May 1, 1998), Black Nationalist Leader, was born in Wabbeseka, Arkansas to Leroy, a dining car waiter, and Thelma Lee Cleaver, a janitor. His family migrated to California soon after his birth. As a youth Cleaver had several run-ins with the law. In 1954 he was sent to reform school and later to Soledad Prison for selling marijuana. After serving two and a half years he was paroled but later arrested again and sentenced to 14 years in prison for assault. In prison he became acquainted with the Nation of Islam and an ardent follower of Malcolm X. His political/racial consciousness inspired him to read widely and write prolifically; national periodicals sponsored a campaign supporting his release. In 1968 he won parole and became a staff writer for *Ramparts* magazine. In the same year, he published *Soul on Ice*, a collection of his prison writings.

He joined the Black Panther Party in 1967 and was soon named minister of information. As a member of the Central Committee, Cleaver was particularly influential. He spoke throughout the nation and wrote for the Black Panther newspaper. In 1968 he and other Panthers were attacked by Oakland police. While attempting to surrender, police killed 17-year old Bobby Hutton who was hiding with Cleaver in the basement of a home. Once arrested, Cleaver was shortly released on a writ of *habeas corpus*. But when the writ expired, he was ordered to return to prison. Instead he fled to Cuba.

From Cuba, Cleaver went into exile in Algeria, where he established the International Section of the Black Panther Party (BPP). He also continued to write polemical essays on race and nationalism. Eventually an ideological split developed between Cleaver and followers of BPP leader Huey Newton. Cleaver believed that the BPP was becoming too reformist and therefore losing its scope of revolutionary ideals. Recent evidence has shown that the rift was exacerbated by the FBI's Counterintelligence Program (COINTELPRO). The split, however, prompted a harsh exchange of words from both sides and the expulsion of Cleaver from the Party in 1971.

Shortly thereafter Cleaver left Algeria and settled in France where he claimed to have had a spiritual rebirth. In 1976 he returned from exile a born-again Christian with a particular new found appreciation for the United States government. In 1978, he opened a boutique in Hollywood selling men's pants with his own, specially designed cod-piece. He later ventured into pottery and recycling in northern California. In 1979, Cleaver founded the Eldridge Cleaver Crusades, an evangelical organization. He had planned to open headquarters in the Nevada desert. He also toured the country, telling of his spiritual conversion and urging others, particularly in Fundamentalist churches, to follow in his path.

Politically, Cleaver became a Republican, supporting both Presidents Ronald Reagan and George Walker Herbert Bush. In 1984, he ran unsuccessfully for Congress as an "independent conservative." Interestingly and ironically, after spending much of his life criticizing the United States and its political system, after his "rebirth," Cleaver once told a group of students at Yale University that the United States of America was the "freest and most democratic country in the world."

Cleaver and his wife Kathleen, once a BPP communications secretary, had two children, prior to their estrangement.

CLEVELAND, JAMES (1931-February 9, 1991) Minister, Entertainer, became a major figure in American gospel music. He was a pianist, composer, arranger, impresario and leader of the James Cleveland Singers. He was also the founder of the Gospel Music Workshop of America. He became a mentor to such illuminaries as Aretha Franklin and Billy Preston and others who went from gospel to soul music.

Cleveland wrote more than 400 gospel songs, including "Everything Will Be Alright," "He's Using Me", "Peace Be Still", "The Love of God" and "The Man Jesus". He recorded more than twenty albums that sold millions of copies and won three Grammy Awards. He was the first gospel singer to have a star on Hollywood's Walk of Fame.

DAVIS, MILES (May 25, 1926-September 28, 1991), Entertainer, was a jazz trumpeter who began playing bebop with Charlie Parker's ensemble in the mid-1940s. In the 1950s he formed his own group and introduced such forms of jazz as "cool", "hard bop" and "jazz rock." Furthermore he experimented with new forms of electrified jazz and funk. His most notable albums included *The Miles Davis Chronicles*, *Birth of the Cool*, *Sketches of Spain*, *Kind of Blue*, *Blue* Sorcere, In a Silent Way, *Bitches Brew*, *Star People*, and *Tutu*.

Davis was one of jazz's greatest innovators. He developed a distinctive sound—sometimes haunting, sometimes melancholy, and virtually free of vibrato. He succeeded in creating more distinctive musical styles than any other jazz artist in history. He also influenced such artists as John Coltrane, Herbie Hancock, Wynton Marsalis, and Wayne Shorter.

DIGGS, CHARLES COLES, JR. (December 2, 1922-August 24, 1998), Politician, the only child of Charles Coles and Mayme (Jones) Diggs, was born in Detroit, Michigan. He received his early education in the Detroit public school system and in high school was an outstanding debater. From 1940 to 1942 Charles Diggs, Jr. attended the University of Michigan in Ann Arbor. In late 1942 he transferred to Fisk University in Nashville, Tennessee. While a student at Fisk, Diggs enlisted in the United States Army on February 19, 1943 and two years later was discharged as a second lieutenant. In September 1945, he enrolled in Wayne State University's School of Mortuary Science in Detroit and graduated in June 1946. He obtained his mortician's license and was employed in the House of Diggs, the family's $1,000,000 business, which was recognized as the largest funeral home in Michigan.

Diggs began his career at an early age. In 1951, while enrolled in the Detroit College of Law, he was elected to the Michigan State Senate and became its youngest member at the age of 27. He defeated his Republican opponent, Robert Ward by a margin of 2 to 1. In 1953, Diggs unsuccessfully ran for a seat on Detroit's City Council, losing by 5,000 votes, but maintained his seat in the legislature.

In spite of the 1953 defeat, Diggs continued to pursue his political career. In August 1954, he sought his second political victory when he entered the Democratic primary race against incumbent George O'Brien and won by 4,600 votes. On November 2, 1954, Diggs defeated Landon Knight, the son of the *Detroit Press* publisher, John Knight, to become Michigan's first black congressman. His victory was, therefore, a historic event in Michigan's political history. Although the odds were against him, with a 55 percent white constituency, Diggs defeated Knight by a margin of 2 to 1 to represent Michigan's 13th District.

Diggs remained active throughout his political career in the fight for African American civil rights. He fought to end segregation in schools and, like Adam Clayton Powell, Jr., he felt that federal appropriations should be denied to those schools which ignored the Supreme Court's 1954 order to desegregate. More importantly, he introduced legislation to establish a civil rights commission, to dispel job bias, and to lower the voting age from 21 to 18. Although none of these measures passed in the 84th Congress, Diggs continued his battle for civil rights.

It was the Emmett Till case, in which a 15 year old black male was killed for allegedly whistling at a white woman in Sumner, Mississippi, Tallahatchie County, in 1954, which left an indelible impression upon Diggs. He soon discovered that 65 percent of the population of Sumner was black while not one black was registered to vote. This prompted him to write a letter to President Dwight Eisenhower requesting that he call a special session of Congress to deal specifically with civil rights. Diggs was concerned with four particular issues: Dissolving black disfranchisement in southern states; giving the Justice Department the authority to enforce the law when civil rights were violated; desegregating interstate travel; and ending discrimination in employment. President Eisenhower did not honor the request of Congressman Diggs.

As a businessman as well as a politician, Diggs supported the establishment of black-owned businesses to increase the economic power of blacks and to eliminate African American unemployment. In 1961, he organized the National Small Business Conference in Washington, D.C. to evaluate the problems of black entrepreneurs and the Inner City Business Improvement Forum, a corporation based in Detroit, to assist blacks in establishing businesses. Diggs also conceived the idea of a cemetery in Michigan for blacks, the Detroit Memorial Park, which became the first in Michigan owned, operated, and financed by black people.

During his long political career, Diggs experienced several setbacks in his efforts to bring attention to the need for civil rights legislation, to increase social security benefits, to secure aid for the United Nations, to eliminate hunger, poverty, and to end unemployment and under-employment in economically depressed areas in the United States and other countries. Nonetheless, Diggs had many successes as a politician In 1954, he was one of five black representatives elected to the 84th Congress and at the age of 33 he was the youngest member and only black member of Congress who was chairman of a full-standing committee, the House Foreign Affairs Sub-Committee on Africa. While chairman of this committee, Diggs noted that while the United States opposed apartheid and supported the United Nations economic sanctions against South Africa, some government programs and private businesses continued to support the economy of South Africa.

He also served as a United States Delegate to the United Nations General Assembly; President of the National Black Political Assembly; Chairman of the Subcommittee on International Resources, Food and Energy; Senior member of the Michigan Democratic Congressional Delegation; Vice Chairman of the Subcommittee on International Operations; founder and past chairman of the Congressional Black Caucus (CBC) and served on the House Committee on the District of Columbia. In 1962, Diggs introduced Senate Bill 2399 for the permanent preservation of the Frederick Douglass Home in Washington, D.C. as a National Memorial and part of the National Capital Park system. This legislation was passed by Congress on July 18, 1962. In 1972, along with Mayor Richard Hatcher and Imamu Amiri Baraka (LeRoi Jones), Diggs convened the first National Black Political Convention in Gary, Indiana. Approximately 2,700 delegates and 4,000 alternates and observers attended this convention.

In October of 1978, Diggs was convicted in a federal district court in Washington, DC of mail fraud and falsifying payroll forms. On June 4, 1980 he resigned his House seat after the U.S. Supreme Court refused to review his 1978 conviction. His 26-year career was tarnished by a formal House censure on July 31, 1979, his resignation from all committee and sub-committee chairmanships as well as his conviction for diverting $60,000 in "payroll kickbacks." He later agreed to pay $40,000 in restitution and "leave Congress with a clear conscious."

FITZGERALD, ELLA (April 25, 1917-June 15, 1996), Entertainer, was born in Newport News, Virginia. She began her career with Chick Webb's band and recorded her first hit in 1938 with a song that she composed, "A-Tisket, A-Tasket." Following Webb's death in 1939, Fitzgerald began to concentrate on a style of singing known as scat and achieved a growing reputation with such songs as "Flying Home" and "Lady Be Good." She is also credited with reviving the popularity of such composers as Ira and George Gershwin, Rodgers and Hart, and Cole Porter by composing songs using their works. She was the recipient of thirteen Grammy Awards.

FULLER, SAMUEL (S. B.) (June 4, 1903-October 24, 1988), Corporate Executive, was born in Monroe, Louisiana, in the parish of Ouachita Paris. Little is known of Fuller's parents, except that they were sharecroppers and his mother died when he was 17 years old. He dropped out of school after the sixth grade. By the age of nine, Fuller was selling "Cloverine Salve" on the streets of Monroe, Louisiana. In 1928, he and his wife hitchhiked to Chicago, where Fuller found work in a coal yard. Later, Fuller worked as an insurance representative for Commonwealth Burial Association. After four years, he was promoted to a managerial position.

Assisted by his wife, Fuller invested in a soap that he peddled from door-to-door. This venture was so successful that he incorporated the business, Fuller Products Company in 1929. By 1939, Fuller's company had become an empire with a value of over several million dollars. In a secret transaction in 1947, he acquired Boyer International Laboratories. Throughout the 1950s, Fuller was known as a master salesman and his companies produced face creams, lotions, perfumes, and a complete line of household products. While cosmetics remained the core of his trade, he also owned shares in newspapers, the *New York Age* and *Pittsburgh Courier* (where he chaired the Board of Directors in 1960). Also, Fuller owned department stores, Chicago's Regal Theater, agricultural interests, and invested in real estate trusts in New York City. He was considered one of the wealthiest black men in the United States and was affectionately known as "the Godfather" of black business. By the early 1960s, Fuller's business interests were worth ten million dollars, with a 60 percent interracial clientele.

During the late 1960s, Fuller's business investments began to decline. Because of the racial tension of the 1960s, Southern White Citizens' Councils tried to destroy the company by boycotting sales throughout the South. White storeowners removed Fuller's products from their shelves and since much of his business came from whites, they devastated Fuller Products Company.

In 1964, the Securities and Exchange Commission (SEC)

charged Fuller with selling unregistered high interest promissory notes on his business and placed him on probation. By 1968, Fuller had lost his publishing and retail stores and Fuller Products Company declared bankruptcy in 1969. At the same time he suffered from a backlash in the African American community, because of his negative statements toward blacks in business. He was alleged to have said: "Negroes lack initiative, courage, integrity, loyalty and wisdom."

In the 1970s, Fuller revived his business under federal bankruptcy laws. Because he had done so much to promote black entrepreneurship, particularly in Chicago, in 1975, a group of businesspeople, led by entrepreneur George Johnson and Johnson Publishing Company executive John H. Johnson, cosponsored a testimonial dinner for Fuller. Illinois Governor Danie Walker declared June 4, 1975, S. B. Fuller Day in his honor as well. At the Chicago event, Fuller was presented with $70,000 and 2,000 shares of stock, valued at $50,000, to help save his company from financial collapse.

By 1962, Fuller had obtained a license to preach and later became an assistant pastor of the St. Andrew Temple of Faith, Truth and Love Baptist Church. He was once the head of the South Side chapter of the NAACP and the first Playwriting Award from Yale University in 1954 and was a John Hay Whitney fellow in 1952. In 1977, he received a citation for Public Service from the University of Chicago Alumni Association, and in 1981 was the recipient of an Equal Opportunity Day Award from the National Urban League and a Distinguished Service Award from the National Conference of Social Welfare.

HANKERSON, JOSEPH ("Big Lester") (1925-August 2, 1988), Civil/Human Rights Activist, was a leader of the civil rights movement in Savannah, Georgia during the 1960s. He subsequently was seen alongside Martin Luther King, Jr. during many of the slain civil rights leaders' marches throughout the South.

On the occasion of his death in 1988, Joesph E. Lowery, president of the Southern Christian Leadership Conference (SCLC), offered that Hankerson was "one of the earliest among the valiant field workers who was a heart and soul of the [Civil Rights] Movement. They did the harsh and dangerous ground-work that made it possible for the captains and generals to claim the victory." And the veteran civil rights leader, Hosea Williams observed: "Big Lester was a true unsung hero....He contributed as much to the street movement as Dr. King did in the suite movement. He didn't go to jail as many times as I, but no one took more beatings and no one shed more blood."

JACKSON, MAYNARD HOLBROOK, JR. (March 23, 1938-June 24, 2003), Politician, was born in Dallas, Texas to May-nard, Sr., a Baptist minister, and Irene (Dobbs) Jackson, a col-lege teacher. He received a B.A. degree from Morehouse College (Georgia) in 1956 and a J.D., cum laude from North Carolina Central State School of Law in 1964. After receiving his under-graduate degree, Jackson worked for the Ohio State Bureau of Unemployment Compensation as a claims examiner (1957-1958) and then did sales work in Boston, Massachusetts and Buffalo, New York, as well as Cleveland, Ohio. He returned to Atlanta, where his father had been a prominent minister, in 1964 to work as an attorney for the regional office of the National Labor Rela-tions Board (NLRB). After only a short while, he became the managing attorney for Emory University's Legal Service Center, also in Atlanta. Meanwhile, motivated by the assassination of civil rights leader Martin Luther King, Jr. to do more in public service, he decided to enter electoral politics.

Two months after King's death in April 1968, Jackson of-fered a somewhat "quixotic challenge" to one of Georgia's in-cumbent US Senators, the venerable, arch-segregationist Herman Eugene Talmadge. Although, as expected, Talmadge trounced Jackson in the Democratic primary, he received surprising sup-port from labor and poor small farmers and ran solidly among blacks. The challenge to Talmadge did give the young lawyer a reputation for "guts" and the visibility, which enabled him to de-feat veteran Atlanta alderman (city councilman) Milton Farris, in 1969, to become Atlanta's first African American vice mayor.

As vice mayor, Jackson became a nemesis to many whites and a hero to many blacks for his vigorous and impassioned challenges to the city's police on the issue of alleged brutality. His courage, articulation, and eruditeness also won him much support among white moderates, particularly intellectuals and recent migrants to the city. Encouraged by these developments, he challenged Mayor Sam Massell, the city's first Jewish mayor in the 1973 elections. Massell, who had been elected four years earlier, on the strength of the black vote, panicked during the campaign, and turned to a "thinly veiled," but nonetheless racist campaign. Even many of Jackson's previous critics, including the white daily newspaper – the *Atlanta Constitution* – could not stomach Massell's tactics. Jackson trounced Massell by a margin of more than two to one, to become not only Atlanta's, but the Deep South's, first black mayor.

As mayor, Jackson moved quickly and vigorously to attack alleged police brutality by creating a new position, the Public Safety Commissioner, and appointing one of his Morehouse College classmates to the office. He pushed an affirmative action program that virtually assured that blacks would receive at least 35% of city contracts. He raised the arts to new prominence by appointing a coordinator for the arts in City Hall. But many whites railed against his "cronyism" and "high handedness" in changing the police department and, particularly, against his affirmative action program, which was launched at the time a new airport was being constructed in the city. Nevertheless, when the airport was completed on schedule and on time, and won national praise, even many of the critics applauded Jackson. Needless to say, he became an even greater hero in Black Atlanta.

Jackson swept to reelection in 1977, with a much greater percentage of white votes. But deep into his second term, several young blacks began to be reported missing or murdered. After it was determined that the crimes were connected, the city became deeply apprehensive. But Jackson and his police chief, Lee P. Brown, were a calming influence, particularly when they refused to concede that the crimes were the work of racists. Later in 1981, a young black man, Wayne Williams, was captured and subsequently convicted in connection with the crimes. The "Atlanta Child Murders" coalesced the city in a way previously unknown. And, by the time Jackson left office later that year, having also achieved some rapport with the white business community, he was given high marks throughout the city and, indeed, the nation. The only major tarnish during his first administrations was a police cheating scandal, in which his public safety commissioner and college classmate, A. Reginald Eaves, was accused of knowing or should have known that several police officers were given advance knowledge of promotional examinations. Jackson reluctantly fired Eaves in 1979.

Jackson returned to the mayor's office in 1989. But in this new term, "much of the fire seemed to have gone out of him." In an era of federal budget cut backs and continued out migration by both whites and blacks to the suburbs, Jackson's programs languished and his overall performance struck many as "lackluster," particularly when compared to his first term and much of the second one. Scandal had also touched Jackson's third term when, during the early 1990s, his airport commissioner Ira Jackson (no relation to the mayor) was convicted of bribery. Jackson did not offer for another term in 1993, and returned to the private practice of law.

Outside of electoral politics, Jackson continued an active role in local political affairs as a "consultant" (some press reports referred to him as a "kingmaker") and as head of voter registration drives for the Democratic National Committee (DNC). He later left the Chicago based firm for which he was working as a bonds lawyer and opened his own bonds and securities company, Jackson Securities—one of the first African American owned companies of this kind in the Deep South. Although, he was out of office, Jackson was also instrumental in bringing the 1996 Olympic Games to Atlanta.

Jackson collapsed and died at the National Airport in Washington, D.C. on June 24, 2003. At his funeral in Atlanta five days later, former president Bill Clinton led the thousands of mourners. *The Atlanta Journal-Constitution* eulogized him as "a giant of a man."

JORDAN, BARBARA (February 21, 1936-January 17, 1996), Politician, was born in Houston, Texas. She studied government at Texas Southern University there, and then earned a law degree at Boston University in 1959. Following her professional studies, she returned to Texas to open a private law practice. During this same period, Jordan also became politically active as a volunteer for John F. Kennedy and Lyndon B. Johnson in the 1960 presidential election.

Her first bid for elective office came in 1962, when she lost a bid to become a member of the Texas House of Representatives. She tried again in 1964 and lost a second time. But in 1966, she aimed for a seat in the Texas senate. Her victory in that election made her the first woman ever elected to the upper branch of the Texas legislature and the state's first black senator since 1883.

After six successful years in office, Jordan ran for the United States House of Representatives and won. She arrived in Washington in January, 1973, to take her seat in Congress, representing Houston's Eighteenth District.

During the impeachment hearings for President Richard Nixon in 1974, Jordan captured national attention with an eloquent condemnation of the president's involvement in the Watergate burglary scandal and an equally eloquent defense of the U. S. Constitution. Two years later at the Democratic National Convention in New York City, she once again electrified a nationwide audience with a speech in which she described her vision of a government that involves all of its citizens.

On December 10, Jordan suddenly announced that she would not seek reelection and also said that she would not seek a seat on the federal bench. She denied rumors of poor health. She did say, however, that "the longer you stay in Congress, the harder it is to leave....I didn't want to wake up one fine sunny morning and say there is nothing else to do."

After retiring from Congress, Jordan accepted a teaching position in the Lyndon B. Johnson School of Public Affairs at the University of Texas at Austin.

KENNEDY, FLORYNCE RAY (FLO) (February 11, 1916-December 21, 2000), Civil/ Women's Rights Activist, was born in Kansas City, Missouri to Wiley, a Pullman porter and waiter, and Zelda, a part-time domestic, Kennedy. In 1942, she went to

New York City to live with her sister, Grayce. In 1948, she received a B.A. degree in pre-law from Columbia University. But when Columbia denied her admission to its law school, despite an "A" cumulative average, she threatened to sue on the grounds of racial discrimination. The university relented and Kennedy received her law degree there in 1951.

Following law school, she entered the private practice of law, representing, among others, the famous singer Billie Holiday. In 1966, she founded the Media Workshop, an organization designed to fight racism in media and advertising. She also became a founding member of the National Organization of Women (NOW). In 1967, while speaking at an anti-Vietnam War Convention in Montreal, Quebec, she protested loudly when organizers tried to deny Black Panther Party (BPP) leader, Bobby Seale, the right to speak. The incident drew widespread media attention and Kennedy became a widely sought lecturer, particularly on issues of the political "left."

She was one of the planners of the first National Conference on Black Power and attended the black political summits in Gary, Indiana in 1968 and 1972. In that same year, she moved from New York to California. Shortly thereafter, she attacked the tax exempt status of the Catholic Church, charging that the church had spent money, politically, to promote and defend its anti-abortion positions. She also joined the legal team that challenged the constitutionality of New York's abortion law, and, with Diane Schuler, co-authored one of the first major books on the abortion debate, *Abortion Rap*.

On her 70th birthday in 1986, Kennedy was honored with a roast at a Playboy Club in New York City. Guests included comedian Dick Gregory, television talk show host, Phil Donahue and famed civil rights attorney, William Kunstler. Even as an octogenarian, Kennedy continued to speak and lecture, especially in support of causes in which she deeply believed.

KING, ALBERT (d. December 21, 1992 at age 69), Entertainer who influenced a generation of rock guitarists such as Eric Clapton and Stevie Ray Vaughn. He was born in Mississippi and began his music career as a drummer, but later switched to guitar. Although, he was left-handed, he played a right-handed guitar and developed a unique style of pulling rather than pushing the strings. His first big hits came during the mid-w960s, when he performed with Booker T and the MGs on blues standards such as "Born Under a Bad Sign" and "Laundromat Blues."

KING, CHEVENE BOWERS (C. B.") (1924-March 15, 1988) Attorney, Civil/Human Rights Leader, Politician, was born in Albany, Georgia.

During the 1960s, King represented Martin Luther King, Jr., Ralph David Abernathy and other civil/human rights leaders as well as student sit-in demonstrators, particularly in his native Albany. He also participated directly in protest demonstrations in Albany and, on one occasion, was beaten on the steps of the Dougherty County (of which Albany is county seat) courthouse.

Beginning in 1964, King sought elective office in Georgia. He ran unsuccessfully for a congressional seat in that year. Then, in 1970, he became the fist African American to run for governor of Georgia since the reconstruction era. In the governor's race, he received 70,424 votes (8.82 percent) in the Democratic Primary. The victorious candidate for governor that year was Democrat Jimmy Carter, who went on to be elected president of the United States.

King, who did not receive the support of major black leaders in Georgia, was embittered by his defeat. He blamed it on "little black political puppets who have exploited politics for their own selfish ends" and on other blacks who still had "social and psychological hang-ups" about voting for a candidate of their own race. King subsequently moved to San Diego, California.

MARINO, EUGENE A. (May 29, 1934-November 12, 2000), Clergyman, was born in Biloxi, Mississippi, the son of Jesus Maria (a native of Puerto Rico) and Lottie (Bradford) Marino. He attended elementary and high school at the Our Mother of Sorrows Church in Biloxi. He received his theological training at the Josephite Minor Seminary in Newburgh, New York. Marino was ordained to the priesthood on June 9, 1962.

In 1974, Marino was named an auxiliary bishop of Washington, D.C., thus becoming only the third African American priest to achieve the rank of bishop in the U.S. Catholic Church. He continued to rise in prominence and prestige in the Catholic Church and was appointed Archbishop of Atlanta in May 1988. This appointment made him the highest ranking African American in the Catholic Church in the United States.

Upon assuming his position in Atlanta, Marino declared that he came "to bring good news to the poor and the poorest are those who do not know Jesus Christ." He also said that the poor must "be supported by visible witness; through education, advocacy, and works of service." He challenged the Archdiocese to "continue to address the great social issues of our times." He reminded his new parishioners that the letter of black bishops, "What We Have Seen and Heard," published in 1984, called "our sisters and brothers to works of evangelism, to reach out with the Gospel challenge... Catholics are a small minority within the black community and we feel this is a good time to come forward with gifts to enrich the Church."

Marino's appointment was hailed internationally as a monumental effort on the part of the Catholic Church to reach out to minorities and the poor. The appointment to Atlanta, a capital of the Civil Rights Movement, also suggested a renewed commitment to the struggle for equal opportunity and justice.

Marino had served as Archbishop of Atlanta for less than two years, when reports began to circulate that he was having romantic relations with an Atlanta woman. Accusations also surfaced that church funds had been given to the woman and that other financial abuses may have occurred. After media in Atlanta published photos of Marino and his alleged lover, the Archbishop left his post in May 1990, claiming that he was suffering from exhaustion and stress. Two months later he submitted his resignation to the Pope. After taking a period off for rest and rehabilitation, Marino ended his career as a spiritual director in an outpatient program for clergy at St. Vincent's Hospital in Harrison, New York. The program counseled clergy in the "areas of substance abuse and sexual behavior issues."

MARTIN, LOUIS EMANUEL (November 18, 1912–January 29, 1997), Political Leader, journalist, was born in Shelbyville, Tennessee, the son of Willa Martin. He received a B.A. degree from the University of Michigan in 1934. Martin began his career as an editor and publisher of the *Michigan Chronicle* in 1936. In 1947, he moved to the *Chicago Defender* as editor-in-chief (1947-1959), editor (1969-1978), and columnist (1987-1997).

Martin became an active national political figure in 1960, when he joined the presidential campaign of John F. Kennedy, with the specific assignment of soliciting black votes for the Massachusetts senator in his race against Vice President Richard Nixon. Martin turned out to be a key figure in getting Kennedy to place a sympathy call to Coretta Scott King, when Martin Luther King, Jr. was sent to Georgia's Reidsville Prison, during the presidential campaign, on a traffic probation violation. King had been previously arrested for participating in a sit-in at an Atlanta department store. The phone call is widely believed to have galvanized black support, nationally, behind Kennedy, the eventual winner of the presidency in 1960. Several years later, Martin intervened to ease tensions between King and President Lyndon B. Johnson, after the civil rights leader came out aggressively against American participation in the Vietnam War.

Once Kennedy assumed the presidency, Martin was named deputy chairman of the Democratic National Committee (DNC). He held this position until 1969, and was also one of the closest advisors on race matters for both Presidents John F. Kennedy and Lyndon B. Johnson. During this same period, Martin was a major broker in securing high level appointments of African Americans in the federal government. Among those believed to have benefited from Martin's brokerings were Federal Reserve Board member, Andrew Brimmer, Army Secretary Clifford Alexander, HUD Secretary, Patricia Roberts Harris, Supreme Court Justice Thurgood Marshall and HUD Secretary Robert Weaver.

Martin left his DNC post in 1968 and returned to journalism in Chicago. Meanwhile, he founded the Joint Center for Political and Economic Studies, one of the nation's first, and still a leading black "think tank." The Joint Center has provided both research and technical support to black politicians and scholars. When Martin retired as chairman of the Joint Center's board after eight years, his successor Eddie Williams dubbed him "the godfather of black politics." Martin, himself, once said that he preferred the title "inside agitator."

After Jimmy Carter returned the Democrats to the White House in 1976, following an absence of eight years, Martin returned to politics as special assistant to the president, for minority and women's affairs. Once Carter was defeated, he took a position at Howard University (D.C.) in 1981, as assistant vice president for Communications. He left this post in 1987 and returned briefly to journalism before suffering a major stroke. Two years later he retired to California.

MCKISSICK, FLOYD B. (March 9, 1922-April 28, 1991), Civil/Human Rights Leader, Jurist, was born in Asheville, North Carolina on March 9, 1922 to Ernest Boyce and Magnolia Ester (Thompson) McKissick. His concern with civil rights spanned his entire lifetime.

Ernest Boyce McKissick was a bellman at the Vanderbilt Hotel in Asheville. He emphasized education and said that there would only be one servant in the family and that was he. Floyd McKissick attended Morehouse College (Georgia), after having served in the U.S. Army during World War II, and graduated from North Carolina College in 1951. Then, he became the first black to graduate from the University of North Carolina at Chapel Hill Law School with an LL.B. degree, after NAACP lawyer Thurgood Marshall filed suit on his behalf.

Upon completion of his studies, McKissick filed suit in 1958 to get his daughter, Jocelyn, into an all-white school in Durham. He subsequently filed suit to get each of his four children into other area schools.

He later became legal counsel for the Congress of Racial Equality (CORE). In 1963, he was elected chairman, and in 1966, director of the organization. He was noted for stepping up CORE's program of civil disobedience. He was an advocate of Black Power and once described his philosophy as follows: "It is a movement dedicated to the exercise of American democracy in its highest tradition...to remove the basic causes of alienation, frustration, despair, low self-esteem, and hopelessness."

After his tenure with CORE, McKissick undertook a Ford Foundation project to help blacks attain positions of responsibility in the cities where they were approaching a majority of the population. Then he took a controversial position as a vocal supporter of President Richard Nixon's reelection effort in 1972. He defended his position claiming that African Americans had been taken for granted by the Democratic Party and that the Republican Party was becoming more main stream. He later said he took this stance in part to get support for his Soul City Project.

In 1974, McKissick formed the Soul City Corporation. His aim was to create a community in which African Americans would control political and economic life. Unfortunately, federal funding was reduced and the city was not able to attract enough business to become self-sufficient. It was projected that the city would have 400,000 inhabitants by the year 2000, but in 1991 the population was only 400.

McKissick, however, remained busy. He had a successful law practice with his son in Durham, North Carolina. In addition, in 1990, Governor Jim Martin appointed him a District Court Judge for North Carolina's Ninth District.

By this time, McKissick was quite ill with lung cancer. He died in his Soul City home on April 28, 1991.

McNAIR, RONALD (1951-January 28, 1986), Astronaut, was one of seven members of the crew of the space ship, *Challenger* who died when the vessel exploded in the skies on January 28, 1986. The space ship had just lifted off from Cape Canaveral, Florida. McNair, a physicist, was the nation's second African American astronaut.

In one of the eulogies for McNair, the famed African American actress Cycely Tyson observed: "Ron and his crewmates touched...us....They touched the other side of the sky for us."

MONK, THEOPHILUS (October 10, 1917-February 17, 1982), Entertainer, was born in Rocky Mount, North Carolina. He moved with his family to New York City in the early 1920s. When he was eleven, he began supplementing his gospel training with weekly piano lessons and soon was accompanying the Baptist choir in which his mother sang. Just two years later, Monk was playing in a trio at a local bar and grill. He eventually won so many of the weekly Apollo Theater amateur contests that he was banned from entering any more. At the age of sixteen, he left school to travel with an evangelical faith healer and preacher. When he returned home the following year, he formed his first group. With the exception of some brief work with the Lucky Millander band and Coleman Hawkins, Monk generally led his own small groups throughout his career. During the early 1940s, Monk found himself in the midst of a new wave of jazz music. Bebop, a faster and more complex style than the older "swing" style of jazz, grew out of late-night jam sessions at jazz clubs. (Perhaps the most famous of these was Minton's, where Monk was the house pianist.) In fact, *Keyboard* magazine claimed "Monk was at the eye of what would become the bebop hurricane." His own music, however, was developing a unique style, and by the early 1950s he had composed the classics "Blue Monk," "Round Midnight," and "Epistrophy." At first, only a small circle of fans appreciated his angular melodies, harmonies marked by jarring surprises, and unusual treatment of notes (and even the absence of notes). But over the years Monk came to be recognized as one of the founding fathers of modern jazz. Some people now consider him to be the most important jazz composer since Duke Ellington. In 1951, Monk's career (which was already faltering) was dealt a serious blow when he was charged with possession of narcotics. He ended up in jail for two months and, more importantly, New York state officials took away his cabaret card. Without it, he could not play any local club dates.

Within a few years, however, his luck changed and his career revived. Monk gave a series of concerts in Paris in 1954, he cut his first solo album, *Pure Monk,* and signed with the Riverside label. In 1957, he had an eight-month engagement at New York's Five Spot, where devoted fans of his music gathered to hear their idol play. It was there that he also met jazz newcomer John Coltrane.

Over the next few years, Monk made several recordings for Riverside, including *Brilliant Corners, Thelonious Himself,* and *Monk with Coltrane.* These recordings were so successful that in 1962 Columbia offered Monk a well-paying contract. In 1964 *Time* magazine featured his picture on the cover, a rare honor for a jazz musician.

MORIAL, ERNEST "DUTCH" (October 9, 1929-December 24, 1989), Politician, was born in New Orleans, Louisiana he became the first black law school graduate of Louisiana State University. His public service career began in 1960 when he was elected president of the NAACP chapter in New Orleans. Working with fellow civil rights activist A.P. Tureard, he filed lawsuits against the city over segregation in public facilities and institutions.

In 1965, Morial became the first black assistant U.S. Attorney in Louisiana. Two years later, he became the first black legislator since the Reconstruction era. He served as a member of the State House of Representatives from 1967 to 1970, then became the first black ever elected to Louisiana's 4th Circuit Court of Appeals in 1973.

In 1977, on the strength of a huge black vote, Morial became the first black mayor of New Orleans. As mayor for two terms (a total of eight years), he had to deal with destructive floods in 1978, a police strike that crippled the city's annual Mardi Gras festival in 1979, and a financially troubled world exposition in 1984. Morial left office in 1986 following an unsuccessful attempt to change the city charger to allow the mayor to serve a third four-year term.

On the national scene, Morial had served as president of the National Conference of Mayors, a member of the Democratic National Committee (DNC), and one of the key black advisors to the Democratic presidential candidate Michael Dukakis in 1988.

MOON, MOLLIE LEWIS (1908-June 25, 1990), Civil/Human Rights Leader, was a founder of the National Urban League

Guild (NULG). The NULG, founded in 1942, was an organization established to raise money to support programs for "racial equality and amity" of the National Urban League (NUL). Under her leadership, the guild grew to eighty units, with thirty thousand volunteers in the major cities of the United States.

The major event for the NULG was an annual Beaux Arts Ball. It began at the old Savoy Ballroom in the Harlem section of New York City and subsequently spread throughout the United Sates. With the assistance of New York philanthropist, Winthrop Rockefeller, the New York ball eventually moved from Harlem to downtown Manhattan, including events held in the Rainbow Room atop Rockefeller Center.

In 1990, two months before Moon's death, New York City's mayor David Dinkins presented her an award for "dedicated and innovative volunteerism" on behalf of President George walker Herbert Bush.

NABRIT, SAMUEL MADISON (February 21, 1905-December 30, 2003), Educator, government official, the son of the Reverend James Madison Nabrit, Sr. and Gertrude West Nabrit, was born in Macon, Georgia. He received his undergraduate degree from Morehouse College in 1925 and became the first African American to receive a doctorate degree from Brown University in 1932. Although Nabrit was a chemistry major at Morehouse, he taught biology there upon his graduation in 1925. However, he received his doctorate in biology and returned to Morehouse in 1932 as a professor of biology and chair of the department. He held these positions until 1947 when he left his alma mater to become dean of the Graduate school of Arts and Sciences at neighboring Atlanta University

In 1955, Nabrit was elected president of Texas Southern University in Houston and held this position until 1966. He won wide attention during the Civil Rights Movement for refusing to expel student demonstrators; although he eventually directed that they remove their protest headquarters from the college campus. Interestingly enough, Nabrit served as president at Texas Southern at the same time that his brother, James Madison Nabrit, Jr. was president of Howard University in Washington, D. C.

In 1927, Nabrit began research on the tail fins of fish. His findings, detailing the size and rate of growth of fins in regeneration, were published in scientific journals and won him wide notoriety in scientific circles. These activities led to an appointment to the board of trustees of the Marine Biological Laboratory Corporation, operators of the highly respected Woods Hole laboratories.

While still president of Texas Southern, President Dwight D. Eisenhower appointed Nabrit to the National Science Board of the National Science Foundation, where he served from 1956 to 1961. During this same time, he also served as a special ambassador to Niger (1961-1962). After retiring from Texas Southern in 1966, Nabrit accepted an appointment from President Lyndon B. Johnson to the U. S. Atomic Energy Commission, where he served from 1966 to 1969. Nabrit ended his long career in public service in 1981, after serving for more than a decade as chair and director of the Southern Fellowship Fund. In this position, he disbursed more than four million dollars to blacks who were seeking advanced degrees.

Despite this latest retirement, Nabrit remained active as a speaker and consultant. He was especially active at his *alma mater*, Morehouse College, and became one of its principal benefactors.

Among Nabrit's awards and honors was a citation from the State Committee on the Life and History of Black Georgians for distinguished service in education in 1985. A science building on the Morehouse campus, the Nabrit, McBay, Mapp Building, carries his name.

PATTERSON, FREDERICK DOUGLASS (October 10, 1901-April 26, 1998), Educator, Association Executive, was born in Washington, D.C., the son of William Ross, a lawyer and school principal, and Mamie Brooks) Patterson, a music teacher. He received a doctorate in Veterinary Medicine from Iowa State University in 1923; a M.S. from the same institution in 1927; and a Ph.D. in Bacteriology from Cornell University (New York) in 1932. He began his career as a teacher of Veterinary Medicine and Chemistry at Virginia State University (Petersburg) in 1923, and became Director of the School of Agriculture at Virginia State in 1927. The next year, he moved to Tuskegee Institute (now Tuskegee University) as instructor of Bacteriology and director of Veterinary Medicine. In 1934, he moved to the School of Agriculture as Director and in 1935 was named President of Tuskegee Institute.

Once in office, Patterson rescued the school from impending bankruptcy; established a new division of domestic service (including programs in nutrition and personal services); launched a program to help farmers build better homes (with concrete blocks); and started the George Washington Carver Foundation (1940) to help encourage and finance scientific research by African Americans.

Patterson is best known, in some places, for establishing the famous Army Air Corps at Tuskegee during World War II. This program led to the recruitment and instruction of the group of black pilots, who achieved acclaim for bravery in the war. His financial success at the school also received widespread media coverage and Patterson was swamped with requests from other schools, particularly African American ones, for "the secrets of his success." In a general response, he advocated a "consortium of black colleges that would raise money for their mutual benefit." In 1944, 27 black schools came together to form the United Negro College Fund (UNCF), the largest "umbrella group" for fund raising for private black institutions of higher education in the country. Patterson is often called "the father of the UNCF." He, himself, served as President of the UNCF from 1964 to 1966.

When Patterson retired from Tuskegee in 1953, he became president of the Phelps Stokes Fund in New York, a 50-year old fund to educate African and Native Americans, as well as African American students. He left this position, in 1980, to head the Robert R. Moton Institute, an organization designed to increase enrollment in black colleges and universities and help stabilize them in an era of reduced federal funding.

In 1987, President Ronald Reagan awarded Patterson the Presidential Medal of Freedom, and shortly before his death in 1988, he was the recipient of NAACP's Spingarn Medal.

PAYTON, WALTER (July 25, 1954-November 1,1999) Athlete, running back for the Chicago Bears, was named the National Football League's Most Valuable Player for 1977. Payton received 57 of 87 votes cast by sportswriters and broadcasters, three from each league city. Quarterbacks Bob Griese of the Miami Dolphins and Craig Morton of the Denver Broncos were the runner ups with ten votes each.

Payton, was born in Columbia, Mississippi and a graduate of Jackson State University in his home state, led the League in rushing with 1,852 yards during the 1977 season, his third year in the NFL (a League record). He ran for 275 yards in one game (November 20 against the Minnesota Vikings), which surpassed the record set by African American O.J. Simpson, Payton also exceeded Simpson's record of 332 carries with 339 of his own. Finally, Payton's 1,852 yards rushing was third only to Simpson's 2,003 and the African American Jim Brown's 1,863 during a season.

PROCTOR, SAMUEL DEWITT (July 13, 1921-May 22, 1997) Clergyman, educator, federal official was born in Norfolk, Virginia, the son of Herbert Quincy and Gladys Velma (Hughes) Proctor. He received a Bachelors degree from Virginia Union University in 1941, a Master of Divinity degree at Crozier Theological Seminary (New York) in 1945, and a Doctor of Theology degree at Boston University in 1950.

A year before he completed his studies at Boston, Proctor became a member of the faculty at Virginia Union University, where by 1960 he had risen to dean and president. He left Virginia Union in 1960 to become President of the North Carolina A&T State University in Greensboro, North Carolina.

In 1964, Proctor resigned from the presidency at North Carolina A&T to become an administrator with the Peace Corps in Nigeria and Washington, D.C. During the period 1964-1969, he was also associate general secretary for the National Council of Churches, special assistant to the director of the Office of Economic Opportunity (OEO), president of the Institute for Services to Education [ISE], and dean of special projects as the

University of Wisconsin. Then, in 1969, he joined the faculty of Rutgers University (New Jersey) where he held the Martin Luther King, Jr. Memorial Chair in the Graduate School of Religion. When he retired from Rutgers in 1984, he was awarded the Rutgers Medal for Distinguished Service.

After leaving Rutgers, as a Professor Emeritus, Proctor continued to teach and lecture at various academic institutions, including Yale University, Vanderbilt University, and Duke University, up to the time of his death.

Meanwhile, after the death of the Reverend Congressman Adam Clayton Powell, Jr. in 1972, Proctor also became pastor of the historic Abyssinian Baptist Church in Harlem, the largest Baptist congregation in the world.

Proctor also served on the governing boards of the National Urban League and the United Negro College Fund (UNCF), as well as Middlebury College, Harvard University, and the Union Theological Seminary of New York. His travels took him to such places as Africa, the Caribbean islands, Scandinavia and Western Europe, Russia and Eastern Europe, the South Pacific and New Zealand.

More than 50 American colleges and universities bestowed honorary degrees on Proctor. He, himself, was the author of numerous scholarly works on theology and public issues, including *The Certain Sound of the Trumpet*, 1995 and *The Substance of Things Hoped For*, 1995. In *The Substance of Things Hoped For*, Proctor spoke of the historical experiences of African Americans. He asserted that "a persistent faith propels [us] – faith in God, faith in [our] own worth and dignity and faith in the idea that

RILES, WILSON CAMANZA (June 27, 1917-April 1, 1999), Educator, was born near Alexandria, Louisiana, the son of a crew chief in a turpentine camp. He was orphaned by the death of both parents in 1917. A childless couple in his father's crew adopted him and took him to Elizabeth, Louisiana, where he attended high school. He received a Bachelor's degree from Northern Arizona University in 1940, before enrolling in the Army Air Corps. After three years of military service Riles returned to Northern Arizona and earned a Master's degree in 1947. Riles began his career as a classroom teacher in a small elementary school on the Apache Indian Reservation at Pistel Creek, Arizona in 1951. By 1965 he had been elevated to the position of Associate Superintendent of the California State Department of Education. In. this capacity, he directed a $ 100 Million-a-Year Federal Compensatory Education Program that was designed to improve the education of disadvantaged children. In 1969, he was promoted to deputy superintendent.

After only a year as deputy superintendent, Riles challenged his boss, a white conservative named Max Rafferty, for the position of state school superintendent. Although Rafferty was popular among "conservatives," and outspoken on the issues, he had not been able to correct the problems in the state schools, many of which seemed to be the result of "poor administration."

Yet Rafferty had served in his post for eight years. But in November 1970, California's voters turned him out of office in favor of Riles. The 6 foot 4 inch, 200 pound black educator gained three and a half million votes, the largest number of ballots "ever cast for a black man in a single election in U.S. history," to become superintendent of one of the nation's largest school systems. At the time of his election, there were more than 11,000 school districts in the state, enrolling four and one-half million pupils. Riles controlled an annual budget of two and one-half billion dollars and supervised a staff of over 2,300 persons. He also won the right to sit on the Board of Regents of the University of California as the first black voting member of this body.

Riles won recognition through the conferral of honorary degrees by several institutions including Pepperdine College (1965), the University of the Pacific (1971), the University of Southern California (1975), the University of Akron (1976), and the Northern Arizona University (1976).

ROBINSON, MAX (1937-December 20, 1988), Journalist, was the first African American news anchorperson on a national network television program. After working for several years at WTPO-TV in Washington, DC, he became a co-anchor with Peter Jennings and Frank Reynolds on the ABC-TV Network's "Evening News" in 1978. However, Carl Bernstein, the chief of the ABC News bureau in Chicago later admitted that Robinson was "deliberately excluded from any decision-making related to the newscast." In a speech at Smith College in February 1981, Robinson, himself, accused ABC of racism. Two years later, following the death of Reynolds, Jennings was named sole anchor of the "Evening News" and Robinson was relegated to weekend anchor positions and "news briefs." The next year he left ABC and joined the news staff of WMAQ-TV in Chicago, Illinois. In June 1985, Robinson was admitted to a hospital, diagnosed with "emotional and physical exhaustion." He never returned to full-time news reporting.

Following Robinson's death in 1988, Roone Arledge, president of ABC News offered: "He made an important contribution to ABC News for which we will always be grateful."

ROWAN, CARL THOMAS (August 11, 1925-September 23, 2000), Journalist, Federal Official, was born in Ravenscroft, Tennessee, to Thomas David and Johnnie (Bradford) Rowan. Rowan went to Bernard High School in McMinnville, Tennessee, where he graduated as his class valedictorian. He attended Tennessee State University in Nashville from 1942 until 1943. Rowan, then, took and passed an examination for a U.S. Navy Commission. He was assigned to Washburn University in Topeka, Kansas, one of the first blacks in Navy history to be accepted into the V-12 Officer Training program. He was eventually commissioned as an officer and served in the Navy until 1946.

He attended Washburn from 1943 to 1944 and then enrolled in Oberlin College where in 1947, he received an A.B. degree in mathematics. In 1948, he graduated from the University of Minnesota with a M.A. degree in journalism.

In the same year, he was hired as a copy editor for the Minneapolis *Tribune*. In 1950, he became the paper's first black reporter. Rowan convinced the *Tribune* staff to let him tour the South and write articles about the effects of Jim Crow laws on blacks. During his trip, he wrote a series of 18 articles in 1951 called "How Far From Slavery," which analyzed southern blacks' racial dilemma. His articles earned him instant fame from the *Tribune* reading constituency and the Sidney Hillman Award for best newspaper reporting in 1952. From 1953 to 1955, he earned three consecutive Sigma Delta Chi Journalism Awards for his articles on court decisions against Jim Crow laws and the country of India and Southeast Asia's volatile political climate. From 1955 to 1961, he wrote numerous articles on the Civil Rights Movement and a book entitled *Go South to Sorrow* in 1957.

In 1961, President John F. Kennedy appointed Rowan Deputy Assistant Secretary of State for Public Affairs of the State Department. He worked at this position until 1963 when Kennedy appointed him ambassador to Finland. In 1964, President Lyndon Johnson appointed him to the position of director of the United States Information Agency (USIA), a position that made him the highest ranking black in the federal government. Later in 1964, Rowan resigned from USIA and took a job as a national columnist for the *Chicago Sun Times* and the *Field Newspaper Syndicate* as well as a commentator on a weekly radio show for the Westinghouse Broadcasting Company. He was also a frequent panelist on the political news television show, "Meet the Press."

Throughout his career, Rowan was an outspoken individual on causes in which he strongly believed. He publicly spoke in favor of Martin Luther King, Jr.'s struggle to end racial inequality while urging the influential black leader to abandon his anti-Vietnam War stance. He also called for the removal of former F.B.I. Director J. Edgar Hoover for abusing his powers. He heavily criticized President Ronald Reagan's "discriminatory policies" as well as former Washington, D.C. Mayor Marion Barry's policies. Rowan defended his comments on Barry by stating that, "I have learned over four decades as a journalist that City Hall becomes more and more corrupt as more and more citizens lose the guts to fight [it]."

In 1999 Rowan filed suit against the *Chicago Sun Times* alleging that after more than 30 years of service, the newspaper had found him to be "too old, too Black, and too liberal." He demanded $1 million in compensatory damages. At about the same time, Rowan received the National Press Club's Fourth Estate Award for lifetime achievement in Journalism.

SANFORD, JOHN ELROY "REDD FOXX" (December 9, 1924-October 11, 1991), was born John Elroy Sanford in St. Louis, Missouri. He began his career performing in various musical groups, including the Bon-Bons, beginning in 1939. He then turned to stand-up comedy in 1941 and recorded numerous comedy albums over the next fifty years. From 1947 through 1951, he teamed up with fellow comedian Slappy White and performed in front of predominantly black audiences. His early routines often featured sex-oriented jokes and profanity.

Foxx's popularity began to soar during the 1970s. He made television history as the star of "Sanford & Son," which ran from 1972 to 1977 and can still be seen in syndication. He also starred in his own "Redd Foxx Comedy Hour," "Redd Foxx Show," and "The Royal Family." His movie credits include *Cotton Comes to Harlem, Norman ... Is That You?,* and *Harlem Nights.*

Foxx won a Golden Globe Award for his performance as best actor in a comedy and received three Emmy Award nominations for best actor in a comedy.

SCOTT, CORNELIUS ADOLPHUS (C. A.) (February 8, 1908-May 7, 2000), Publisher and Editor, was born to the Reverend William Scott, Sr. and Emmiline Southall Scott. On February 4, 1934, W. A. Scott, the founder of *The Atlanta Daily World*, the nation's first black daily newspaper, was shot and killed in Atlanta. C. A. Scott subsequently succeeded his brother as publisher and editor of the newspaper.

Continuing and expanding upon traditions established by his brother during his brief tenure of leadership of the newspaper, the World, under Scott, covered lynchings, police brutality incidents and segregation and discrimination issues. Scott championed African American voting rights and once these were won, the registration and voting by blacks. He and his newspaper also supported the campaigns of African Americans for public office. The *World* was also one of the first newspapers in the nation to report "black on black" crimes. It encouraged support for black businesses and was one of the first newspapers to pay extensive attention to the black sports world. In 1944, a World reporter, Harry S. Alpin, was the first African American to serve as a White House correspondent.

During the Civil Rights Era, Scott and his newspaper became the objects of considerable controversy, when they opposed direct action sit-ins in Atlanta. Scott defended his position on the grounds that desegregation in education, political rights and participation and economic self sufficiency were more important than sitting and eating with whites at lunch counters. A long-time Republican, even after most African Americans in the Atlanta and the nation had become staunch Democrats, Scott once said that "he was a natural conservative....My mama sort of made me that way."

SENGSTACKE, JOHN HERMAN (November 25, 1912-May 28, 1997), Publisher, was born in Savannah, Georgia, the son of Herman Alexander, a minister and newspaper publisher, and Rosa (Davis) Sengstacke. He received a B.A. degree from Hampton Institute in 1933. Upon graduation, he went to work with his uncle, Robert Abbott, attended school to learn printing, and wrote editorials and articles for three of Abbott's papers. In 1954, he became Vice President and General Manager of the company.

During World War II, Sengstacke was an advisor to the U.S. Office of War Information, during a period of severe tension between the government and the black press. He also headed the Chicago rationing board.

In 1940, after the death of his uncle, Sengstacke became President of the Robert S. Abbott Publishing Company, which included the weekly *Chicago Defender*, founded by his uncle in 1905. In 1956, Sengstacke founded the *Daily Defender*, one of only three black dailies in the country at that time. In 1940 he founded the Negro Newspaper Publishers Association, now known as the National Newspaper Publishers Association, and served six terms as its president. He was also president of Tri-State Defender, Inc., Florida Courier Publishing Company, New

Pittsburgh Courier Publishing Company, and Amalgamated Publishers, Inc., and chairman of Michigan Chronicle Publishing Company and Sengstacke Enterprises, Inc., and treasurer of Chicago Defender Charities, Inc.

Sengstacke served in leadership positions with many professional, educational, and civic organizations, received a number of presidential appointments, and was the recipient of several academic awards. He was a trustee of Bethune-Cookman College (Florida), Chairman of the Board of Provident Hospital and Training School Association in Chicago, a member of the board of directors of the American Society of Newspaper Editors and the Advisory Board of the Boy Scouts of America.

By the 1970s, many African American readers were dismayed at Sengstacke's insistence on backing white Democratic politicians rather than progressive black candidates. Meanwhile, advertisers were putting their money into mainstream papers rather than black ones, whose readership numbers were declining. Speaking at the 40th annual black publisher's convention in Chicago in 1980, Sengstacke declared that on issues of racism and discrimination, "the Black press recently has not been as vocal as it should be.... As a result, our circulation is limited to the restricted perimeter of the Black community and our political influence is waning." By the 1990s, circulation of the *Chicago Defender* had dropped to 25,000, from a peak of 160,000 in the 1940s. The Sengstacke chain as a whole, however, remained the largest conglomeration of African American owned newspapers in the United States. In 1992, Sengstacke was named "International Man of the Year" by the International Biographical Centre of Cambridge, England, in recognition of his decades of community service, including his leadership in the campaign to build Provident Hospital, and later after it had closed to have it reopened and modernized under the auspices of Cook County Hospital.

SHAKUR, TUPAC (Tupac) (June 16, 1971-September 13, 1996), Entertainer, was born in New York City, the son of Aleni Shakur (aka Alice Faye Williams), a political activist. He attended the Baltimore School for the Arts. Shakur began acting as early as 1983 with the 127th Street Ensemble in New York City. In the early 1990s he also appeared in *A Raisin in the Sun*. Shakur began his career as a rap artist with the Digital Underground in 1990 and was heard on their recording, "This is an EP Release" in 1991. That same year he signed a contract with Interscope Records and produced a solo album entitled "2PACalypse Now." Meanwhile, he also appeared in film; having roles in "Juice", "Poetic Justice" and "Above the Rim" between 1992 and 1994. In that same year he formed his own rap group, Thug Life, which recorded "Volume One" and contributed to the soundtrack for "Above the Rim".

Also, in 1994, Tupac established his own recording label, Out Da Gutta, which was affiliated with Interscope Records. He, then, established his own production company. The next year Tupac found himself in prison, having been convicted of sexual abuse. After his release from incarceration the next year, he signed a contract with Death Row Records and worked on an album called "The Don Kulluminati: The 7 Day Theory. In September 1996, after leaving a boxing match in Las Vegas, Nevada, he was shot and mortally wounded by unknown assailant (s). Following his death, "The Don Kullumianti: The 7 Day Theory" was released under the name Makaveli.

In his lifetime, Tupac was awarded Platinum records for the soundtrack from "Above the Rim" and "Strictly4 My N.I.G.G.A.Z" and a Gold record for "2 Pacalyspse Now."

The life and death of Shakur typified the stories of many young African American men, some of them apparently gifted students, who drifted into the world of Rap Music and other aspects of Hip Hop Culture. Many of them, no matter what their earlier circumstances, became idols to Hip Hoppers and obtained considerable wealth. Their songs, attitudes, and actions which allegedly portrayed the realities of core everyday life in African communities, although often profane, vulgar, sexist and replete with self-hatred soon attracted audiences beyond "core" African American communities and became a world-wide phenomenon. Still the base of support for Tupac and similar artists was among young African Americans, particularly males. Thus, to them, even in death he became "larger than life" and, in some places, virtual Tupac cults appeared,

STANFORD, JOHN HENRY (September 14, 1938-November 28, 1998), Soldier, Municipal Official, was born in Darby, Pennsylvania. He received a Bachelors degree in political science from Pennsylvania State University in 1961. One day after graduation, he joined the United States Army, beginning his service in Germany as an air and battalion operations officer. He later rose to commander of the transportation division.

Stanford spent more than three years in Germany and began his next major assignment in Korea as a fixed-wing aviator. He later served in Vietnam as a fixed-wing aviator and commander of a transportation battalion. Stanford was back in the United States in the 1970s and earned a Masters degree in personnel management and administration from Central Michigan University.

In the decade between 1970 and 1981, Stanford served the military as a personnel management officer; battalion commander and commander of division support in Korea; assistant to the undersecretary of the Army; and executive assistant to the special assistant to the Secretary of Defense in Washington, D.C.

Between November 1981 and June 1984, Stanford was an executive secretary to the Secretary of Defense Casper Weinberger. He left the Pentagon in June 1984 to serve as commander of Military Traffic Management Command in Oakland, California; deputy commander for research and development in St. Louis, Missouri; commanding general, Military Traffic Management Command; director of plans, U.S. Transportation Command at Scott Air Force Base, Illinois. In this position he oversaw all of the transportation plans and programs for "Operation Desert Storm." Stanford described this latter assignment as equivalent to "setting up a town the size of Atlanta [Georgia] in the middle of the desert."

Following "Desert Storm," Stanford retired from the military with the rank of major general in July 1991. He returned to civilian life, after 30 years in the armed services, by accepting the position of county manager for Fulton County, of which Atlanta is the county seat, in Georgia.

Stanford received "high marks" as the first African American county manager for Fulton County. He oversaw a budget of nearly one-half billion dollars and managed more than 5,000 employees; streamlined the bureaucracy; and helped to lower taxes. He, thus, anguished over an offer he received, in 1995, to serve as superintendent of schools in Seattle, Washington. After concluding that the opportunity and the challenge of reforming a major, urban school system was an extremely appealing venture in this stage of his life, Stanford accepted the position. In his initial visits to Seattle, Stanford shocked some and pleased others when he accepted the challenges presented by the school system, declaring that he had never failed at anything. This declaration was made amid skepticism among some in Seattle, particularly over the fact that he did not have a background in education.

On September 1, 1995, his first day on the job, Stanford proposed that the central office staff of the school system should spend at least one day a week helping in the schools and announced that "poor customer service" on the part of any employee would result in a firing. He, then, quickly proceeded to propose tougher academic standards for the school system, including holding students back if they did not meet academic requirements and a community wide "reading offensive" that led to the donation of thousands of books to the city's school libraries.

Stanford labeled himself a "children's crusader" and chastised pessimists by declaring that if it's never been done "we will do it." This attitude and the business-like policies and procedures that he initiated won Stanford considerable support from Seattle's business community. Many parents, including those of minority students, soon came to applaud his initiatives. Most principals and teachers, who initially expressed skepticism and alarm about the breadth of the reforms and the accountability procedures that Stanford proposed, also endorsed his programs.

Among Stanford's most successful, and most applauded, programs were the principal as CEO, in which businesses supported a new leadership institute; a linkage of school spending with the educational challenges of the students which called for extra spending in schools where students had language problems or came from poor homes; and a four day work week for teachers, with the fifth day being used for parent conferences, planning or additional training.

Although Stanford had done much in his first two years as superintendent of Seattle's schools, as was evidenced by the continued rise in students' test scores, he had many ideas and plans which were yet unfulfilled. As he outlined in his book, *Victory in Our Schools: We Can Give Our Children Excellent Public Education* (New York, Bantam Books edition, 1999), he intended to demonstrate in Seattle that every child enrolled in public school could succeed. But, Stanford's plans were cut short when he lost a long battle with leukemia on November 28, 1998.

Commenting on Stanford's death, President Bill Clinton said: "After 30 years of military service, the General brought his own infectious brand of courage and optimism to a new battle. He streamlined and reinvigorated Seattle's schools, inspiring his students to strive for excellence, and an entire community to believe once again in their public schools."

STEWART, BENNETT McVEY (August 6, 1912-April 26, 1998), Politician, was born in Huntsville, Alabama. He attended public schools in Huntsville and received a B.A. degree from Miles College (Alabama) in 1936. From 1936 to 1938, he was an assistant principal of the Irondale High School in Birmingham. In 1938, Stewart returned to Miles College as an associate professor of sociology. He left this position in 1940 to become an executive in an insurance company.

In 1950 Stewart became the Illinois state director for the company, a position he held for 18 years. He, then, left the insurance business to become an inspector with the city of Chicago's building department and a rehabilitation specialist with the Chicago Department of Urban Renewal, where he advised property owners on the financing of renovations. In 1971, he was elected to the Chicago City Council from the 21st Ward, and was elected Democratic committeeman for the same ward in 1972. He held both of these offices until 1978.

After Congressman Ralph H. Metcalfe died in October 1979, Stewart offered as a candidate to fill this vacancy. In the general elections in November, he defeated former Chicago Alderman A. A. Rayner and was sworn into the 96th Congress on January 3, 1979.

In the Congress, Stewart was a member of the powerful Appropriations Committee. He supported federal loan guarantees for the financially troubled Chrysler Motor Corporation, which employed more than 1,500 workers in his district. And he advocated and tried to extend the time low-income persons could spend in public service employment programs.

After allegations of mismanagement in the Chicago Housing Authority surfaced, Stewart requested and received a General Accounting Office (GAO) review of the agency, in 1980. The investigation revealed that the agency's mismanagement had led it to the verge of bankruptcy. Stewart also carried on the tradition of Ralph Metcalfe and reintroduced resolutions calling for the celebration of Black History Month in February of each year. He often spoke out against proposed constitutional amendments to prohibit busing to achieve desegregation in public schools. He attacked the proposals as a "subversion" of the 14th Amendment and an attempt to reestablish segregation in the country.

In 1980, Stewart sought reelection for a full term in the House, but was defeated by a more charismatic candidate, Harold Washington. Stewart, then, returned to Chicago as interim director of the Chicago Department of Inter-Governmental Affairs (1981-1983). After 1983, he retired from public life.

STOKES, CARL BURTON (June 21, 1927-April 3, 1996), Politician, was born in Cleveland, Ohio, son of Charles, a laundry worker, and Louise (Stone), a domestic worker. His father died when he was only two years of age. Stokes attended East Technical High School in Cleveland, but dropped out in 1944 to take a job in a foundry. The next year he joined the U.S. Army, where he served in Germany and attained the rank of corporal. Following his military duties, Stokes returned to Cleveland and graduated from high school in 1947. He began his higher education at West Virginia State College and Cleveland College of the Western Reserve University and received a B.S. degree in law from the University of Minnesota, in 1954, and a LL.B. degree from the Cleveland-Marshall Law School in 1957. He began practicing law in Cleveland in 1957.

Fresh out of law school, Stokes became very active in civic and political affairs in his community. He served on the elective committee of the Democratic Party in Cuyahoga County (of which Cleveland is the seat and largest city), and on the executive committee of the local NAACP. In 1958, Cleveland Mayor Anthony Celebreeze named Stokes his assistant city prosecutor. He held this post until 1962, when he quit to form a law firm with his brother, Louis. Yet, he remained active in politics, and that same year, was elected to the Ohio House of Representatives, becoming the first black Democrat ever to sit in the state legislature. He earned a reputation as a "moderate" lawmaker and was reelected for two additional terms.

By 1965, many blacks in Cleveland had become disillusioned with their mayor, Ralph Locher, because he refused to meet with them to discuss an allegation that his police chief was racist. They, then, offered Carl Stokes as a candidate to oppose Locher in the 1965 city elections. In a three-man race, Stokes nearly upset Locher, polling 85,375 votes to the incumbent's 87,833.

As Locher returned to office, charges of police brutality against blacks continued. These allegations, coupled with growing unemployment in the black ghettoes, helped spark a serious race riot in the city in 1966. The next year, Carl Stokes, again, was asked to challenge Mayor Locher. In another three-man race, on October 3, 1967, Stokes handily defeated Locher. He still, however, faced stiff opposition in the general election in the Republican candidacy of Seth C. Taft, the nephew of the late Ohio Senator Robert A. Taft and grandson of President William Howard Taft. Nevertheless, Stokes held onto his block of black support and through his skill as a debater and "moderate" platform won over almost 43,000 white voters. He defeated Taft by a margin of 2,500 ballots.

In November 1967, when Carl Stokes took over as mayor of Cleveland, he became the chief executive of the eighth largest city in the United States. He moved quickly to improve housing and reduce unemployment. He reformed the police department and improved the relationship between police officers and the black ghettoes. Yet, crime continued to be a major problem in the city. Thus, in the 1969 election both his Democratic and Republican challengers ran on "law and order" themes. However, Stokes defeated the Democrat, Robert Kelly by a margin of 60 to 40% and squeaked past Ralph Perk, the Republican nominee by a margin of almost 4,000 votes out of 240,000 cast in the general elections.

Stokes left the mayor's office in 1972 and became a television news correspondent and anchorperson in New York City from 1972 through 1980. He returned to Cleveland in 1980 as a senior partner in a firm specializing in labor law. He returned to public office in 1983, as a presiding administrative judge in the Cleveland Municipal Court. In 1986, Stokes became the court's chief judge until 1994. Appointed by President Bill Clinton, he became the United States Ambassador to the Republic of the Seychelles, an island nation off the coast of Africa. Stokes served as the U.S. Ambassador for a year, but had to leave the post because of illness.

STOUT, JUANITA (KIDD) (March 7, 1919-August 23, 1998), Jurist, was born in Weweolia, Oklahoma, the daughter of Henry M. and Mary A. (Chandler) Kidd, both school teachers. She earned a BA degree from the State University of Iowa in 1939. From 1939 to 1941, she was an elementary music school teacher in Oklahoma; then an instructor of business at Florida A and M University (1948) and at Texas Southern University (1949); an administrative secretary for the U. S. Court of Appeals in Philadelphia (1949-1954).

During World War II, Stout's fiancé went into the Army and she went to Washington, D. C., where she found work as a secretary with the National Housing Authority. She quit this position on account of low pay and went to work for Houston, Houston and Hastie, a prestigious black law firm. She worked directly for the famous Charles Hamilton Houston, who later described her as "the best lawyer I have ever met."

With encouragement from Charles Houston, Stout began legal training at Howard University. She later transferred to Indiana University in Bloomington, where her husband was completing his doctoral studies. Six years after completing a bachelors degree in law, she obtained a master of law degree, specializing in legislation.

Stout passed the Pennsylvania Bar exam in 1954 and began private practice with Mabel G. Turner, who would go on to become an assistant U. S. Attorney. In April, 1956, Stout joined the Philadelphia district attorney's office. Three-and-one-half years later she was promoted to chief of appeals.

In September 1959, Governor David L. Lawrence appointed Stout an interim judge of the municipal court of Philadelphia, making her the first black woman jurist in the city's history. Two months later, in a citywide election, Stout won a ten-year term on the court (beating her opponent by a two to one margin), and, thus, becoming the country's first elected black woman to sit on the bench.

Stout began to attract national attention in the mid-1960s for handling a series of cases involving youth gangs. Some of these gangs were turning some neighborhoods into war zones. In administering her swift justice against the gang members, the American Civil Liberties Union (ACLU) contended that she did not pay enough attention to the "constitutional niceties." Stout responded that she did not understand what the criticism was all about.

After thirty years of service in the trial courts, Stout, in 1989, became the first black woman in American history to serve on a state supreme court.

In addition to authoring several opinions that legal scholars lauded for their "clarity"; Stout wrote several articles for periodicals in her field. Her professional memberships included the American Bar Association (ABA), National Association of Women Lawyers and an English teacher."

SULLIVAN, LEON HOWARD (October 16, 1922-April 26, 2001), Civil/Human Rights Leader, was born in Charleston, West Virginia. He received a B.A. degree from West Virginia State College in 1943 and a M.A. from California University (1947). He also studied at Union Theological Seminary (New

York) and Virginia Union University (Richmond).

From the beginning of his professional career, Sullivan mixed religion and civil rights. He pastored churches and led Church Conferences in South Orange, New Jersey and Philadelphia, Pennsylvania until 1988. He emerged as a national civil rights leader with the founding of Opportunities Industrialization Centers (OIC) of America in 1982 and the organization of one of the first African American Summits in 1991.

The OIC was principally a privately operated job training agency. It eventually operated in 75 urban areas of the country and prepared almost two million people for work. As early as 1977, Sullivan had issued his "Sullivan Principles" calling for fair and equitable business practices in South Africa. Despite the cooperation of many corporations, discrimination in American-owned facilities continued during the apartheid era in South Africa. Sullivan, then, became one of the first American leaders to urge economic and other sanctions against the South African regime. On a wider scale, he spearheaded the organization and convening of the first African–African American Summit, which met in Abidjan, Ivory Coast in April 1991. The meeting aimed to help address and redress the lack of black American involvement in African affairs. At the time, Sullivan told the *New York Times* that blacks had been "…brainwashed to believe that Africa was the dark continent, a place of crocodiles, trees and Tarzan." He sought African American investments in Africa, as one way to link the peoples of the two continents.

In his last years, Sullivan was the president of the International Foundation for Education and Self-Help, a non-profit organization to train skilled workers and farmers, and to train semi-literate and illiterate persons. In 1999, he also published an autobiography, *Moving Mountains.*

Sullivan's awards and honors include the Franklin D. Roosevelt Four Freedoms Medal (1987) and the Presidential Medal of Freedom (1991). He was the recipient of honorary degrees from Dartmouth, Princeton, and Yale Universities as well as the University of Pennsylvania, among others.

SUN RA (1914-May 30, 1993), Entertainer was born Herman Blount in Birmingham, Alabama, but he later liked to claim he was born on the planet Saturn about 5,000 years ago. As Sonny Blount, he played in Fletcher Henderson's jazz orchestra during the mid-1940s and also was active in experimental music circles in Chicago, Illinois.

Blount was already a well-known musician when he changed his name to Sun Ra during the 1950s. Along with the name change, he created a whole new identify for himself by drawing from the Bible, black spiritualism, science, fiction, and Egyptian mythology. (Ra, in fact, was the name of the ancient Egyptian sun god.) Beginning in 1956, Sun Ra traveled with a multimedia group known as Arkestra that included musicians as well as exotically costumed dancers.

Ra's career spanned sixty years. During that time, he recorded more than 200 albums, including *Saturn, Magic City, Savoy,* and *It's after the End of the World.* They encompassed a wide range of sounds and styles, including bop, gospel, blues, and electronic synthesizers.

Ra considered himself to be a bridge between different generations, and in February, 1993, *Rolling Stone* magazine seemed to confirm that judgment when it called him "the missing link between Duke Ellington and Public Enemy." Yet he was not especially well known in his native country (he spent most of his later years in Europe) and never had the recognition and success that many bigger stars enjoyed.

TEMPTATIONS One of the most popular soul quartets from the 1960s to the 1980s. The lead singers were Eddie Kendricks and David Ruffin.

KENDRICK, EDDIE (1940-October 5, 1992), Entertainer, was a tenor in one of the most popular soul group of the 1960s, 70s and 80s—"the temptations". He was a standard setter for falsetto singing and led the Temptations to fame with such recordings as "Get Ready", "Just My Imagination", and "The way You Do the Things You Do." The temptations, during Kendricks' tenure with the group, had thirteen top ten hits and became one of the nation's most popular male singing group.

Kendricks left the Temptations in the 1970s and went solo with such major recordings as "Keep on Trucking." However, he rejoined the Temptations for a short reunion tour in 1982. Kendricks was preceded in death, the previous year, by another leading member of the Temptations, David Ruffin.

RUFFIN, DAVID (January 18, 1941-June 1, 1991), Entertainer, was born in Meridian, Mississippi. He joined the famous singing group the Temptations in the early 1960s. One of the group's three lead singers (the others were Eddie Kendrick and Paul Williams), he was the baritone voice behind the hits "My Girl", "Since I Lost My Baby" and "Ain't Too Proud to Beg". In 1969, Ruffin launched a solo career that lasted throughout most of the 1970s.

During the 1980s Ruffin teamed up with Kendrick and another former Temptation, Dennis Edwards, on several projects. In 1985, for example, he and Kendrick recorded an album with Darryl Hall and John Oates. The album, "Live at the Apollo with David Ruffin and Eddie Kendrick", went gold. Later they performed at the Live Aid benefit concert for African famine relief and then on the anti-apartheid album "Sun City". By the late 1980s, Ruffin, Kendrick and Edwards were performing together regularly. In fact Ruffin had returned to Philadelphia just three weeks before his death of an apparent drug overdose after a successful tour of England with his fellow Temptations.

WALKER, JAMES ("Walker") (1926-October 30, 1992), Entertainer, was born in Mileston, Mississippi. In 1854, after being discharged from the U. S. Navy, he joined "the Dixie Hummingbirds" quartet. Walker soon became the lead singer and one of "the Hummingbirds" most powerful singers as well as a composer, writing more than seventy songs for his group. Under his leadership, "The Hummingbirds" became one of the nation's best known gospel quartets.

WASHINGTON, WALTER EDWARD (April 15, 1915-October 27, 2003) Politician, was born in Dawson, Georgia. His family later moved to Jamestown, New York, an industrial city that was relatively hospitable to its small Black Community. His father worked as a hotel bellhop, shoeshine man and ball bearing polisher. When his mother died, while Walter was in grade school, he went to live with a Miss Evelyn Andrews, a close friend of the family and later received notoriety in high school as a track star. After moving to Washington, D. C., Washington earned bachelor's and law degrees from Howard University there in 1938 and 1948, respectively. At Howard, he became a member of the student council and played football. One of his instructors, Ralph Bunche, advised Washington to pursue a career in public administration.

From 1941 to 1945 Washington served as a housing manager for the National Capital Housing Authority. Then, from 1945 to 1961, he served in various other executive positions with the Authority. In 1966, he became head of the New York City Housing Authority. But after only one year in this position, President Lyndon B. Johnson named him to the new position of mayor-commissioner of Washington, D. C., in a reorganized triumvirate commission system that governed the city. He was reappointed for two additional terms by President Richard M. Nixon.

Washington had been on the job for a mere six months when rioting broke out in Washington in the wake of the assassination of Martin Luther King, Jr. The mayor-commissioner won high marks for his dispassionate handling of the violence and for restoring order quickly. He, personally, walked through the city urging calm and resisted calls to have looters shot.

In 1973 the U. S. Congress approved home rule for the District of Columbia. In the city's first mayoral elections, in 1974, Washington was elected the city's first mayor. However, the city was still responsible to a southern-dominated Congress in several respects, particularly for much of its budget. Washington once complained that he was "unique. I have a great deal more responsibility than I have authority." As mayor, Washington won praise from federal officials and others for his careful, moderate approaches to his job and in his infrequent public pronouncements and for his frugal management of government. However, the city's black neighborhoods continued to be plagued by poor housing, drug infestation and crime. True to his low-key approach, Washington approached these problems slowly and cautiously. Thus, when he ran for re-election in 1978, a more passionate and fiery candidate, running on a platform of community-based issues, Marion Barry easily defeated Washington.

One of the principal tributes to Washington's leadership, at least in the view of federal officials, was that he left a forty million dollar surplus in the city's budget. After leaving public service, Washington became a partner in a Washington law firm. He also devoted much time to an effort to establish a National Museum of Art and a city museum in the District of Columbia.

Following Washington's death in 2003, D. C. congressional delegate Eleanor Holmes Norton eulogized him for the "legendary...way which he dealt with the president and the Congress."

During his long career in public service, Washington served as vice chairman of the Human Resources Development Commission of the National League of Cities; was on the advisory board of the U. S. Conference of Mayors and a trustee of the John F. Kennedy Center for Performing Arts. He was given awards and citations by the

WEAVER, ROBERT CLIFTON (December 29, 1907-July 19, 1997), Federal Official, educator, was born in Washington, D.C., to Mortimer G., a postal clerk, and Florence (Freeman) Weaver. He attended Dunbar High School in Washington, while running his own electrical business.

He graduated, with honors, from Harvard University in 1929 and received a Master's degree in Economics; then two years later, a Ph.D. in economics from the same institution in 1934. Between studies for his master's and doctorate degrees, Weaver was a member of the faculty at North Carolina A&T College (1931-1932). Then, he moved immediately into governmental service; first as adviser on Negro Affairs to Secretary of the Interior Harold Ickes from 1933 to 1937; then special assistant to the administrator of the United States Housing Authority, from 1937 to 1940; and from 1940 to 1944 administrator in the National Defense Advisory Commission, the Office of Production Management, the War Manpower Commission, and the

War Production Board. In all of these positions, Weaver worked on matters of employment and training of blacks and other minorities. He used his experiences in these areas to produce a book, *Negro Labor: A National Problem* in 1946. He also rose to the ranks of those intimate advisors, who President Franklin D. Roosevelt used to counsel him on Negro affairs, known as "the Black Cabinet."

At the end of the Second World War, Weaver left the federal government to serve as executive director of the Mayor's Committee on Race Relations in Chicago, 1945-1946. Then, he held administrative positions with the Metropolitan Housing Council of Chicago and the National Council on Housing. From these experiences, he authored a book, in 1948, entitled, *The Negro Ghetto*. Before returning to teaching in 1947, Weaver went to Russia, where he worked as a supply officer, reports officer and deputy chief of mission for the United States Relief and Rehabilitation Administration in the Ukraine.

In 1947, Weaver took a position on the economics faculty at Northwestern University. For the next four years, he also taught at Columbia University's Teachers College, the New York School of Education, and the New School for Social Research. Between 1949 and 1954, he was the director of the John Hay Whitney Foundation's Opportunity Fellowships Program.

An active Democrat, Weaver returned to governmental service with an appointment as Deputy Commission of the Division of Housing for the state of New York in 1955. He served less than a year in this post, before being named to Governor Averell Harriman's "Cabinet" as the State rent Administrator. He left this post in January, 1959, when Republican Governor Nelson Rockefeller came into office, and became a consultant for the Ford Foundation. By this time, Weaver was widely recognized as one of the nation's leading experts on housing. Not one to be long out of government, Weaver received an appointment, in 1960, as vice chairman of New York City's Housing and redevelopment Board. But he was in this office for barely a year, when President-elect John F. Kennedy asked him to take a job as Administrator of the Housing and Home Finance Agency (HHFA) in his new administration. This was, at the time, the highest position ever held by an African-American in the executive branch of the federal government. At the HHFA, Weaver supervised thousands of employees and directed a budget of over $340,000,000. In 1966, the HHFA was merged into the new Department of Housing and Urban Development (HUD). President Lyndon B. Johnson named Weaver the first Secretary of HUD, thus giving him the distinction of being the first African American ever to sit in the Cabinet of the President of the United States. After the Republicans regained the White House, in 1969, Weaver returned to academia as president of the Barnard M. Baruch College of the City University of New York. Always a scholar as well as a bureaucrat, Weaver also wrote *The Urban Complex* (1964) and *Dilemmas of Urban America* (1965).

WILLIAMS, HOSEA LORENZO (January 5, 1926-November 16, 2000), Civil Rights Leader, state legislator, county official, was born in Attapulgus, Georgia. He received a B.A. degree from Morris Brown College (Georgia) and a M.S. from Atlanta University. He began his professional career as a high school science teacher (1951-1952). Then he became a research chemist for the U.S. Department of Agriculture (1952-1963) and publisher of *The Chatham County Crusader* in Savannah, Georgia (1961-1963). Also, in 1963, Williams joined the Southern Christian Leadership Conference (SCLC) as special projects director (1963-1970). He rose quickly in the ranks of SCLC leaders, becoming national program director (1967-1969); regional vice president (1970-1971); and national executive director (1969-1971 and (1977-1979).

Williams entered elective politics in 1974 as a Georgia State Representative. He served in the Georgia House from 1974 to 1985; then sought and won a seat on the Atlanta City Council, where he served for five years, before winning a seat on the DeKalb County (of which Decatur is the county seat) Commission in 1990. Williams left the Commission in 1994, and announced his retirement from elective politics, saying: "I'm giving up the prestigious suite of elected politics and returning to the streets to struggle against inhumanities that are destroying Americans." Williams had also undergone back and neck surgery prior to his retirement announcement, but said this had nothing to do with his decision.

In the Civil Rights Movement, Williams became best known as a "ramrod" in protests and demonstrations. Most often, dressed in blue denim overalls, and speaking ungrammatically, he openly confronted white racists and attracted members of black disadvantaged classes, including "street people" to the Movement. He left negotiations and other "niceties" of the protests to Martin Luther King, Jr., Andrew Young, and others. He was a leader of the original march from Selma to Montgomery, Alabama to dramatize voting rights on March 7, 1965, when Alabama state troopers broke up the demonstration in a brutal attack on the marchers. The subsequent march, led by Martin Luther King, Jr. reached Montgomery two weeks later, under the protection of the National Guard. Williams once called the events: "The greatest triumphs of the civil rights movement.... That's when we crushed the mightiest of the mighty forces of racism." Williams, who has often compared Martin Luther King, Jr. with the greatest leaders and martyrs in world history, including Jesus, was on the balcony of the Lorraine Motel in Memphis, Tennessee, on the evening of April 4, 1968, when the civil rights leader was slain. He then helped guide King's mule-drawn casket through the streets of downtown Atlanta, on April 9, for his final rites.

Williams' reputation as a "grass roots" leader of Black America was also enhanced by his "Feed-the-Hungry" program in metropolitan Atlanta. Beginning in 1970, as a small effort to feed a few hundred hungry and homeless persons on the Thanksgiving and Christmas holidays, by 1999, the annual feasts had grown so large that they had to be held in gymnasiums and stadiums. The events now draw an army of bi-racial volunteers and feed more than 100,000 persons a year. Williams missed his first meal with the hungry during the holidays of 1999, while recovering from major surgery. He continued, through his last illnesses, to speak out against racial and class injustices, while attending to his several business enterprises and writing an autobiography.

YOUNG, COLEMAN ALEXANDER (May 24, 1918-November 29, 1997), Politician, was born in Tuscaloosa, Alabama to Coleman and Ida Reese (Jones) Young. The family moved to Detroit, Michigan, when Coleman was only five years old. He graduated from the Eastern High School in Detroit, but his family was unable to raise enough money to supplement scholarships in order for him to attend college. Thus, he enrolled in an electrician's apprentice school operated by the Ford Motor Company. After completing his apprenticeship, he joined the assembly line at the Ford Motor Company, where he became involved in "underground" union activities.

After leaving Ford Motor Company, Young took a job with the U.S. post office, Detroit, where he also engaged in labor organizing.

During the Second World War, Young became a Second Lieutenant in the Army Air Corps. He was arrested at Freeman Field, Indiana for demanding service at the segregated officer's club. Shortly thereafter the U.S. War Department declared that all military facilities must be open to all officers regardless of race or religion.

After the War, Young returned to the labor movement as Director of Organization for the Wayne County (for which Detroit is the county seat and largest city) AFL-CIO. In 1951, he founded the National Negro Labor Council, whose pickets forced the Sears, Roebuck Company and several other large businesses in Detroit to employ black workers.

Even before the Second World War, Young had been active in the Civil Rights Movement and civic and political organizations in the Detroit area. In 1961, he was elected a delegate to a convention that drafted a new state constitution for Michigan. The next year, after losing a race for a seat in the state legislature, he was named Director of the Democratic gubernatorial campaign in Wayne County.

In 1964, Young ran for and won a seat in the Michigan State Senate, where he became a Democratic floor leader and a Democratic National Committeeman. In the Senate, he supported abortion reform, consumer protection, a civilian review board for police conduct, housing reforms, and welfare benefits for the poor. By 1969, he wanted to offer for mayor, but was prohibited by a state law that barred state legislators from holding office while running for mayor. The Michigan Supreme Court overturned this restriction in 1973. Young, again, sought the mayor's office and won the election, becoming the first black mayor in the history of Detroit.

The voters of Detroit returned Young to office for five successive terms, despite growing problems of unemployment and crime in the city. Detroit had consistently ranked among the highest U.S. cities in murders per capita. Yet Young also presided over a "renaissance" in downtown economic development and was the host mayor for the 1980 Republican National Convention.

Young considered retirement in 1985, but then changed his mind. He was returned to office that year, and, again in 1989, even in a city with high unemployment, a high crime rate, and a shortage of money. In 1993, Young did withdraw and threw his support to the unsuccessful campaign of Sharon McPhail. He was succeeded by Dennis Archer.

REFERENCES

BOOKS and PERIODICALS

African American Biography, 3 vols., UXL Gale Research Inc., 1994

Almanac of America Politics, 1990-2004, National Journal

Atlanta Constitution, 1920-2004

Atlanta Journal, 1920-2003

Atlanta Journal- Constitution, 1960-2005

Bibliography of African American Leadership, Greenwood Press, 2000

Congressional Black Caucus Foundation, *Point of View*, Fall 1984

Contemporary Black Biography, 1-26, Gale Group Inc., 1992-2002

Davis, Abraham L., *Blacks in the Federal Judiciary: Neutral Arbiters or Judicial Activists*, Wyndham Hall Press, 1989

Ebony, 1955-2003, Johnson Publishing Co.

Estell, Kenneth, *African America: Portrait of a People*, Visible Ink Press, 1994

Freund, M. P. and Annette McQuirter, *The Young Oxford History of African Americans*, 11, Oxford University Press, 1997

Hine, Darlene Clark, ed., *Black Women in America: An Historical Encyclopedia*, 1-2, Carlson Publishing Co., 1993

Hornsby, Alton, Jr, *Chronology of African American History*, 2 editions, 1992, Gale, 1992-1997

Hornsby, Alton, Jr., editor-in-chief, *Dictionary of Twentieth Century Black Leaders*, E-Book-Time Publishers, 2005

Jet, 1960-2004 Johnson Publishing Co.

The Journal of Black Studies, July 1996

Newsmakers, '92, Gale Research, Inc., 1992

The New York Times, 1930-2004

Outstanding Educators of America, OEA Inc., 1975

Reference Library of Black Americans, I-III, Gale Research, Inc., 1997

Smith, Jesse Carney, *Epic Lives: 100 Black Women Who Made a Difference,* Gale Research, Inc., 1993

The Washington Post, 1950-1999

Who's Who Among African Americans, 2000-2004

Who's Who in America, Marquis Who's Who Co., 1950-1999

Who's Who in Black America, 1985-1999

Who's Who in the South and Southwest, 1993-1997

Who Was Who, Marquis Who's Who Co., 1997-1999

WEBSITES

African American Biographies
(http://www.infoplease.com.//ipa/A0878436.html)
© 2000-2005 Pearson Education, publishing as Infoplease

African Americans in Science
(http://www.ericdigest.org/1996-1/african.htm)

http://www.britannica.com/women/articles/Hope_Lugenia_Burn
s.html

http://www.spartacus.schoolnet.co.uk/USAmurrayA.htm

http://statelibrary.dcr.state.nc.us/nc/bio/afro/brown.htm

https://webfiles.uci.edu/mcbrown/display/walker.html

https://webfiles.uci.edu/mcbrown/display/latimer.html

Infoplease
(http://www.factmaster.com)

The New Georgia Encyclopedia
(http://www.georgiaencyclopedia.org)

Wikipedia, the free encyclopedia
(http://www.wikepedia.org)

ABOUT THE AUTHOR

Alton Hornsby, Jr. is Fuller E. Callaway Professor of History at Morehouse College. From 1976 to 2001, he was the Editor of the *Journal of Negro History*. He is also the editor of "The Papers of John and Lugenia Burns Hope." His previous publications include *Chronology of African American History* 2 editions), *Milestones in Twentieth Century African American History*, *A Short History of Black Atlanta, 1847-1990*, *Death and Remembrance in the African American South: The Transition of Mayor Maynard Holbrook Jackson, Jr.*; *A Companion to African American History* (edited with an introduction), *The Atlanta Urban League, 1920-2000* (with Alexa Benson Henderson; winner of the Adele Mellen Prize for distinguished scholarship, 2005) and *Dictionary of Twentieth Century Black Leaders*. He also wrote the Introduction to the 17th edition of *Who's Who Among African Americans* and is writes frequent guest commentaries for the *Atlanta Daily World*.

INDEX OF SUBJECTS

A

Abbott, Robert S., 30
Abernathy, Ralph David, 92
Adderley, Julius "Cannonball", 94
Ailey, Alvin, 221
Aldridge, Ira Frederick, 1
Allen, Richard, 1
Anderson, Marian, 30
Armistead, James Lafayette, 3
Armstrong, Louis, 95
Ashe, Arthur, 221
Attucks, Crispus, 3

B

Baker, Ella Jo, 96
Bailey, Pearl, 222
Baldwin, James A., 97
Banneker, Benjamin, 4
Barbadoes, James, 4
Barber, Jesse Max, 32
Barrow, Joe Louis, 32
Barthe, Richmond, 33
Basie, William "Count", 223
Bates, Daisy, 224
Bearden, Harold Irvin, 226
Beckwourth, James Pierson, 5
Berry, Leonidas Harris, 99
Bethune, Mary McCleod, 33
Bethune, Thomas, 5
Black Panther Party, 101
Blackwell, Lucien E., 227
Blakely, Art, 99
Bolden, Dorothy, 101
Bowman, Thea, 229

Bouchet, Edward A., 35
Bradley, Thomas, 229
Branson, Herman, 231
Branton, Wiley A., 103
Brooks, Gwendolyn, 35
Brown, Charlotte Hawkins, 36
Brown, Ronald Harmon, 231
Bragg, Janet Harmon, 102
Bruce, Blanche K., 37
Bryan, Andrew, 6
Bunche, Ralph Johnson, 104

C

Caesar, John, 6
Calloway, Cab, 233
Campanella, Roy, 233
Carmichael, Stokeley, 106
Carver, George Washington, 38
Cherry, Gwendolyn, 108
Chisholm, Shirley Anita, 234
Cinque, Joseph, 7
Clark, Septima Poinsetta, 235
Cleage, Albert Buford, 236
Cleaver, Eldridge, 238
Cleveland, James, 240
Coles, Nathaniel (Nat King), 109
Collins, George, 111
Coltrane, John, 112
Cook, Will Marion, 39
Cornish, Samuel, 23
Crockett, George, 113
Cromwell, Oliver, 7
Crummell, Alexander, 39
Cuffe, Paul, 7

D

Dabney, Austin, 8
Dandridge, Dorothy, 40
Davage, Matthew, 41
Davis, Benjamin J., 114
Davis, Benjamin, O. Sr., 116
Davis, Benjamin, O. Jr., 117
Davis, Miles, 240
Davis, Sammy, 117
Delany, Martin R., 8
Depriest, Oscar, 42
Dett, Nathaniel, 43
Diggs, Charles, 240
Dixon, Willie, 43
Dorsey, Thomas A., 44
Douglass, Frederick, 9
Drew, Charles, 45
DuBois, W.E.B., 45
Dunbar, Paul, 46
Dunn, Oscar, 47
DuSable, Jean Paul, 10

E

Eldridge, Eleanor, 10
Ellington, Duke, 118
Estevanico (Esteban), 11
Evers, Medgar, 120

F

Farmer, James, 120
Fitzgerald, Ella, 243
Flipper, Henry Ossian, 48
Forten, James, 11
Fortune, T. Thomas, 48
Franklin, C.L., 122
Frazier, E. Franklin, 122
Fuller, Samuel B. ("S.B."), 123

G

Gardner, Newport, 12
Garnet, Henry Highland, 49

Garvey, Marcus, 55
Gaston, A. G., 125
Gaye, Marvin, 125
Gibson, Althea, 126
Gillespie, Dizzy, 127
Granger, Shelton B., 128

H

Hale, Clara, 129
Hale, William Jasper, 56
Haley, Alex, 130
Hall, Prince, 12
Hammon, Jupiter, 13
Hamer, Fannie Lou, 130
Handy, W. C., 56
Hankerson, Lester, 245
Hansberry, Lorraine, 133
Harris, Patricia Roberts, 134
Hastie, William, 135
Hayes, Charles Arthur, 136
Hayes, Roland, 57
Healey, James, 13
Healey, Patrick, 13
Hemings, Sally, 14
Henderson, Vivian, 138
Henry, Aaron, 137
Henson, Matthew, 58
Hill, Peter, 14
Holiday, Billie, 58
Hollowell, Donald, 139
Holman, M. Carl, 141
Hope, John, 59
Hope, Lugenia Burns, 60
Horton, George Moses, 15
Houston, Charles, 61
Hughes, Langston, 143
Hull, Agrippa, 15
Hurley, Ruby, 144
Hurston, Zora Neale, 62

J

Jackson, Maynard H., 246
James, Daniel ("Chappie"), 146
Jenkins, Esau, 147

Jockeys, 62
Johnson, Charles Spurgeon, 149
Johnson, Frances (Frank), 15
Johnson, Jack, 63
Johnson, James Weldon, 62
Johnson, John Harold, 150
Johnson, Mordecai, 151
Jones, Casey, 64
Jones, John, 16
Jones, Sissieretta
   ("Black Patti"), 64
Joplin, Scott, 65
Jordan, Barbara, 248
Julian, Percy, 152
Just, Ernest, 66

K

Kennedy, Florynce, 249
Kenny, Bill, 152
King, Albert, 250
King, Alberta, 153
King, Chevene Bowers
   ("C.B."), 251
King, Martin Luther, Sr., 154
King, Martin Luther, Jr., 154

L

La Fontant-Mankarious, Jewel, 156
Lane, Isaac, 67
Langston, John Mercer, 16
Latimer, Lewis, 67
Laveau, Marie, 68
Leidesdorff, William, 17
Little, Malcolm (Malcolm X), 157
Loguen, Jermain Wesley, 17
Looby, Z. Alexander, 159
Lowery, Peter, 18
Lyle, George, Jr., 161
Lyke, James Patterson, 160
Lyons, Judson, 18

M

McKay, Claude, 69

McQueen, "Butterfly", 69
Malvin, John, 18
Marino, Eugene, 251
Marshall, Thurgood, 162
Martin, Louis, 253
Matzeliger, Jan, 69
Mays, Benjamin E, 164
Marrant, John, 19
Micheaux, Oscar, 70
Mitchell, Arthur, 170
Mitchell, Nannie, 71
McNair, Ronald, 167
McPherson, Alan, Jr., 167
Metcalfe, Ralph, 168
Miller, Dorie, 70
Molineaux, Tom, 20
Moon, Mollie, 257
Moore, Harry, 171
Morial, Ernest, 257
Muhammad, Elijah, 174
Murray, Pauli, 175

N

Nabrit, Samuel, 258
Newby, Dangerfield, 20
Nix, Robert N., Sr., 177
Nixon, E. D., 170

O

Owens, Jesse, 178

P

Paige, Leroy "Satchel", 71
Parsons, James Benton, 179
Patterson, Frederick D., 259
Payne, Ethel Lois, 180
Payton, Walter, 261
Pendleton, Clarence, 181
Pickett, Bill, 71
Pinchback, PBS, 73
Perry, Lincoln
   ("Steppin Fetchit"), 183

Pleasant, Mary Allen
("Mammy"), 20
Plessy, Homer Adolf, 73
Plummer, Henry Vinton, 21
Powell, Adam Clayton, 183
Prince, Lucy Terry, 21
Proctor, Samuel D., 261
Prosser, Gabriel, 22

R

Rainey, Joseph H., 74
Randolph, A. Philip, 186
Ranger, Joseph, 22
Revels, Hiram R., 75
Riles, Wilson, 262
Rillieux, Norbert, 75
Robinson, Jackie, 187
Robinson, Max, 189
Rowan, Carl, 264
Russwurm, John Brown, 23
Rustin, Bayard, 189

S

Sampson, Edith Spurlock, 191
Sanderson, Jerimiah Brown, 23
Sanford, John Elroy
(Redd Foxx), 266
Sash, Moses, 24
Schomburg, Arturo Alfonso, 76
Scott, C.A., 266
Scott, Dred, 24
Scott, Emmett, 77
Scottsboro Boys, 77
Sengstacke, John H., 267
Shakur, Tupac, 268
Simmons, Althea, 192
Smalls, Robert, 24
Smith, Antonio Maceo, 194
Spaulding, Clinton C., Jr., 195
Stanford, John Henry, 270
Stanley, Frank L., 78
Stewart, Bennett McVey, 196
Stokes, Carl, 273
Stout, Juanita (Kidd), 275

Sullivan, Leon Howard, 276
Sun Ra, 278

T

Tanner, Henry O., 78
Taylor, Hobart, 198
Temptations, 278
Terrell, Mary Church, 79
Terrell, Robert Herberton, 80
Thierry, Camille, 25
Trotter, William Monroe, 80
Truth, Sojourner, 82
Tubman, Harriett, 25
Turner, Henry McNeal, 82
Turner, Nat, 26

U

Uncle Tom, 83

V

Vassa, Gustavious
(Olaudah Equino), 26
Vaughn, Sarah, 199
Venture, 27
Vesey, Denmark, 27

W

Walden, A. T., 199
Walker, David, 27
Walker, James ("Walker"), 201
Walker, Madame C.J., 84
Washington, Booker T., 86
Washington, Harold, 201
Washington, Walter, 204
Waters, Ethel, 206
Weaver, Robert, 281
Wheatley, Phillis, 28
White, George, 88
White, Walter Francis, 88
Wilkins, Roy, 207
Williams, Daniel Hale, 89

Williams, Hosea, 283
Williams, Paul Revere, 210
Williams, Robert, 211
Williamson, Q. V., 214
Woods, Granville T., 90
Woodson, Carter G., 90
Wright, Jonathan Jasper, 88
Wright, Richard, 216
Wright, Theodore Sedwick, 28

Y

Yerby, Frank, 218
Young, Charles, 91
Young, Coleman Alexander, 285
Young, Whitney, 218
York, 29

Printed in the United States
40929LVS00003B/34